French Course Handbook

Instructions
Explanatory Notes
Vocabularies

The Linguaphone Institute

Linguaphone Institute Limited
207 Regent Street
London W1R 8AU

First published   1971
2nd (revised) edition   1973
3rd (revised) edition   1974
4th (revised) edition   1976
5th (revised) edition   1977

Printed photolitho in Great Britain by
J. W. Arrowsmith Ltd, Bristol

Course written by

Max Bellancourt, L. ès L., D.E.S., Chevalier de l'Ordre des Palmes
Académiques,
Lecturer, University of London.

Recorded with the participation and under the direction of Max Bellancourt by the following French actors:

Jo Charrier	Michèle Dumontier	Yves-Marie Maurin
Jacqueline Dufranne	Pierre Fromont	Philippe Ogouze
		Jane-Val

Contents

Learning with Linguaphone

The Linguaphone French course

Your Linguaphone course has been carefully constructed in the most up-to-date scientific way to build up the language you are learning from an absolute beginning to the point where, if you have followed the instructions, you will be able to speak, read and write the language and to understand it when it is spoken. You will be able to cope confidently with everyday situations in the country where the language is spoken.

Instructions

Regular study and practice with this course is much more effective than attempting large amounts at irregular intervals. 'A little and often' is preferable to 'a lot but seldom'.

For the introduction and each lesson:

1 **Recording** Listen to the recording of Part 1 once. Don't try to understand at this stage. Just listen to the sounds of the language.

2 **Handbook** Read the summary of Part 1. This will give you an idea of what happens in this part. (For the Introduction only, you have a complete translation.)

3 **Recording** Listen to the recording of Part 1 several times more. You will now begin to associate the sounds with what happens. You will find that you are becoming accustomed to the sounds of the language.

4 **Illustrated book   Recording** Listen to the recording of Part 1 and follow the text in the book several times.
You will now be able to relate what you hear to what you see written. At the same time, the pictures will help you to understand a little more.

5 **Handbook** Work out the meaning. Use the word list and notes. (For the Introduction only, you have a complete translation.) Try to understand first of all the meaning of the phrases, and then of whole sentences.

6 **Recording** Listen to the recording again now that you understand the meaning. Continue to listen until you can understand everything as you hear it.

7 **Illustrated book   Recording**   Read the text to yourself and then read it aloud several times. If you have any doubts about the pronunciation of any word or phrase, listen to that part of the recording again. You can also listen to the recording of the sounds of French (*Sons du français*).

8 Now repeat instructions 1–7 for Part 2 and then for Part 3.

9 **Handbook**   Study the tables, which show you the sentence patterns and grammatical structures you have absorbed while working through the text.

10 **Written exercises (Exercices écrits)** Do the exercise to see if you have fully understood the lesson. Est-ce que vous comprenez la leçon?
   i Read the four sentences a, b, c and d.
   ii Write down the letter which is alongside the one correct sentence. The other sentences are wrong.
   iii Check with the answers at the end of the book.
N.B. Write your answers on a separate sheet of paper, not in the book.

11 If you have made no more than one mistake in the exercise, go on to instruction 12. If you have made more than one mistake, go back to instruction 4 and work through the lesson again.

12 **Written exercises (Exercices écrits)**   Do the written exercises 1–6 on a separate sheet of paper, not in the book.
   i Read the examples: they show you what you have to do.
   ii Write out each sentence in full, including the first two, which are the same as the examples.
   iii Check your sentences with the answers at the end of the book.
   iv If you have made a mistake and cannot understand why, refer to the text and the tables again.
   v If you have made more than two mistakes in one exercise, do the exercise again, but study the lesson first.

Begin the next lesson.

The books and the recordings

The illustrated book

The Introduction shows you some of the elementary sentence patterns and sounds of the language.

Each of the thirty lessons has three separate parts so that, once you have understood the Introduction, you have ninety carefully graded, easily paced stages to work through. Each stage is long enough to give you meaningful language practice and short enough to enable you to understand everything in it in a single study period.

Part 1 is a monologue which brings in the main teaching points of the lesson. This means that you have only one voice to listen to while you absorb the new language.

In **Part 2** you will hear the characters of the story using the new language and adding to it in everyday situations.

In Parts 1 and 2 you will meet a family and their friends in everyday life. We hope you will become their friend and learn to speak their language as well as they do.

Part 3 consists of conversations set in different situations. This part is based on the language you have learnt in Parts 1 and 2 and gives you the chance to practise it in varied situations.

The illustrations to the lessons are there to show you at a glance the meaning of individual words and phrases and to help you to understand what is happening in the story.

The recordings

The Introduction and all the lessons are recorded. The professional speakers have been carefully selected for their correctness and clarity of speech. The early lessons have been recorded as slowly as possible without distorting the language. Gradually, the speed of speech is increased through the course. There is a separate section on the sounds of the language which is designed to enable you to recognize and practise the key sounds. Refer to this section regularly throughout the course. Remember that the same letters or combination of letters are often pronounced in quite different ways in different languages. Practice makes perfect.

This handbook

After this section you will find a translation of the Introduction and then a guide to each lesson which gives you:
  i A short account of what happens in the lesson.
  ii A list of the new words used in the lesson.
  iii Notes on the meaning of the lesson, with the language points carefully explained; these notes progressively build up to give an understanding of the whole language.

iv Tables which show you the sentence patterns and grammatical structures introduced in the lesson.

The alphabetical vocabularies at the end of the book give you the meaning of every word used in the course.

The appendix consists of a grammatical analysis of the verb.

The written exercises (Exercices écrits)

This book is programmed to make sure you have understood the lessons and it enables you to practise in writing the language you have learnt.

Introduction

Part one

M. Delon	Hello! Listen, please. My name is Olivier Delon. I'm French. I'm a teacher. I'm speaking French. You aren't French. You're learning French. This is a book. This is a tape. This is a cassette. This is a record.

Part two

M. Delon	Hello!
You	Hello, M. Delon.
M. Delon	How are you?
You	I'm very well, thank you. And how are you?
M. Delon	I'm very well, thank you. Are you French?
You	No.
M. Delon	Are you learning French?
You	Yes.
M. Delon	Have you got a book?
You	Yes, I've got a book.
M. Delon	Good. Where is it?
You	There.
M. Delon	Where?
You	It's on the table.

Part three

M. Delon	I'll introduce my family. This is my wife.
Mme Delon	Hello! My name is Yvonne Delon. I'm French.

	I'm forty-two.
	I'm a nurse.
	Goodbye.
M. Delon	This is my daughter.
Valérie	Hello!
	My name is Valérie.
	I'm French too.
	I'm nineteen.
	I'm a secretary.
	See you soon!
M. Delon	And my son . . .
Paul	Here I am.
	My name is Paul.
	I'm French.
	I'm sixteen.
	I'm a schoolboy.
	See you soon!
M. Delon	Here are our friends:
	This is Guy.
Guy	Hello!
	My name is Guy Martin.
	I'm French too.
	I'm twenty-eight.
	I have an advertising agency.
	Bye for now!
M. Delon	And this is Marie-Claire.
Marie-Claire	I'm seventeen.
	I'm Guy's sister.
	I'm a schoolgirl.
	Goodbye. See you soon!
M. Delon	There you are. Goodbye. See you soon!

Leçon un   *Lesson one*
Première leçon   *First lesson*

En route pour Paris!   Off to Paris!

What happens

PART 1

Le rendez-vous: *The meeting*
Guy Martin introduces himself. He's at Orly Airport, Paris, waiting for
Monsieur and Madame Delon and their children, Paul and Valérie, to
arrive from Montreal. They arrive, go through passport control and
customs and then they all get into the airport bus.

PART 2

À l'aéroport d'Orly; au contrôle des passeports: *At Orly airport; at the
passport control*
This scene is a flashback of the Delon family showing their passports.
We learn that, although they live in Canada, they are French.
Vous avez quelque chose à déclarer? *Have you anything to declare?*
The customs officer asks each member of the Delon family if they have
anything to declare.
Dans le grand hall à Orly: *In the main hall at Orly*
Guy meets the Delon family and asks them how they are.

PART 3

Dans le hall de l'aéroport: *In the airport hall*
Madame Hébert puts Charles in his place.
Dans l'avion: *In the plane*
Pierre and Marcel chat.

Words in this lesson

à at, to
(elle) admire (she) admires
admirer to admire
l'aéroport (m) airport
l'after-shave after-shave
j'ai I have, I've got
l'ami (m) friend
je m'appelle my name is
s'appeler to be called

il arrive he is arriving
arriver to arrive
au at (the)
au revoir good-bye
aussi too, also
avec with
vous avez you have (got)
l'avion (m) plane
avoir to have

3

1

les bagages (*m*) luggage
bien well
bon good
bonjour hello
ça va all right
le Canada Canada
canadien Canadian
le car bus
comment how
comment allez-vous? how are you?
le contrôle des passeports passport
  control
dans in
de (d') of, from
déclarer to declare
le demi-litre half-litre
des of (the)
des some
deux two
deuxième second
le disque record
le douanier customs officer
du of (the), from
eh bien well
en route pour off to
l'enfant (*m*) child
il est it is, he is
et and
vous êtes you are
être to be
il examine he examines
examiner to examine
fatigué tired
le flacon bottle
français French
grand large
vous habitez you live (in)
habiter to live (in)
le hall hall, terminal
l'hôtel (*m*) hotel
il he, it
ils they
je (j') I
le (l') the
la leçon lesson
les the
M. Mr.
Madame Mrs., madam
Mademoiselle Miss
mais but

merci thank you
mes my
Messieurs-Dames ladies and
  gentlemen, sir and madam
le microsillon L.P.
Mme Mrs.
moi me
moi, je . . . I
mon my
Monsieur Mr., sir
il monte (dans) he gets into
monter (dans) to get into
ne . . . pas not
ne . . . rien nothing
non no
j'observe I'm watching
observer to watch
oui yes
le parfum perfume
la partie part
pas not
le passeport passport
petit small
le policier immigration officer
pour for
première first
le quart d'heure quarter of an hour
quelque chose anything
il regarde he's looking at
regarder to look at
le rendez-vous meeting
s'il vous plaît please
le sac bag
le sac à main handbag
ils sont they are
je suis I'm, I am
très very
troisième third
un a, one
un instant just a moment
l'uniforme (*m*) uniform
je vais très bien I'm very well
voilà there is, there are, here is,
  here are
vos your
votre your
vous you
le voyageur passenger
le whisky whisky

4

Notes

PART ONE

1 **Leçon un** *Lesson one*
The accent under the **c** is called a cedilla accent, and **ç** is pronounced like an **s**.

2 **En route pour Paris!** *Off to Paris!*
When **en route** is followed by **pour** it means something similar to our English expression *off to*.

3 **Première partie** *Part one* (lit. *first part*)
You can see the second **e** of **première** — **è** — has an accent above it; we refer to it by its French name: a GRAVE accent.

4 **Le rendez-vous** *The meeting*
You will have noticed that **rendez-vous** has the word **le** in front of it.

5 **Bonjour!** *Hello*!
The literal meaning is *good day*, and is used where in English we might say *good morning* or *good afternoon* instead of *hello*.

6 **Je m'appelle Guy Martin.** *My name is Guy Martin.*
If you compare a French sentence with an English one, it becomes obvious that you cannot substitute for each French word its English equivalent, and still keep the original meaning. In fact, a word for word translation would often end up meaning nothing. In certain situations, the French use a French turn of phrase, where an Englishman would use one peculiar to his own language. Naturally, the words of the French phrase do not correspond to those of the English speaker. You have to accept this difference when you learn a foreign language. So we must now say that **Je m'appelle Guy Martin** is equivalent to *My name is Guy Martin* or *I am Guy Martin*.

7 **Je suis français.** *I am French.*
a **Je** corresponds to the English *I*. It is written with a capital only when it comes at the beginning of a sentence or paragraph.
b **je suis**: *I am*
c **français**: *French* Notice that **français** is written with a small **f**.

8 **Je suis à Orly.** *I am at Orly.*
a **à Orly**: *at Orly* Orly is the airport which serves Paris.
b **À** often means *at*. It has a GRAVE accent.

9 Orly est l'aéroport de Paris. *Orly is the Paris airport.*

a You already know how to say *am, I am*: **je suis. Est** is the French for *is*.

Guy Martin est français *Guy Martin is French.*

b **l'aéroport de Paris**: *The Paris airport* We say **le rendez-vous** but **l'aéroport.** In English we tend to pronounce *the* as *thee* before a word which begins with a vowel (a, e, i, o, u,): *the airport* (*thee airport*). In French also, **le** changes before a vowel:

le rendez-vous **le** before the consonant **'r'**

l'aéroport **l'** before the vowel **'a'**.

c **l'aéroport**: *the airport* The accent on the **e** of **aéroport** is an ACUTE accent.

d **l'aéroport de Paris**: *the Paris airport* Here is another example of a French phrase which cannot be translated literally. In the vocabulary list you will find:

l': *the*

aéroport: *airport*

de: *of*

Paris: *Paris*

which gives: *the airport of Paris.* This sounds unnatural in English; we would be much more likely to say *Orly is the Paris airport.*

10 Je suis dans le hall de l'aéroport. *I'm in the airport terminal.* (lit. *I'm in the hall of the airport*).

a Again, **je suis**: *I am.*

b **le hall**: lit. *the hall* If you listen carefully you will notice that Guy Martin does not pronounce the **h** in **hall. H** is never pronounced in French, but since, when it is written, **hall** does begin with the consonant **h,** the French say *le* **hall.**

c **le hall de l'aéroport** Compare:

l'aéroport de Paris

le hall de l'aéroport

d In French, all syllables receive roughly the same amount of emphasis. Listen again to the last sentence:

Je/suis/dans/le/hall/de/l'a/é/ro/port.

There may be slightly more emphasis on the final syllable **/port/,** but apart from this, the syllables are even.

11 J'observe les voyageurs. *I'm watching the travellers.*

a **j'observe**: *I am watching* Just as **le** becomes **l'** before a vowel, so **je** becomes **j'** in front of a word beginning with **a, e, i, o,** or **u.**

b **les voyageurs**: *the travellers* **Le** means *the* and is used before a singular word. **Le voyageur** means *the traveller.* **Les** also means *the* and is used before plural words: **les voyageurs**: *the travellers.*

In French, as in English, a plural noun generally ends in **s**.

le hall — les halls

le voyageur — les voyageurs

If you listen carefully to the pronunciation of **voyageurs** you will notice that the final **s** is silent.

12 Dans un quart d'heure, Monsieur Delon arrive. *Monsieur Delon is arriving in a quarter of an hour.* (lit. *In a quarter of an hour Monsieur Delon is arriving.*)

a un quart d'heure This expression is equivalent to the English, *a quarter of an hour.* At this stage you have to learn such expressions by heart. Later you will see how they are constructed. One point however, the first word, **un** means *a* in English.

un quart d'heure: *a quarter of an hour*

un hall: *a hall*

You may have noticed that the **n** of **un** is not pronounced. The word **un** has a nasal quality, the **n** is not sounded separately.

b Monsieur Delon: lit. *Mister Delon* Listen very carefully to the pronunciation of **monsieur** and try to imitate it. The final **r** is silent.

c Monsieur Delon arrive.: *Monsieur Delon is arriving.*

Arrive means *is arriving.*

13 Il arrive avec Madame Delon. *He's arriving with Madame Delon.*

il arrive: *he is arriving* (lit. *he arrives*).

Be careful, there is no **s** at the end of the French word.

Il replaces **Monsieur Delon** and means *he.*

14 Paul et Valérie arrivent aussi. *Paul and Valérie are arriving too.*

Paul et Valérie arrivent: *Paul and Valérie are arriving*

The **-nt** ending shows that more than one person is arriving.

Monsieur Delon *ARRIVE.*

Madame Delon *ARRIVE.*

Monsieur et Madame Delon *ARRIVENT.*

15 Paul et Valérie sont les enfants de M. et Mme Delon. *Paul and Valérie are Monsieur and Madame Delon's children.*

a Paul et Valérie *sont* **les enfants de M. et Mme Delon.**: *Paul and Valérie are M. and Mme Delon's children.*

Sont: *are* is the plural of **est**: *is.*

Paul *est* **l'enfant de M. et Mme Delon.**

Paul et Valérie *sont* **les enfants de M. et Mme Delon.**

les **enfants**: THE *children* Here again we find **les**, as **enfants** is plural. Notice that even though **enfants** begins with a vowel, **les** is still used. **Les** is the plural of both **le** and **l'**.

1

If you listen very carefully to the pronunciation of **les enfants,** it seems as if only one word is being pronounced. There seems to be a **z** sound between the two words, linking them together, as if the word were **zenfants.** This is because, when **les** comes before a word beginning with a vowel, the **s** is pronounced as a **z** and sounds as if it were attached to the word which follows. This linking of words is called a LIAISON.

Be careful with the pronunciation of **enfants.** Both syllables, in spite of their different spelling, have the same nasal quality which is not found in English. The **n** is not sounded separately.

Monsieur and Madame are often abbreviated to **M.** and **Mme. Mme** is not followed by a full stop.

16 Ils arrivent de Montréal. *They're arriving from Montreal.*

a When he was speaking about Monsieur Delon, Guy Martin used **il**:
Il arrive avec Mme Delon.
When he refers to both M. and Mme Delon he says:
Ils **arrivent de Montréal.**
il (sing.): *he*
ils (pl.): *they*

b REMEMBER: **les enfants de Monsieur et Madame Delon**: lit. *the children of Monsieur and Madame Delon.*
De can mean *of* or *from*, depending on the context in which it is used:
Je suis à l'aéroport *de* **Paris.** (*of*)
BUT:
J'arrive de Paris. (*from*)
J'arrive *de* **l'aéroport** *de* **Paris.** (*from . . . of*)

17 M. Delon est français. *Monsieur Delon is French.*

18 Ils ne sont pas canadiens. *They are not Canadian.*

a The negative — *not* in English — is formed in French by placing **ne** before the verb, and **pas** after it:
Je suis français.
Je *ne* **suis** *pas* **français.**

b Notice that in French **canadiens** has an s in the plural.

19 Ils sont français. *They're French.*
You have already seen **français** in the singular:
Monsieur Delon est français.
To make **canadien** plural an s was added; but **français** already ends in s in the singular, so it does not follow the usual rule, but remains unchanged in the plural:
Il est français.
Ils sont français.

20 Je suis un ami des Delon. *I'm a friend of the Delons.*

1

a **un ami**: *a friend*
If you listen carefully you will notice that here Guy Martin does pronounce the **n** in **un** (cf. N12a). It even sounds as though the word were **nami** (and not **ami**). Since **ami** begins witĥ a vowel the last letter of the preceding word is run on, into **ami**.
This is another example of a LIAISON. There is a liaison each time **un** precedes a word beginning with a vowel.

b **un ami des Delon**: *a friend of the Delons*
The words *de* and *les* cannot be used together in French. Instead **des** (which is a contraction of **de** + **les**) is used.

c There is no **s** at the end of **Delon**. In French, names of families do not take an **s** in the plural.

21 Ah! Voilà l'avion. *Ah! Here's the plane.*
l'avion: *the plane*
L' is used because **avion** begins with a vowel.

22 Voilà les Delon. *Here are the Delons.*
In N12a above (**un quart d'heure**), you learnt that the **n** of **un**, was not pronounced, and that **un** had a nasal sound. Now listen to Guy Martin say: **Voilà l'avion; Voilà les Delon.** The **n** is still not pronounced, but it sounds as though Guy were speaking through his nose, when he pronounces the **on** in **avion**, and in **Delon**. The sound is quite different from **un** but it, too, is nasal.

23 Un policier regarde les passeports. *An immigration officer is looking at the passports.*

a The British immigration officer has no exact counterpart in France. The job of checking passports at the frontier is performed by the **Sécurité du Territoire** or, at airports, by the **Police de l'Air** or, most frequently, by the **C.R.S. (Compagnies Républicaines de Sécurité).**

b **un policier**: *an immigration officer*
Un can mean *an* as well as *a*. In English we use *an* before·a word which begins with a vowel and *a* before one beginning with a consonant. In French **un** is always used.
un rendez-vous   un + consonant
un aéroport   un + vowel
Don't forget that there is a liaison before a vowel.

c **un policier regarde les passeports.**: *an immigration officer is looking at the passports.*
If you want to say *he is arriving; they are looking (at)* do not translate *he is* or *they are* and then try to add a word to mean *arriving* or *looking.* You must remember:

9

he is arriving: **il arrive**
they are looking at: **ils regardent.**

24 **Des douaniers regardent les bagages.** *Some customs officers are looking at the luggage.*

  a **un douanier**: *a customs officer*; **des douaniers**: lit. *customs officers*
The plural of **un**: *a* or *an* is **des.** This is sometimes translated as *some*, but often *some* is not necessary in English.
Be careful not to confuse **des** (plural of **un**) and **des** (**de** + **les**: *of the*).
Je suis un ami *des* Delon.: *I am a friend* OF THE *Delons.*
***Des* douaniers regardent les bagages.**: SOME *customs officers are looking at the luggage.*

  b **Des douaniers regarde*nt* les bagages.** Notice the same ending **-nt** as in **ils arrive*nt*, ils so*nt*.**

  c **Les bagages**: *the luggage* is almost always used in the plural, while in English *luggage* is always singular.

25 **Un douanier examine les bagages de M. Delon.** *A customs officer examines M. Delon's luggage.*

  a So far, Guy Martin has been DESCRIBING the scene around him; he has been telling us what is GOING ON.
M. Delon *arrive*, Paul et Valérie *arrivent*: *M. Delon* IS ARRIVING, *Paul and Valérie* ARE ARRIVING.
He also describes what the immigration officer and the customs officers ARE DOING at the airport.
Des douaniers *regardent* les bagages.: *Some customs officers* ARE LOOKING AT *the luggage.*
But now, he starts to REPORT a sequence of events. The first being:
Un douanier *examine* les bagages de M. Delon.: *A customs officer* (NOW) *examines M. Delon's luggage.*
Examine, like **arrive** and **regarde,** can, in English, mean either: *is examin*ING *or examin*ES.

  b **les bagages de M. Delon**: *M. Delon's luggage* (lit. *the luggage of M. Delon*) Remember that in French, it is not possible to say *M. Delon's luggage,* you have to say *the luggage of M. Delon.*

26 **Mme Delon admire l'uniforme du douanier.** *Mme Delon admires the customs officer's uniform.*

  a **l'uniforme du douanier**: lit. *the uniform* OF THE *customs officer*
In N20b above, you saw **des** as a contraction of **de** + **les** (*of the,* plural); now we have **du,** which is the contraction of **de** + **le** (*of the,* sing.)

b Listen carefully to the last four sentences. Notice the number of -e's that are not pronounced:
Un policier regardé les passéports.
Des douaniers regardént les bagagés.
Un douanier examiné les bagagés de M. Delon.
Mme Delon admiré l'uniformé du douanier.

27 **Il ne regarde pas le sac de Mme Delon.** *He doesn't look at Mme Delon's bag.*
il *ne* regarde *pas* . . . : *he doesn't look at* . . .
Remember the negative was formed by placing **ne** before **sont**, and **pas** after it (see N18a above). Other verbs are made negative in exactly the same way:
il **regarde** . . . : *he looks at* . . .
il **ne regarde pas** . . . : *he doesn't look at.* . . .

28 **Il regarde Valérie.** *He looks at Valérie.*
Be careful with **il regarde**: *he looks* (*at*). It does not end in **s**.

29 **Valérie regarde le douanier.** *Valérie looks at the customs officer.*

30 **Le douanier admire Valérie.** *The customs officer admires Valérie.*

31 **Il n'examine pas le sac de Valérie.** *He doesn't examine Valérie's bag.*
Il *n'*examine *pas* le sac.: *He doesn't examine the bag.*
Just as **le** becomes **l'** before a vowel (**l'aéroport**), and **je** becomes **j'** (**j'observe**), **ne** becomes **n'**:
Le douanier *n'* examine pas le sac.

32 **Voilà les cars de l'aéroport.** *Here are the airport buses.*
a **Voilà** comes from the phrase **Vois là!** *See there! Behold!* and so it can express *there is, there are, here is* or *here are.*
b Compare: **l'aéroport de Paris**: *the Paris airport with* **les enfants de M. et Mme Delon**: *M. and Mme. Delon's children.*

33 **M. Delon monte dans le car.** *M. Delon gets into the bus.*
Je suis *dans* le hall de l'aéroport.: *I am* IN *the airport terminal.*
M. Delon monte *dans* le car.: *M. Delon gets* INTO *the bus.*
Dans, therefore, can mean *in* or *into*, depending upon the context.

34 **Mme Delon et les enfants montent dans le car.** *Mme Delon and the children get into the bus.*
We find once again that when several people *arrive, look at, get into*, the verb ends in *-nt*:
il **arrive,** *ils arrivent*
il **regarde,** *ils regardent*
il **monte,** *ils montent*

1

35 **Moi aussi.** *So do I* (lit. *I too*).
Moi aussi is a simple French expression used where in English we would say, *so do I, I do too*.

PART TWO

36 **Deuxième partie** *Part two* (lit. *second part*)

37 **À l'aéroport d'Orly;** *At Orly airport;*
  a **À l'aéroport:** *at the airport* cf. N8 above
  b **à l'aéroport d'Orly:** lit. *at the airport of Orly*
  De becomes **d'** before a vowel just as:
  le becomes **l'** (**l'aéroport**)
  je becomes **j'** (**j'observe**)
  ne becomes **n'** (**n'examine pas**).

38 **au contrôle des passeports:** *at the passport control*
  À + le becomes **au**; **à** and **le** (meaning *the*) are never found together, but **à** followed by **l'** remains **à + l'**:
  Je suis au contrôle des passeports.
  BUT:
  Je suis à l'aéroport d'Orly.
  In N20b above, you saw that **de les** becomes **des** and that **de le** becomes **du**. Similarly, **à + le** becomes **au**.
  b **au contrôle *DES* passeports:** lit. *at the control of the passports.*
  Des here is **de + les**.

39 **Votre passeport, s'il vous plaît?** *Your passport, please?*
  a If you listen carefully to the speaker's intonation, you will notice that his voice rises towards the end of the sentence. It is this intonation that tells us that the sentence is, in fact, a question.
  b **votre passeport:** *your passport*
  votre **sac:** YOUR *bag*
  votre **car:** YOUR *bus*
  Listen carefully and you will hear that the **re** of **votre** is not sounded. The word is pronounced as though it were *vot'* **passeport.**
  c **s'il vous plaît:** *please*
  As you learn this expression, pay great attention to the pronunciation of **plaît.** You may think it sounds like the English word, *play*, but really the sound is nearer to the *e* in *let*.

40 **Voilà mon passeport.** *Here is my passport.*
  mon: MY
  mon **sac:** MY *bag*
  mon **car:** MY *bus*

Now you can say *my bag* and *your bag*, *my passport* and *your passport*:

mon sac, **mon** passeport; **votre** sac, **votre** passeport.

41 Merci, Monsieur . . . *Thank you.* (lit. *Thank you, Sir*)

a You now know *please* and *thank you*: **s'il vous plaît** and **merci.**

b Notice how often, for politeness, **Monsieur, Madame** or **Mademoiselle** is added to the expressions for *please* and *thank you*.

42 Ah! Vous êtes français, *Oh! You're French,*

a **vous êtes**: *you are*
Remember, **Je suis français.**: *I am French.*
Il est français.: *He is French.*
Ils sont français.: *They are French.* Here now is **Vous êtes français.**: *You are French.*

b Remember to put the accent ˆ over the first **ê** of **vous êtes.** This accent is called a circumflex.

43 mais vous habitez le Canada. *but you live in Canada.*

a This is the first time we have come across a verb (other than **vous êtes**) in the **vous** form. In the **vous** form, the verb ends in **-ez.** You can now make the **vous** forms of all the verbs you have met.
j'arrive, vous arrivez
je regarde, vous regardez
j'examine, vous examinez
j'admire, vous admirez
je monte, vous montez.

b *le* **Canada**: *Canada*
Canada is preceded by a word for *the* in French, but there is no need for a word for *in*, as **habiter** may mean *live in.*

44 Oui; j'arrive du Canada. *Yes, I've just arrived* (lit. *I'm arriving*) *from Canada.*
du Canada: *from Canada* You learnt (N16 above) that *from Montreal* is **de Montréal.** Because *Canada* is **le Canada** in French (N43b above), FROM *Canada* is **du (de + le) Canada.**

45 Votre passeport, s'il vous plaît, Madame? *Your passport, please.*
The customs officer addresses Mme Delon as **Madame.** This is the polite form of address in French, when talking to a woman.

46 Euh . . . un instant, s'il vous plaît, Monsieur . . . *Er, just a moment, please . . .*

47 Il est dans mon sac à main. *It's in my handbag.*
il est: *it is* **Il** means both *he* and *it*; here it refers to *passport*, so of course here **il** means *it*.

48 **Vous aussi, vous arrivez du Canada.** *You've just arrived from Canada, too.*
vous aussi: *you too.* cf. **moi aussi**: *I too* (N35 above)

49 **Merci, Madame** ... *Thank you* ... (lit. *Thank you, Madame.*)
In such expressions, **Monsieur, Madame** and **Mademoiselle** are not followed by the family name, even when it is known.

50 **Merci, Messieurs-Dames.** *Thank you.* (lit. *Thank you gentlemen and ladies* — that is, *Ladies and Gentlemen*). This phrase may be used in addressing a number of men and women or one man and one woman only.

51 **Voilà vos passeports.** *Here are your passports.*
***votre* passeport**: YOUR *passport* but ***vos* passeports**: YOUR *passports*
***votre* sac**: YOUR *bag* but ***vos* sacs**: YOUR *bags*.

52 **Vous avez quelque chose à déclarer?** *Anything to declare?* (lit. *You have got anything to declare?*)
We know this sentence is a question because of the intonation (the voice goes up towards the end).
vous avez: *you have got* Notice the **-ez** ending — the sign of the **vous** form.

53 **Est-ce que vous avez quelque chose à déclarer?** *Anything to declare?*
There is no difference between this question and the previous one, as regards meaning. When **est-ce que** (lit. *is it that*) is put in front of a statement, it turns the statement into a question.
Now we have a choice of question forms, either: **Monsieur Delon est français?** or **Est-ce que Monsieur Delon est français?**

54 **J'ai un demi-litre de whisky canadien**; *I've got a half-bottle of Canadian whisky*; (lit. a *half-litre*)
a **j'ai**: *I have*, or *I've got.* In the Introduction you met **j'ai quarante-deux ans**: lit. *I have forty-two years.*
b **un demi-litre de whisky canadien**: *a half-bottle of Canadian whisky*
   1   2   1   2
In French the adjective **(canadien)** usually follows the noun, **(whisky).**

55 **il est dans mes bagages.**: *it's in my luggage.*
mes bagages: *my luggage*; **mes**: *my*, is the plural form of **mon** and is used with plural nouns.
mon sac: *my bag*; **mes sacs**: *my bags*

56 **Bon, ça va.** *Good, that's all right.*

57 **Et vous, Madame?** *What about you?* (lit. *And you?*)

58 **Non; je n'ai rien à déclarer.** *No; I haven't got anything to declare.*

a Notice the same nasal sound in **non** as in **mon, Delon, bon.**

b **ne . . . rien** Ne placed before the verb and **rien** after it mean *nothing* or *not anything.* Note that you cannot use **pas** as well.

59 **Et vous, Mademoiselle?** *And what about you?* (lit. . . . , *Miss*)

60 **J'ai un petit flacon de parfum . . .** *I've got a small bottle of perfume . . .*
Petit: *small* comes before the noun:
un *petit* sac; un *petit* flacon de parfum.
Un flacon refers to a fairly small bottle.

61 **Et un grand flacon de parfum.** *And a large bottle of perfume.*
Grand, like **petit,** goes in front of the noun:
un grand sac; un grand flacon de parfum
Petit and **grand** are exceptions to the rule that the adjective usually follows the noun it describes (N54c above).

62 **Le petit flacon est pour Jacqueline.** *The small bottle is for Jacqueline.*
pour Jacqueline: *for Jacqueline*

63 **Le grand flacon est pour moi!** *The large bottle is for me!*
This is the same *moi* as in the expression *moi aussi.*

64 **Il est pour vous?** *It's for you?*
pour vous: *for you*
Il est pour *moi*.: *It's for* ME.
Il est pour *vous*.: *It's for* YOU.

65 **Bon, ça va . . .** *That's all right.*

66 **Et vous, Monsieur?** *And what about you?*

67 **Des disques:** *Records*
un disque: *a record*
des disques: *records* (N24a)

68 **Pas *des* disques, mais *un* disque: un microsillon.** *Not records but a record, an L.P.*
You probably recognize **pas** from **ne . . . pas.**
Vous avez un sac?
Non, pas *un* sac, des sacs.

69 **Et j'ai deux petits flacons d'after-shave.** *And I've got two small bottles of after-shave.*

deux: *two* We could have translated **un disque** as *one record*. You now know the first two numerals:

un disque: *one record*
deux disques: *two records*

un flacon: *one bottle*
deux flacons: *two bottles*

70 **Dans le grand hall, à Orly.** *In the entrance hall at Orly.*

71 **Bonjour, Madame.** *Hello, Mme Delon.*
As in the case of **s'il vous plaît**, it is polite to follow **Bonjour** by **Madame, Mademoiselle** or **Monsieur**. At the beginning of the course, Guy Martin simply said **Bonjour**. Had he known your name, he would almost certainly have added: **Madame, Mademoiselle,** or **Monsieur.**

72 **Comment allez-vous?** *How are you?* (lit. *How go you?*)
Madame Delon replies: **Je vais très bien, merci.**: *I am very well, thank you* (lit. *I go very well, thanks*).

73 **Et vous, Monsieur? Comment allez-vous?** *And what about you? How are you?*

74 **Très bien, merci.** *Very well, thank you.*
A slightly shortened version of **Je vais très bien, merci.**

75 **Moi, je suis fatigué.** *I am tired.*
Moi, **je suis fatigué** is the same as saying in English: *I am tired,* when *I* is emphasized.
This is the same **moi** as in **moi aussi**: *I do too;* **pour moi**: *for me.*
The following example shows how *moi je* can be used:
Je suis français.: *I'm French.*
Moi, je suis canadien.: *I am Canadian.*

76 **Eh bien, voilà le car.** *Well, here's the bus.*

77 **En route pour l'hôtel!** *Off to the hotel!*
a Hôtel has a circumflex accent on the **o**: **ô**.
b Earlier (N10b above) you saw that words beginning with **h**, such as **hall**, are thought of as beginning with a consonant, even though it is a silent one. But there are some words beginning with **h** in French which are thought of as beginning with a vowel. **Hôtel** is one of these words, and therefore **l'** not **le** must be used.
You have to learn these as you go along. We shall have to refer again to this type of h. We shall call it silent h.

78 **Moi, j'habite Paris.** *I live in Paris.* Another silent **h**, before which **je** and **ne** become **j'** and **n'**.

The language you have learnt

He, it

Guy Martin Il	est à Orly.
Le passeport Il	est dans mon sac.

He, they + verb in the present tense

M. Delon Il Un douanier	*arrive*	à Orly.
	observe	les voyageurs.
	examine	les bagages.
Les Delon Ils Des douaniers	*arrivent*	à Orly.
	observent	les voyageurs.
	examinent	les bagages.

I arrive, you arrive

*J'*arrive *Vous* arrivez	à Orly.

Asking 'yes' or 'no' questions

Vous avez *Est-ce que* vous avez	quelque chose à déclarer?

Not

Je	*ne* suis *pas*	canadien.
Il	*n'*est *pas*	
Ils	*ne* sont *pas*	canadiens.
Je Il	*ne* regarde *pas*	les passeports.
Je Il	*n'*arrive *pas*	de Montréal.

1 **Where?**

Je suis	à	Orly.
Guy Martin est	à l'	aéroport d'Orly.
M. Delon est	au	contrôle des passeports.
Mon passeport est	dans	mon sac.

Where from?

	de	Montréal.
	de l'	aéroport.
Les Delon arrivent	d'	Orly.
	du	Canada.

Whose?

Le sac	de	Madame Delon.
Le hall	de l'	aéroport.
L'aéroport	d'	Orly.
L'uniforme	du	douanier.
Un ami	des	Delon.

Singular and plural adjectives

Un	petit grand	flacon de parfum.
Deux	petits grands	flacons de parfum.

My, your, with singular and plural nouns

	mon votre	passeport. sac à main.
Voilà	mes vos	passeports. sacs à main.

18

À l'hôtel At the hotel

What happens

PART 1
La chambre de Paul: *Paul's room*
Paul Delon tells us about himself, and his family. He doesn't like Paris, the hotel or his room, but he does like French girls.

PART 2
À la réception de l'Hôtel du Nord: *At the reception desk of the Hôtel du Nord*
The receptionist has three rooms for the Delon family, which will cost one hundred francs a day, everything included. He tells them which floor their rooms are on. Monsieur and Madame Delon and Paul take the lift. Valérie prefers to walk up to her room.

PART 3
Monsieur Blois à l'hôtel: *Monsieur Blois at the hotel*
Monsieur Blois checks in at his hotel.

New words in this lesson

à in
(elle) a (she) has
j'adore I love
adorer to love
(il) aime (he) likes, loves
aimer to like, to love
allons well
alors so, then
l'année (*f*) year
l'ascenseur (*m*) lift
le beurre butter
la bicyclette cycling
la bicyclette bicycle
c'est (=ce+est) it's, that's, is this?
c'est parfait, that's good, fine
c'est tout that's all
c'est vrai it's true
c'est vrai? really?

ça fait that's, that comes to
cent hundred
la chaise chair
la chambre room
cher expensive
cinq five
cinquième fifth
la clef key
compris included
comprise included
la confiture jam
convenable nice, decent
le croissant croissant (roll)
la cuisine kitchen
de (la) some
dix ten
la douche shower
du some

2

elle she
elles they
enfin well
l'escalier (*m*) stairs, staircase
les escaliers (*m*) stairs
l'étage (*m*) floor
la famille family
fatiguée tired
la fiche form
la fleur flower
le football football
le franc franc
la Française French girl,
  Frenchwoman
le frère brother
le garage garage
le grand lit double bed
grande large
la gymnastique gymnastics
il y a there is, (there's), there are
l'infirmière (*f*) nurse
le jambon ham
le jardin garden
jeune young
je joue I play
jouer (à) to play
le jour day
la the
le lavabo washbasin
le lit bed
le lycéen schoolboy
ma my
magnifique marvellous
la mère mother
monter (dans) to go up (in),
  to get into
n'est-ce pas? isn't it? aren't they?
  haven't you?
non alors! Oh, no!
le numéro number
l'œuf (*m*) egg
(ils) ont (they) have
le pain bread
par jour a day, per day
pardon sorry

le parent parent
parfait perfect, fine
le père father
le petit déjeuner breakfast
petite small
la poubelle dustbin
je préfère I prefer
préférer to prefer
premier first
prèsque almost
le professeur teacher
quatre four
la réception reception (desk)
le réceptionniste receptionist
la salle de bains bathroom
la secrétaire secretary
la semaine week
le service service charge
seulement only
signer to sign
la sœur sister
le sport sport
sur on, onto
la taxe tax
le tennis tennis
tous les jours every day
tout everything, all
tout le monde everyone
toute la famille the whole family
toute l'année all the year round
toutes les chambres all the rooms
toutes les semaines every week
la tranche slice
trois three
une a, one
la valise suitcase
venez come
venir to come
la ville city, town
je voudrais I'd like, I want
vous voulez will you, would you,
  you want to
vouloir to want to
vrai true
la vue view

Notes

PART ONE

1 La chambre de Paul *Paul's bedroom* (lit. *the room of Paul*)
la chambre: *the room*

20

All French nouns belong to one of two groups: masculine or **2**
feminine. You already know the word for *the* which is used with
masculine nouns: **le**. **La** is the word for *the* which is used with
feminine nouns. It is easy to see why a noun such as *father* belongs
to the masculine group, or *mother* to the feminine; but there is no
apparent reason why the majority of nouns in French belong to one
group rather than the other. The best way to remember which
nouns are masculine and which feminine is to learn each new noun
with either **le** or **la** as it appears in the lesson vocabulary.

2 **J'arrive du Canada.** *I've just arrived* (lit. *I am arriving*) *from Canada.*

3 **Je suis lycéen.** *I'm a schoolboy.*
There is no equivalent of *a* in the French sentence: lit. *I am
schoolboy.* Whenever *I am, he is* etc. is followed by a job, profession
or by a nationality, the French say *je suis, il est*, etc. plus the noun for
the job, profession or nationality: **Il est policier.**: *He is an immigration
officer.* **Je suis douanier.**: *I am a customs officer.*

4 **Mon père est professeur de français à Québec.** *My father's a French
teacher in Quebec.*
a **est professeur** Remember that there is no need for the equivalent
of *a* in the French sentence (N3 above).
b **à Québec** In lesson 1 you learnt **à**: *at* (L1, N8). It also means *in*
when you are saying *in* a town or place.
c **Québec** Listen to the pronunciation: **qu** is pronounced k.

5 **Ma mère est infirmière.** *My mother is a nurse.*
ma: *my* You have already learnt two words for *my*: **mon** (L1, N47)
and **mes** (L1, N55). **Mon** is used with masculine nouns, **mon père,**
and with feminine nouns which begin with a vowel, **mon infirmière;**
mes is used with all plural nouns, **mes bagages, mes enfants. Ma** is
used with feminine singular nouns: **ma mère**: *my mother*, **ma
chambre**: *my room.*

6 **J'ai une sœur, Valérie.** *I have a sister, Valérie.*
une sœur **Une** is the feminine form of **un** and is used with feminine
nouns. It means *a* or *one.*

7 **Elle est secrétaire.** *She's a secretary.*
a **elle est**: *she is* Remember, **il est**: *he/it is* (L1, N47).
b **... est secrétaire** Again, there is no word for *a* before **secrétaire**
because it describes her job (N3 above).

8 **Je suis à Paris.** *I'm in Paris.*
Je suis à l'hôtel. *I'm at the hotel.*

2

à Paris ... à l'hôtel In English we say *in* a town but *at* a hotel; in French **à** stands for both *in* and *at* (L1, N8b and N4b above).

9 **Tout le monde aime Paris.** *Everyone likes/loves Paris.*
Tout le monde: lit. *all the world*, means *everyone, everybody.*

10 **Moi, je n'aime pas Paris.** *I don't like Paris.*
a **moi, je ...** As you saw in lesson 1 (N75), the word **moi** is used to emphasize **je.**
b **je n'aime pas** Remember that **ne** is shortened to **n'** when the verb which follows begins with a vowel, (L1, N31).

11 **Paris est une grande ville.** *Paris is a big city.*
a **une ville** Ville is a feminine noun, so **une** ville: A *city*, **la** ville: THE *city.*
b **Grande**: *big, large* is the feminine form of **grand,** which we saw in **un grand flacon** (L1, N61). The feminine form is used here to agree with the feminine noun **ville.** In French all adjectives agree with the noun they describe. If the noun is masculine, then the masculine form of the adjective is used; if the noun is feminine, the feminine form of the adjective. Most masculine adjectives not already ending in **e** add a final **e** to make the feminine form.

12 **Je n'aime pas les grandes villes.** *I don't like big cities.*
a **Les** is the plural of both **la** and **le.**
b **Grandes** is the plural of **grande.**
c **les grandes villes**: *big cities* lit. *the big cities* In French you use **le, la, l'** or **les** with the noun when you are making a generalization. In English this *the* is omitted.

13 **J'aime le sport.** *I like sport.*
le sport: *sport* c.f. N12 above.

14 **J'aime le tennis, le football et la gymnastique.** *I like tennis, football and gymnastics.*
Notice that *the*: **le, la** is repeated for each noun.

15 **À Québec, je joue au tennis tous les jours.** *In Quebec, I play tennis every day.*
a **Je joue au tennis.**: *I play tennis.*
Je joue au football.: *I play football.*
In lesson 1 you saw **il regarde**: *he looks at* (no word for *at* in French). Now you see the reverse: a preposition (*au*) in French where one is not used in English.
b **au** As you saw in lesson 1, (N38) **le** may not follow **à** in French. You must therefore say, **Je joue au tennis (jouer à + le tennis).**

c **tous les jours**: *every day*, lit. *all the days* **Tous** is the plural of **tout** which you have already seen in the phrase **tout le monde**: *everyone* (N9 above). **Tous** is used with masculine plural nouns.

MASCULINE SINGULAR: **tout le monde**
MASCULINE PLURAL: **tous les jours**

16 **Et je joue au football toutes les semaines.** *And I play football every week.*
toutes les semaines: *every week* (lit. *all the weeks*)
Toutes is the feminine plural of **tout** (N9 and N15c above) and is used with feminine plural nouns, in this case **semaines.** So you now know three forms, **tout, tous** and **toutes.**

17 **J'adore la bicyclette.** *I love cycling.*
J'adore: *I love* is a much stronger expression than **j'aime** (N13 and N14 above).

18 **À Québec, j'ai une bicyclette magnifique.** *In Quebec, I've got a marvellous bicycle.*
magnifique Adjectives such as **magnifique** which end in **e** in the masculine singular, remain exactly the same in the feminine singular: **un disque magnifique, une bicyclette magnifique.**
Remember that in French the adjective usually follows the noun (L1, N54c). A few common adjectives such as **grand** and **petit,** are placed before the noun.

19 **Ma chambre est petite.** *My room's small.*
Petite: *small, little,* is the feminine form of **petit** and agrees with **la chambre,** which is feminine. Listen carefully to the pronunciation of **petite**: the second **t** is sounded, **pétite.**
Incidentally, neither **e** is pronounced.

20 **Dans ma chambre, il y a une chaise.** *In my room there's a chair.*

21 **C'est tout.** *That's all.*
a **c'est = ce + est** Here **ce** means *that*; **est** means *is.* So **c'est** means *that is.*
b **tout**: *all, everything*

22 **Ma sœur a une chambre avec douche.** *My sister has a room with a shower.*

Mes parents ont une chambre avec salle de bains. *My parents have a room with a bathroom.*
a **Mes**: *my,* is a plural here, to agree with **parents.**
b **Ont**: *have,* when it means *they* (here **mes parents**) *have.*
Il a une chambre.: *He has a room.*
Ils ont une chambre.: *They have a room.*

2

2 **23** **Il y a des salles de bains dans l'hôtel, c'est vrai.** *There are bathrooms in the hotel, it's true.*

a **il y a**: *there are* In N20 above you saw that **il y a** means *there is*; it also means *there are*. Be careful not to confuse **il y a** with **voilà**, which also means *there is, there are*. **Il y a** is used for statements of fact, whereas **voilà** is used when pointing out or noticing something. Thus you would say:
Voilà les Delon!: *Here are/There are the Delons!*
but:
Il y a une chaise dans ma chambre.: *There's a chair in my room.*
In this latter sentence you would not be indicating where the chair is in the room; you would be stating the fact that there *is* a chair in the room.
N.B. **il y a** never means *here is*.

b **des salles de bains** Just as the plural of both **le** and **la** is **les**, and the plural of **mon** and **ma** is **mes**, so **des** is the plural of both **un** and **une**. Notice that the plural of **salle de bains** is **salles de bains**.

24 **J'aime bien le petit déjeuner canadien**: *I do like Canadian breakfasts*: (lit. *the Canadian breakfast:*)

a **bien**: lit. *well*, is used here for emphasis.

b **canadien** has a small **c** because it is an adjective here.

25 **un œuf et une tranche de jambon.** *an egg and a slice of ham.*

a **un œuf**: *an egg*, another word with **œ** (N6 above).

b **et une** Note that there is no liaison after **et**: *and*.

26 **Je n'aime pas le petit déjeuner français**: *I don't like French breakfasts*: (lit. *the French breakfast*):

27 **du pain, du beurre, de la confiture et des croissants.** *bread, butter, jam and croissants* (lit. *some bread, some butter*, etc.).

a **Du** in **du pain** and **du beurre** means *some*. So does **de la** in **de la confiture**. In this context *some* does not need to be used in English. As we know **des** in **des croissants** is the plural of **un**.
le pain, *le* beurre   *du* pain, *du* beurre
la confiture   *de la* confiture
les croissants   *des* croissants
Notice that the word for *some* is repeated before each noun, even if they are both masculine: *du* **pain**, *du* **beurre** . . .

b A **croissant** is a kind of crescent-shaped roll.

28 **Je n'aime rien.** *I don't like anything.*
You know how to form the negative *not* by putting **ne (n')** before

the verb and **pas** after it (L1, N18a):
Je *n'aime pas* la chambre.: *I do not like the room.*
When you put **ne** before the verb and **rien** after it, it means *not . . .
anything . . ., nothing:*
Je n'aime rien.: *I do not like anything.*
Il ne regarde rien.: *He is not looking at anything.*

29 **Oh, pardon! J'aime les jeunes Françaises!** *Oh, sorry! I like French
girls!* (lit. *young Frenchwomen*).

a **Jeunes**: *young*, is feminine plural here to agree with **Françaises.**
The masculine and feminine singular forms of this word are the
same: **jeune** (cf. **magnifique**, N18 above). The masculine or
feminine plural is **jeunes.**

b **les . . . Françaises**: lit. *Frenchwomen* **Françaises** is a noun here, not
an adjective, so it is written with a capital letter.
les Français: (*the*) *Frenchmen* or *the French*
la Française: (*the*) *Frenchwoman*
les Françaises: (*the*) *Frenchwoman*
Note the pronunciation of **Françaises**. The first **s** is sounded as a **z**
and the ending **-es** is silent.

PART TWO

30 **À la réception de l'Hôtel du Nord** *At the reception desk of the Hotel
du Nord*

31 **Oui; j'ai vos chambres.** *Yes, I've got your rooms.*
vos chambres Remember, **vos**: *your* is used with plural nouns.

32 **J'ai une chambre à deux lits, avec salle de bains: la chambre
numéro trois.** *I've got a double room with a bathroom: room number
three.*

a **à deux lits**: lit. *with two beds*

b **la chambre numéro trois** Notice that in French you say *la* **chambre
numéro . . .** where in English we say *room number . . .*

33 **Alors, ça fait cent francs par jour.** *That's a hundred francs a day,
then.*

a **Ça fait** is the French equivalent of *that comes to, that is* (*will cost*).

b **cent**: *a* (*one*) *hundred* In French you say simply **cent**, in English *a*
or *one hundred.*

c **par jour**: *a* (*per*) *day*
par semaine: *a* (*per*) *week*

34 **Allons, le petit déjeuner est compris, n'est-ce pas?** (*Well*), *breakfast
is included, isn't it?*

2   **a**   **le petit déjeuner** Again, **le** is needed in French where *the* is not used in English.

     b   **n'est-ce pas?** is the French equivalent of *isn't it, aren't they, aren't you, haven't you, doesn't it,* etc.

The speaker invites the listener to agree with him. In English there are a variety of ways of doing this; in French there is only one: **n'est-ce pas?**

M. Delon est français, n'est-ce pas?: *M. Delon is French, isn't he?*

Vous avez deux chambres, n'est-ce pas?: *You have two rooms, haven't you?*

35   **Oui, Monsieur. Tout est compris: le petit déjeuner et le service.**
Yes sir. Everything is included: breakfast and the service charge.
tout: *everything, all* (cf. N21 above). The second **t** of **tout** is pronounced here to make a liaison with **est** — **tout est.**

36   **Et les taxes?** *And taxes? (Taxes too?)*

37   **Oui, elles sont comprises.** *Yes, they are included.*

     a   **elles**: *they* When *they* refers to a feminine plural noun you must use **elles. Ils** refers only to masculine plural nouns. Here **elles** is used because it refers to **les taxes,** which is a feminine plural.

     b   **Comprises** is a feminine plural, agreeing with **elles.**

38   **C'est parfait.** *That's fine.*
Parfait: lit. *perfect* is used colloquially in the sense of *very good, fine.*

39   **Voilà, Monsieur: une fiche, une fiche pour toute la famille** *Here you are, sir: a form, one form for the whole family.*

     a   **une fiche . . . une fiche** Here you see **une** meaning both *a* and *one.* When you register at a French hotel you are given a form to fill in.

     b   **toute la famille** You already know **tout** (m. sing, N9 above), **tous** (m. pl., N15c above) and **toutes** (f. pl., N16 above). Here is the feminine singular form, **toute.**

You saw the word **tout** on its own in N21 and N35 above, where it was translated by *all* or *everything.* When it is followed by a noun, as in N9, N15c, N16 above and here, it is the equivalent of *every* or *all* in English.

40   **Voilà.** *There you are.*
Voilà means *here is/are* and *there is/are* — so it can mean *there you are* as well as *here you are.*

41   **Vous voulez signer la fiche, Monsieur?** *Would you sign/would you mind signing the form, sir?/ Will you sign . . .* (lit. *You want to sign the form, sir?*)

a **Vous voulez . . . ?:** lit. *you want . . . ?* is the equivalent of *will you . . . ? would you mind . . . ? would you like to . . . ?* etc.

b **signer** The verb forms TO *sign*, TO *like*, TO *look at* are called the INFINITIVE. The infinitive of many French verbs ends in **-er**: **aimer**: *to like*, **regarder**: *to look at*, **arriver**: *to arrive*

2

42 **C'est votre valise, Mademoiselle?** *Is this your suitcase, miss?* (lit. *That's/It's your suitcase, miss?*)
You have seen **c'est** with adjectives — **c'est vrai, c'est parfait, c'est cher.** Now we find it with a noun, **C'est votre valise?**

43 **c'est la valise de mon père.** *it's my father's suitcase.*
la valise de mon père Remember, you have to say *the suitcase of my father* in French (L1, N9d).

44 **La chambre numéro trois est au premier étage.** *Room number three is on the first floor.*
a **au premier étage:** lit. *at the first floor*
b **Premier:** *first* is the masculine singular form. You have seen the feminine singular form, **première**, in **Première partie:** *Part one* (lit. *first part*) (L1, N3).
Adjectives which end in **-er** in the masculine singular end in **-ère** in the feminine singular.

45 **Toutes les chambres sont au premier étage, n'est-ce pas?** *All the rooms are on the first floor, aren't they?*
N'est-ce pas? here means *aren't they?* (N34c above).

46 **Votre chambre, Mademoiselle, est au cinquième.** *Your room, miss, is on the fifth (floor).*
a **cinquième** It is not necessary to add **étage:** *floor.*
b **est au** Note the liaison — est͜ au.

47 **Vous avez une vue magnifique sur le jardin.** *You have a marvellous view of the garden.*
une vue sur: lit. *a view on*, or *on to* In English we say *a view of.*

48 **Il y a des fleurs toute l'année, Mademoiselle.** *There are flowers all the year round, (miss).*
a **Il y a des fleurs** Again, in French *des fleurs*, in English, just *flowers.*
b **toute l'année:** lit. *all the year* The feminine **toute** is used because **l'année** is a feminine noun (N39c above).

49 **C'est vrai?** *Really?* (lit. *That's true?*)
The intonation tells us that this is a question.

2   50   **Est-ce que j'ai une 'vue magnifique', moi aussi?** *Have I got a*
'magnificent view', too? (lit: *me too?*)
Remember, when **est-ce que** is put in front of a statement, it turns
the statement into a question.

51   **Vous, vous êtes au deuxième étage.** *You're on the second floor.*
Vous, vous . . . is the emphatic way of saying *you*. Remember, **Moi
je** . . . (L1, N75).
Moi, je suis au deuxième étage.: *I'm on the second floor.*
Vous, vous êtes au deuxième étage.: *You're on the second floor.*

52   **Oh! Il n'aime rien, mon frère.** *Oh, my brother doesn't like anything.*
As in N50 above, the emphasized words, **mon frère**, come at the
end of the sentence. **Il n'aime rien, mon frère** is more emphatic than
mon frère n'aime rien.

53   **Voilà vos clefs: la clef de la chambre numéro trois, la clef de la
chambre quatre et la clef de la chambre dix.** *Here are your keys;
the key to room number three, the key to room four and the key to
room ten.*
   a   **la clef de la chambre**: lit. *the key of the room*   You already know
de: *of*, **du**: *of the* (m) and **des**: *of the* (pl.). Here we have **de la**:
of the. This form is used with feminine singular words.
   b   **la chambre quatre**   All the numbers except **un/une** have one form for
both masculine and feminine.

54   **Vous voulez monter dans l'ascenseur, Messieurs-Dames?** *Would you
like to go up in the lift?*
   a   **vous voulez** . . . ? (c.f. N41a above)
   b   **Monter dans** usually means *to get into* (L1, N33); here it means
to go up in.

55   **Oh, oui, merci! Je suis fatiguée.** *Oh, yes, thank you! I'm tired.*
Fatiguée: *tired*, is the feminine form of **fatigué**. Adjectives which
end in **é** in the masculine take an **e** in the feminine, but are
pronounced in the same way.
The feminine form **fatiguée** is used here because it is Madame Delon
who is tired.

56   **Et vous, Mademoiselle, est-ce que vous voulez monter aussi?** *And you,
miss, would you like to go up too?*

57   **Merci.**: *No, thank you.*
Merci can mean either *thank you* or *no thank you.*

58   **Vous n'aimez pas les ascenseurs?** *You don't like lifts?/Don't you like
lifts?*

59 **Non, je n'aime pas les ascenseurs. Je préfère les escaliers.** *No, I don't like lifts . . . I prefer (the) stairs.*

je préfère: *I prefer* This part of the verb *to prefer* has one acute accent é and one grave accent è; the **vous** form, *you prefer*, has two acute accents, **vous préférez** and so has the infinitive: **préférer**: *to prefer.*

60 **Moi aussi. Voilà l'escalier. Venez avec moi!** *So do I. There are the stairs. Come with me!*

L'escalier, the singular form of **les escaliers,** also means *the stairs, (staircase).*

The language you have learnt

I'd like, I'd like to

Je voudrais	une chambre.
	examiner vos bagages.

Would you like . . . ? Would you like to . . . ?

Vous voulez	votre clef?
	jouer au tennis?

He, she, it is; they are + adjective

Guy Martin Il		français.
Valérie Delon Elle		française.
Le sac Il	*est*	petit.
La chambre Elle		grande.
Les Delon Ils		français.
Mme Delon et Valérie Elles		françaises.
Les sacs Ils	*sont*	petits.
Les chambres Elles		grandes.

2 **Some**

Du	pain. beurre.
De la	confiture.
Des	croissants.

My, your (singular and plural)

Voilà	*mon* *votre*	père. sac.
	ma *votre*	mère. valise.
	mes *vos*	frères. valises.

It's a, my

C'est	*un* sac à main. *ma* valise.

Moi, je; vous, vous

Moi, je	monte dans le car.
Vous, vous	montez dans le car.

Moi and vous with et and pour

Vous voulez monter dans l'ascenseur? Vous voulez monter dans le car?	*Et moi?* *Et moi?*	Est-ce que je monte, moi aussi? Est-ce que je monte, moi aussi?
J'aime le jambon. Elle adore la confiture.	*Et vous?* *Et vous?*	
La chambre numéro deux Le petit déjeuner Le flacon de parfum	est	*pour moi.* *pour vous.*

30

N'est-ce pas?

Je suis Vous êtes	jeune, fatigué,	
Les Delon sont	canadiens,	*n'est-ce pas?*
J'ai Vous avez Ils ont	une bicyclette magnifique, une chambre à deux lits,	

Leçon trois *Lesson three*
Troisième leçon *Third lesson*

La chambre numéro trois   Room number three

What happens

PART 1
L'Hôtel du Nord: *The Hôtel du Nord*
Georges Louvier, the hotel receptionist, talks about his job, and about the hotel. He likes the Delon family — especially Valérie.

PART 2
Dans la chambre numéro trois: *In room number three*
Georges shows Monsieur and Madame Delon their room.

Dans la salle de bains: *In the bathroom*
They look over the bathroom. Monsieur Delon wants to see his children's rooms. His wife wants to have a bath.

PART 3
Les clients sont difficiles.: *The guests are difficult.*
A chambermaid is complaining to the receptionist.

Un hôtel confortable: *A comfortable hotel*
The manager is very proud of the Hôtel du Canada.

New words in this lesson

aimable nice
l'ampoule (*f*) bulb
aujourd'hui today
aux at (the)
nous avons we've got, we have
la baignoire bath
le bain bath
le bidet bidet
le bouton switch
ce it
certainement certainly
chaque each
charmant lovely
chaud hot
le chauffage heating
le chauffage central central heating

chérie dear, darling
le cintre coat-hanger
le client guest
la commode chest of drawers
confortable comfortable
la couverture blanket
(il) demande (he) asks for
demander to ask for
difficile difficult
l'eau (*f*) water
électrique electric
en général generally, usually
est-ce qu'il y a? is there?
l'étagère (*f*) shelf
excellent excellent

facile easy
la femme de chambre chambermaid
froid cold
le gérant (d'hôtel) (hotel) manager
gratuit free
ici here
jeter un coup d'œil to have a look at
  (glance at)
joli pretty
là there
la lampe lamp
(il) marche (it) works
marcher to work
le matin morning
même even, quite
naturellement of course
nous we
l'oreiller (m) pillow
le placard wardrobe

le plateau tray
je porte I carry, take
porter to carry, to take
prendre to take
la prise de courant socket
quelquefois sometimes
le rasoir électrique electric razor
remplacer to replace
sans without
sept seven
la serviette towel
six six
surtout especially
sympathique nice, pleasant
le téléphone telephone
téléphoner (à) to telephone
le traversin bolster
vider to unpack, to empty
vingt twenty

3

Notes

PART ONE

1 **Je suis réceptionniste.** *I am a receptionist.*

2 **Je suis le réceptionniste de l'Hôtel du Nord.** *I am the receptionist at* (lit. *of*) *the Hôtel du Nord.*
   Georges Louvier says **Je suis *le* réceptionniste** here, because he is talking about his particular job (cf. L2, N3).

3 **Je voudrais être gérant d'hôtel.** *I'd like to be a hotel manager.*
   French verbs may be divided into certain definite categories, i.e. groups of verbs which behave in the same way. You will see how these categories work later. There are, however, several verbs which do not fit into any category, but which are formed in a quite different way. These are the IRREGULAR VERBS, and must be learned individually. **Être** is one of these verbs. You have already learnt **je suis, il est, vous êtes, ils sont,** which are all parts of this verb. **Être** is the infinitive (See Appendix).

4 **Ce n'est pas un hôtel cher.** *It's not an expensive hotel.*
   Notice that **cher** comes AFTER the noun to which it refers.

5 **Mais c'est un hôtel excellent.** *But it's an excellent hotel.*
   Georges uses *c'est* here and *ce* n'est pas in the previous sentence. If you look back you will see that **c'est** and NOT **il est** is used when you want to follow *it is* by an article (**le, la, un, une**) and a noun:

3

It is a suitcase.: **C'est une valise.**
It is the Hôtel du Nord.: **C'est l'Hôtel du Nord.**

6 **Nous avons le chauffage central.** *We've got central heating.*
nous avons: *we have (got)*

7 **Naturellement, nous avons aussi l'eau chaude et l'eau froide.** *Of course we've also got hot and cold water.*
a **chaude**: *hot, warm* The feminine form **chaude** (with the **d** sounded) is used here because **l'eau** is feminine. (The masculine singular is **chaud.**)
b **froide**: *cold* Again **froide** is feminine (with the **d** sounded) to agree with **l'eau.** (The masculine singular is **froid.**)

8 **Dans chaque chambre, il y a le téléphone.** *In each room, there's a telephone.*
a **Chaque**: *each* is another adjective which is the same in both the masculine and the feminine singular forms. (L2, N18).
b **le téléphone** In this French sentence *le* **téléphone**, in English A *telephone.*

9 **Le gérant est très aimable.** *The manager is very nice.*
Note the liaison — **très aimable.**

10 **Les femmes de chambre sont très aimables. Et moi aussi.** *The chambermaids are very nice. And so am I.*
a **les femmes de chambre**: *the chambermaids*
la femme de chambre: *the chambermaid*
b **moi aussi** In lesson 1 (N35) and lesson 2 (N60) **moi aussi** meant *so* DO *I.* Here the English equivalent is *so* AM *I.*

11 **L'hôtel a vingt chambres.** *The hotel has twenty rooms.*

12 **Les chambres ne sont pas chères.** *The rooms are not dear.*
Chères is the feminine plural of **cher**: *expensive.* Remember (L2, N44b) that adjectives ending in **-er** in the masculine singular end in **-ère** in the feminine.

13 **En général, l'ascenseur marche très bien.** *Generally, the lift works very well.*

14 **Tous les matins, je porte les petits déjeuners dans les chambres.** *Every morning I take the breakfasts to* (lit. *into*) *the rooms.*
a **tous les matins**: lit. *all the mornings* Remember, **tous les jours**: *every day* (L2, N15c), **toutes les semaines**: *every week* (L2, N16).

15 Quelquefois, je porte trois petits déjeuners, sur trois plateaux. **3**
Sometimes, I carry three breakfasts, on three trays.
les plateaux: *the trays*
le plateau: *the tray*
Nouns ending in **-eau** in the singular take an **x**, not an **s**, in the plural.

16 Ce n'est pas facile! C'est même difficile . . .
It's not easy! In fact, it's quite (lit. *even*) *difficult . . .*
facile: *easy* **Facile** here is masculine, even though it ends in **e**.

17 En général, les clients de l'hôtel sont sympathiques. *Generally, the guests* (lit. *of the hotel*) *are nice.*

18 Mais quelquefois, il y a des clients difficiles. *But sometimes there are difficult guests.*

19 Quelquefois un client demande une salle de bains avec le téléphone
Sometimes a guest asks for a bathroom with a telephone
a **(il) demande**: (*he*) *asks* FOR   Remember **il regarde**: *he looks* AT;
j'habite . . . : *I live* IN . . .

20 Les Delon sont sympathiques. *The Delons are nice.*
les Delon   Remember that French surnames do not take an **s** in the plural (L1, N20c).

21 J'aime surtout Valérie. Elle est très jolie. *I like Valérie best.* (lit. *I like especially Valérie*). *She's very pretty.*
a **surtout**: *especially, particularly*   Note the position of **surtout**.
b **jolie**: *pretty* is feminine here, to agree with Valérie. The masculine form is **joli**.

PART TWO
22 Est-ce que les lits sont confortables? *Are the beds comfortable?*
a Here is another example of a question with **est-ce que** . . . :
Les lits sont confortables.: *The beds are comfortable.*
Est-ce que les lits sont confortables? *Are the beds comfortable?*
b **Confortable** ends in **e** in the masculine singular, so the feminine singular is also **confortable** (L2, N18). Notice that **confortable** is spelt with an **n** in French.

23 Oui, Monsieur. Nous avons le chauffage central. *Yes, sir. We've got central heating.*

24 Mais oui, *Oh yes!* **Mais** (lit. *But*) is commonly put in front of **oui** to give it added emphasis. Listen to the pronunciation: there is no liaison between **mais** and **oui**.

25 **Est-ce qu'il y a un placard?** *Is there a wardrobe?*
The statement **il y a un placard** is turned into a question by adding **est-ce que.**

b **Placard**: *wardrobe, cupboard,* looks deceptively like an English word, but it has a different pronunciation and a different meaning. (Remember **le car**: *the bus*; **le professeur**: *the teacher.*)

26 **C'est parfait! Je voudrais vider mes valises.** *That's fine! I'd like to unpack* (lit. *empty*) *my suitcases.*

27 **Un instant, chérie.** *Just a moment, dear.* (lit. *One moment, dear.*)
Chérie: *dear, darling,* is the feminine form. The masculine form is **chéri.**

29 **Non?** *Isn't it?* (lit. *No?*)

30 **Vous voulez remplacer l'ampoule?** *Would you replace the bulb?*
(lit. *You wish to replace the bulb?*)
vous voulez remplacer As you saw in lesson 2 (N41a and 54a) when **vous voulez?** is used in this way it means *would you? will you? would you like?*
Each time **vous voulez** has occurred ʿo far it has been followed by the infinitive form of a verb:
Vous voulez signer la fiche?: *Would you like to sign the form?*
Vous voulez monter dans l'ascenseur?: *Would you like to go up in the lift?*
In the sentence here **remplacer** is also an infinitive. From these examples you can, therefore, see that whenever **vous voulez . . .** is followed by a verb, the verb is in the infinitive.

31 **Oui, Madame. Là, sur l'étagère.** *Yes, Madam. There, on the shelf.*
a **Là**: *there* has a grave accent to distinguish it from **la**: *the.* **Là** is also used in certain cases where *here* is used in English.
b Notice that French speakers give slightly more emphasis to the last syllable of every sentence: . . . **étagère.**

32 **Je voudrais téléphoner à Marie-Claire Martin.** *I'd like to telephone Marie-Claire Martin.*
a You have already seen **je voudrais** twice in this lesson: **Je voudrais être gérant d'hôtel** and **Je voudrais vider mes valises.** Now we have: **Je voudrais téléphoner à Marie-Claire Martin.** As you can see from these three examples, **je voudrais**, like **vous voulez** (N30 above), is always followed by a verb in the infinitive form.
b **je téléphone à**: *I telephone.*

33 **Un instant, chérie. Je voudrais jeter un coup d'œil à la salle de bains.** *Just a moment, dear. I'd like to have a look at the bathroom.*
jeter un coup d'œil à: *to have a look at, to glance at.* Note the pronunciation of the word **œil.**

34 **Voilà la salle de bains: la baignoire, le lavabo, le bidet.** *Here's the bathroom: the bath, the wash-basin and the bidet.*
La baignoire means the actual *bathtub*, as opposed to the bath you take, which is **le bain.**

35 **Je voudrais jeter un coup d'œil aux chambres des enfants.** *I'd like to have a look at the children's rooms.*
jeter un coup d'œil aux chambres . . . Aux (à + les) is the plural of **au (à + le).**
Je voudrais jeter un coup d'œil *à la cuisine.* (with f. sing.)
Je voudrais jeter un coup d'œil *au passeport.* (with m. sing.)
Je voudrais jeter un coup d'œil *aux chambres.* (with pl.)

36 **Vous voulez prendre l'ascenseur, Monsieur?** *Will you take the lift, sir?*
prendre: *to take* Like **être**: *to be*, **prendre** is an irregular verb.

37 **Oui, très bien.** *Yes, all right, (very well).*

38 **Et moi, je voudrais prendre un bain.** *I'd like to have* (lit. *take*) *a bath.*

The language you have learnt

We have

Nous avons	le téléphone. le chauffage central. un réceptionniste sympathique.

Position of adjectives

C'est	une	*petite*	chambre.
	le	*premier*	étage.
Nous avons	une vue	*splendide.*	
	un professeur	*excellent.*	

37

3 Each

Georges téléphone à Valérie	chaque jour.
Il y a le téléphone	dans chaque chambre.

Leçon quatre   Lesson four
Quatrième leçon   Fourth lesson

À table!   Come and eat!

What happens

PART 1
Jules Levoisin
Jules Levoisin introduces himself to us; he is a taxi driver, but is
retiring tomorrow. He talks about his wife and his house. Today he is
lunching with Monsieur Delon.

Part 2
À la réception de l'Hôtel du Nord: *At reception in the Hôtel du Nord*
M. Levoisin suggests they go to the Restaurant des Chauffeurs.

Au Restaurant des Chauffeurs. Monsieur Levoisin consulte le menu.:
At the Restaurant des Chauffeurs. Monsieur Levoisin looks at the menu.
Monsieur Levoisin and Monsieur Delon decide what to have for lunch.
Monsieur Delon is watching his weight.

PART 3
Dans un restaurant: *In a restaurant*
Monsieur Legros asks the waiter about the food.

New words in this lesson

à table come and eat! let's eat!
aller to be going to
amusant funny
l'argent (*m*) money
assez enough
avec plaisir with pleasure, certainly
la banlieue suburbs
beaucoup very much
beaucoup de many
bien cuit well done
bon good
bon appétit enjoy your meal
bonne good
c'est ça that's right
ça that
le café coffee

la campagne country
le champignon mushroom
le chauffeur driver
le chauffeur de taxi taxi driver
cher dear
comme like, as
comment ça va? how are you?
je connais I know
vous connaissez you know
nous connaissons we know
connaître to know
(il) consulte (he) consults, studies
consulter to consult, to study
content pleased
cuit cooked
la dame lady

4 je déjeune I'm having lunch
déjeuner to have lunch
demain tomorrow
depuis for
depuis longtemps for a long time
désirer to want
vous désirez you want (what will you have?)
le dessert dessert
dur hard (boiled)
l'eau minérale mineral water
enfin finally
ensemble together
ensuite next, then
eux them
la femme wife
le fils son
le Français Frenchman
les frites (f) chips, fried potatoes
le fromage cheese
le garçon waiter
garder to keep
garder la ligne to keep one's figure
le gâteau cake, pastry
le grand magasin (department) store
gros fat
grosse big
le gruyère gruyère
le hors-d'œuvre hors d'œuvre
la laitue lettuce
le légume vegetable
longtemps a long time
lui (aussi) he (too)
lundi Monday
le magasin shop
la maison house
ils mangent they eat, they're eating
manger to eat
marié married
même same
le menu menu
les messieurs (m) gentlemen
nos our
notre our
nous us

l'œuf dur mayonnaise (m) egg mayonnaise
l'oignon onion
ou or
le paysan peasant
les petits pois (m) peas
le plat principal main course
le poisson fish
la pomme apple
la pomme (de terre) potato
le potage aux légumes vegetable soup
le poulet chicken
le poulet rôti roast chicken
prendre la retraite to retire
je prends I take, I'll have
vous prenez you take, you'll have
(nous) prenons (we) take, we'll have
quatrième fourth
qu'est-ce que . . . ? qu'est-ce qu' . . . ?
what . . . ?
le restaurant restaurant
la retraite retirement
rouge red
saignant rare
la salade salad
la salade niçoise niçoise salad
la soupe soup
la soupe à l'oignon onion soup
la soupe du jour soup of the day
le steak steak
le steak aux pommes steak and chips
la table table
tant pis too bad, never mind
le taxi taxi
tous les deux both
la truite trout
je vais (prendre) I'm going to (have)
varié mixed
la vendeuse assistant
le vin wine
le vin rouge ordinaire (ordinary) red wine
voir to see
voisin next, neighbouring
vous (aussi) you (too)
voyons let's see

Notes

PART ONE

1 **Comme beaucoup de Français,** *Like many Frenchmen,*

a beaucoup de Français Beaucoup must always be followed by **de** if it precedes a noun: **beaucoup de Français; beaucoup de chambres.**

b Français: *Frenchmen* You have already seen the feminine form of this noun — **Françaises** (L2, N29b). Both words are written with a capital **F**, to distinguish them from the adjective **français** (L1, N7c).

2 je suis fils de paysans. *I come from a peasant family.* (lit. *I am the son of peasants.*)

a (le) fils: (*the*) *son* Listen to the pronunciation. The **s** at the end is always pronounced.

b de paysans: *of peasants, of country people* **Le paysan** is someone who lives in the country. This is not necessarily a derogatory word in French.

3 J'aime beaucoup la campagne. *I like the country very much.*

a beaucoup: *very much* There is never a separate word for *very* before **beaucoup.** Be careful not to confuse **beaucoup:** *very much* with **beaucoup de:** *many.*
Compare the word order here:
J'aime beaucoup la campagne.: *I like the country very much.*

    1   2   3   1   3   2

4 Ma femme est vendeuse dans un grand magasin. *My wife is an assistant in a store* (lit. *a big shop*).

5 Elle aime beaucoup la campagne, elle aussi. *She likes the country very much, too* (lit. *she too*).
elle . . . elle aussi: lit. *she . . . she too* Remember, **Vous aussi, vous arrivez du Canada.** (L1, N48).

6 Moi, je suis chauffeur de taxi depuis longtemps. *I've been a taxi driver for a long time.* (lit. *Me, I'm a taxi driver since a long time.*)

a moi, je . . . Monsieur Levoisin is emphasizing **je** (L1, N75).

b depuis longtemps: lit. *since a long time* In English we say *I* HAVE BEEN *something* FOR *a long time*; in French we say I AM . . . SINCE *a long time*:
Je suis professeur depuis longtemps.: lit. *I am (a) teacher since a long time.* = *I've been a teacher for a long time.*

7 Mais demain, je prends ma retraite. *But, tomorrow, I'm retiring* (lit. *I take my retirement.*)
je prends In lesson 3 (N36) you saw the infinitive form of this verb: **prendre,** *to take* (App. IIIE).

8 Nous habitons dans une petite maison. *We live in a little house.*

a By now you have come across quite a few verb forms. In lesson 1

4 you learnt that **-nt** at the end of verbs shows that the subject of the verb is plural: **ils arrivent** (N14), **ils regardent** (N24), **ils montent** (N34).

Also in lesson 1 you met: **vous habitez** (N43), **vous arrivez** (N48), and the phrase: **comment allez-vous?**

In all these cases the **vous** form of the verb ends in **-ez.** Now, in lesson 4, we have the **nous** form of the verbs, which also has its own ending: **-ons: nous habitons, nous connaissons, nous prenons.**

(You saw the **nous** form of the irregular verb **avoir** in lesson 3 (N6), **nous avons.**)

b **Nous habitons dans une petite maison.** *We live in a little house.*
Remember **vous habitez le Canada** (L1, N43). If **habiter** is followed by the name of a country or a town, there is no need to add **dans.**

9 **Notre maison est dans la banlieue de Paris.** *Our house is in the suburbs of Paris.*
Notre: *our* is the same in the masculine and feminine.
la maison: notre maison: *our house*
le jardin: notre jardin: *our garden*

10 **Nos enfants sont mariés depuis longtemps.** *Our children have been married for a long time.*

a **Nos:** *our* is the plural of **notre** and is used here to agree with the plural noun **enfants.**

b **L'enfant:** *the child* can be either masculine or feminine.

c **mariés:** *married* Listen to the effect of the acute accent on the sound of **e. Mariés** is plural, to agree with the plural noun **enfants.**

11 **Alors, notre maison est assez grande pour nous.** *So our house is big enough for us.*

a **assez grande:** *big enough* Notice that **assez:** *enough* comes before **grande.**

b **pour nous:** *for us* You have already seen **pour moi:** *for me* and **pour vous:** *for you* (L1, N63 and N64). The same word, **nous,** means both *we* and *us.*

12 **Je connais M. Delon depuis longtemps.** *I've known M. Delon for a long time.*
je connais: lit. *I know* (a person or a place)

13 **Aujourd'hui, lundi, je déjeune avec Monsieur Delon.** *Today, Monday, I'm having lunch with Monsieur Delon.*
lundi: *Monday* In French, days of the week are NOT written with a capital letter.

14   **J'adore manger.** *I love eating* (lit. *to eat*). You have already seen   **4**
J'adore la bicyclette (L2, N17). Now **j'adore** is followed by a verb
and, just as **je voudrais** is followed by the verb in the infinitive
(L3, N32), so is **j'adore.**

15   **M. Delon adore manger, lui aussi.** *M. Delon loves eating, too* (lit.
he too).
lui aussi: lit. *he too*   You have already met **moi aussi**: *me too*, **vous
aussi**: *you too*, and **elle aussi**: *she too*.

16   **Ma femme n'est pas contente.** *My wife isn't pleased.*
Contente: *pleased*, is the feminine form, to agree with **ma femme.**

17   **Aujourd'hui, je vais prendre de la soupe.** *Today, I'll have some soup.*
(lit. *Today, I am going to have some soup.*)
a   **je vais . . .** : lit. *I am going to*   When **je vais** is followed by another
verb it means *I will*. Compare this with the English future form
I am going to . . . Notice that the second verb, **prendre** is in the
infinitive.
b   **prendre**   You have already seen **prendre** in **prendre un bain** (L3,
N38): *to take* or *to have a bath*. In English we sometimes say *have*
where a part of the verb **prendre**: *to take*, would be used in French:
Je vais *prendre* **mon petit déjeuner.**: *I am going to **have** my breakfast.*
c   **prendre de la soupe**   Remember **de la** means *some*; it is used with
feminine singular nouns and it must be used even where *some* in
English is omitted (L2, N27a).

18   **J'aime beaucoup la soupe à l'oignon.** *I like onion soup very much.*
soupe à l'oignon: *onion soup*
Some compound nouns in French are formed with a preposition:
sac à main: *handbag;* **chambre à deux lits**: *double room*. In English
we simply put the nouns side by side.

19   **Ensuite, je vais prendre des hors-d'œuvre variés et du poisson.** *Next
I'll have a choice of* (lit. *mixed*) *hors-d'œuvres and some fish.*
a   **des hors-d'œuvre**   There is no liaison between **des** and **hors-d'œuvre**.
Hors-d'œuvre is an unusual noun — it doesn't take **s** in the plural.
You will notice, however, that **variés** is nonetheless in the plural.
b   **du poisson**: *some fish*   Remember, you must use **du** (L2, N27a) here,
as **poisson** is masculine.

20   **Ensuite, des légumes et une salade.** *Then* (*some*) *vegetables and a
salad.*
Une salade: *a salad* in French means lettuce, or chicory, with
French dressing, rather than the more elaborate English salad.

4　**21**　**Ensuite, du fromage — du roquefort ou du gruyère — et une grosse pomme.** *Next (then), cheese — roquefort or gruyère — and a big apple.*

　　a　**et une**　Remember, there is NEVER a liaison after **et**.

　　b　**Grosse**: *big* is the feminine form of **gros**, agreeing with the feminine noun **la pomme**. **Grosse** is a rather unusual feminine form: an extra **s** is added as well as an **e**.

22　**Je vais prendre du vin rouge et enfin du café.** *I'll have some red wine and last of all some coffee.*
Rouge: *red* is the same in both the masculine and feminine singular forms.

PART TWO

23　**Bonjour, mon cher Olivier. Comment ça va?** *Hello, (lit. my dear) Olivier. How are you?*

　　a　**Mon cher Olivier** is a friendly form of address. In lesson 2 you saw this same word **cher**, which was translated by *expensive*. This time, in the phrase **mon cher Olivier**, it is the equivalent of the English word *dear*.

　　b　**Comment ça va?** *How are you?/How are things?* This is a more familiar greeting than **Comment allez-vous?** — which can only mean *How are you?* (L1, N73 a & b).

24　**Ça va très bien, merci.** *Very well, thank you.*
This is the usual reply to the question **Comment ça va?**

25　**Olivier, est-ce que vous voulez connaître un bon petit restaurant?** *Olivier, would you like to get to know a good little restaurant?*
Connaître is the infinitive of a verb you have already learnt: **je connais**: *I know* (N12 above). It means *to know* (a person or place). (See also App. IIIC).

26　**Mais oui, avec plaisir.** *Oh yes, I'd like to* (lit. *with pleasure*).

27　**Ah, vous aussi, vous connaissez le Restaurant des Chauffeurs!** *Oh, you know the Restaurant des Chauffeurs, too!*
Vous connaissez is the **vous** form of the irregular verb **connaître** (App. IIIC).

28　**C'est amusant! Nous connaissons le même restaurant, tous les deux!** *That's funny! We both know the same restaurant!*

　　a　**amusant**　Note the liaison — **C'est amusant.**

　　b　**Nous connaissons** is the **nous** form of **connaître** (App. IIIC).

　　c　**même**: *same*　Try not to confuse this with the same word **même** which you saw in lesson 3: **c'est même difficile.**

　　d　**tous les deux**: *both*

29 **Parfait! En route et à table!** *Fine! Let's go and eat!*
À **table** can also mean *Let's sit down to breakfast/lunch/dinner*, etc.,
or *Come to the table, Come and sit at the table*, etc.

30 **Voyons . . .** Let's see. . .

31 **Voyons: potage aux légumes, deux francs . . . soupe du jour, un
franc . . . œuf dur mayonnaise, trois francs . . .** *Let's see: vegetable
soup, two francs . . . soup of the day, one franc . . . egg mayonnaise,
three francs . . .*

  a **(le) potage**: *(the) soup* **Potage** is a more refined word for soup than
soupe.

  b **potage aux légumes**: *vegetable soup* (cf. **soupe à l'oignon** (N18
above).

  c **(un) œuf dur**: lit. *a hard (boiled) egg* Note that the **f** is pronounced.

32 **Qu'est-ce qu'ils mangent à la table voisine?** *What are they eating at
the next table?*

  a **Qu'est-ce qu' . . . ?**: *What . . . ?* You already know that **est-ce que**
turns a simple statement into a question:
Ils regardent les voyageurs.: *They are looking at the travellers.*
Est-ce qu'ils regardent les voyageurs?: *Are they looking at the
travellers?*
When **qu'est-ce que** is put at the beginning of a statement, it means
what . . . ?:
Ils regardent les avions.: *They are looking at the planes.*
Qu'est-ce qu'ils regardent?: *What are they looking at?*

33 **Parfait! Prenons de la soupe à l'oignon, nous aussi.** *Fine! Let's have
onion soup too* (lit. *we too*).

  a **prenons**: *let's take*, from the verb **prendre** (App. IIIE). Remember
voyons: *let's see* (N30 above). Note that the **-ons** ending is used in
both cases.

  b **nous aussi**: lit. *we too* Compare N15 above, **moi aussi, vous aussi,
elle aussi, lui aussi.**

34 **Bonjour, Messieurs. Vous désirez?** *Good morning.* (lit. *Gentlemen*)
What will you have?

  a **Messieurs** is the plural of **Monsieur** (cf. **Messieurs-Dames**: *Ladies
and Gentlemen* in L1, N50).

  b **Vous désirez?**: lit. *You want?* This is the equivalent of *Can I help
you?* or *What will you have?*

35 **Bien, Monsieur: nous avons de la soupe. Et nos soupes sont
excellentes.** *Right, sir: we have soup. And our soups are excellent.*

  a **bien**: lit. *well* It is more natural in English to say *Right* here.

4

b **excellentes** Note the feminine plural ending **-es**, to agree with **soupes.**

36 **Alors, garçon, deux soupes à l'oignon, s'il vous plaît, comme eux.** *Two onion soups then, please, waiter,* (lit. *Then two onion soups . . .*) *like them.*
comme eux: *like them* After prepositions (**comme, pour,** etc.) *them* (m.) is **eux.**

37 **Comme eux?** *Like them?* Notice the intonation, which indicates that this is a question.

38 **Comme le monsieur et la dame de la table voisine.** *Like the lady and gentleman at* (lit. *of*) *the next table.*
le monsieur et la dame: lit. *the gentleman and the lady*
(cf. **Messieurs-Dames**: lit. *Gentlemen and ladies.*)

39 **Et notre salade niçoise est très bonne aussi.** *And our niçoise salad is very good too.*

a **salade niçoise** Niçoise is an adjective, from **Nice,** the town in southern France. It is feminine here, to agree with **la salade.** A **c** with a cedilla, **ç,** is pronounced like an **s.** Otherwise **c** is pronounced as **k** when it comes before an **a, o,** or **u**: e.g. **car, comme, cuisine.**

b **Bonne:** *good* is the feminine form of **bon,** agreeing with **la salade.** Note the clear **n** sound and lack of nasal quality in **bonne** compared with **bon** (**L1 N22**). However, when **bon** precedes a vowel or silent **h** (**bon hôtel**) it sounds like **bonne.**

40 **Ah! Je prends ça.** *Ah! I'll have that.*
Je prends: lit. *I take,* here means *I'll have.*
You would use this phrase when you order in a restaurant or buy something in a shop (Note 17b above).

41 **Vous prenez deux salades niçoises?** *You'll have two salades niçoises?*
Vous prenez is the **vous** form of **prendre** (App. IIIE).

42 **Oui, c'est ça.** *Yes, that's right.*
C'est ça: lit. *it's that,* is the usual way of saying *that's right, that's it.*

43 **Qu'est-ce que vous prenez comme plat principal?** *What will you have as the main course?*
qu'est-ce que . . .? See N32 above.

44 **Le steak est excellent.** *The steak is excellent.*
le steak Occasionally, French adopts the English name of a

particular dish; but for the names of most French dishes there are no English equivalents.

45 **Oui, je prends un steak aux pommes, s'il vous plaît.** *Yes, I'll have (a) steak and chips* (lit. *potatoes*), *please.*

steak aux pommes: *steak and chips* As you have seen (N21 above), **pommes** can also mean *apples;* in fact this is the more usual translation. The full form of *potato* is ***la pomme de terre.***

46 **Un steak saignant ou bien cuit?** *Steak rare or well done* (lit. *cooked*)?

47 **Ensuite, une salade; je voudrais garder ma ligne.** *Then a salad; I'd like to keep my figure.*

48 **Et de l'eau minérale, s'il vous plaît.** *And mineral water, please.*

a **de l'eau minérale**: (*some*) *mineral water* Again the equivalent of *some* is necessary in French.

b **Minérale** has a final **e** to agree with **l'eau,** which is feminine.

49 **Moi, des frites. Ensuite des champignons, des petits pois et une salade.** *I'll have chips.* (lit. *Me, chips.*) *Then mushrooms, peas and a salad.*

des petits pois: (*some*) *peas* (lit. *little peas*) *A pea* is **un pois.**

50 **Comme dessert: un gâteau et une pomme.** *For dessert a pastry and an apple.*

Here we have another use of **comme,** which, in this case, is the equivalent of *as*, or *in the way of,* in English.

51 **Je vais prendre du vin rouge ordinaire et enfin du café.** *I'll have ordinary red wine and coffee to finish* (lit. *and finally some coffee*). **Vin ordinaire** is cheap table wine (not vintage).

52 **Bon appétit, mon cher Jules.** *Enjoy your meal, Jules.* (lit. *Good appetite, my dear Jules.*)

The language you have learnt

I am going to . . .

| *Je vais* | jou*er* au tennis. |
| | télépho*ner* à Georges. |

Nous . . . -ons

	av*ons*	nos passeports.
Nous	ador*ons*	manger.
	pren*ons*	l'ascenseur.

4 **To know someone/thing**

Je voudrais	connaître	M. Levoisin. Québec. l'Hôtel du Nord. un bon petit restaurant.

How are you?

Comment allez-vous? Comment ça va?	Ça va, merci. Ça va très bien, merci. Je vais très bien, merci. Bien, merci. Très bien, merci.

I have been . . . since/for . . .

Je suis	professeur infirmière réceptionniste	depuis	deux jours. une semaine. longtemps.

Our with singular and plural nouns

Nous avons Il a	notre	sac. disque.
Vous avez	nos	sacs. disques.

I, he, she, we, you . . . too

Moi		j'aime	
Lui		il aime	
Elle	aussi,	elle aime	le café.
Nous		nous aimons	
Vous		vous aimez	

Leçon cinq   *Lesson five*
Cinquième leçon   *Fifth lesson*

5

Mon père est le frère   My father is my
de ma tante.   aunt's brother.

What happens

PART 1
Drôle de famille: *A strange family*
Louise Louvier talks about her family and her flat. Today her nephew
Nicolas is being baptised and his relatives are coming.

PART 2
Dans l'appartement des Louvier: *In the Louviers' flat*
Madame Louvier talks to Uncle Charles, and to other members of the
family. The grandmother thinks the baby is lovely, but Jean-Luc says
he's ugly.

PART 3
Madame Gaston n'est pas Madame Hébert.: *Madame Gaston is not
Madame Hébert.*
Madame Fabre is quite mistaken.

New words in this lesson

à la campagne in the country
à part apart from
adorable gorgeous
l'an (*m*) year
l'âne (*m*) donkey
l'appartement (*m*) flat
le baptême christening
beau beautiful
beaucoup de place plenty of room
beaucoup trop much too much
le bébé baby
le canapé settee
le cousin cousin (male)
la cousine cousin (female)
le docteur doctor
drôle (de) (a) strange
écouter to listen to
l'écrivain (*m*) writer

en effet indeed
en province in the provinces
enchanté pleased, delighted
les environs (*m*) outskirts
l'étudiant (*m*) student (male)
l'étudiante (*f*) student (female)
excuse (-le) excuse (him)
excuser to excuse
faire votre connaissance to meet you
la fille daughter
la grand-mère grandmother
le grand-père grandfather
les grands-parents grandparents
heureuse happy
heureux happy
l'ingénieur (*m*) engineer
l'invité (*m*) guest
la jambe leg

49

5

le journaliste journalist
long long (time)
maman mother, mummy
le mari husband
le neveu nephew
la nièce niece
l'oncle (*m*) uncle
où where
par by
par alliance by marriage
pas mal not bad
le petit-fils grandson
je présente I introduce (let me . . .)
présenter to introduce
qui who
qui est-ce? who's that? who is it?
il refuse he refuses
refuser to refuse
les rhumatismes (*m*) rheumatism
la rue street
sa his, her, its
ses his, her, its
le singe monkey
le sofa sofa
nous sommes we're (we are)

son her, his, its
la tante aunt
têtu stubborn
têtu comme un âne stubborn as a mule
tiens! look!
toi you
ton your
tous all
tout va bien everything's fine
il travaille he works
travailler to work
je me trompe I'm wrong, I've made a
    mistake
se tromper to be wrong, to make a
    mistake
trop too much
tu you
l'usine (*f*) factory
(toute la famille) va arriver (the whole
    family) is coming, (is going to come)
vilain ugly
vingt et un twenty-one
vingt-quatre twenty-four
vingt-trois twenty-three
il voudrait he'd like

Notes

PART ONE

1 **Drôle de famille** *A strange family*

2 **Mon mari s'appelle Pierre.** *My husband's called Pierre.*

3 **Il travaille beaucoup.** *He works hard* (lit. *a lot*).

4 **l'appartement numéro 4, 15 rue des Fleurs, Paris IXe.** *flat 4, 15 rue
    des Fleurs, Paris IXe.*

a **rue des Fleurs**: lit. *street of the flowers*, or *Flower Street*. Notice that
    rue, the word for street, does not have a capital letter.

b **Paris IXe** In full, **Paris neuvième** (lit. *Paris ninth*). **Neuvième**: *ninth*
    refers to the **arrondissement** or *postal district*.

5 **Nous sommes contents d'avoir un grand appartement.** *We're glad
    we've got* (lit. *to have*) *a large flat.*

a **Nous sommes**: *we are*, is part of the verb **être**: *to be* (See Appendix).

b **Contents d'avoir**: *glad to, pleased to have* **Contents** is plural here, to
    agree with **nous**. Note that **contents de** is followed by the infinitive
    of a verb, here **avoir** (See Appendix).

6   **Nous avons un fils, Georges.** *We have a son, Georges.*

7   **Il a vingt-trois ans.** *He's twenty-three.* (lit. *He has twenty-three years.*)
To give your age in French you use the verb **avoir**: *to have*, rather than the verb *to be*, as in English. You must also include the word **ans**: *years.* Thus: **il a vingt-trois ans**: *he's twenty-three.*

8   **Je suis mariée depuis vingt-quatre ans.** *I've been married for twenty-four years.*
mariée   The second e shows that **mariée** is feminine; it refers to **Mme Louvier.**

9   **C'est long.** *That's/it's a long time.*
Long: lit. *long* is used here in the sense of **longtemps,** which you saw first in lesson 4 (N6b).

10   **Aujourd'hui, c'est le baptême de Nicolas**: *Today is* (lit. *it is*) *Nicolas's christening.*
a   **le baptême**: *the christening*   The p in **baptême** is not pronounced.
b   **Nicolas**   Note the spelling of this name: there is no **h.**

11   **Nicolas, c'est le fils de mon neveu, Jean-Luc.** *Nicolas is the son of my nephew Jean-Luc.*
a   **C'est** usually means *he/she/it/that is.* But it can also be used to emphasize the word which precedes it: **Nicolas, c'est . . .**

12   **Alors, il y a beaucoup de place pour tous les invités.** *So there's plenty* (lit. *a lot*) *of room for all the guests.*

13   **Toute la famille va arriver pour le baptême.** *The whole family* (lit. *all the family*) *is coming* (lit. *is going to arrive*) *for the christening.*
la famille va arriver: *the family is going to come*
You already know **je vais** + infinitive: *I am going to.* Now we have **la famille va,** also followed by an infinitive. **Va** is another part of the irregular verb **aller** (App. ICa).

14   **Nicolas a une grand-mère, deux grands-pères, quatre tantes, et deux oncles, deux cousins, et trois cousines.** *Nicolas has a grandmother, two grandfathers, four aunts and two uncles, and five cousins* (lit. . . . *two male cousins and three female cousins*).
a   **une grand-mère**: *a (one) grandmother*   Note that **grand** is followed by a hyphen and has no **e**, in spite of the fact that **mère** is a feminine noun.
b   **deux grands-pères**: *two grandfathers*   Here **grand** has an **s** to agree with **pères.**

5　**15**　**Les grands-parents habitent tous en province.** *The grandparents all live in the provinces.*

a　**grands-parents**　Again, **grands** is plural to agree with **parents.**

b　**Tous** refers to **grands-parents** and is therefore plural. Note its position after the verb and that the final **s** is pronounced.

16　**Les quatre tantes, elles, habitent toutes dans les environs de Paris.** *The four aunts all live on the outskirts of Paris.* (lit. *The four aunts, they . . .*)

a　**Elles**: *they,* refers to the aunts. It is used here for emphasis.

b　**Toutes** refers to **les tantes,** and is placed after the verb (N15b above).

17　**Les deux oncles, eux, habitent à la campagne.** *The two uncles live in the country* (lit. *the two uncles, they . . .*).

a　**Eux**: *they* is the emphatic form of **ils,** just as **moi** is the emphatic form of **je.**

b　You have now met several different prepositions translated by *in* in English: **à la campagne,** etc. These should be learnt as set expressions; e.g. **à Paris** (L2, N8).

18　**Les cousins et les cousines habitent, eux aussi, à la campagne.** *The cousins live in the country too.* (lit. *The cousins live, they also . . .*)

19　**Ils s'appellent M. et Mme Galet.** *They're called M. and Mme Galet.*

20　**M. Galet, Jean-Luc, mon neveu, a vingt et un ans.** *M. Galet — Jean-Luc, my nephew, is twenty-one.*
vingt et un　Note **et** between **vingt** and **un.**

21　**Sa femme, Sylvie, est étudiante, elle aussi.** *His wife, Sylvie, is also a student.*
Sa can mean either *his* or *her.* You remember **mon, ma, mes** in **mon père, ma mère, mes bagages. Mon** agreed with **père, ma** with **mère** and **mes** with **bagages.** In the same way, in **sa femme, sa,** a feminine form, agrees with **femme,** the noun which follows:
sa mère: *his/her mother*; **sa cousine**: *his/her cousin*

22　**Elle, elle a vingt ans.** SHE *is twenty.*
elle, elle　You learnt how to emphasize **je**: *I* by adding **moi**: **Moi, je suis fatigué** (L1, N75). You have also learnt how to emphasize **vous,** just by repeating **vous** (L2, N51): **Vous, vous êtes au deuxième étage. Elle** is emphasized in the same way: **Elle, elle a vingt ans.**

23　**Lui, il voudrait être professeur ou écrivain.** *He'd like/he wants to be a teacher or a writer.*
lui, il　**Lui** is the emphatic form of **il.** We have already met **lui** in the phrase **lui aussi** (L4, N15). Here it is used in the same way as **moi, je . . .** in the sentence: **Moi, je suis fatigué.**

PART TWO

24 Et toi? *And what about you?*

In French there are two ways of addressing people; the formal way, using **vous**, which you have already seen in the phrase **et vous** and a more familiar way, which is used between members of a family, with children and with friends. Because Mme Louvier is younger than he is, Uncle Charles uses the familiar form and says: **Et toi?** not **Et vous?** But, as her uncle is older than she is, Mme Louvier uses **vous** when she talks to him.

Toi, is always singular; but **vous** is both *you* (sing.) and *you* (pl.).

25 Il refuse d'écouter son docteur — et sa femme. *He refuses to listen to his doctor — and his wife.*

a **refuser de**: *to refuse to* (*do something*)   You will be meeting other verbs which take the preposition **de** before an infinitive (here écouter). Think of the verb and preposition together as a phrase.

b **son docteur**: *his doctor* — or *her doctor*   Here it must be *his* because Louise is talking about M. Louvier's doctor. **Son**: *his* or *her* is the form used with masculine singular nouns and with feminine singular nouns beginning with a vowel.

26 Je connais ton mari. *I know your husband.*

ton mari: *your husband*   In lesson 1 you saw **votre passeport**: *your passport*. Here is the familiar form of *your*: **ton mari**: *your husband*. Like **mon** and **son**, **ton** is used before all masculine singular nouns and before feminine nouns which begin with a vowel:

ton frère: *your brother*   **ton infirmière**: *your nurse.*

27 Toi aussi, Louise, tu travailles trop. Toi aussi, tu es têtue. YOU *work too hard as well, Louise.* YOU'RE *stubborn as well.*

a **Toi . . . tu**: *you* is another example of emphasis, **toi** being added to emphasize **tu**. Compare this with **moi . . . je**: *I.*

b **tu travailles**: *you work*   The ending of the **tu** form of all regular -er verbs is -**es**.

28 Où est Pierre? *Where's Pierre?*

After question words such as **où** the subject is placed after the verb. Remember **comment allez-vous** (L1, N72). An exception is **comment ça va?** (L4, N23).

29 Venez, je vais vous présenter Monsieur Duhamel . . . *Come on* (lit. *come*), *I'll introduce Monsieur Duhamel to you.*

je vais *vous* présenter . . . : *I'll introduce* TO YOU

Here **vous** means *to you* and comes before **présenter**.

30 Je vous présente Monsieur Duhamel . . . *Let me introduce Monsieur Duhamel to you.* (lit. *I to you introduce M. Duhamel.*)

Je vous présente ma femme: *Let me introduce my wife* (*to you*).

5

31 Je suis très heureux de faire votre connaissance, Monsieur. *I'm very happy to meet you, (sir).*

32 Enchanté. *Pleased to meet you.*
Enchanté: *pleased/delighted* is short for **enchanté de faire votre connaissance.** Enchanté is quite enough in ordinary circumstances.

33 Tiens! Voilà Maman. *Look! there's Mother.*
Tiens! is an idiomatic expression implying mild surprise.

34 Bonjour, Maman. Comment vas-tu? *Hello, Mother. How are you?*
Comment vas-tu? is the familiar form of *Comment allez-vous?* It is quite natural for a daughter to use **tu** to her mother.

35 À part mes rhumatismes dans ma jambe. *Apart from the* (lit. *my*) *rheumatism in my leg.*
(Les) rhumatismes: *rheumatism* is often plural in French.

36 Ah . . . je suis heureuse! Et toi? *Oh . . . I'm happy! Are you?* (lit. *and you?*)
Heureuse is the feminine form of **heureux.** Adjectives ending in **-eux** in the masculine singular and plural, end in **-euse** in the feminine singular and **-euses** in the feminine plural.

Il est heur*eux*.   Elle est heur*euse*.
Ils sont heur*eux*.   Elles sont heur*euses*.

37 Excuse-le; il est fatigué. *Excuse him; he's tired.*
a   Excuse is the familiar form of **excusez.**
b   Excuse-le: *excuse him* Le can be a pronoun (*him*, or *it*, in English). After a command (an imperative) le comes after the verb, as in English, but is joined to it by a hyphen.

38 Je voudrais admirer mon petit Christophe. Où est-il? *I want to* (lit. *I'd like to*) *admire my little Christophe. Where is he?*

39 'Christophe', qui est-ce? *'Christophe'? Who's that?*
qui est-ce? *who's that?* It can also mean, *who is it?*

40 Mais c'est mon petit-fils! *He's my grandson!* (lit. *But he's my grandson!*)
Petit-fils: *grandson* is always written with a hyphen.

41 Oh, pardon, je me trompe. *Oh sorry, I'm wrong.*
Je me trompe is a phrase which means *I've made a mistake, I'm wrong.*

42 Je vais demander à son père. *I'll ask* (lit. *I'm going to ask*) *his father.*

demander à: to *ask* (someone) (L3, N9), **demander**: *to ask for*.
Thus, note the difference between:
Je demande à la femme de chambre: *I'm asking the chambermaid.*
Je demande la femme de chambre: *I'm asking* FOR *the chambermaid.*

43 Il est là, sur le canapé, avec ses tantes. *He's there, on the settee with his aunts.*
ses tantes Ses is the plural of **son** and **sa** and means *his* or *her*. It must be used here because **tantes** is plural.

44 Oh! C'est un beau bébé. Il est adorable! *Oh! He's a beautiful baby. He's gorgeous.*

a **C'est un beau bébé.** Remember that when you want to say *he/she/it/that is* followed by an article and a noun you use **c'est** (L3, N5):
C'est *un hôtel* **excellent,**
C'est *la valise* **de mon père.**

b **il est adorable** Here the baby is being described; — there is no noun in the sentence; therefore **il est** plus the adjective is used.

45 Il est beau comme son père, n'est-ce pas? Oui, il est beau comme lui. *He's handsome like his father, isn't he? Yes, he's handsome like him.*
comme lui: *like him* Lui is the special form of **il** which is used after prepositions such as **comme, pour** etc. (L4, N37).

46 Nicolas est beau comme moi? Il est vilain comme un singe! *Nicolas is handsome like me? He's as ugly as* (lit. *like*) *a monkey!*

The language you have learnt

To be called — some important forms

Je	m'appelle	Paul. Valérie.
Il	s'appelle	Olivier.
Elle		Yvonne Delon.
Ils	s'appellent	M. et Mme Galet.
Elles		Yvonne et Valérie Delon.

5 **Glad to . . .**

Nous sommes Vous êtes Ils sont	*contents*	*de* travailler. *d'*être à Paris. *d'*habiter le Canada.

To ask, telephone someone

Je vais	*demander à* *téléphoner à*	Valérie. ta sœur.

You; formal and familiar forms

Madame Delon, *vous*	habit*ez* à la campagne?
Valérie, *tu*	habit*es* à la campagne?

Toi, tu, ton

Et *toi*, Paul *tu*	téléphones à ——— préfères	*ton*	ami, ——— steak saignant,	*toi* aussi?

His, her, with singular nouns

Paul Valérie	a	*son*	passeport.
		sa	fiche.
		son	eau minérale.

N.B. Whether the "owner" is masculine or feminine is irrelevant.

His, her, with plural nouns

Paul Valérie	a	*ses*	croissants.
			serviettes.

N'est-ce pas?

Il s'appelle Paul, Elles habitent la province, Elle travaille beaucoup,	*n'est-ce pas?*

Où se trouve . . . ? Where is . . . ?

What happens

PART 1
Je veux acheter une robe . . . : *I want to buy a dress . . .*
Valérie Delon tells us she is a bilingual secretary on holiday in Paris
with her family. She is going shopping and wants to buy a dress. She
likes French fashion and is going to the boulevard Haussmann, but
she doesn't know how to find it.

PART 2
À la réception de l'Hôtel du Nord: *At reception in the Hôtel du Nord*
Georges, the receptionist, directs Valérie to the boulevard Haussmann.

Dans la rue: *In the street*
Valérie asks passers-by the way to the boulevard Haussmann.

PART 3
Pardon, où se trouve . . . ?: *Excuse me, can you tell me the way to . . . ?*
Alain and Claire are looking for the same hotel.

Madame Duclos et ses trois fils: *Madame Duclos and her three sons*
Jean, Pierre and Marc all want to go to the cinema.

New words in this lesson

à droite (on/to the) right
à gauche (on/to the) left
à ma taille my size
(ils) accompagnent (they) go with,
  accompany
accompagner to go with, to
  accompany
acheter to buy
l'agent de police (*m*) policeman
aider to help
aller to go
allez-vous-en! go away!
au coin on the corner
l'avenue (*f*) avenue
avoir peur to be afraid

belle lovely, beautiful
bilingue bilingual
blanc white
blanche white
le boulevard boulevard
canadienne Canadian
le carrefour crossroads
ce that, this
certain certain, sure
ces these, those
cet this, that
cette this, that
je chausse du 35 I wear (take) size 35
  shoes
chausser to wear (shoes)

6

la chaussure shoe
le chemisier blouse
je cherche I'm looking for
chercher to look for
le cinéma cinema
le coin corner
de rien not at all, don't mention it
déjà already
descendez go down
descendre to go down
devant in front of
en in
s'en aller to go away
en vacances on holiday
exactement exactly
s'excuser to be sorry, to excuse
  oneself
excusez-moi I'm sorry, excuse me
faire to do
faire des courses to go shopping
la femme woman
(ils) ferment (they) close, shut
fermer to close, to shut
la fois time
la France France
le genre kind
gentil nice
l'histoire (f) story
l'homme (m) man
j'invite I invite
inviter to invite
le jeune homme young man
jusqu'à/au as far as
les them
leur their
la maison d'édition publishing house
le manteau coat
le marchand de tabac tobacconist
me me
mesdames ladies
la minute minute
la mode fashion
monsieur l'agent (m) officer
noir black
ou bien or (rather)

la paire pair
le passage clouté pedestrian crossing
peut-être perhaps
je peux I can
le plan map
plusieurs several
la pointure size
la porte door
pour in order to
pouvoir can, to be able to
(ils) prennent (they) take
se promener to go for a walk
puis then
je reconnais I recognize
vous reconnaissez you recognize
reconnaître to recognize
rendre visite à to visit
revenez come back
revenir to come back
la robe dress
je sais I know
vous savez you know
savoir to know
nous savons we know
sixième sixth
sortez go out
sortir to go out
le tabac tobacco
la taille size
toujours always
tourner to turn
tournez turn
tous les deux ans every two years
tout droit straight on
traverser to cross
traversez cross
trente-cinq thirty-five
trente-huit thirty-eight
trouver to find
(où) se trouve is (where is . . .)
se trouver to be (situated)
les vacances (f) holidays
ils veulent they want (to)
je veux I want (to)
elles vont they go, they're going

Notes

PART ONE

1 **Vous me connaissez déjà.** *You know me already.* Note the word
  order — **me** comes before the verb.

58

2 Je suis en vacances, avec mon père, ma mère, et mon frère Paul. **6**
I am on holiday with my father, mother and my brother Paul.

3 Tous les deux ans, mes parents prennent leurs vacances en France.
Every two years, my parents go to France for their holidays (lit: *take their holidays in France*).

a **(ils) prennent**: (*they*) *take* is another form of the verb **prendre**: *to take.*

b **leurs vacances**: *their holidays* **Leurs**: *their* is plural, to agree with **vacances** which is always plural in French.

4 Naturellement, leur fils et leur fille les accompagnent. *Of course their son and daughter go with them.*

a **leur fils et leur fille**: *their son and their daughter* **Leur** is the singular form of **leurs**: *their*. It is the same in both masculine and feminine. Like the words for *my* (**mon, ma, mes**) it must be repeated.

b **(Ils) les accompagnent**: (*they*) *go with them, accompany them* You know that **le** means *him* in **excuse-le**. Here now is the French for *them*: **les**. Like **me** in **vous me connaissez** (N1 above) it comes before the verb.

5 Je veux acheter un chemisier blanc *I want to buy a white blouse*
je veux: *I want* (*to*)
Je veux is part of the same verb as **vous voulez**, the verb **vouloir**. As is the case with **vous voulez**, (L3, N30), any verb following it must be in the infinitive form.

6 et surtout une belle robe, une belle petite robe blanche. *and above all a nice dress, a nice little white dress.*

a **belle**: *lovely, beautiful, nice* is the feminine form of **beau** (L5, N44). It is an irregular feminine form. Both **beau** and **belle** are placed in front of the noun: **une belle robe, un beau bébé.**

c **blanche**: *white*, the feminine form of **blanc** (N5 above) Note that **petite** comes before **robe** (one of the few adjectives that always does) but that **blanche,** like most adjectives, comes after.

7 J'adore les robes françaises; elles sont belles. *I love French dresses; they are beautiful.*

8 Le noir va avec tout. *Black goes with everything.*
le noir: *black* When you put **le** before an adjective such as **noir** (the masculine form) it becomes a noun.

9 Je n'aime pas la mode canadienne. *I don't like Canadian fashion.*
Canadienne: *Canadian* is written with a small **c** because it is an adjective. This is the feminine form. Notice that there is a double **n** before the **e**.

59

6 **10** **Elle ne me va pas.** *It doesn't suit me.*
In lesson 5 (N13), you met the phrase — **toute la famille va arriver.**
Va was translated as *is going to;* it was part of the verb **aller,** *to be going to.* In the sentence **elle ne me va pas,** va is the same part of **aller;** but **aller** is used in a quite different sense; in this case it is the equivalent of the English verb *to suit.*

11 **Et puis, ici, à Paris, je peux trouver des robes à ma taille.** *And (then) here, in Paris, I can find dresses* (lit. *to) my size.*
je peux: *I can* As was the case with **je veux** (N5a above) you must use the infinitive form of the verb after *je peux:*
Je peux acheter un manteau.: *I can buy a coat.*

12 **Je prends du trente-huit.** *I take size thirty-eight.*
du trente-huit: *thirty-eight* (Continental size; the equivalent English size is 32.) **Du** is always used with sizes.

13 **À Québec, je ne peux pas trouver ce genre de robe.** *In Québec, I can't find that kind of dress.*
ce genre: *this/that kind* **Ce** stands for *this* or *that* before masculine singular nouns beginning with a consonant: **ce disque**: *this/that record;* **ce chemisier blanc**: *this/that white blouse.*

14 **Je chausse du trente-cinq.** *I wear size thirty-five shoes.*
a **Chausser** must be followed by **du.**
b **trente-cinq**: *thirty-five* (Continental size; the equivalent English size is 3).

15 **Au Canada, je ne peux pas trouver cette pointure.** *In Canada, I can't find this size.*
a **au Canada** **Au** (à + le) is used for *in,* with countries that are masculine.
b **cette pointure**: *this/that size* **Cette** is the form used before all feminine singular nouns: **cette robe, cette infirmière.**
c **La pointure** is the word to use for the size of shoes; *la taille* for the size of clothes.

16 **Mais aujourd'hui, je vais aller dans les grands magasins pour acheter une robe.** *But today I'm going to the big stores to buy a dress.*
a **aller**: *to go* When you saw this irregular verb before, it was used with a second verb to make a future tense:
Je vais prendre du vin rouge.: *I'm going to have red wine.* (L4, N22)
On its own, **aller** means **to go.**
b **dans les grands magasins**: lit. *into the big stores*
c **pour** You already know **pour** meaning *for,* **pour moi**: *for me;* **pour vous**: *for you.* When **pour** is followed by a verb it means *in order to,* or *to.*

17 **Je vais aller au boulevard Haussmann.** *I'll* (lit. *am going to*) *go to the*
boulevard Haussmann.
au boulevard **Au** can mean *at the*, or *to the*. Here it means *to the*.

18 **Mais . . . où se trouve le boulevard Haussmann?** *But where's the*
boulevard Haussmann?
où se trouve . . . ? *where is . . . ?*

19 **Je ne sais pas.** *I don't know.*
Je sais is part of an irregular verb **savoir**: *to know* (App. IVb).

20 **Je vais demander à ce beau jeune homme.** *I will* (lit. *am going to*) *ask*
that handsome young man.

21 **C'est le réceptionniste de l'hôtel.** *He is the receptionist at the hotel.*
C'est: *He is . . .*
When *he is . . . .* answers the question *What is he? What does he*
do? **il est** must be used:
Il est professeur de français.
When it answers the question *Who is he?* **c'est** must be used:
C'est le réceptionniste.

22 **Il est gentil, très gentil . . .** *He's nice, very nice . . .* (cf. L5, N44b).

PART TWO
23 **Vous me reconnaissez?** *Do you recognize me?*
me Notice that, once again, this sort of pronoun (object pronoun)
me, comes before the verb (N1 above).

24 **Naturellement; je vous reconnais.** *Of course, I recognize you.*
je vous reconnais **Vous,** the object pronoun, comes before the verb.

25 **Non; ils veulent se promener tous les deux dans Paris** *No; they both*
want to go for a walk in Paris
a **ils veulent**: *they want; they wish*
You already know **je veux**: *I want/wish (to);* and **vous voulez**:
you want/wish (to); **ils veulent** is another part of the same verb *to*
want/wish (App. IVb). It too, is followed by the infinitive of the verb.
b **se promener**: *to go for a walk*
c **dans Paris**: *in Paris, around Paris* At or in a town is usually **à** but
here it means *around* the streets — within the city.

26 **et rendre visite à leurs amis.** *and visit their friends.*
a **rendre visite à**: *to visit (people)*
b **leurs**: *their* is plural, to agree with **amis.**

61

6 27 **Et vous, qu'est-ce que vous allez faire?** *And what are* YOU *going to do?* (lit. *And you, what are you going to do?*)

a **Vous allez**: lit. *you are going, you go,* is from the verb **aller** (App. ICa).

b **faire**: *to do* is the infinitive of an irregular verb (App. IIIE).

28 **Sortez de l'hôtel.** *Go out of the hotel.*

Sortez: *go out!* (**vous sortez**: *you go out*)

When you know the **vous** form of a verb you can make a request or give a command:

vous regardez: *you look (at)* **regardez!**: *look!*
vous venez: *you come* **venez!**: *come!*

29 **Tournez à droite. Prenez la deuxième rue à gauche.** *Turn right. Take the second street on the left.*

a **Tournez**: *turn,* is the command form (*vous tournez*: **you turn**).

b **Prenez**: *take* is the command form. Remember that **vous prenez** is the **vous** form of **prendre** (L4, N41).

30 **Traversez la rue. Ensuite, prenez la première à droite,** *Cross the street. Then take the first on the right,*

a **traversez**: *cross;* **vous traversez**: *you cross*

b **La première**: *the first,* stands for **la première rue**.

31 **Descendez cette avenue, tout droit, jusqu'au carrefour.** *Go down that avenue, straight on, as far as the crossroads.*

a **descendez**: *go down;* **vous descendez**: *you go down*

b **cette avenue**: *this/that avenue*   **Cette** is used because **avenue** is a feminine noun.

c **tout droit**: *straight on*

d **jusqu'au carrefour**   **Carrefour** is masculine so **jusqu'à** + **le** becomes **jusqu'au.**

32 **De rien, Mademoiselle.** *Not at all/Don't mention it, (Miss).*

De rien is a polite response to **merci**.

33 **et je prends la deuxième à droite — ou bien est-ce que c'est la première . . . ou la troisième peut-être . . . ?** *and I take the second on the right . . . or is it the first . . . or the third perhaps . . . ?*

est-ce que c'est . . . ? The statement **C'est la première**: *It is the first,* has been made into a question by adding **Est-ce que**: *Is it . . . ?*

34 **. . . Je vais demander à cet homme . . .** *I'll* (lit. *I am going to*) *ask this man . . .*

cet homme: *this man/that man*   Remember that we use **l'** and not **le** with masculine nouns beginning with a silent h: **l'hôtel, l'homme** (L1, N77).

Similarly, **Cet** and not **ce** is used before this type of noun: **cet homme, cet hôtel.**

35   **Je cherche les grands magasins.** *I am looking for . . .*
je cherche . . .   Remember, two words in English, one in French:
cf. **Je regarde cet homme.**: *I look* AT *that man.*
J'habite le Canada.: *I live* IN *Canada.*

36   **non, n'allez pas dans les grands magasins. Venez prendre un café avec moi.** *no, don't go to the big stores. Come and have a coffee with me.*

a   **n'allez pas!** *don't go!*   You have seen the command form **allez!**: *go!*
Here is the negative command form of the verb. As usual, you put **ne (n')** before the verb and **pas** after it:
Venez!: *Come!*
Ne venez pas!: *Don't come!*

b   **Venez prendre un café**: *Come and have a coffee*   **Venez** is always immediately followed by the infinitive when it means *come* AND . . .:
Venez regarder ma robe.: *Come and look at my dress.*

37   **Vous avez peur, Mademoiselle?** *Are you afraid (Miss)?*
vous avez peur: lit. *you have fear*
Remember the parts of the verb **avoir**: *to have* that you already know. You can say: **J'ai peur, vous avez peur, il/elle a peur, nous avons peur, ils/elles ont peur.**

38   **Allez-vous-en . . . !** *Go away!*
You already know **allez!**: *go!* This is an idiom, meaning *go away!*

39   **Oh, ces hommes!** *Oh, (these) men!*
ces hommes: *these/those men*
Ces is the plural of **ce, cet** and **cette**:
ce sac   ces sacs
cet hôtel   ces hôtels
cette rue   ces rues.
Note the liaisons: **ces hommes, les hommes.**

40   **Ils veulent vous aider, c'est certain . . .** *They want to help you, that's for sure . . .*
ils veulent vous aider   Notice that **vous** comes before **aider** and not before **veulent**; this is because **vous** is the object of **aider. Ils veulent** is part of the same verb as **je veux, vous voulez, nous voulons** (App. IVB).

41   **Ah oui, il y a plusieurs beaux magasins boulevard Haussmann . . .**
Oh yes, there are several fine shops on the boulevard Haussmann . . .

a   **Beaux** is the plural of **beau** (cf. **un plateau, des plateaux; l'eau, les eaux**).

6 **b** **boulevard Haussmann** When stating a location in a particular street or road, the preposition (**sur, dans**) is generally suppressed: **Je vais acheter une robe boulevard Haussmann**: *I'm going to buy a dress in the boulevard Haussmann.*
Il habite boulevard Haussmann: *He lives on the boulevard Haussmann.*

42 **Ce n'est pas facile, vous savez, Mademoiselle.** *It isn't easy, you know.*
vous savez: *you know* The English verb form *you know* has two equivalents in French: **vous connaissez** and **vous savez**. **Vous connaissez**, which you saw in lesson 4 can only mean *you know* in the sense of *you are acquainted with*:
Vous me connaissez.: *You know (are acquainted with) me.*
If you want to say *you know* in French in any other sense, you must use **vous savez**.

43 **Elles vont peut-être savoir où se trouve ce boulevard.** *They will perhaps know where this boulevard is.*
a **elles vont**: lit. *they go, they are going* (*to*) This is another part of the verb **aller**: *to go* (App. ICa).
b **savoir**: *to know* Remember, **je sais, vous savez** (App. IVB).

44 **Excusez-moi, Mademoiselle. Nous ne savons pas.** *I'm sorry. We don't know.*

45 **Je vais demander à cet agent de police . . .** *I'll ask that policeman.*
cet agent de police: *that/this policeman* **Cet** is used before masculine nouns beginning with a vowel (N34 above). A policeman on point duty etc. in a town is **un agent de police**. He is sometimes referred to simply as **un agent**.

46 **Monsieur l'agent, le boulevard Haussmann, s'il vous plaît?** *Officer, the boulevard Haussmann, please?*

47 **Ah, non alors!** *Oh, no!*
Alors usually means *then, so*. Here it emphasizes **non**.

48 **Revenez demain!** *Come back tomorrow!*
Revenez!: *Come back!*

The language you have learnt

Je veux + infinitive

Je veux Je ne veux pas	prendre un bain. rendre visite aux Delon.

Je peux + infinitive

Je peux Je ne peux pas	travailler aujourd'hui. monter dans l'ascenseur.

In order to

Je vais dans un grand magasin	*pour*	acheter une robe.
Je veux aller à la campagne		rendre visite à mes cousins.

Him, them (object)

Je	l' les	excuse. accompagne.
	le les	regarde.

Even

Il demande	*même*	une chambre sans chauffage central.
Il prend du vin rouge		avec du poisson.

The same

Nous prenons	*le même*	plat principal. dessert.
Nous avons	*la même*	taille. pointure.
Nous aimons	*les mêmes*	disques. fleurs.

6   To know where

Je voudrais *savoir* Je *sais* Nous *savons* Vous *savez*	*où se trouve* le boulevard Haussmann.

Orders and requests

Ven*ez* Sort*ez*	aujourd'hui. toutes les semaines.

Me (object)

Vous	*me*	connaissez.
	m'	écoutez bien.

You, him, them (object)

Je	*le* *vous* *les*	reconnais. regarde.
	l' *les*	accompagne jusqu'à l'aéroport? examine.

Voilà

Voilà	son	sac.
	sa	valise.
	ses	sacs.

Leçon sept *Lesson seven*
Septième leçon *Seventh lesson*

L'argent   Money

What happens

PART 1
Monsieur Lecerf parle à ses clients. Il vous parle.: *Monsieur Lecerf talks to his customers. He talks to you.*
Jacques Lecerf tells us about his job as a bank clerk.

PART 2
Dans la chambre numéro trois: *In room number* 3
Madame Delon wants to go to the hairdresser's. Her hair looks dreadful and Valérie suggests she buys a wig. Madame Delon can't find the hairdresser's address. She has to go to the bank because she has no money.

À la banque: *At the bank*
Madame Delon cashes two traveller's cheques.

PART 3
Madame Langlois va chez le coiffeur.: *Madame Langlois goes to the hairdresser's.*
Madame Langlois is mistaken.

Où se trouve . . . ? *Where is . . . ?*
Monsieur Fabre really wants to go to the airport.

New words in this lesson

à propos by the way
à tout à l'heure see you later
à votre service at your service
l'adresse (*f*) address
affreux terrible
allons bon! there now!
approuver to endorse
au bon endroit in the right place
au mauvais endroit in the wrong place
la banque bank
barrer to cross out

bon right
(ne) bouge (pas) (don't) move
bouger to move
ça y est right, that's it
le caissier cashier
le carnet cheque book
changer to change
le chèque cheque
le chèque de voyage traveller's cheque
les cheveux (*m*) hair
chez at, to (the shop of etc. . . .)

7
le client customer
le coiffeur hairdresser
comment est-ce que ... ? how ... ?'
d'abord first
la date date
distrait absent minded
le dollar dollar
(elles) donnent (they) give
donner to give
égarer to mislay, to lose
vous égarez you mislay, you lose
l'employé (m) clerk, employee
en avance early
en retard late
l'endroit (m) place
n'exagérons pas let's not exaggerate
exagérer to exaggerate
favorable favourable
la (voilà) here it is/there it is
le (voilà) here it is/there it is
les (voilà) here/there they are
loin far, a long way
la main hand
je me maquille I (do my) make-up
se maquiller to make oneself up
mauvais wrong
mauvaise wrong

vous mettez you put
mettre to put
papa father, daddy
parce que because
(il) parle (he) talks
parler to talk
la perruque wig
la poudre de riz powder
pourquoi? why?
pourquoi est-ce que? why?
pourquoi pas? why not?
prêt ready
qu'est-ce qu'il y a? what's the matter?
quoi? what?
le rouge à lèvres lipstick
s'il te plaît please
le salon de coiffure hairdresser's
septième seventh
la signature signature
sous under
le taux de change rate of exchange
te you, to you
le ticket slip, ticket
urgent urgent
tu vas you're going
vraiment really

Notes

PART ONE

1 **Monsieur Lecerf parle à ses clients. Il vous parle.** *Monsieur Lecerf talks to his customers. He talks to you.*
Il *vous* parle.: *He talks* TO *you.* (cf. L6, N24)
Je vous reconnais.: *I recognize you.*
Il vous parle.: *He talks* TO *you.*
As you can see, **vous** can be *to you* or just *you.*

2 **Vous ne me connaissez pas.** *You don't know me.*
When **me** and **vous** are used in front of the verb, **ne** comes before **me** or **vous.**

3 **Comment est-ce que je les connais?** *How do I know them?*
comment est-ce que ... You have learnt **comment** in the phrases **comment allez-vous?** (L1, N73) and **comment ça va?** (L4, N23). Here is **comment est-ce que ...** which, when added to a statement, turns the statement into a HOW question.

68

4 Je connais vos mains parce que je les regarde. *I know your hands*
because I look at them.
je les regarde: *I look at them*   Remember **regarder** means *to look* AT.
This is the same **les** you saw in L6, N4b:
Leur fils et leur fille *les* **accompagnent.:** *Their son and daughter*
accompany THEM.
Like **vous** and **me** it comes before the verb except in commands,
where it comes after the verb.
Remember, **excusez-les:** *excuse them;* **excuse-le:** *excuse him*
(L5, N37); **excusez-moi:** *excuse me* (L6).

5 Vos mains me donnent des chèques de voyage, et les signent. *Your*
hands give me (to me) traveller's cheques, and sign them.
me: *me, to me*   Like **vous** (L7, N1), **me** can mean either *me* or *to me.*

6 Je vous donne un ticket. *I give you a slip.*
In most French banks the bank clerks give you a slip which you
then give to the cashier.

7 Ce ticket, vous le donnez au caissier. *You give this slip to the*
cashier.
vous le donnez: *you give it*   Le: *it,* when *it* refers to a masculine
noun — in this case, **le ticket.** Note the construction of this
sentence. **Ce ticket** is placed at the beginning, for emphasis.

8 Vous êtes quelquefois distraits. *Sometimes you are absent-minded.*
a vous êtes distraits   **Vous** refers here to more than one person, so
distraits is plural.

9 Vous vous trompez. *You make mistakes.* Remember, **je me trompe:**
I am wrong (L5, N41).

10 N'exagérons pas. *Let's not exaggerate.*
In lesson 4 you saw **voyons** (N31), and **prenons de la soupe à**
l'oignon (N33a)   **N'exagérons pas:** *Let's not exaggerate,* is the
same construction, but in its negative form.

11 Et vous mettez la bonne date . . . *And you put the right date . . .*
a vous mettez: *you put*   This is part of the irregular verb **mettre:** *to put*
(App. IIIE).
b la bonne date: *the right date*   This is a less usual use of the adjective
bon, which normally means *good.*

PART TWO
12 Tu es fatiguée? *Are you tired?*
Valérie uses **tu es,** the familiar form, rather than the formal **vous**
êtes, as she is speaking to her mother.

7 **13** **Où vas-tu?** *Where are you going?*
Vas-tu is the question form of **tu vas**: *you are going, you go.* **Tu vas**
is another part of the verb **aller**: *to go* (App. I Ca).

14 **Chez le coiffeur. J'ai un rendez-vous ce matin.** *To the hairdresser's. I*
have an appointment this morning.
chez means *at* or *to the shop of* . . .

15 **Regarde mes cheveux. Ils sont affreux!** *Look at my hair. It's terrible!*
a **regarde**: *look at* This is the familiar command form. The polite
command form would be **regardez!** which is, as you know, the
same as the **vous** form, **vous regardez** (L6, N28).
The familiar command form of **-er** verbs is the same as the **tu** form
— **tu regardes** — but without the final **s.**
Tu signes la fiche.: *You sign the form.*
Signe la fiche.: *Sign the form.*
Tu écoutes ton père.: *You listen to your father.*
Écoute ton père.: *Listen to your father.*
b **mes cheveux**: *my hair*
In English we speak of *hair*, in the singular. In French you always
speak of **les cheveux**, unless you are referring to a single hair.
c **ils sont affreux**: lit. *they* ARE (because *cheveux* is plural) *terrible*
Affreux, a plural adjective here, ends in **-x.** It has the same form in
the masculine singular.
un singe affreux: *a horrible monkey*
des singes affreux: *horrible monkeys.*

16 **En effet. Pourquoi est-ce que tu n'achètes pas une perruque?** *Yes*
(*indeed*). *Why don't you buy a wig?*
a **tu n'achètes pas** **Tu achètes** is the familiar form of **vous achetez**:
you buy. Be careful with the accents on the verb **acheter,** *to buy.*
j'achète   **nous achetons**
tu achètes   **vous achetez**
il achète   **ils achètent** (App. IBf).
b **pourquoi est-ce que** . . . ? *Why* . . . ? We learnt how to form
HOW . . . ? questions with **comment** + **est-ce que** at the beginning
of this lesson (L7, N3). WHY . . . ? questions are formed in the
same way, using **pourquoi**: *why*:
Tu achètes une perruque.: *You are buying a wig.*
Est-ce que tu achètes une perruque?: *Are you buying a wig?*
Pourquoi est-ce que tu achètes une perruque?: *Why are you buying a*
wig?
The negative is formed in the usual way, by putting **ne** before the
verb, and **pas** after it.

70

17 **Allons bon! Je ne trouve pas son adresse.** *There now! I can't* (lit. *don't*) *find his address.*
son adresse: *his address*   **Adresse** is feminine, but remember that **son** is used before feminine words beginning with a vowel (L5, N25b). Note that there is only one **d** in the French word **adresse**.

18 **Elle est peut-être dans ton sac à main.** *Perhaps it's in your handbag.*
elle est: *it is*   Remember that **elle** can mean *it* as well as *she*. Here it refers to **l'adresse,** which is feminine.

19 **Donne-moi mon sac, s'il te plaît.** *Give me my bag, please.*
a **Donne-moi**: *give me* is the familiar form of **donnez-moi.**
Remember that **moi** is the pronoun used after a command, not **me.**
b **S'il te plaît** is the familiar form of **s'il vous plaît.**

20 **Mais, où est-il, mon sac à main?** *But where is my bag?* (lit. *But where is it, my bag?*) This word order is used for emphasis. Remember **Il n'aime rien, mon frère,** (L2, N52) which is more emphatic than **Mon frère n'aime rien.** And, in this lesson (N7) **Ce ticket, vous le donnez au caissier,** which is more emphatic than **Vous donnez ce ticket au caissier.**

21 **Vraiment, Maman; tu égares toujours ton sac!** *Really, Mother (Mummy); you are always losing your bag!*
Tu égares is the familiar form of **vous égarez.**

22 **Je sais, je l'égare toujours.** *I know, I'm always losing it.*
Je l'égare. *I lose it.* In N7 you saw **vous le donnez**: *you give IT*. In this sentence **l'** is used and not **le,** (*it*), as the next word begins with a vowel.

23 **Le voilà, là, sur la chaise.** *There it is, there, on the chair.*
le voilà: *there it is*   Remember **voilà** means *there is/are, here is/are.* **Le voilà** means *there* IT *is* when *it* refers to a masculine noun, in this case **le sac.**

24 **Ne bouge pas. Je vais te donner ton sac . . .** *Don't move. I'll give you your bag . . .*
a **Ne bouge pas.**: *Don't move* is the familiar form of **ne bougez pas.**
b **je vais te donner . . .** : lit. *I'm going to give you . . .* When **te** comes in front of a verb it can be *you* or *to you*. Notice that **te** comes in front of **donner** and not in front of **vais.**

25 **Non; je ne la trouve pas . . . Oh! Pardon! La voilà . . .** *No, I can't* (lit. *don't*) *find it . . . Oh! sorry! Here it is.*

7 **a je ne la trouve pas** La is used because *it* refers to a feminine noun,
adresse.

b la voilà See L7, N23. Again, **la**: *it*, refers to the feminine noun,
adresse.

26 **Je n'ai pas d'argent.** *I haven't got any money.*
After a negative such as **ne . . . pas,** *de, d'* should be used and not
du or **de l'.**
Nous avons du pain.: *We have got some bread.*
Nous n'avons pas de pain.: *We have not got any bread.*

27 **Où est-il, Papa?** *Where's Daddy?* (lit. *Where is he, Daddy?*)
The use of both **il** and **Papa** makes this question more emphatic
(L7, N20).

28 **Chez les Martin, peut-être.** *At the Martins', perhaps.*
a **chez les Martin**: at the Martins' You have learnt that **chez** means
at/to the shop of (L7, N14). **Chez** can also mean at someone's home, or
house.
chez Pierre: *at Pierre's home,*
at Pierre's house,
at Pierre's.

29 **Les voilà sous la chaise.** *There they are under the chair.*
les voilà: *there/here they are*
le voilà: *here it* (m.) *is* (L7, N23)
la voilà: *here it* (f.) *is* (L7, 25b)
les voilà: *here they* (m. or f.) *are*

30 **Merci . . . Eh bien, ça y est, je suis prête.** *Thanks . . . Well, that's it,*
I'm ready.
Prête: *ready* is the feminine form. The masculine is **prêt.** Notice that
the **t** of **prête** is sounded.

31 **Où est mon carnet?** *Where's my cheque book?*
mon carnet: *my book* (*of cheques*) **Un carnet** is a small book, in this
case a cheque book.

PART THREE
32 **Mais vous n'avez pas de rendez-vous, Madame.** *But you haven't got*
an appointment, Madam.
vous n'avez pas de rendez-vous This is the negative corresponding
to the positive: **Vous avez un rendez-vous.**
Un, like **du, de l',** becomes **de** in a negative sentence (L7, N26):
J'ai un sac.
Je n'ai pas de sac.

33   **regardez-les**: *look at them;*
     Je les regarde.: *I look at them.*
          1   2   1   2
     Regardez-les.: *Look at them!*
        1   2   1   2
     Vous les mangez.: *You are eating them.*
        1   2   1   2
     Mangez-les!: *Eat them!*
       1   2   1   2

The language you have learnt

Why ... ? How ... ?

Pourquoi est-ce que *Comment est-ce que*	vous téléphonez à Québec? vous fermez cette porte? vous allez à l'aéroport?

Why ... ? Because ...

Pourquoi est-ce que	vous préférez cette chambre?	Parce qu'elle est grande.
	vous aimez cet hôtel?	Parce qu'il est confortable.
	vous invitez les Delon?	Parce que je les connais bien.

Where is ... ?

Où est-il,	mon sac à main? ce livre?
Où est-elle,	ta valise? votre fèmme?

It, them (object)

Je	*le* *les*	signe. reconnais. prends. veux.

7 Me, to me; you, to you

Il	me	cherche. regarde.
	vous	connaît. parle.
	te	donne la clef. téléphone.

Pronouns and commands

Excusez- Regardez- Écoutez- Aidez- Accompagnez-	moi. nous. le. la. les.

Here it, she is; Here they are

Vous cherchez	votre mari? son sac?	Le voilà!
	Mme Delon? votre femme?	La voilà!
	les Delon? vos sacs?	Les voilà!

I've got some

J'ai	du fromage. de la salade.
	de l'argent.

I haven't got any

Je n'ai pas	de	fromage. salade.
	d'	argent.

Late/early

Je suis	*en retard.*
J'arrive	*en avance.*

Chez

Il est		le coiffeur.
	chez	le marchand de tabac.
		les Martin.
Je vais		ma tante.
		Guy.

Leçon huit   *Lesson eight*
Huitième leçon   *Eighth lesson*

La Capitale des Parisii   The Capital of the Parisii

What happens

PART ONE
Paul Delon n'est pas content.: *Paul Delon isn't happy.*
Paul doesn't like his room, it's too small and the view from the window
is dreadful. His father is out, and his mother and sister have gone
shopping as usual, leaving him all alone. He has no money so he can't
go shopping. He decides to go to the Eiffel Tower.

PART TWO
Au pied de la Tour Eiffel, Paul rencontre Monsieur Levoisin.: *At the foot
of the Eiffel Tower, Paul meets Monsieur Levoisin.*
Monsieur Levoisin invites Paul to go up the Eiffel Tower with him.

Le vieux Paris: *Old Paris*
Monsieur Levoisin tells Paul that the Parisii inhabited Paris in the
fourth century — but Paul isn't interested. However, he is interested in
visiting the sewers, but Monsieur Levoisin makes an excuse not to go
with him.

PART THREE
Monsieur et Madame Lejeune: *Monsieur and Madame Lejeune*
Monsieur and Madame Lejeune have a present from a friend.

New words in this lesson

à bientôt! see you soon!
à côté de near, beside
à la maison at home
elle ajoute she adds
ajouter to add
amuse-toi enjoy yourself
s'amuser to enjoy oneself
(elle) apporte (she) brings
apporter to bring
l'après-midi (*m*) afternoon
l'arbre (*m*) tree
assez rather

assez d' (**de**) enough
(elle) attend (she) is waiting for
attendre to wait for
au pied de at the foot of
un autre another
avoir besoin de to need
bien entendu of course
le billet ticket
le bureau de tabac tobacconist's
ça ne fait rien that doesn't matter
ça ne m'intéresse pas that doesn't
   interest me

le cadeau present
la capitale capital
ce sont they are
le centime centime
la chose thing
combien? how much?
comme how
la cour courtyard
délicieux delicious
je déteste I hate
détester to hate
dire to say
elle dit she says
(venez) donc (come on) then
les égouts (m) sewers
elles (aussi) they (too)
en ce moment at the moment
ennuyeuse annoying
ennuyeux annoying
l'entrée (f) entrance
l'entrée (f) admission charge
faire beau to be fine
faire chaud to be warm
faire froid to be cold
faire noir to be dark
tu fais you do, make
nous faisons we make, do
elle fait she does, she makes
vous faites you are doing, you make
la fenêtre window
(elles) font they do, make
formidable! wonderful!
gagner to win
le guide guide
l'habitant (m) inhabitant
l'histoire (f) history
huit eight
huitième eighth
l'importance (f) importance
intéresser to interest

laid ugly
la loterie lottery
national national
ne . . . pas assez not enough
l'odeur (f) smell
ordinaire ordinary
ouvert open
par out of
paresseuse lazy
paresseux lazy
partout everywhere
pas du tout not at all
le pied foot
le plein air open air
vous pouvez you can
nous pouvons we can
près de near
quand when
le rat rat
regardez-moi ça! just look at that!
(il) rencontre (he) meets
rencontrer to meet
rien nothing
seul alone
si if
le siècle century
le spectacle sight
la statue statue
tellement so much
tenez here you are
la tour tower
tout près quite near, very near
trente mille thirty thousand
va-t-en go away
vieil old
vieille old
vieux old
visiter to visit

Notes

PART ONE

1 **Moi, je ne vais pas bien du tout.** *I don't feel at all happy.*
pas . . . du tout: *not . . . at all*

2 **Je voudrais aller dans un autre hôtel.** *I'd like to go to* (lit. *into*)
another hotel.
Un autre: *another* — two words in French, one word in English.

8

3 **Ou je voudrais une autre chambre.** *Or I'd like another room.*
une autre Notice that **autre** is the same in both the masculine and
feminine.

4 **Il n'y a pas assez de place.** *There's not enough room.*

5 **Quand je regarde par la fenêtre,** *When I look out of the window,*
Par, which usually means *by,* is here the equivalent of *out of.*

6 **le spectacle est affreux: une cour, un garage et pas d'arbres.** *it's a*
horrible sight; a courtyard, a garage and no trees.
pas d'arbres: *no* (lit. *not any*) *trees*

7 **Quand la fenêtre est ouverte, l'odeur est affreuse.** *When the window is*
open, the smell is horrible.
a **ouverte:** *open* There is an **e** on the end of **ouverte** because it refers
to **la fenêtre,** which is a feminine noun. The masculine form is
ouvert.
b **affreuse** is the feminine form of **affreux.**

8 **Elle dit: 'Voilà des croissants délicieux!** *She says: 'Here are some*
delicious rolls.
a **elle dit:** *she says.* This is part of the irregular verb **dire:** *to say*
(App. IIIE).
b **délicieux:** *delicious* Remember, if a word already ends in **s** or **x** in
the singular, the plural is unchanged (L7, N15c).

9 **Et elle ajoute: 'Et notre confiture est délicieuse!** *And she adds:*
'And our jam is delicious!
Délicieuse is the feminine form of **délicieux.**

10 **Nous la faisons ici, à l'hôtel.'** *We make it here at the hotel.'*
a **Nous . . . faisons:** *we make, we do* is part of the irregular verb
faire: *to do, to make,* (App. IIIE).

11 **Elle fait des courses.** *She's shopping.*
elle fait des courses Notice the **il/elle** form of the verb **faire**
(App. IIIE).

12 **Valérie et ma mère font des courses presque tous les jours.** *Valérie*
and my mother go shopping almost every day.
(Elles) font des courses This is the **ils/elles** form of the verb **faire.**

13 **Tous les matins, ma mère me dit: 'Amuse-toi bien, Paul!' Tous les**
matins, Valérie me dit: 'Comme tu es ennuyeux! Va-t-en!' *Every*
morning my mother says (to me): 'Enjoy yourself Paul!' Every
morning Valérie says to me: 'How annoying you are! Go away!'
Va-t-en!: *go away!* is the familiar form of **Allez-vous-en!**

14 **Tous les matins, mon père me dit: 'Va à la Tour Eiffel!'** *Every morning my father says to me: 'Go to the Eiffel Tower.'*

a **Va!**: *Go!* is the familiar form of **allez!**

b **La Tour Eiffel** *The Eiffel Tower* was built near the Seine by a French engineer on the occasion of the 1899 Exposition Universelle. It is 320 metres high.

15 **Ennuyeux, moi? Valérie est ennuyeuse.** *Me, annoying? Valérie is annoying.*

ennuyeux . . . ennuyeuse: *annoying* These are the masculine and feminine forms.

PART TWO

16 **Qu'est-ce que vous faites ici?** *What are you doing here?*

Vous faites: (*you do*) *you are doing* is another part of the verb **faire** (App. IIIE).

17 **Moi, je monte à la Tour.** *I'm going up* (lit. *to*) *the Tower.*

je monte: *I'm going up* You have seen this verb before in L1, N34, where it meant *to get into* (a bus) and in L2, N61, 63 where it meant *to go up* (in the lift).

18 **Il fait beau aujourd'hui.** *It's fine today.*

Il fait chaud. *It's warm.*

You have already seen **elle fait** from the irregular verb **faire.** Here is *il* **fait**: lit. *it/he makes/does.* When you talk about the weather, you say: **Il** *fait* **beau, Il** *fait* **chaud, Il** *fait* **froid.**

19 **Combien est-ce que vous avez?** *How much have you got?*

Combien est-ce que . . . ?: *How much . . . ?*

Notice that **combien est-ce que?** looks like **comment est-ce que . . . ?** *How . . . ?* (L7, N3) and like **pourquoi est-ce que . . . ?** *why . . . ?* (L7, N16b).

20 **Cinq centimes.** *Five centimes.*

There are a hundred centimes in a franc.

21 **Oh, Monsieur Levoisin, vous êtes trop aimable.** *Oh, M. Levoisin, you are too kind.*

trop aimable: *too kind* (*nice*)

In lesson 7, (N8) you had the sentence: **vous êtes quelquefois distraits. Distraits** had an s as it was a plural **vous** in this sentence. Here you see **vous** used in the singular, as the formal form of address; the adjective is therefore also in the singular: **aimable.**

22 **Pas du tout. C'est un petit cadeau. Mais, venez donc!** *Not at all. It's a little present. Do come!*
When **donc** is used immediately after a verb, it adds emphasis to the verb.

23 **Paris, c'est la vieille capitale des Parisii.** *Paris is the old capital of the Parisii.*
a **la vieille capitale**: *the old capital* Notice the spelling and pronunciation of **vieille,** the feminine of **vieux.**
b **des Parisii**: *of the Parisii* **Parisii** was the name given by the Romans to the tribe of Gauls who lived in the area which is now Paris.

24 **Les habitants de l'Île de la Cité, au quatrième siècle.** *The inhabitants of the 'Île de la Cité' in the fourth century.*
a **l'Île de la Cité**: lit. *the island of the city.* This is an island in the Seine; it is the oldest part of Paris.
b *au* **quatrième siècle**: IN *the fourth century*

25 **Ah, l'histoire!** *Oh, history!*
In L6, we saw **histoire** used in the sense of *story.*

26 **J'aime ne rien faire.** *I like doing nothing.*
Ne and **rien** BOTH come together before the verb in the infinitive. You have seen that the infinitive is used after **j'adore** in **j'adore manger** (L4, N14). The infinitive is also used after **j'aime, j'aime manger.**

27 **Ma femme me dit toujours: 'Jules, tu ne fais rien.**: *My wife is always telling me: 'Jules, you don't do anything.*
tu fais: *you do,* is·from the verb **faire** (App. IIIE).

28 **Les femmes sont paresseuses, elles aussi.** *Women are lazy too.*
a **Les femmes** means *women* in general, so the article is used.
b **paresseuses**: *lazy* The ending -ses, agrees with **les femmes,** a feminine plural.

29 **Vous pouvez faire des choses amusantes ici à Paris.** *You can do amusing things here in Paris.*
vous pouvez: *you can* In L6, N15, we saw **je ne peux pas**: *I cannot.* **Vous pouvez** is the **vous** form of the same verb (App. IVB). As was the case with **je peux,** if **vous pouvez** is followed by another verb, that verb must be in the infinitive form.

30 **Oui; nous pouvons les visiter ensemble, si vous voulez.** *Yes, we can visit them together, if you like.*
nous pouvons: *we can* (App. IVB).

31 **Et puis, il fait noir.** *And it's dark.*

a **Et puis** — lit. *and then*, more emphatic than *and* on its own.

b Remember, *it is warm*: **il fait chaud**, *it is cold*: **il fait froid**. *It's dark* is translated in the same way, **il fait noir.**

32 **Je ne peux pas vous accompagner cet après-midi.** *I can't come with you this afternoon.*
cet après-midi: *this afternoon* **Cet** is used here because **après-midi** begins with a vowel.

33 **Ma femme m'attend à la maison.** *My wife is waiting for me at home.*
(elle) m'attend: *(she) is waiting for me*, *(she) waits for me* **Attend** is part of one of a group of verbs whose infinitive ends in **-re** (App. IIIA). The infinitive of **attend** is **attendre**: *to wait for*.

34 **Je voudrais tellement pouvoir vous accompagner.** *I'd like so much to be able to go with you.*
pouvoir: *to be able* This is the infinitive of the verb whose parts, **je peux, nous pouvons, vous pouvez**, you already know (N29, 30 above and App. IVB).

35 **Où se trouvent-ils, ces égouts?** *Where* ARE *these sewers?*
Où se trouvent-ils . . . ? is the plural form of **il se trouve** which we saw in L6, N36. Note the construction. In the same way as **mon sac à main** is emphasized in **Où est-il, mon sac à main?** (L7, N36), **ces égouts** is emphasized here.

36 **Ils sont assez loin d'ici: l'entrée est près de la statue de Lille, sur la place de la Concorde.** *They are quite a way from here; the entrance is near the statue of Lille, on the place de la Concorde.*

a **assez loin**: *quite a way*, *rather far* **Assez** means *rather/quite*, as well as *enough*.

b **près de la statue**: *near the statue* **Près** must be followed by **de** when followed by a noun.

c **La place de la Concorde** is a large square in the centre of Paris.

37 **Mais non. La place de la Concorde est tout près.** *Oh no, it isn't. The place de la Concorde is quite near.*

a **mais non** is more emphatic than **non** on its own (**mais oui**: *oh yes*).

b **tout près**: *quite near* A moment before, M. Levoisin said that the sewers were **assez loin**: *rather far away*, but seeing that Paul was inclined to be put off by that, he now tries to encourage him.

8

8 **38** C'est un vieil homme, très gentil — un vieil ami. *He's a very nice old man, an old friend.*

a c'est: *he is* Remember when *he is* is followed by an article and a noun you must use **c'est** (L3, N5).

b vieil: *old* **Vieil** and not **vieux** is used before masculine singular nouns which begin with a vowel and those which begin with a silent h.

SUMMARY

Masculine singular in front of a consonant:

le *vieux* sac   **les *vieux* sacs**

Masculine singular in front of a vowel:

le *vieil* agent de police   **les *vieux* agents de police**

Masculine singular in front of a silent **h**:

le vieil hôtel   **les vieux hôtels**

Feminine:

la vieille ville   **les vieilles villes**

39 Et l'entrée, c'est combien? *And how much is the admission charge?* Note the word order; because of this construction, **l'entrée** is emphasized.

...c'est combien?: ... (lit.) *it's how much?* Learn this way of asking the price.

Le sac, c'est combien?: *How much is the bag?*

40 Tenez, voilà dix francs ... *Here you are, here's ten francs ...* dix francs: *ten francs* The x of **dix** (and **six**) is not pronounced when the next word begins with a consonant.

41 Non, Monsieur Levoisin! C'est trop! *No, M. Levoisin, it's too much!* trop: *too much* As you know, **trop** can also mean just *too*, when it is followed by an adjective.

42 Écoutez: allez au bureau de tabac, à côté de la Tour Eiffel, et achetez un billet de la loterie nationale. *Listen: go to the tobacconist's near the Eiffel Tower and buy a national lottery ticket.* loterie nationale A national lottery was started by the State in 1933. There is a draw every week.

43 Avec un billet, vous pouvez gagner trente mille francs. *With one ticket, you can win thirty thousand francs.*

44 Amusez-vous bien. *Have a good time.*

PART THREE

45 Ce sont des billets *They are tickets*

IT IS *a ticket.*: *C'est* un billet.

THEY ARE *tickets.*: *Ce sont* des billets.

82

We equated *it is* and **il est** in **Il est dans mon sac** (L1, N43a). But we know that when *it is* is followed by an article and a noun, the French for *it is* is **c'est**. (N38a above).

e.g. IT IS *a ticket*.: **C'est un billet.**

The plural of *It is a ticket* is: *They are tickets*; the plural of **C'est un billet** is **Ce sont des billets.**

The language you have learnt

It's hot, dark

Il *fait*	chaud. noir.

To be able to

Je voudrais	*pouvoir*	faire de la gymnastique. vous accompagner.

Not at all

Je	*ne*	l'aime	*pas du tout.*
Ça		m'intéresse	

Nothing

Il	*ne*	fait mange	*rien.*

To do, take nothing

Je voudrais Nous pouvons	*ne rien*	faire. prendre.

To need

J'ai Ils ont	*besoin d'*	argent. un plan.

8 How . . . it is

Comme c'est	difficile!
	joli!

Far, near . . .

Il habite	*loin.*
	loin de Paris.
	tout *près.*
	près de Paris.

Beaucoup (de), assez (de), trop (de)

Il gagne	*beaucoup.*
	*beaucoup d'*argent.
	assez.
	*assez d'*argent.
	trop.
	*trop d'*argent.

Too

Vous êtes	*trop*	gentil.
		fatigué.

Ma chère Anne, . . .   My dear Anne, . . .

What happens

PART ONE

Voilà Monsieur Redon: *Here's Monsieur Redon*
Monsieur Redon owns a tobacconist's. He is not usually busy in the
morning, and this morning it is cold and wet. Monsieur Levoisin is a
regular customer; he buys a lottery ticket every week. M. Redon has
only ever won three francs on the lottery; his wife once won ten
francs, a year or so ago.

PART TWO

Au bureau de tabac: *At the tobacconist's*
Paul buys some postcards, stamps, a newspaper and some chocolate from
M. Redon. Marie-Claire meets him and they go off to the Post Office together.

Au bureau de poste: *At the post office*
Marie-Claire asks Paul to make two phone calls for her. Then she goes.

PART THREE

Le concierge gagne toujours.: *The caretaker always wins.*
In five years the caretaker has won twenty-five thousand francs.

New words in this lesson

elle a de la chance she's lucky
aimer bien to like very much
après after
avoir de la chance to be lucky
beaucoup de monde a lot of people
bien sûr certainly
la boîte à lettres letter box
le bonbon sweet
le buraliste tobacconist
le bureau de poste post office
c'est dommage it's a pity, that's a pity
c'est la vie! that's life!
la caisse till
la carte postale postcard
le cendrier ashtray

le chocolat chocolate
la cigarette cigarette
cinquante fifty
le comptoir counter
le concierge concierge
consoler to console
(ils) coûtent (they) cost
coûter to cost
d'accord all right
de temps en temps from time to time
des quantités de lots of
(il) dit he says
elle her
en couleurs (in) colour
envoyer to send

9

fidèle loyal
je fume I smoke
fumer to smoke
le gagnant winner
le gros lot big prize
il y a ago
le jeton "jeton"
le journal newspaper
je laisse I leave
laisser to leave
la lettre letter
leur to them
lui to her/him
mauvais bad
moins minus
ne . . . jamais never
neuf nine
neuvième ninth
nous us
par exemple for instance, for example
un peu a little
peu de few
(elle) peut (she) can
(ils) peuvent (they) can
la pipe pipe

il pleut it's raining
pleuvoir to rain
plus more
poster to post
le prix price
le propriétaire owner
quarante forty
quatre-vingts eighty
la revue magazine
la santé health
si yes
le soir evening
soixante-dix seventy
souvent often
soyez les bienvenus . . . ! welcome!
la tablette bar
le télégramme telegram
le timbre stamp
le timbre-poste postage stamp
tout de suite immediately
tout seul all alone, on one's own
le travail work
trente thirty
je vends I sell
vendre to sell

Notes

1 **Soyez les bienvenus dans mon bureau de tabac!** *Welcome to my tobacconist's shop!*
Soyez . . . !: lit. *be . . . !* is the polite command or request form of the verb être.

2 **Je vends des journaux, des revues, des bonbons, des cartes postales, des timbres-poste.** *I sell newspapers, magazines, sweets, postcards, stamps.*
je vends: *I sell* In L8, N33, you learnt that attend belongs to the -re group of verbs. Je vends also belongs to this group (*to sell*: vendre) (App. IIIA). The tu form of -re verbs is always the same as the je form:
je vends, tu vends.

3 **Je vends aussi des pipes, des cendriers, et, naturellement, du tabac et des cigarettes.** *I also sell pipes, ashtrays and, of course, tobacco and cigarettes.*
je vends aussi . . . : lit. *I sell also* . . . Note the word order.

4 C'est très mauvais pour la santé. *It's very bad for the health.*
Mauvais here means *bad.* You have already seen that it can mean *wrong, incorrect* (L7). Remember that **bon** also has two meanings: *good* (L4, N39) and *right, correct* (L7, N11).

5 Quelquefois, je la laisse toute seule et je lui laisse les clefs de la caisse. *Sometimes I leave her on her own and I leave her the keys of the till.*
a Je la laisse.: *I leave her.*
Je lui laisse les clefs.: *I leave her the keys.* In the second sentence, *her* means TO *her* — therefore you use **lui** in French. As you can see, **lui** comes before the verb.

6 Ce matin, il y a peu de clients: il fait froid et il pleut un peu. *This morning there are few customers; it's cold and it's raining a little.*
a peu de clients: *few customers* As was the case with **beaucoup** and **assez**, **peu** must be followed by **de** when it precedes a noun.
b un peu: *a little* Be careful not to confuse **peu de:** *few* and **un peu:** *a little.*

7 En général, le matin, j'ai peu de travail. *I'm not usually very busy in the morning.* (lit. *Generally in the morning I have little work.*)
a le matin: *in the morning* Note that the French for *in the morning* is simply **le matin.**
b peu de travail This time, **peu de** means *little.* Remember that it can also mean **few** (N6 above).

8 En général, nous vendons peu le matin. *We usually sell (very) little* (lit. *little) in the morning.*
a Nous vendons is the **nous** form of **vendre:** *to sell.*
b Nous vendons peu: *We sell little.* Careful!
Nous vendons *peu*: *We sell* LITTLE.
Nous vendons *un peu* le matin.: *We sell* A LITTLE *in the morning.*

9 Mais, l'après-midi et le soir, nous avons beaucoup de monde. *But in the afternoon and the evening we're very busy* (lit. *we have a lot of people*).

10 Je lui vends un billet chaque semaine. *I sell him a ticket every week.*
je lui vends: *I sell him* In this sentence, *him* means *to him* — in French **lui.** As you can see, **lui** is used for both (*to*) *him* and (*to*) *her* (N5 above).

11 Je vends beaucoup de billets à trois francs. *I sell a lot of three franc tickets* (lit. *tickets at three francs*).

9

12 **Mais il est plus difficile de vendre les billets à trente ou à cinquante francs.** *But it's more difficult to sell thirty or fifty franc tickets.*

vendre is the infinitive of the verb *to sell*: You have already learnt:

je vends	**nous vendons**
tu vends	**vous vendez**
il/elle vend	

Remember, once you know these forms of **vendre**, you can use the same forms of all other verbs of the same type, that is, verbs which end in **-re**, such as: **attendre** (L8, N33), **descendre** (L6, N31). (See App. IIIA.)

13 **Les gagnants peuvent gagner trente mille francs.** *The winners can win thirty thousand francs.*

(ils) peuvent: *(they) can* is another part of **pouvoir** (App. IVB.)
Remember:

je peux	**vous pouvez**
nous pouvons	**ils/elles peuvent.**

14 **De temps en temps, un de mes clients gagne un gros lot.** *From time to time one of my customers wins a big prize.*

15 **Bien entendu, d'autres ne gagnent jamais rien.** *Of course, others never win anything.*

a **d'autres**: *others*
un autre: *another*   Note carefully that the plural of **un autre** is **d'autres**.

b **ne ... jamais**: *never*   The equivalent of *never* in French is **ne ... jamais**. As is the case with **ne ... pas** (L1, N18), and **ne ... rien** (L2, N28), **ne** is placed before the verb and **jamais** is placed after it.

16 **Quelquefois, pour les consoler, je leur donne un billet gratuit.** *Sometimes, to console them, I give them a free ticket.*

a **pour les consoler**: *(in order) to console them* (c.f. L6, N16c).

b **je leur donne**: *I give them* (lit. *to them*)   You have learnt **je lui laisse ...** : *I leave her (to her)* ... (L9, N5) and **je lui vends ....** *I sell him (to him)* (L9, N10). *I leave/sell* THEM *(to them)* is **je leur laisse/vends ...**;
I give THEM *(to them)* ... is **je leur donne.**

17 **Monsieur Levoisin, lui, a gagné cent francs.** *M. Levoisin won a hundred francs.*

(il) a gagné   This is the first time you have learnt how to form a past tense in French. **Il a gagné** is the equivalent of both *he's won* and *he won*. If you look at the word order you will see that this tense is formed in the same way as in English:

il a + gagné

he has + won

9

gagné, like *won*, is the past participle. The past participle of all French verbs of the **-er** kind is obtained by substituting **é** for **er**.

18 **Il y a dix ans peut-être.** *Ten years ago perhaps.*
il y a You have learnt **il y a** meaning *there is* (L2, N20) and *there are* (L2, N23).
The same phrase corresponds to *ago* when it is used with an expression of time: **il y a dix ans**: *ten years ago*.

19 **Ma femme, elle, m'a acheté un billet, il y a un an ou deux.** *My wife bought me a ticket a year or two ago.*
(elle) m'a acheté . . . : (*she*) *has bought me* (*to me*)/*she bought me*
she has bought HIM . . . : **elle *lui* a acheté . . .**
she has bought HER . . . : **elle *lui* a acheté . . .**
she has bought THEM . . . : **elle *leur* a acheté . . .**
she has bought ME . . . : **elle *m'*a acheté . . .**
Just as **j'** and **l'** are used instead of **je** and **le** in front of a vowel, **m'** is used instead of **me**.

20 **En vingt ans, j'ai gagné trois francs!** *In twenty years I have won three francs!*
En vingt ans means *in twenty years* in the sense of IN THE COURSE OF *twenty years*.

PART TWO
21 **Oui, voilà, soixante-dix centimes.** *Yes, here you are, seventy centimes.*
soixante-dix: *seventy* (70) (lit. *sixty ten*) **soixante**: *sixty* Strangely enough, the French for *seventy* is **soixante-dix**, *sixty ten*.

22 **Vous ne vendez pas de timbres?** *You don't sell stamps?*
Remember that after a negative, **du, de l'** and **de la** become **de** (L7, N26 and L8). **Des** also becomes **de** after a negative:
Vous avez *des* timbres.
Vous n'avez pas *de* timbres.

23 **Si, bien sûr.** *Yes, I do* (lit. *Yes certainly*).
If a question contains a negative and you want to answer *yes*, you must use **si** and not **oui.**
Vous ne vendez pas de timbres? Si.: *You don't sell stamps, do you? Yes we do.*

24 **'L'Équipe', et deux tablettes de chocolat.** *The 'Équipe' and two bars of chocolate.*
'l'Équipe' is a French sporting paper.

9   25   **Ça fait combien?** *How much is that?*

26   **Ça fait sept francs quatre-vingts.** *That's seven francs eighty.*
   quatre-vingts: *eighty* (lit. *four twenties*), that is, eighty centimes.

27   **Ça va?** *How are you?*
   Remember **comment ça va?** (L4, N23) **Ça va?** is a shortened, more casual greeting.

28   **Pas mal, merci.** *Not bad, thanks.*
   Pas mal is short for **Ça ne va pas mal.**

29   **Écoute, Paul. Guy m'attend. Tu veux lui téléphoner pour moi?**
   Listen Paul. Guy is expecting me. Will you phone him for me?
   a   **Écoute:** *listen* is the familiar form of **écoutez.**
   b   **Tu veux** is the familiar form of **vous voulez** (App. IVB).

30   **Bien sûr. Je peux faire ça pour toi.** *Certainly. I can do that for you.*
   Pour toi: *for you,* is the familiar form of **pour vous.**

31   **Je veux envoyer un télégramme.** *I want to send a telegram.*
   Envoyer: *to send* is a slightly unusual -er verb: the y becomes i in four forms: **j'envoie, tu envoies, il/elle envoie, ils/elles envoient** (App. ICb).

32   **Alors, qu'est-ce que je dis à Guy?** *So what shall I say to Guy?*
   (lit. *So, what do I say to Guy*).
   je dis à . . . : *I say to . . . I tell . . .* from **dire** (App. IIIE).

33   **Dis-lui:** *Tell him:*
   Remember that the ending of the polite command form is the same as that of the **vous** form, **vous sortez:** *you go out*; **sortez:** *go out* L6, N28). Similarly, the familiar command form is, in the case of most French verbs, the same as the normal **tu** form: **tu lui dis:** *you tell him* — **dis-lui:** *tell him.*
   Remember that there is a small difference in spelling in the case of an -er verb (L7, N15), where the familiar command form is **e,** and not **es.** Notice that in a command, the pronoun, whether it is **les** or **lui,** comes after the verb. (cf. L7, N33).

34   **Et s'il n'est pas là?** *And what if he's not there?* (lit. *And if he's not there?*)
   s'il = si il (cf. **s'il vous plaît** (L1, N39c))

35   **Parle à la concierge.** Speak to the concierge.
   Parle: *speak* is the familiar command form from the verb **parler** (cf. L7, N15a), an -er verb, therefore there is no s at the end of **parle**

36 Eux, ils sont certainement là. *They're certainly there.*
eux, ils: *they* The pronoun **eux** is used to emphasize **ils.**
You now know how to emphasize *I, you, he/she, we, you* (pl.),
they: in French:
moi, je: **Moi, je suis fatigué.** (L1, N75)
toi, tu: **Toi aussi, Louise, tu travailles trop.** (L5, N27)
lui, il: **Lui, il voudrait être professeur.** (L5, N23)
elle, elle: **Elle, elle a vingt ans.** (L5, N22).
nous, nous: **Nous, nous vendons les cartes postales.**
vous, vous: **Vous aussi, vous arrivez du Canada.** (L1, N48)
eux, ils: **Eux, ils sont certainement là.**
elles, elles: **Elles, elles vont peut-être savoir.** (L6, N43)

37 Qu'est-ce que je leur dis à eux? *What do I say to* THEM?
a je leur dis: *I say to them, I tell them* **Leur** is the object pronoun, *to*
THEM (L9, N16b).
b à eux: *to them*
The word **eux** which is used to emphasize **ils**: *they,* can also be used
to emphasize **leur**: *to them.*

38 Dis-leur: 'Marie-Claire et Guy ne peuvent pas venir ce soir.': *Tell*
them: 'Marie-Claire and Guy can't come this evening.'
dis-leur: *tell them (to them).* Remember **dis-lui**: *tell him (to him)*
(L9, N33).

39 Tu peux acheter deux jetons au comptoir. *You can buy two 'jetons'*
at the counter.
deux jetons Some public telephones can be operated with coins; for
others you have to buy special tokens (**jetons**), either from a post
office or from the café or restaurant from where you are phoning.

40 Deux francs vingt moins quatre-vingts centimes, ça fait un franc
quarante. *Two francs twenty minus eighty centimes is one franc forty.*
a Moins means *minus* when it is used in subtraction.
b ça fait: lit. *that makes.*

41 ce n'est pas assez pour les égouts. *it's not enough for the sewers.*
ce n'est pas assez Ce corresponds to *it* in phrases built on this
pattern.

The language you have learnt

Perfect tense -er verbs

J'ai	gagné déjeuné	un gros lot. au Restaurant des Chauffeurs.

9 **Perfect tense with ago**

J'ai	gagné déjeuné envoyé	un gros lot, au Restaurant des Chauffeurs, une carte à Paul,	il y a une semaine.

How much

Combien d'argent *est-ce que* vous avez gagné? Vous avez gagné *combien*?

(To) him, them, with verbs which take an indirect object

Je veux	*lui* *leur*	dire bonjour. téléphoner tout de suite. parler.

Le, l' with regarder and écouter

Je	*le*	regarde.
	l'	écoute.

Position of lui and leur after a command

Donnez- Demandez-	*lui* *leur*	de l'argent. une chambre.

Oui, si

Vous venez?	*Oui.*
Vous *ne* venez *pas*?	*Si.*

Little, few

Vous avez	*peu de*	travail. salade. clients.

A little, little

Il pleut	*un peu.*
Il mange	*peu.*

En + time

Il a gagné mille francs	*en*	cinq ans.
Il a acheté deux rasoirs électriques		trois semaines.

Dans + time

Il va arriver	*dans*	une semaine.
Il va téléphoner		un quart d'heure.

In the morning, etc.

Il	arrive toujours	*le* matin.
	téléphone	*l'*après-midi.
	travaille	*le* soir.

This morning, etc.

Il	a téléphoné	*ce* matin.
	a travaillé	*cet* après-midi.
	m'a invité	*ce* soir.

Another, other(s)

Je voudrais	*un autre*	croissant.
	une autre	chambre.
	d'autres	disques.
D'autres	ne gagnent jamais.	
	ne travaillent pas.	

Leçon dix *Lesson ten*
Dixième leçon *Tenth lesson*

Au bureau de poste At the post office

What happens

PART ONE
La sœur de Guy Martin se présente.: *Guy Martin's sister introduces herself.*
Marie-Claire lives with her brother in a flat in Paris. Their parents died ten years ago. She is hoping to go to University, if she passes her exams. Meanwhile she works for Guy in his advertising agency.

PART TWO
Paul téléphone à Guy Martin.: *Paul phones Guy Martin.*
Paul has great difficulty trying to ring Guy. Marie-Claire tries but the number is engaged.

PART THREE
Un paysan arrive en ville.: *A countryman comes to town.*
The countryman doesn't know how to use a telephone.

New words in this lesson

elle a raison she's right
à vrai dire really, in fact
l'agence (*f*) agency
l'agence de publicité (*f*) advertising agency
allô hello
appeler to call, to phone
j'appelle I call, I phone
vous avez appuyé you (have) pressed
appuyer to press
attendre to expect
autoritaire bossy
avoir raison to be right
le bac baccalauréat (examination)
le bouton button
c'est-à-dire (que) that is . . . (that's to say . . .)
c'est bien simple it's quite simple

la cabine téléphonique telephone booth, kiosk
la carrière career
chacun each (one)
nous avons choisi we've chosen
choisir to choose
le combiné receiver
nous avons conservé we've kept
conserver to keep
mon correspondant the person I'm calling
le courrier post
d'habitude usually
d'un certain âge middle-aged
décrocher to pick up (receiver)
décrochez pick up
désagréable unpleasant
le dessinateur designer

10

le **directeur** director
dixième tenth
dur hard
engager to take on, to employ
(il) entend (he) hears
entendre to hear
j'espère I hope
espérer to hope
être obligé (de) to have to, to be obliged to
les études (f)-studies
l'expert comptable (m) accountant
la faculté University (Faculty)
la fente slot
fonder to start, (to found)
j'ai formé I dialled
former to dial
l'instruction (f) instruction
introduire to put in
introduisez put in
la jeune fille (young) girl
lire to read
lisez read
malheureusement unfortunately
le mois month
Mon Dieu! Good heavens!
mort dead
nouveau new
nouvel new
nouvelle new
occupé engaged
l'opératrice (f) operator
passer to sit/take an exam.

pendant during
le personnel staff
plutôt rather
(elle se) présente (she) introduces herself
se présenter to introduce oneself
prochain next
que that
je raccroche I hang up
raccrocher to hang up
les réclamations (f) complaints
je recommence I start/begin again
recommencer to begin again
la référence reference
le résultat result
réussir to succeed
je réussis I succeed
je me sauve I'm off
simple simple
la sténo-dactylo shorthand typist
je surveille I supervise
surveiller to supervise
je tape à la machine I type
taper à la machine to type
terminer to finish
la tonalité dialling tone
venir de to have just
nous venons de we have just
ils viennent de they have just
je viens de I have just
(il) vient de (he) has just
la voix voice
nous voudrions we would like (to)

Notes

PART ONE

1 Nous voudrions trouver un appartement plus petit et moins cher.
We'd like to find a smaller and less expensive flat.

a nous voudrions: *we would like* Remember **je voudrais**: *I would like* (L2).

b plus petit: *smaller* In lesson 9 you learnt the comparative of the adjective **difficile**: *plus difficile* (L9, N12a). To form this sort of comparative, add **plus** to all adjectives.

c moins cher You learnt **moins** meaning *minus* in subtraction (L9, N75a). Here it means *less*.

2 À vrai dire, nous voudrions trouver un appartement chacun. *In fact, we'd like to find a flat each.*

95

10   **chacun**: lit. *each one*   You already know **chaque**, which is always followed immediately by a noun: (L3, N8) **chaque chambre.** **Chacun** is used alone, instead of a noun: *each one.*

3 **Nous sommes donc obligés d'attendre.** *So we'll have to wait.* (lit. *We are therefore obliged to wait.*)

4 **Guy vient de fonder une agence de publicité.** *Guy has just started an advertising agency.*
   Guy vient de fonder . . . : *Guy has just started . . .* The phrase **vient de** + infinitive corresponds to *has just* + past participle in English.

5 **Il travaille dur pour réussir.** *He works hard to succeed.*
   pour réussir   cf. L6, N16 (lit. *in order to*)
   In the English sentence *He works hard to succeed,* to again stands for *in order to,* so the French for it is again *pour.*
   Réussir is the infinitive of a verb belonging to the third main group of French verbs, those ending in **-ir** (App. IIA). (You are already familiar with the **-er** and the **-re** groups).

6 **Moi, je suis lycéenne.** *I am a schoolgirl.*
   (La) lycéenne is the feminine of **le lycéen** (L2, N3).

7 **Je viens de passer mon bac.** *I have just taken my bac.*
a **Je viens de passer . . .** *I have just taken . . .* Once again *je viens de* + infinitive is *I have just* + past participle.
b **passer mon bac**   Bac is short for **baccalauréat,** the nearest equivalent to the English GCE 'A' level examination.
   Passer in the phrase **passer le bac** is *to take,* not *to pass.*

8 **Si je réussis, j'espère aller à la faculté.** *If I pass,* (lit. *succeed*) *I hope to go to University.*
a **si je réussis**   Notice the **-is** ending for the **je** form of this verb.
b **à la faculté**: lit. *to the faculty*   A university is composed of **facultés** (*schools*) and **la faculté** is often used in French where *University* would be used in English.

9 **Ensuite, je veux choisir une carrière.** *Then, I want to choose a career.*
   Choisir is an **-ir** verb, like **réussir** which you have just learnt.

10 **Nous venons d'engager un nouveau dessinateur et un nouvel expert comptable.** *We have just engaged/taken on a new designer and a new accountant.*
a **nous venons de . . .** : *we have just . . .* (cf. N4 and 7 above)
b **un nouveau dessinateur . . . un nouvel expert comptable**   Nouveau: *new* is the form used with the masculine noun **dessinateur. Nouvel** also means *new* and is also masculine. But it is used before a masculine noun beginning with a vowel or silent 'h.'

11 Ils viennent tous les deux de terminer leurs études. *They have both just finished their studies.*
ils viennent de . . . : *they have just* . . . (see N4 and 7a above).

12 Ils nous ont donné des références excellentes. *They gave us excellent references.*
ils nous ont donné Remember this past tense is formed with **avoir** + past participle (L9, N17). Notice that **nous** meaning *to us* here comes before both parts of the verb **ont donné**.

13 Ils vont arriver la semaine prochaine. *They will* (lit. *they're going to*) *arrive next week.*
la semaine prochaine **Prochaine** is the feminine form of **prochain**.

14 Aujourd'hui, nous attendons une nouvelle sténodactylo. *Today we are expecting a new shorthand-typist.*
une nouvelle sténodactylo **Nouvelle** is the form used before feminine nouns. You now know three words for new:
nouveau un *nouveau* directeur
nouvel un *nouvel* employe
nouvelle ، une *nouvelle* concierge

15 Quelquefois, nous réussissons, quelquefois pas. *Sometimes, we succeed, sometimes we don't* (lit. *sometimes not*).
nous réussissons: *we succeed* The **nous** form of **-ir** verbs (*here*, **réussir**) ends in **-issons** (App. IIA).

16 Cette fois, nous avons choisi, *This time, we chose/have chosen,*
a cette fois: *this time* When *time* means *occasion*, e.g. *on this occasion*, use **fois** (cf. L6).
b nous avons choisi: *we chose/we have chosen*
You know how to make the past tense of **-er** verbs (L9, N17). The past tense of **-ir** verbs is formed in the same way.
il **a gagné** = il **a** + past participle
he has won = *he has* + past participle
il **a choisi** = il **a** + past participle
he has chosen = *he has* + past participle
The past participle of an **-ir** verb is obtained by substituting **-i** for **-ir**. choisir — choisi, réussir — réussi.

17 ou plutôt Guy a choisi, une jeune fille très jolie. *or rather Guy has chosen, a very pretty girl.*
a une jeune fille: *a girl* Une **fille** can also mean *a daughter* (L6, N4). Une **jeune fille** means *a young girl*.
b très jolie: *very pretty* **Joli** is one of the few adjectives which normally come before a noun; when it is coupled with **très**, it can be used after the noun.

10

97

10   **18   Espérons!** *Let's hope!/let's hope for the best!*

PART TWO

19   Allô . . . ? Allô . . . ah, . . . Guy ne m'entend pas. *Hullo . . . ? Hullo?
. . . Guy can't* (lit. *doesn't*) *hear me.*

a   **Allô** means *hullo,* but it is only used on the telephone. It is not a
greeting.

b   **(il) ne m'entend pas:** (*he*) *can't hear me*   An Englishman says
CANNOT *hear* when a Frenchman just says **il** *ne* **m'entend** *pas.*
Il entend is another form of the -re verb **entendre:** *to hear.*

**20   Je raccroche et j'appelle les réclamations. Voyons . . . réclamations:
13**   *I'll ring off* (lit. *I hang up) and call the operator. Let's see . . .
complaints: 13*

a   **Je raccroche:** *I'll ring off* (lit. *I hang up*). Here the present tense is
used to describe an action which is about to take place. We do the
same in English when we say *I'm coming* in the sense of *I'm coming
in a minute.*

b   **et j'appelle**   You have already seen **Je m'appelle:** *My name is* (L1),
which was part of the verb **s'appeler:** *to be called.* Now you have
appeler: *to call.* This is a slightly unusual **-er** verb. There is only one
l, in the **nous** and **vous** forms (App. IBa).

c   **les réclamations**   When you have a complaint you dial 13, a
service called **les réclamations.**

21   Je ne vous entends pas . . .   *I can't hear you . . .* (lit. *I don't hear you*).
Again there's no word in the French sentence corresponding to the
English *can't.*

22   Avez-vous un jeton? *Have you got a jeton?*
avez-vous . . . ? : *have you . . . ?* You learnt in lesson 1 that
intonation alone can turn a statement into a question. Then in
lesson 2 you learnt that you can do the same thing by adding
est-ce que to the statement.
There is a third method, a slightly more sophisticated one, which
involves changing the word order.
Vous avez quelque chose.: *You have something.* **Avez-vous quelque
chose?**: *Do you have anything?*
Notice the hyphen between **avez** and **vous** in this question form.

23   Oui. J'ai mis mon jeton dans la fente: *Yes. I've put my jeton in the
slot.*
j'ai mis   **Mis** is the past participle of **mettre.**

24 **J'ai entendu sa voix; j'ai attendu** . . . *I heard his voice; I waited* . . .
j'ai entendu . . . ; **j'ai attendu**: *I heard* . . . *I waited* . . .
You remember that the past participles of **-er** verbs end in **é** (L9, N17) and that of **-ir** verbs end in **i** (N16 above). To make the past participle of **-re** verbs remove the **-re** from the infinitive and substitute **u**:
entendre, entendu
The past tense can then be formed using **avoir** in the usual way:
j'ai entendu, etc.

25 **Recommencez!** *Start again!*
commencer: *to begin*; **recommencer**: *to begin again*. **Re** at the beginning of a verb usually means *again*. **Venez!**: *Come!* **Revenez!**: *Come again!* (L6, N49).

26 **Si vous ne réussissez pas?** *If you don't succeed?*
vous réussissez: *you succeed* The **vous** form of **-ir** verbs ends in **-issez** (App. IIA).

27 **Malheureusement, elle a raison: je n'ai pas appuyé sur le bouton.**
Unfortunately she's right: I didn't press the button.

28 **Eh bien, je recommence** . . . *Well, I'll start again* . . .
Again a present tense is used in French to describe an action which is about to take place (N20a above).

29 **As-tu envoyé ton télégramme?** *Have you sent your telegram?*
as-tu envoyé . . . ?: *Have you sent* . . . ? uses the third method described in this lesson (N22 above).

30 **As-tu téléphoné à Guy?** *Did you ring/have you rung Guy?*
Remember, you must say **téléphoner à** . . .

31 **Qu'est-ce qu'il a dit?** *What did he say?*
Il a dit is the past tense of the irregular verb **dire**: *to say* (L8, N8a; App. IIIE).

32 **Comment non?** *What do you mean, no?*
You have learnt **comment** in the phrases **comment allez-vous?** and **comment ça va?**
We also know **comment est-ce que** . . . ?: *How* . . . ? (L7, N3)

33 **Eh bien, laisse. Je vais téléphoner** . . .: *Well leave it. I'll ring up.*
Laisse is the familiar command form from the regular **-er** verb **laisser**: *to leave*.

10 The language you have learnt

Perfect tense: attendre, entendre

Hier,	j'*ai* tu *as* il *a* elle *a* nous *avons* vous *avez* ils *ont* elles *ont*	attend*u* entend*u*	Valérie.

Perfect tense: choisir, réussir

Je suis content,	j'*ai* tu *as* il *a* elle *a* nous *avons* vous *avez* ils *ont* cllcs *ont*	chois*i*! réuss*i*!

The main forms of venir in the phrase "I have just . . ."

Je *viens* Il ⎫ Elle ⎬ *vient* Nous *venons* Vous *venez* Ils ⎫ Elles⎭ *viennent*	*de*	téléphoner à Guy. jouer au tennis. choisir un billet de loterie.

Each one

Nous avons Vous avez Ils ont	une secrétaire un cendrier un journal	*chacun*.

More, less

Je préfère la chambre No 10. Elle est	*plus*	grande. belle.
	moins	chère. froide.

100

Leçon onze *Lesson eleven*
Onzième leçon *Eleventh lesson*

Georges et Valérie Georges and Valérie
sortent ensemble. go out together.

What happens

PART ONE
Georges Louvier parle.: *Georges Louvier speaks.*
Georges tells us about his work in the hotel. There are always staff problems to sort out, and he is exhausted. His parents are not happy about his choice of job; his mother thinks he works too hard, his father does not think it is a good career.

PART TWO
À la réception de l'Hôtel du Nord: *At the reception desk in the Hôtel du Nord*
Georges asks Valérie if he can spend the afternoon with her.
À la terrasse d'un restaurant: *At a restaurant*
Georges and Valérie look at the menu and order their meal. They talk about their jobs.

PART THREE
Il y a tant de choses à faire à Paris: *There are so many things to do in Paris.*
Unfortunately, Jean is interested in sport.

New words in this lesson

apprendre to learn
s'asseoir to sit down
asseyez-vous sit down
au lieu de instead of
au régime on a diet
l'augmentation (*f*) rise
aussi . . . qu' (e) as . . . as
autant que as much as
la blanquette de veau 'blanquette' of veal
la carafe carafe
combien de temps? how long?
croire to think

je crois I think
je crois que non I don't think so
le cuisinier cook
d'ailleurs moreover
d'autres others
j'ai décidé I have decided
décider to decide
le détergent detergent
dimanche Sunday
du moins at least
en réalité in fact
en tout in all, all together
en ville into town

11

épuisé exhausted	peu little, not much
j'espère que oui I hope so	(ils) se plaignent (they) complain
gagner to earn	se plaindre to complain
gérer to manage	(il) se plaint (he) complains
gras rich	plus . . . (que) more . . . than
les haricots verts (m) French beans	propre clean
l'hôtellerie (f) hotel management	que faire? what can you do?
immédiatement immediately	quelqu'un someone
impossible impossible	quelques some
(elle s') inquiète (she) worries	refaire to make (to remake)
s'inquiéter to worry	refait made (remade)
intéressant interesting	le régime diet
l'un . . . l'autre one . . . another	relire to read back (re-read)
le lait milk	rester to stay
laver to wash	rien de spécial nothing special
laver la vaisselle to wash up	servir to serve
léger light	snob snobbish
libre free	sois be
mardi Tuesday	la sole meunière 'sole meunière'
le métier job, career	solennel solemn
moins . . . que less . . . than	la sténo shorthand
montrer to show	sûr sure
ne . . . pas encore not yet	tant de so many
ne . . . personne no one (not anyone)	tantôt . . . tantôt first . . . then
ne . . . plus no more	le temps time
non plus neither	la terrasse terrace
onze eleven	le théâtre theatre
onzième eleventh	travailleur hardworking
je paie I pay	la vaisselle washing-up
pas encore not yet	le veau veal
passer (quelques jours) to spend (a few days)	le veilleur de nuit night porter
	(elle) veut (she) wants
passionnant thrilling	je veux bien all right, by all means
le patron boss	(il) vient (he) comes
payer to pay	le vin blanc white wine
vous permettez you allow	je voudrais bien I'd really like to
permettre to allow	voyager to travel

Notes

1 **Georges et Valérie sortent ensemble.** *Georges and Valérie go out together.*
(**Ils**) **sortent** (*they*) *go out* is part of the irregular verb **sortir** (App. IIB).

PART ONE

2 **toujours quelque chose à faire,** *always something to do,*
Something to + infinitive is **quelque chose à** + infinitive in French.
Remember **quelque chose à déclarer** (L1, N52).

3 **toujours quelqu'un à servir,** *always someone to serve,*
Someone to + infinitive is **quelqu'un à** + infinitive in French:
J'ai quelqu'un à accompagner.: *I have someone to accompany.*

4 **Le personnel non plus, d'ailleurs.** (lit. *Moreover*) *Neither are the staff.*
non plus: lit. *neither* The following examples will help you to see
how **non plus** is used:
Valérie n'est pas là. Paul *non plus*: *Valérie is not here. Neither is Paul.*
M. Delon n'est pas arrivé. Mme Delon *non plus*: *M. Delon hasn't
arrived. Neither has Mme Delon.*

5 **Tout le monde se plaint.** *Everybody complains.*
(Il) se plaint: *(He) complains* This is part of the verb **se plaindre,**
which is a similar type of verb to **s'appeler** (L1, N6).

6 **L'un vient me dire:** *One comes and says (to me)*:
a **l'un** If you want to say *one . . . another . . .*, use **l'un** for *one.*
b **(il) vient me dire** *(he) comes and says (to say) to me* Notice that
vient: *comes* is followed by an infinitive. Compare the French and
the English constructions: **il vient me dire**: *he comes and says to me.*

7 **L'autre vient se plaindre parce que sa chambre n'est pas propre.**
Another comes and complains because his room isn't clean.
a **L'autre . . .** is the word for *another* in the phrase *one . . . another*
(cf. N6 above).
b **(il) vient se plaindre** Again there is no word equivalent to *and* in
the French sentence. **Se plaindre** is the infinitive of the verb form
you saw in N5 above, **il se plaint.**

8 **L'un me dit: 'Il n'y a plus de lait à la cuisine.'** *One says: 'There is
no more milk in the kitchen.'*
il n'y a plus de lait Ne . . . plus de . . .: *no more . . .* Ne . . . plus
behaves like ne . . . pas, ne . . . rien, ne . . . jamais. Ne (n')** is
placed before **y a,** the verb, and **plus** after.

9 **Un autre ne veut plus travailler le dimanche.**: *Another doesn't want
to work on Sundays any more.* (lit. *Another no longer wants . . .*)
a **(Il) veut**: *(he) wants* is another part of the verb *to want*: **vouloir.**
You now know all the forms of this verb in the present tense
(App. IVB).
b **(il) ne veut plus travailler le dimanche.** Here, **ne . . . plus**
corresponds to *no . . . longer.* In the sentence **je n'ai plus de lait,**
it corresponded to *no . . . more.*
c *le* **dimanche**: *on Sundays* Compare these two sentences:
Il travaille le dimanche. *He works on Sundays* (every Sunday).
Il travaille dimanche. *He is working on Sunday* (one particular
occasion).

10   **D'autres ne veulent plus travailler le lundi.** *Others don't* (lit. *no longer*) *want to work on Mondays any more.* **D'autres** is the plural of **un autre**: *another.*

11   **'Jeanne est plus jeune que moi, et elle gagne plus que moi.** *'Jeanne is younger than I (am) and she earns more than I (do).*
a   **plus que moi**   Notice that **moi** is used for *I* after **plus que**.
b   **elle gagne**: *she earns*   You have learnt **gagner** in the sense of *to win* (L9, N13). It also means *to earn*.

12   **Je veux gagner plus qu'elle.'** *I want to earn more than she does.'*
plus qu'elle   Elle is used for *her* after **plus que**.

13   **Alors, je la paie plus.** *So I pay her more.*
Je paie: *I pay* is from the -er verb **payer**. In this tense, **payer** behaves exactly like **envoyer** (L9, N31): **y** becomes **i** except in the **nous** and **vous** forms.

14   **'Marie est moins jeune que moi, c'est vrai;** *'It's true that Marie is older than I;* **Moins . . . que**: *less . . . than*   Remember **moins cher**: *less expensive* (L10, N1c). You also know **moins** in the sense of *minus* (L9, N40d).

15   **mais je suis aussi travailleuse qu'elle.** *but I'm as hard-working as she is.*
aussi . . . que . . .: *as . . . as*   He is AS tired AS I am: **Il est *aussi* fatigué *que* moi.**

16   **Alors, je veux gagner autant qu'elle.'** *So, I want to earn as much as she does.'*
autant que: *as much as*
He works AS MUCH as I do.: **Il travaille *autant que* moi.**

17   **Tous les employés se plaignent** *All the staff complain*
(Ils) se plaignent: *(They) complain* is part of the verb **se plaindre** (N5 and 7 above).

18   **parce qu'ils ne gagnent pas assez.** *because they don't earn enough.*
ne . . . pas assez: *not enough*

19   **Mais, je ne gagne pas assez, moi non plus.** *But I don't earn enough either.* (lit. *But I don't earn enough, me neither.*)
moi non plus lit. *me neither* (cf. N4 above). The following examples will show you the meaning of . . . **non plus** and how it is used:
Je ne travaille pas, *moi non plus*.: *I don't work either.*
Tu ne manges pas, *toi non plus*.: *You don't eat either.*
Moi non plus can also be used alone, as a response to someone's remark. In this case it stands for *Neither do I.*

20 **'Tu travailles trop,' me dit-elle.** *'You work too much,' she tells me.*
me dit-elle Compare: **Elle me dit, 'Tu travailles trop'** and **'Tu travailles trop,' me dit-elle.**

21 **Du moins, j'espère que non** *At least, I hope not*
j'espère que non Do not leave **que** out of this phrase.

22 **Il est un peu snob, mon père.** *My father's a bit of a snob.*

23 **'Combien d'argent est-ce que tu vas gagner?** *'How much money are you going to earn?*
a **Combien d'argent?**: *How much money?*
b **Tu vas** is the **tu** form of **aller** (App. ICa).

24 **Sois ingénieur comme moi!'** *Be an engineer like me!'*
Sois: *Be!* Remember **Soyez les bienvenus!** (L9, N1).
Sois is the familiar form of **soyez!**

25 **C'est aujourd'hui mardi.** *Today is Tuesday.* (Lit. *It's today Tuesday.*)

26 **Je suis toujours libre le mardi après-midi.** *I am always free on Tuesday afternoons.*
a **libre** *free* Remember that *free* meaning *free of charge* is **gratuit** (L3).
b **le mardi après-midi** You have learnt **le lundi**: *on Mondays*, **le mardi**: *on Tuesdays*. **Le mardi après-midi** is *On Tuesday afternoons*.

27 **Elle est très gentille** . . . *She's very nice* . . .
b **Gentille** is the feminine form of **gentil** (L6, N22).

PART TWO
28 **Vous allez rester à Paris longtemps?** *Are you going to stay in Paris for long?* (lit. *You are . . . .?*)
a **rester** Careful! **Rester** means *to stay, to remain*, and NOT *to rest*.
b **longtemps**: *for a long time*

29 **Connaissez-vous beaucoup de monde à Paris?** *Do you know many people in Paris?*
connaissez-vous?: *do you know?* You have already seen this kind of question in **Avez-vous . . .?** where **vous** is placed after **avez** to form a question (L10, N22). The **vous** form of any other French verb can be treated in the same way to form a question. **Vous connaissez Valérie.**: *You know Valérie.* **Connaissez-vous Valérie?**: *Do you know Valérie?* You can make questions in the same way with the **tu, nous, il, elle, ils, elles** forms of all verbs (but not as a rule with the **je** form). The following chart summarizes what you have learnt about turning a statement into a yes or no question.

105

Statements

Yes or no questions

Statements	formula 1	formula 2	formula 3
Tu vas rester ici.	Tu vas rester ici?	Est-ce que tu vas rester ici?	Vas-tu rester ici?
Il connaît Valérie.	Il connaît Valérie?	Est-ce qu'il connaît Valérie?	Connaît-il Valérie?
Nous allons visiter les égouts.	Nous allons visiter les égouts?	Est-ce que nous allons visiter les égouts?	Allons-nous visiter les égouts?
Vous avez votre sac.	Vous avez votre sac?	Est-ce que vous avez votre sac?	Avez-vous votre sac?
Ils vont manger au restaurant.	Ils vont manger au restaurant?	Est-ce qu'ils vont manger au restaurant?	Vont-ils manger au restaurant?

Should you want to say *Do I wait here?* (*shall I wait here?*) *Do I keep . . . ? Do I . . . .?*

use either formula 1 or 2.   Je reste ici?   Est-ce que je reste ici?
Je garde . . .?   Est-ce que je garde . . .?

Formula no. 3 is the least colloquial of the three.

30   **Non. À vrai dire, je ne connais presque personne.** *No. To tell the truth, I hardly know anyone.*
    Je ne connais . . . personne.: *I don't know anyone.* **Ne . . . personne** is constructed like **ne . . . pas, ne . . . rien, ne . . . jamais, ne . . . plus**; **ne** comes before the verb, **personne** after.

31   **Vous allez sortir?** *Are you going out?*
    Sortir is the infinitive of the verb you saw in N1 above (**ils sortent**).

32   **Est-ce que vous me permettez de sortir avec vous,** *May I go out with you,*
    Permettre takes **de** before an infinitive (**L5, N25**).

33   **si vous n'avez rien de spécial à faire?** *if you haven't anything special to do?*

 a   **ne . . . rien de spécial**: *nothing special*   Remember that **de** must be used between **rien** (and **quelque chose**) and the adjective which follows. **Rien** *de* **spécial**: *nothing special*; **quelque chose** *de* **spécial**: *something special.*

 b   **ne . . . rien . . . à faire**: *nothing to do.* cf. **Je n'ai rien à déclarer** (L1 note 58); and **quelque chose à faire** (N2 above), **quelqu'un à servir** (N3 above).

34   **Je voudrais bien pouvoir vous accompagner.** *I'd really like (to be able) to come with you.*
    Je voudrais bien *I would really like to . . .* **bien** reinforces **je voudrais.**

35   **Je veux bien.** *By all means.*
    je veux bien   Strangely enough **bien** added to **je veux,** as distinct from **je voudrais,** does not reinforce it. **Je veux bien** is much less emphatic. The equivalent English phrase would be *by all means.*

36   **Il y a tant de choses intéressantes à voir à Paris!** *There are so many interesting things to see in Paris!*

37   **Alors, je vais vous montrer un restaurant bien.** *Then I'll show you a good restaurant.*
    un restaurant bien: *a good restaurant*   **Bien,** which usually means *well,* is sometimes used colloquially with a noun in the sense of *good*: **une chambre bien, un hôtel bien.**

38   **À la terrasse d'un restaurant** *On the 'terrasse' of a restaurant*
    la terrasse   In France many cafés and restaurants have tables on the pavement outside. This area is **la terrasse.**

39   **Qu'est-ce qu'il y a de bon?** *What is there that's nice (good)?*
    There's something nice.: **Il y a quelque chose de bon.** *Is there anything nice?*: **Est-ce qu'il y a quelque chose de bon?** Similarly: **Qu'est-ce qu'il y a de bon?**

40 **Oui, mais je veux manger peu.** *Yes, but I don't want much (to eat).* (lit. *I want to eat little*).
manger peu Remember, **peu**: *little (not much)*; **un peu**: *a little* (L9, N6).

41 **Je vais prendre une blanquette de veau aux champignons.** *I'll have a 'blanquette' of veal with mushrooms.*
aux champignons: *with mushrooms* Compare this construction with **un steak aux pommes** (L4, N45).

42 **Eh bien, quelque chose de léger et de pas trop gras.** *Well, something light and not too rich.*
a **quelque chose de léger**: *something light* Something followed by an adjective is **quelque chose de**. Remember **rien de spécial** (N33a above). Try not to confuse (i)
something/nothing to + infinitive: **quelque chose/rien à** + infinitive.
J'ai *quelque chose* **à faire.**
Je *n*'ai *rien* **à faire.**
and (ii)
something/nothing + adjective: **quelque chose/rien** *de* + adjective.
something light: **quelque chose de léger**
nothing special: **rien de spécial**
b *de* **pas trop gras** De must be repeated. **Gras** is the French word for *rich* when speaking of food.

43 **Ah, oui, je veux bien. Mais votre 'voulez-vous des frites?' est bien solennel!** *All right. But your (way of saying) 'Will you have some chips?' is very formal!*
je veux bien: *all right/I don't mind* Do not forget that **bien** rather weakens **je veux** in the phrase **je veux bien** (N35 above).

44 **Et ensuite des haricots verts et une salade pour tous les deux . . .** *And then French beans and a salad for both (of us) . . .*
des haricots verts: *French beans* There is no liaison between **des** and **haricots**. The **h** of haricot is not the 'silent h' type, but is like the h in **hall** (L1, N10b).

45 **La semaine prochaine, je vais passer quelques jours en province.** *Next week, I'm going to spend a few days in the country.*
a **Passer** here means *to spend* (time) (cf. L10, N7).
b **en province**: *in the provinces* Note that the French phrase is in the singular.

46 **Je vais apprendre à gérer un hôtel de province.** *I'm going to learn to manage a provincial hotel.*

Apprendre à . . . *to learn how to* . . . is an irregular **-re** verb, conjugated like **prendre** (App. IIIE). Since you know **je prends, nous prenons, vous prenez,** you can deduce the corresponding forms of **apprendre.**

47 **Tu trouves ça intéressant?** *Do you find that interesting?*
Trouver, which basically means *to find* something you have been looking for, can also mean, as in English, *to think. I find this difficult (I think this is difficult).*: **Je trouve ça difficile.**

48 **Tu es une bonne secrétaire?** *Are you a good secretary?*
Note the difference between **Tu es secrétaire?**: *Are you a secretary?* and **Tu es une bonne secrétaire?**: *Are you a good secretary?* Georges is not asking Valérie *what* her job is but what *sort* of secretary she is.

49 **J'espère que oui, mais je crois que non!** *I hope so, but I don't think so!*
je crois que non: *I don't think so. I think so* would be **je crois que oui.** Practise these phrases:

J'espère que oui.	**J'espère que non.**
Je crois que oui.	**Je crois que non.**

Je crois: *I think, believe* is one of the forms of an irregular verb which you will learn later (App. IIIE).

50 **Je ne peux pas me relire!** *I can't read what I have written!* (lit. *to read myself again*)
me relire: re + lire: *re + read* (cf. L6. N48).
lire: *to read*
Remember **lisez!** which you saw in L10.

51 **Oui . . . combien d'années d'hôtellerie est-ce que tu as fait?** *Yes . . . how many years of hotel work have you done?*
a **combien d'années?** *how many years?* Remember **année** is the first word for *year* that you learnt, **Il y a des fleurs toute l'année.**: *There are flowers all the year round* (L2, N48b). Then you learnt another word for year in L5, N7: **Jean-Luc a vingt et un ans.**: *Jean-Luc is 21.* Through practice you will learn when to use **année** or **an** for *year.* Remember from now on that *all the year round* is always **toute l'année**; *How many years?*: **Combien d'années?**; and that you must always use **an** when you are speaking of age.
b **Tu as fait**: *you have done* is the familiar form of **vous avez fait.**

52 **je veux être gérant d'un hôtel vraiment bien.** *I want to be the manager of a really good hotel.*
d'un hôtel vraiment bien Remember that **bien,** which basically means *well* and is usually used with a verb, can be used in conversation with a noun, in the sense of *good* (N39 above).

11 The language you have learnt

Two ways of asking a 'yes' or 'no' question

Est-ce que vous avez *Avez-vous*	déjeuné?
Est-ce que vous aimez *Aimez-vous*	ce vin?

There is/are . . . to + verb

Il y a	*beaucoup de travail*	*à*	*faire.*
	quelques valises		*porter.*

Reporting conversations

'Venez avec moi,'	me *dit-il.*
'Téléphonez-lui',	me *dit-elle.*

I hope/think so

J'espère Je crois	*que*	oui. non.

Comparisons

Guy est	*plus* *moins* *aussi*	fatigué vieux	*que*	Paul. moi.

Le cuisinier gagne	*plus* *moins* *autant*	*que*	le veilleur de nuit. moi.

no longer, more

Je *ne* veux Il *n'*y a	*plus*	de vin.
Il *ne* peut Je *ne* peux		travailler ici.

Negative phrases

Je *ne* suis *pas* content,	*moi*	
Tu *n'*as *pas* d'argent,	*toi*	
Il *ne* gagne *pas* assez,	*lui*	*non plus.*
Elle *n'*aime *pas* ça,	*elle*	
Ils *ne* peuvent *pas*,	*eux*	
Elles *ne* veulent *pas*,	*elles*	

	mange	*rien.* *jamais.* *plus.* *pas assez.* *pas du tout.*
Je *ne*	cherche	*personne.* *personne non plus.*
	travaille	*pas encore.*

Something, nothing

Il y a *quelque chose* Il n'y a *rien*	*de*	bon. spécial.

Many, so many

Il y a Je connais	*beaucoup de* *tant de*	Canadiens. secrétaires.

On Sundays, Mondays, etc.
Every Sunday, Monday, etc.

Il	vient nous voir ne travaille pas joue au tennis	*le*	dimanche. lundi matin. mardi après-midi.

Leçon douze *Lesson twelve*
Douzième leçon *Twelfth lesson*

Le train de Niort   The Niort train

What happens

PART ONE
Monsieur Blond vous parle de son travail.: *Monsieur Blond is telling you about his work.*
Working at the Information desk in the Gare du Nord, Monsieur Blond is used to all sorts of strange questions. Most people are polite and friendly, especially women, but even they are often anxious about catching their train.

PART TWO
Nous partons dimanche matin.: *We are leaving on Sunday morning.*
Monsieur Aimé asks Georges about train times.

Aux réservations. Il est sage de louer sa place.: *At the reservations office. It is wise to book one's seat.*
There is really no need to book seats for a Sunday, but Monsieur Aimé insists.

PART THREE
À la gare: *At the station*
Mademoiselle Olivier can always catch another train.

New words in this lesson

à la réflexion come to think of it
absolument definitely
aimablement politely, nicely
l'aller (*m*) single ticket
l'aller et retour (*m*) return (ticket)
après-demain the day after tomorrow
(il) s'arrête (it) stops
s'arrêter to stop
l'arrivée (*f*) arrival
l'attente (*f*) wait
bien (nerveux) very (excitable)
ce n'est pas la peine it's not worth it
certains some

le compartiment compartment
la correspondance connection
debout standing
la demi-heure half-hour
le départ departure
dix-huit eighteen
douze twelve
douzième twelfth
le drapeau flag
l'employé (*m*) booking office clerk
en pleine nuit in the middle of the night
en première first class

en provenance de (coming) from
en seconde second class
l'express (m) express (train)
la gare station
généralement generally
les gens (m) people
grossier rude
l'heure (f) time
l'heure (f) clock, hour
l'heure d'arrivée (f) arrival time
l'heure de départ (f) departure time
l'horaire (m) timetable
l'horloge parlante (f) 'speaking clock'
impatient impatient
impoli impolite
la journée day
juillet July
lequel which (one)
louer to book
manquer to miss
mettre to take
minuit midnight
nerveux nervous
non-fumeurs non-smoker
la nuit night
l'omnibus (m) stopping train
optimiste optimistic
par cœur by heart
parfois sometimes, at times
je pars I leave
(il) part (it) leaves
ils partent they leave
vous partez you leave
partir to leave
nous partons we leave
la peine bother, trouble
pessimiste pessimistic
la place seat
poli polite

(ils) posent (des questions) (they) ask (questions)
poser des questions to ask questions
précis exactly
le quai platform
le quart quarter
quel which, what
quelle which, what
quelle heure est-il? what time is it?
quelques-unes some
quelques-uns some
la question question
quinze fifteen
rapide fast
le rapide fast train
rare rare, unusual
les renseignements (m) enquiries
répondre to answer
je réponds I answer
la réservation reservation
vous avez réservé you have reserved
réserver to reserve
retéléphoner to phone back
ridicule ridiculous
sage wise
le service des renseignements enquiries (service)
six heures et demie half past six
tard late
le terminus terminus
tôt early
tout à l'heure in a minute, a minute ago
toute la journée all day long
le train train
le train direct through train
treize thirteen
vendredi Friday
le wagon-restaurant restaurant car

12

Notes

PART ONE

1 **Allô? Ici la Gare du Nord, les renseignements . . .** *Hullo, this is the Gare du Nord, information . . .*

a **La Gare du Nord** is the Paris station from which trains go to the north and north-east of France and to Belgium.

b **Les renseignements**: *information* is used in the plural when it describes the information service or office at a railway station, an airport, etc.

2 Toute la journée, je réponds au téléphone. *All day I answer the phone.*

a toute la journée: *all day* You learnt **tous les jours**: *every day* in L2, N15c. **Journée** tends to be used when by *day* you mean a whole day, a period of twenty-four hours or a working day.

b je réponds (à): *I reply (to), answer* (App. IIIA)

3 Je suis employé à la S.N.C.F. *I work for the S.N.C.F.*
La S.N.C.F., la Société Nationale des Chemins de Fer Français: *French State Railways.*

4 Par exemple: 'Le train de Lyon part à quel quai?' *For instance: 'What platform does the train for Lyons leave from?'*

a (il) part: *it leaves* is part of an **-ir** verb **partir** (App. IIB).

b le train de Lyon: lit. *the train of Lyons, the Lyons train.* **Le train de Lyon** is as ambiguous in French as the *Lyons train* is in English. It can mean the train *to* Lyons and *from* Lyons. Only the context or the situation makes the meaning clear.
Notice that there is no **s** on **Lyon** in French.

c à quel quai?: lit. *at what platform?* Because the train is standing AT a platform before it leaves, the French say: **le train part *au* quai n° 1.**
Quel is the form used for *what* and *which* when they are followed by a masculine singular noun.

5 'Le train de Niort arrive à quelle heure?' *'What time does the Niort train arrive?'* (lit. *The Niort train arrives at what time?*)

a le train de Niort: *the train* TO *Niort or the train* FROM *Niort* Niort is a small town in the West of France, between Poitiers and la Rochelle.

b à quelle heure?: *what time?* lit. AT *what time* The French for *at*: **à** cannot be omitted in this sort of question. **Quelle** is used before feminine singular nouns: **À quel quai? À quelle heure?**

6 (Le Mistral, c'est le rapide de Marseille). (*The Mistral is the express to Marseille.*)
Marseille In French, **Marseille** is never spelt with an **s**.

7 'Quels sont les trains les plus rapides pour aller à Bordeaux?' *Which are the fastest trains to Bordeaux?*

a Quels?: *which? what?* is the masculine plural form, which agrees here with **trains.**

b les trains les plus rapides: *the fastest trains*
***plus* rapide**: *fastER*
le plus rapide: *the fastest* (sing.)
les plus rapides: *the fastest* (pl.)

8 **'Quelles sont les heures d'arrivée des trains en provenance de Toulouse?'** *What are the arrival times of trains from Toulouse?*
Quelles?: *what? which?* is the feminine plural form.
You have now met all the possible forms of the French equivalent of *what? which?*: **quel** (masc. sing.), **quelle** (fem. sing.), **quels** (m. plural), **quelles** (f. plural).

9 **Par exemple, une femme m'a téléphoné un jour à cinq heures.** *For instance, a woman rang me up one day at five o'clock.*
à cinq heures: *at five o'clock* At one o'clock would be **à une heure**; *at two o'clock*: **à deux heures,** etc.

10 **'Est-ce que le train de quatre heures est en retard?' m'a-t-elle demandé.** *'Is the four o'clock train late?' she asked (me).*
m'a-t-elle demandé. The natural word order **elle m'a demandé**: *she asked me* has been inverted. Remember this is done when such phrases as **il me dit, il me demande,** etc. are added after a quotation (L11, N20). The t in **a-t-elle demandé** makes the pronunciation of this phrase easier.

11 **Une autre m'a dit: 'Je voudrais prendre le train le plus rapide de France.** *Another said to me: 'I would like to go on the fastest train in France.*
le train le plus rapide de France: lit. *the fastest train of France*

12 **Est-ce que c'est le Mistral ou le Drapeau?'** *Is it the Mistral or the Drapeau?'*
Le Mistral is a fast train on the Paris-Marseille line. **Mistral** is normally the name of the dry cold wind which blows down the Rhône valley to the Marseille area.
Le Drapeau is the name of a fast train on the Paris-Bordeaux line. **Drapeau** normally means *flag*.

13 **Tout à l'heure, un homme m'a téléphoné.** *A man rang me a moment ago.*
tout à l'heure: *a moment ago* Strangely enough, **tout à l'heure** can mean either *in a minute, soon* or *a moment ago, just now*. Earlier in this lesson you saw it meaning *in a minute*.

14 **'Est-ce que le train d'Amiens s'arrête à la gare du Nord?' m'a-t-il demandé.** *'Does the Amiens train stop at the Gare du Nord?' he asked me.*
a **Il s'arrête**: *it/he stops* is part of the verb **s'arrêter**; it is the same type of verb as **s'appeler** and **se plaindre**.
b **m'a-t-il demandé** Remember **a-t-elle demandé** (N10 above).

12

15 **Mais certains voyageurs sont impatients.** *But some travellers are impatient.*
certains voyageurs When **certain** is used in the sense of *some*, it comes before the noun:
un certain voyageur; pl. certains voyageurs.

16 **Généralement, les gens me disent aimablement merci:** *Generally people thank me politely (nicely):*

a **généralement:** *generally* A certain number of French adverbs can be made by adding **-ment** to the feminine of an adjective. **Certainement** (L3 and earlier in this lesson) comes from the feminine of **certain, certaine; naturel,** f. **naturelle,** adverb **naturellement** (L3, N7).

b **(ils) me disent:** *(they) say to me* **Disent** is another form of **dire** (L8, N8a; L9, N32 and App. IIIE).

c **aimablement:** *pleasantly, nicely* See N16a above.

17 **À la réflexion, quelques-unes sont parfois bien nerveuses.** *Now I think of it, some are very excitable at times.*
Quelques-unes: *some* is the feminine of **quelques-uns.**

18 **Monsieur, si vous voulez savoir l'heure, appelez l'horloge parlante!',** *'If you want to know the time, sir, phone the speaking clock!'*

a **appelez:** *phone* (See L10, 20b)

b **parlante:** *speaking*, ends in **e** to agree with **l'horloge.**

PART TWO

19 **Nous partons dimanche matin.** *We're leaving on Sunday morning.*
Nous partons: *we are leaving* is part of the verb **partir** (N4a above).

20 **J'ai besoin de renseignements sur les trains de Niort.** *I want some information about* (lit. *on*) *the trains to Niort.*
j'ai besoin de: lit. *I have need of* **Avoir besoin** is followed by **de.**

21 **Nous sommes vendredi . . . 21 juillet aujourd'hui, n'est-ce pas?** *Today is Friday . . . the 21st of July, isn't it?*

a **nous sommes vendredi . . .** lit. *we are Friday* This is a common way of saying *today is Friday.*
vingt et un juillet: *twenty-first of July* (lit. *twenty-one July*) When you give the date, use the cardinal numbers (**vingt** and not **vingtième**), except for the first day of the month: **vendredi, premier juillet; vendredi, vingt et un juillet.** There is no article between the name of the day and the date; there is no preposition before the name of the month:
Friday THE *twenty-first* OF *July*: **vendredi** ∧ **vingt et un** ∧ **juillet**
Saturday THE *twenty-second* OF *July*: **samedi** ∧ **vingt-deux** ∧ **juillet.**

Though one says: **Nous sommes** ∧ **vendredi,** when the date is added to the name of the day it is usual to say: **Nous sommes *le* vendredi vingt et un juillet. Nous sommes *le* samedi vingt-deux juillet.** In this case M. Aimé hesitates, hence the absence of **le.**

22 **Le matin, vous avez un train direct; il part à sept heures précises.** *In the morning, you have a through train; it leaves at seven o'clock precisely.*

à sept heures précises: *at seven o'clock precisely* **Heure,** which was equivalent to *time* in the phrases **Quelles sont les heures des trains?** and **Quelle heure est-il?** here equals *o'clock:*
It's seven O'CLOCK.: **Il est sept *heures.***

23 **À sept heures du matin! C'est trop tôt.** *At seven o'clock! That's too early.*

a **sept heures du matin:** *seven o'clock in the morning* **Il est dix heures *du* matin; il est dix heures *du* soir.**

b **tôt:** *early* Do not confuse this with **en avance,** which also corresponds to *early* in English. **Tôt** means *early in the day, early in the year;* **en avance** means *early* — before a specified time (L7).

24 **Je ne pars jamais très tôt le dimanche.** *I never set out very early on Sundays.*
Je pars: *I set out, I leave,* is from the verb **partir** (N4a, 19 above).

25 **Vous avez un express à onze heures quinze et, l'après-midi, un omnibus.** *You have an express at eleven fifteen and a stopping train in the afternoon.*
à onze heures quinze: *at eleven fifteen*
nine fifteen: **neuf heures quinze**
Don't leave out the word **heures.**

26 **L'omnibus met cinq heures; il s'arrête à toutes les gares.** *The stopping train takes five hours; it stops at all stations.*
(Il) met is part of the verb **mettre,** which you saw in lesson 7 and which was translated by *to put*; here it is the equivalent of *it takes.* As you can see, **heure** can also be the equivalent of *hour.*
SUMMARY
Quelle *heure* est-il? *What* TIME *is it?*
Il est cinq *heures*: *It is five* O'CLOCK.
Le train *met* cinq *heures*: *The train takes five* HOURS.

27 **Et vous arrivez à dix-huit heures.** *and you arrive at* 18 *hours* (6 p.m.)
dix-huit heures: *eighteen hours* (6 p.m.). The French tend to use the twenty-four hour clock when they talk about times of trains, planes, etc.

28 **Vous changez au Mans, vous avez la correspondance,** *You change at*
le Mans, you've got the connection (*there*),
au Mans: The name of the town is *le* **Mans,** so *at le* **Mans** must be
au **Mans.**

29 **mais il y a une demi-heure d'attente.** *but there's half an hour's wait.*
une demi-heure: *half an hour,* (lit. *half hour*) There is a hyphen
between **demi** and **heure.** Note that **demi** is not spelt with an **e,**
though **heure** is feminine.

30 **C'est trop tard!** *It's too late!*
tard: *late* Do not confuse **tard** with **en retard** (L7), which means
late in the sense of *behind time.*

31 **Bon, partons au train de neuf heures et quart!** *All right, let's leave on*
(lit. *at*) *the quarter past nine train!*
a **Partons**: *let's leave* is another form of the verb **partir.**
b **neuf heures et quart**: *a quarter past nine*
a quarter past ten: **dix heures et quart**
a quarter past eleven: **onze heures et quart,** etc. (cf. N51 above).

32 **Il est sage de louer sa place.** *It's wise to reserve one's seat.*
The same possessive adjective is used in connection with **il/elle**:
he/she, personal pronouns, as with **il** (*it*), indefinite pronoun.
He is reserving HIS *seat.*: **Il réserve** *sa* **place.**
It is wise to reserve ONE'S *seat.*: **Il est sage de réserver** *sa* **place.**

33 **Deux allers, en seconde — et dans un compartiment de non-fumeurs.**
Two singles, second class and in a non-smoker (lit. *a compartment of*
non-smokers).
en seconde: lit. *in second* **Seconde** is feminine because it refers to a
feminine noun — **classe,** which is understood here. The traveller
is booking **deux allers en seconde classe.**

34 **Je veux absolument louer ma place.** *I insist on reserving my seat.*

35 **Je ne voudrais pas rester debout pendant trois heures.** *I wouldn't*
like to stand for three hours.
rester debout: *to stand* (lit. *to stay standing*)
There is no single verb for *to stand* in French. **Debout** means
standing and it is often used with **être**:
Il est debout.: *He is standing.*
and with **rester**:
Il reste debout.: *He stands.*

36 **Mais . . . je veux une place assise!** *But . . . I want a seat!*
Une place usually means *a seat,* but as it can also mean *some room*

(whether standing or sitting); the French distinguish when necessary **12**
between **une place debout**: *standing room* and **une place assise**: *a seat.*

37 **'Départ à neuf heures quinze,' vous dites!** *'Departure at 9.15', you
say!*
Vous dites: *you say* is the **vous** form of **dire** (App. IIIE).

38 **Vous n'avez pas bien regardé l'horaire.** *You haven't looked at the
timetable very closely* (*well*).
Following the general rule, the adverb **bien** is placed between **avez**
and **regardé** (between the auxiliary **avoir** and the verb).

39 **Ils partent au quai numéro 9.** *They go from platform nine.*
ils partent: *they go/leave* You have now learnt most of the present
tense of **partir: je pars, il part, nous partons,** and **ils partent.**
You can guess the **tu** form, **tu pars**, as there is always an s at the
end of the second person singular. You also know how to make the
vous form by substituting **-ez** for the **-ons** ending of the **nous** form
(this works with most verbs).

40 **Lequel choisissez-vous?** *Which* (*one*) *will you choose?*
a **Lequel?**: *Which one?* is the masculine singular form. **Quel train
choisissez-vous? Lequel choisissez-vous?**
b **Choisissez-vous?** is the question form corresponding to the
statement **vous choisissez.**

41 **Le train de huit heures du soir.** *The 8 p.m. train.*
huit heures du soir: *eight o'clock in the evening* (8 *p.m.*) (cf. N23a
above).

42 **Mais je veux louer ma place. Et en première!** *But I want to reserve
my seat. And I want to go first class!*
en première: lit. *in first* **Première** is feminine to agree with *classe*
which is again not used. Remember, **en seconde** (N33 above).

PART THREE
43 **Mais il est sept heures moins dix!** *But it's ten to seven!*
Sept heures moins dix: lit. *seven o'clock less ten* shows you how to
say the minutes before the hour.
Compare:
ten to seven: **sept heures moins dix**
five to seven: **sept heures moins cinq**
Do not leave out **heures.**

119

12   The language you have learnt

When . . .

Quand est-ce que	vous allez manger? vous jouez au tennis?

What is . . . what are . . . ?

Quel	est	le prix du billet?
Quelle		la chambre de Paul?
Quels	sont	les prix des chambres?
Quelles		les heures d'arrivée?

Addition

Deux et un,	ça fait	trois.
Trois et deux,		cinq.

Reporting conversations in the past

'Vous partez?' 'Vous aimez prendre le train?'	m'a-t-il m'a-t-elle	demandé.

The date

C'est Nous sommes	vendredi,	aujourd'hui.
Nous sommes le 21 juillet,		

At what, which . . . ?

Elle va arriver	à quel	quai?
Elle part	à quelle	heure?

Which one, ones?

Lequel *Laquelle* *Lesquels* *Lesquelles*	choisissez-vous? voulez-vous? préférez-vous?

The time

Il est	neuf heures (du matin). dix heures (du matin). midi.	
	une heure (de l'après-midi). trois heures (de l'après-midi). minuit.	(treize heures). (quinze heures).
	une heure et quart. quinze.	(treize heures quinze).
	unè heure et demie. trente.	(treize heures trente).

Superlatives

Le Mistral est le train	*le plus*	rapide	*de*	France. Paris.
L'Hôtel du Nord est l'hôtel		confortable		

Tout à l'heure = a few minutes ago and presently

Il a téléphoné	*tout à l'heure.*
Il va venir	

13 Leçon treize *Lesson thirteen*
Treizième leçon *Thirteenth lesson*

Chez les Louvier   At the Louviers'

What happens

PART ONE
Madame Louvier est chez elle.: *Madame Louvier is at home.*
Madame Louvier, whom we met earlier, in Lesson 5, now describes her
flat. She would really prefer to have a house and a garden out of Paris,
but is quite enthusiastic about her present home.

PART TWO
Dans l'appartement des Louvier: *In the Louviers' flat*
Pierre Louvier entre.: *Pierre Louvier comes in.*
Monsieur Louvier comes home in a bad mood after a busy day at the
office.

PART THREE
Chez le dentiste: *At the dentist's*
The dentist is very reassuring.

New words in this lesson

à la fin de at the end of
l'acier inox (*m*) stainless steel
j'ai eu I had
allume turn on (the radio)
allumer to turn on (the radio)
au contraire on the contrary
avoir de la visite to have visitors
le batteur électrique electric food whisk
beige beige
bleu blue
bleu clair light blue
bleu foncé dark blue
la boiserie woodwork
bonsoir hello, good evening
bref in short
le bureau office
calme calm, peaceful
le carrelage tiles
la chambre d'amis guest room
le ciment armé reinforced concrete

la cocotte minute pressure cooker
comme toujours as always
compter to count
le confort comfort
tu connais you know
la cuisinière électrique electric cooker
de la journée all day
le dentiste dentist
dîner to have dinner
le dîner dinner
le document document, paper
j'en ai assez I've had enough
en avoir assez to have had enough
en hiver in winter
en pierre (in) stone
en plein cœur de right in the heart of
énormément de enormous amount of
entre between
(il) entre (he) comes in
entrer to come in

l'évier (m) sink
la façade front
faire la navette entre to commute
  between
faire pousser to grow
le fauteuil armchair
la fin end
finalement finally
le four oven
le frigidaire fridge
le gadget gadget
gai gay
gâter to spoil
tu gâtes you spoil
le grille-pain toaster
gris grey
l'hôtel particulier (m) private house
  (large old town house)
l'idiot (m) idiot
immense enormous
l'immeuble (m) block
important important
insupportable unbearable
intérieur interior
les jeunes (m or f) young people
laisser tranquille to leave alone, to
  let alone
lis read
le locataire tenant
le loyer rent
la machine à laver la vaisselle dishwasher
la maîtresse de maison housewife
marron brown
même pas not even
le mètre metre
minuscule minute
le mixer food mixer
moderne modern
le mur wall
obliger to make, to force, to oblige
par terre on the floor
passer une bonne journée to have a
  good day

patient patient
pauvre poor
peint painted
la pendule clock
la petite amie girl-friend
la pièce room
le plafond ceiling
plutôt qu'(e) rather than
ponctuel punctual
le portail doorway
prendre à la légère to take lightly
prendre au sérieux to take seriously
prendre rendez-vous to make an
  appointment
je prépare I prepare
préparer to prepare
il a pris rendez-vous he made an
  appointment
le quartier area
qu'est-ce qu'ils veulent encore? now
  what do they want?
la radio radio
je me rappelle I remember
se rappeler to remember
il a renversé he spilt
renverser to spill
le repas meal
le repos rest
la salle à manger dining-room
le salon sitting-room
sauf except
me semble-t-il it seems to me
sembler to seem
si so
situé placed, situated
soyez be
sur by
tout petit very small
tranquille quiet
treizième thirteenth
le trimestre term
une fois once
le vestibule hall
les waters (m) toilet

Notes

PART ONE

1 **Madame Louvier est chez elle.** *Mme Louvier is at home.*
  chez elle: *at home* Remember **chez les Martin**: *at the Martins'*

13

(*home*) (L7, N28). Instead of saying **chez Madame Louvier,** you can replace **Madame Louvier** by **elle—chez elle**: *at her home/house.*
at my house: **chez moi**
at your house: **chez toi/vous**
at his house: **chez lui,** etc.

2 Mon mari et moi habitons un appartement à Paris. *My husband and I live in a flat in Paris.*
habitons The **-ons** form is used because **mon mari et moi** is a plural subject which could be replaced by **nous.**

3 J'aimerais habiter une maison plutôt qu'un appartement. *I'd rather live in a house than in a flat.*
j'aimerais: *I would (should) like* You learnt **je voudrais**: *I'd like* in L2. Just as **je voudrais** is related to **je veux,** so **j'aimerais** is related to **j'aime**:
j'aime: *I like* **j'aimerais**: *I should like (I'd like).*

4 J'aimerais avoir un jardin et faire pousser des légumes et surtout des fleurs. *I'd like to have a garden and grow vegetables and, above all, flowers.*
faire pousser: lit. *to make grow*
Les fleurs poussent.: *The flowers are growing.*
Les légumes poussent.: *The vegetables are growing.*
Je fais pousser des fleurs.: *I grow flowers.*
Je fais pousser des légumes.: *I grow vegetables.*

5 pas dans un de ces immeubles modernes en ciment armé. *not in one of those modern blocks of flats made of reinforced concrete.*
a Moderne ends in **e** in both masculine and feminine forms.
b en ciment armé **Ciment** means *cement* (there is a technical word for *concrete*) but usage has sanctioned the technically incorrect phrase: **du ciment armé** (lit. *reinforced cement*). In this case, **en** means *made of*; it is followed by the name of the material.

6 La maison a une belle façade en pierre, *The house has a fine stone front,*
en pierre: lit. *in stone, made of stone* (See N5b above)

7 Je le vois à la fin de chaque trimestre quand je vais lui payer le loyer. *I see him at the end of every quarter when I go to pay him the rent.*
je vois: *I see,* from **voir** (App. IVB)

8 Notre appartement a sept pièces sans compter le vestibule et les waters. *Our flat has seven rooms, without counting the hall and the toilet.*

a **sept pièces**: *seven rooms* **Pièce** means any sort of room in a house. **Chambre** is *bedroom*.

b **sans compter**: *without counting* After all prepositions, including **sans**: *without*, the verb must be in the infinitive form.

c **Les waters** is short for **les water-closets**. It is often written **W.-C.** **La toilette** is also used.

9 **Nous avons trois chambres, une pour mon fils,** *We have three bedrooms, one for my son,*

a **la chambre**: *(the) bedroom* Remember **chambre** is only used for *bedroom*, and not for other rooms (N8a above).

b **une pour mon fils**: *one for my son* The feminine **une** is used, because it refers to the feminine noun **chambre**.

10 **une pour mon mari et pour moi, et une chambre d'amis.** *one for my husband and me, and a spare bedroom* (lit. *a room of friends*).

11 **Le salon est immense: il a sept mètres sur six.** *The sitting-room is huge: it is seven metres by six.*
il a sept mètres sur six: lit. *it has seven metres on six* Remember **Il a vingt-trois ans**: *He is twenty-three* (L5, N7). This is another example of **avoir** being used in French where *to be* would be used in English: **Le salon a sept mètres sur six.**: *The lounge* IS *seven metres by six.*
A metre is slightly longer than a yard.

12 **une cuisinière électrique avec un bon four, un grand frigidaire, un évier en acier inox, et tous les gadgets modernes:** *an electric cooker with a good oven, a big refrigerator, a stainless steel sink, and all (sorts of) modern gadgets:*

a **un frigidaire**: *a refrigerator* **Frigidaire** is in fact a brand name, but it is used colloquially for *fridge*.

b **en acier inox**: lit. *of stainless steel* cf. N5b and 6 above.

13 **Les murs sont peints en bleu clair et en bleu foncé,** *The walls are painted light blue and dark blue,*

a **sont peints**: *are painted* **Peints** is from the verb **peindre**: *to paint* (App. IIIE).

b **en bleu clair . . . en bleu foncé** When you use **peindre** with a colour, you must use **en**:

Il est peint **Il sont peints**	{ en bleu. en blanc. en noir.

Foncé is used for *dark* when *dark* refers to colour; **clair** for *light*.

13 14 **les boiseries et le plafond en gris.** *the woodwork and the ceiling (are painted) grey.*
en gris (*in*) *grey* Light grey would be **gris clair**; *dark grey*: **gris foncé.** Note that **en**, the preposition, is repeated before each colour.

15 **Ah, voilà mon mari: donc il est sept heures moins le quart.** *Oh, there's my husband: so it's a quarter to seven.*
sept heures moins le quart: *a quarter to seven* (lit. *seven minus the quarter*) Remember **neuf heures et quart**: *a quarter past nine* (L12, N31).

16 **Il est sept heures moins dix à la pendule.** *It's ten to seven by the clock.*

PART TWO
17 **Oui, pas mauvaise. Mais j'ai eu énormément de travail.** *Yes, not bad. But I had an enormous amount of work.*
a **pas mauvaise**: *not bad* Mauvaise is the feminine form of **mauvais**; the **s** is pronounced.
b **J'ai eu**: *I had* is the past tense of **j'ai**: *I have.* Eu is the past participle:

j'ai eu	**nous avons eu**
tu as eu	**vous avez eu**
il a eu	**ils ont eu**

18 **Cet idiot de Pujos a téléphoné trois fois à sa petite amie.** *That fool Pujos rang up his girl-friend three times.*
a **cet idiot de Pujos**: *that fool Pujos* An idiomatic **de** has to be used between **cet idiot** and the name which follows: **Cet idiot** *de* **Paul.**
b **trois fois**: *three times* Remember when *time* means *occasion* it is **fois** (L6).
c **Sa petite amie** means *his girl-friend* (lit. *his little friend*). **Amie,** the feminine of **ami,** means *female friend.*

19 **Il la voit tous les jours!** *He sees her every day!*
Il voit: *he sees* is another part of the verb **voir** (N7 above).

20 **Puis, il a pris rendez-vous avec son dentiste.** *Then he made an appointment with his dentist.*

21 **Laisse-le tranquille, ce pauvre jeune homme!** *Leave him alone, poor young man!*
a **laisse-le tranquille**: lit. *leave him quiet* **Laisser** means *to leave* or *to let*; *to leave someone alone* is **laisser quelqu'un tranquille.**
b **pauvre**: *poor* When **pauvre** means *poor* in the sense of *pitiful, unfortunate* (someone, or something you are sorry for), it comes before the noun.

126

22 **Les jeunes ne voient pas les choses comme nous: tu le sais bien.**
Young people don't see things as we do: you know that.

a **ils ne voient pas**: *they do not see* You now know all parts of the present tense of the verb **voir**: *to see*:

je vois	**nous voyons**
tu vois	**vous voyez**
il/elle voit	**ils/elles voient** (App. IVB)

b **tu le sais bien**: lit. *you know it well* An idiomatic **le** is often used with **savoir**:
He's coming tomorrow.: **Il arrive demain.**
Yes I know.: **Oui je le sais.**

23 **Bref, il n'a rien fait de la journée.** *In fact, he did nothing all day.*
(lit. *In short, he didn't do anything all day.*)

a **Il n'a rien fait.**: *He did nothing.* In the past tense **rien** — like **pas, personne**, etc. — comes between the verb **avoir** and the past participle.

b **De la journée** is an idiomatic way of saying *all day*, in the sense of *during the day*, after a verb with **ne . . . rien, ne . . . pas, ne . . . personne**, etc.
Il *ne* mange pas *de* la journée.

24 **Au contraire, il a fait énormément de choses, me semble-t-il.** *On the contrary, it seems to me that he did a lot (of things).*
me semble-t-il Normally *it seems to me* is **il me semble.** But if this phrase comes as an incidental remark, between commas, instead of beginning the sentence, **il** must be put after the verb. You have seen similar examples of this sort of construction in L11 and in L12, N10, when a **t** is inserted between **e** and **il** to avoid a meeting between two vowels. (L12, N10).

25 **Oh, Pierre, ne sois pas si dur.** *Oh, Pierre, don't be so hard.*
ne sois pas si dur: *don't be so hard* Remember **sois patient** (earlier in this lesson).

26 **Écoute, chéri, assieds-toi là, dans le fauteuil,** *Listen dear, sit down there in the armchair,*
Assieds-toi: *sit down* is the familiar form of **asseyez-vous!** (L11)

27 **allume la radio ou bien lis ton journal.** *put on the radio or read your paper.*

a **Allumer** is used for *to put on, switch on, turn on* a radio or a television set.

b **Lis**: *read* is the familiar form of **lisez!** (L10) and is part of the verb **lire**: *to read.* Remember **relire**: *to read back, to read again* (L11, N50).

13

28 **Moi, je te prépare un bon petit dîner.** *I'm making you some nice dinner.* (lit. *Me, I'm preparing a nice little dinner for you.*)
je te prépare: lit. *I prepare for you*

29 **J'ai beaucoup travaillé aujourd'hui et j'ai besoin de repos.** *I've worked very hard today and I need some rest.* (lit. *I've worked a lot . . .*)

  a **J'ai beaucoup travaillé**: *I have worked a lot* Notice the position of **beaucoup**: it comes after **ai** and before **travaillé**.

  b **J'ai besoin de repos.**: *I need some rest.* Remember **j'ai besoin** must be followed by **de**.

30 **Je ne veux surtout pas manger.** *I certainly don't want to eat.*
Je veux manger.
Je *ne* veux *pas* manger.
Je *ne* veux surtout *pas* manger.
surtout pas: *above all, particularly*

31 **Non . . . euh . . . une toute petite tranche?** *No, er . . . a very small slice?*
une toute petite tranche: *a very small slice* Remember that **tout**, which, with a noun means *all* (**toute l'année**) means *very* or *quite* when it is placed in front of an adjective.

PART THREE

32 **Soyez calme, Monsieur. N'ayez pas peur,** *Relax.* (lit. *Be calm*) *Don't be afraid.*
Soyez: *be* in an order or request.
Ayez: *have* in an order or request.
As the French equivalent of *to be afraid* is **avoir peur**, the command form corresponding to *Do not be afraid* is **N'ayez pas peur.**

33 **J'ai eu, une fois, un dentiste affreux.** *Once I had an awful dentist.*
une fois: *once* Une fois, like its English literal translation can mean *once* as distinct from *twice*, or *once* in the sense of *once upon a time*.

The language you have learnt

Welcome!

Sois	le bienvenu,	Paul!
	la bienvenue,	Valérie!
Soyez	le bienvenu,	M. Delon!
	la bienvenue,	Mme Delon!

128

Commands + pronouns

Laisse- Laissez-	*moi!*
Regarde- Regardez-	*le!* *la!*
Ecoute- Ecoutez-	*nous!* *les!*

Sans + infinitive = without + present participle

Il fait son travail	*sans*	parle*r* à personne. fume*r*. bouge*r*.

The time

	deux heures	moins le quart. quarante-cinq.
Il est	deux heures	moins dix. moins cinq.
	quatorze heures	quarante-cinq. cinquante. cinquante-cinq.

Adjectives used as nouns

Ils sont jeunes :	*les jeunes* ne sont pas toujours heureux.
Ils sont pauvres :	*les pauvres* sont quelquefois heureux.
Il est pessimiste :	*les pessimistes* sont ennuyeux.
Votre robe est noire :	j'aime *le noir*.

13 Chez

Paul	est	chez	le coiffeur. moi. lui. elle. nous. vous. eux. elles.
	va		

Leçon quatorze   *Lesson fourteen*
Quatorzième leçon   *Fourteenth lesson*

14

Le dîner est servi.   Dinner is served.

What happens

PART ONE
Guy Martin est invité chez les Louvier.: *Guy Martin is invited to the Louviers.*
Guy and his sister, Marie-Claire, have been invited to the Louviers' flat for dinner. He usually likes going out in the evening but the Louvier family seem to annoy him.

PART TWO
Guy et Marie-Claire arrivent chez les Louvier.: *Guy and Marie-Claire arrive at the Louviers.*
Madame Louvier chats to her young guests.

Dans la salle à manger: *In the dining-room*
They all sit down at table.

Conversation à table: *Table-talk*
They chat.

PART THREE
Jean ne sait jamais l'heure.: *Jean never knows the time.*
Jean is always late; his watch doesn't work.

New words in this lesson

à elle hers
à eux theirs
à la droite (de) on the right (of)
à lui his
à ma (la) gauche on my (the) left
à moi mine
à toi yours
ils ont adopté they adopted
adopter to adopt
elle agace she annoys
agacer to annoy
tu as bonne mine you look well
tu as tort you're wrong
avoir bonne mine to look well
avoir tort to be wrong

bel beautiful
la boucle d'oreilles ear-ring
le bouton de manchettes cuff-link
le buffet sideboard
celle that (the one)
celles those (the ones)
celui that (the one)
ceux those (the ones)
chercher to fetch
la conversation conversation
croire to think, to believe
elle croit she thinks
de temps à autre from time to time
dépenser to spend
dresser to train

14

en somme more or less
(cette) espèce de (that) kind of
vous êtes quittes you're even
être quitte to be even
(il) se fâche (he) gets angry
se fâcher to become, get angry
falloir to be necessary, to have to
il faut one must, you must etc.
les gros (m) fat people
grossir to put on weight
l'initiale (f) initial
l'invitation (f) invitation
se laver les mains to wash one's hands
maigre thin
maigrir to lose weight
se marier to get married
mets (-le) put (it)
le mien mine
la mienne mine (my one)
la montre watch
la mort death
ne . . . guère hardly (ever), rarely,
   not much
ne vous en faites pas don't worry
occupé busy
(elle) ose (she) dares
oser to dare
particulièrement particularly
passer to pass
le plat plate, dish
porter (une robe) to wear

tu pourrais you could
prêter to lend
quatorze fourteen
quatorzième fourteenth
qu'est-ce que c'est que ça? what on
   earth's that?
rarement rarely
rentrer to come in, to come back
reposant relaxing, restful
le rond de serviette serviette ring
(il) sait (he) knows
sans arrêt continuously
le sel salt
je sers I serve
la serviette serviette
la sienne his (one)
la soirée evening
je sors I go out
elle sort she goes out
nous sortons we go out
ta your
tellement . . . que so . . . that
tes your
la tienne yours (your one)
le tiroir drawer
la vie life
vite quickly
vivre to live
la voiture car
vous voyez you see
y (j'y vais) there (I'm going there)

Notes

PART ONE

1 **Marie-Claire, ma sœur, est invitée elle aussi.** *Marie-Claire, my sister, is invited too.*
   Invitée is the feminine form of **invité**. This is a past participle, but it agrees as if it were an adjective: **Marie-Claire** (fem.) **est invitée** (fem.).

2 **Nous sommes invités à dîner.** *We are invited to dinner.*
   Invités is plural, as it agrees with **nous**. **Nous** stands for Marie-Claire and Guy, and as the masculine gender prevails in the case of mixed genders, **nous** is treated as masculine and **invités** is in the masculine plural.

3 **Marie-Claire, elle, sort beaucoup plus souvent.** *Marie-Claire goes out much more often.*
   Elle sort is another form of **sortir** (App. IIB).

132

4 **Nous sortons rarement ensemble.** *We rarely go out together.*

a **nous sortons:** *we go out* You now know the whole of the present tense of **sortir**:

je sors	**nous sortons**
tu sors	**vous sortez**
il/elle sort	**ils/elles sortent**

(cf. App. IIB).

b **ensemble:** *together* Remember, **ensemble** never has a plural ending.

5 **Elle a ses amis, et moi, j'ai les miens.** *She has her friends and I have mine.*

Les miens: *mine* is the masculine plural of **le mien,** referring to **amis,** a masculine plural noun. This is a new type of word — a POSSESSIVE PRONOUN. You will learn other forms of it in this lesson.

6 **Après la mort de nos parents, nous avons décidé de vivre chacun notre vie.** *After the death of our parents, we each decided to live our own lives.*

chacun notre vie: lit. *each* (*one*) *our life*

7 **Les Louvier sont de vieux amis de la famille.** *The Louviers are old friends of the family.*

de **vieux amis:** lit. SOME *old friends* Very often **de** and not **des** is used for *some* when an adjective comes in front of the noun.

8 **Quand nos parents sont morts, ils nous ont adoptés en somme.** *When our parents died, they more or less adopted us.*

a **sont morts:** *died* (App. IIE) You know how to say: *they worked, they looked, they ate,* etc., **ils *ont* travaillé, ils *ont* regardé, ils *ont* mangé.**

But here we are equating *they died* and **ils sont morts.** This is because the past tense of a certain number of verbs, is formed with **être** and not **avoir.** The French for *he/she/they died* has to be: **il *est* mort, elle *est* morte, ils *sont* morts, elles *sont* mortes.**

We shall come across other verbs which behave in this way.

Travaillé, the past participle of **travailler,** does not take an **s** in **ils ont travaillé;** but **mort** does in **ils sont mort*s*.** The reason is that a past participle used after **être** is felt to be an adjective; it consequently agrees, as **content** or **fatigué,** or any other adjective would:

ils sont mort*s*	**elles sont mort*es***

b **ils nous ont adoptés:** *they adopted us* You already know that in the past tense, the French pronouns for *me, us, him, her,* etc. (**me,**

133

nous, le, la, etc.) are placed before the verb:
ils nous ont adoptés

1   2

The past participle does not usually change after **avoir** (ils *ont* travaill*é*)(N.a. above), but it DOES if the direct object pronoun comes before the verb. This is the case in

ils nous	**ont**	**adoptés.**
dir. ob. pron.	avoir	verb
1		2

Compare: **Ils ont adopté Georges et Guy** and **Ils les ont adoptés.**

9 **Nous sommes obligés d'aller les voir de temps à autre.** *We have to* (lit.: *We are obliged to*) *visit them from time to time.*

a **nous sommes obligés** *de* . . . : *we are obliged* TO . . . Careful! You saw **obliger** followed by à in L13 : **Je ne voudrais pas l'***obliger à* **faire la navette. De,** not à must be used after *être obligé:* **Il** *est obligé de* **faire la navette.**

b **aller les voir**: *to go and see them* **Aller voir** is often used to mean *to visit.* Remember, you use **visiter** for *to visit* in the sense of to visit a monument, a museum, a town or . . . the Paris sewers.
You cannot use **visiter** if you want to say *to visit* PEOPLE; you must use either **rendre visite à** (L6), or **aller voir.**

10 **Madame Louvier a un peu pris la place de ma mère.** *Mme Louvier has to some extent taken the place of my mother.*
elle a pris: *she has taken* The past participle of **prendre**: *to take* is **pris**: *taken.* As it comes after **a** (**avoir**), and not **être**, **pris** does not agree with **elle** (See N8a and N8b above).

11 **Elle me dit de me marier.** *She tells me to get married.*
dire . . . **de** . . . : *to tell* . . . *to* . . .

12 **Elle me dit de ne pas trop dépenser.** *She tells me not to spend too much.*

13 **Elle croit bien faire.** *She thinks she is doing the right thing.*

14 **Elle lui dit de ne pas trop mettre de rouge à lèvres.** *She tells her not to put on too much lipstick.*
a **elle lui dit de** . . . : *she tells her to* . . .
b **ne pas trop mettre**: *not to put on too much*
Mettre means *to put on* as well as *to put* (App. IIIE).
c **ne pas mettre de rouge à lèvres. De** is used here because it comes after the negative *ne pas* (L7, N32).

15 **Elle lui dit de ne pas rentrer trop tard le soir.** *She tells her not to come home too late at night.*
de ne pas rentrer Again **ne** and **pas** are both used before the verb because it is in the infinitive.

16   **Sa femme lui pose des questions sans arrêt.** *His wife keeps cn asking him questions.*

17   **Son père se fâche et lui dit de changer de métier.** *His father gets angry and tells him to change his job.*

a   **Il se fâche** means *he gets annoyed, angry.* **Se fâcher** is the same type of verb as **s'appeler, s'ennuyer.**

b   **changer de métier**: *to change jobs, to change one's job*

18   **Une soirée chez les Louvier n'est pas une soirée particulièrement reposante.** *An evening at the Louviers is not a particularly restful evening.*

a   **Une soirée**: *an evening* describes the evening seen as a whole; **soir** is the part of the day which follows the afternoon and precedes the night.
     Je pars ce soir.: *I am leaving this evening.*
     Je vais passer la soirée chez des amis.: *I am going to spend the evening with some friends.* (cf. **journée** and **jour,** L13).

b   **particulièrement**   Remember, quite a number of adverbs are made by adding **-ment** to the feminine of an adjective: **particulier** (masc.), **particulière** (fem.), **particulièrement** (adverb).

PART TWO

19   **Qu'est-ce que c'est que ça?** (lit. *What's that?*) *What on earth is that?*
     This apparently long and complicated phrase corresponds to the short and simple English *What's that?*

20   **je ne vais pas vous la donner!** *I'm not going to give it to you!*
     Notice that here there are two object pronouns, **vous** and **la,** before the verb. When this happens **vous** always comes before **la** (or **le**).

21   **Elle est à moi . . .** *It's mine . . .*
     This is an idiomatic way of saying *it is mine.*

22   **c'est un bel homme! Tenez, le voilà.** *he is a fine figure of a man! Look, there he is.*
     bel *beautiful* is the masculine form of **beau** used before a vowel or silent **h**: **un bel enfant**: *a beautiful child.*
     Tenez is used colloquially in the sense of *look, I say*, etc.

23   **Je sers immédiatement.** *I'll serve up at once.*
     Je sers: *I serve (up)* is the **je** form of the irregular verb **servir** (App. II E).

24   **Allons, Pierre, va vite le leur dire.** *Come on Pierre, go and tell them quickly.*
     va le leur dire: *go and tell them* (lit. *go and tell it to them*)   In such a sentence with **dire, le** cannot be omitted. Notice the order of the pronouns. **Le** precedes **leur**: **je** *le leur* **dis, je** *le leur* **donne.**

14

25 **Bon, bon, j'y vais.** *All right, I'm going.*
j'y vais: *I'm going, I'm on my way* **Y** in **j'y vais** is a pronoun meaning *there*. **Je vais** cannot be used alone as *I'm going* can in English.

26 **Valérie, asseyez-vous là, à la droite de mon mari; et toi, Marie-Claire, assieds-toi à sa gauche . . .** *Valérie, sit here on my husband's right; and you, Marie-Claire, (sit) on his left . . .*

27 **Georges, va les chercher, veux-tu?** *Georges, go and get them will you?*
va les chercher **Aller chercher** means literally to *go and look for* i.e. *to go and get, to fetch.*

28 **Dans le tiroir du buffet, voyons.** *In the drawer of the sideboard, of course.*
Voyons means *let us see*, but it is also an exclamation: *of course, surely.*

29 **Il y a la mienne, celle de ton père et la tienne.** *There's mine, your father's and yours.*
a **La mienne:** *mine* is the feminine of **le mien** (N5 above). It refers to **serviette,** which is feminine.
b **Celle de . . . :** lit. *that of . . .* is a new phrase to be learnt by heart. It is feminine because it agrees with **la serviette.**
c **La tienne:** *yours* is the feminine of **le tien;** it refers to **la serviette.**

30 **Et toi, Pierre, va chercher le vin et mets-le sur la table, veux-tu?** *Pierre, will you fetch the wine and put it on the table?* (lit. *And you, Pierre, go and get the wine and put it on the table, will you?*)
mets-le: *put it* **Mets,** is the familiar command form of **mettre.**

31 **Vous voyez, Valérie, il faut dresser les hommes.** *You see, Valérie, you have to train men.*
Il faut is a very useful phrase which never changes in the present. When **il faut** is followed by an infinitive, as it is here, it is comparable to the phrases *one has to, one must, it is necessary to.*

32 **Mais si, c'est la sienne: cette serviette est à lui.** *Yes, it's his; this serviette is his.*
a **mais si:** *(but) yes* Remember to use **si** not **oui** for *yes*, when you are giving an affirmative answer to a negative question.
b **La sienne:** *his* or *hers* is the feminine form of **le sien;** it agrees with **cette serviette.** (cf. **le mien** and **le tien,** N29 above).
c **À lui:** *his*, an alternative to **le sien, la sienne, les siens** or **les siennes.** (cf. **à moi:** *mine*, N21 above).

33 **Je te demande pardon.** *I beg your pardon.*

34 **Ce rond de serviette, c'est bien celui de ton père: mais la serviette** **14**
est à moi. *This serviette ring is certainly your father's: but the*
serviette is mine.
celui de ton père: *your father's* (lit. *that of your father*)
Celui de is the masculine form of **celle de** (N29b above).

35 **Oui, oui; mettez-le là.** *Yes, put it there.*
Mettez-le: *put it;* the **vous** form of **mets-le.**
You now know the present tense of **mettre:**

je mets	**nous mettons**
tu mets	**vous mettez**
il/elle met	**ils/elles mettent**

(App. IIIE)

36 **Guy, il est près de toi: veux-tu le lui passer?** *Guy, it's near you: will*
you pass it to him?
le lui passer: *pass it to her, to him* This is a new combination of
object pronouns to memorize: **le** precedes **lui** (as it preceded **leur** in
N24 above).
It would be a good idea to learn by heart the three combinations
you have learnt so far:
Je vous le donne.: *I give it to you.*
  1 2
Je le leur donne.: *I give it to them.*
  1 2
Je le lui donne.: *I give it to him.*
  1 2

37 **Elle n'est pas à moi! Elle est à ma mère.** *It's not mine! It's my*
mother's. (cf. N21 above).

38 **Elle est à elle, mais elle me la prête; la mienne ne marche pas.**
It is hers, but she lends it to me; mine doesn't work.
 a **elle est à elle:** *it's hers* You can now say, of a feminine object, *it's*
MINE, HIS, HERS: **elle est** *à moi,* **elle est** *à lui,* **elle est** *à elle.*
 b **elle me la prête:** *she lends it to me* **Me** like **vous** (N20 above),
precedes **la** (and **le**):
Il vous la/le donne.
  1 2
Il me la/le donne.
  1 2
From this, you can deduce that **nous** also precedes **la** or **le**:
Il nous la/le donne.
  1 2
As **l'** stands for the direct object **la** (a feminine) and is placed before
the verb **prête**, the past participle (**prêtée**) in the perfect tense would
have the feminine ending **e** (see N8b above).

14

39 **Toi, aussi, tu as de la chance: tes boucles d'oreilles ne sont pas à toi.**
You're lucky too: your ear-rings aren't yours.
à toi: *yours*

40 **Pardon! Ce sont celles de ma mère; mais elle me les a données.**
Excuse me! They are my mother's, but she gave them to me.
  a **celles de ma mère**: *my mother's* Celles is the feminine plural of **celle**
  (N29b above).
  b **elle me les a données** Me precedes **le** and **la** (N38b above); it also
  precedes **les**:
  Elle me les donne.
  1   2
  The past participle **données** agrees with the object **les** (cf. N8b and
  38b above).

41 **Ce ne sont pas ceux de ton père?** *They aren't your father's?*
  ceux de ton père: *your father's* Ceux is the masculine plural of **celui**
  (cf. N34 above).
  Now you know **celui de . . . , celle de . . . ,** *(that of . . .)* and **celles
  de . . . , ceux de . . .** *(those of . . .).*

42 **Non, ma chère; il me les a donnés.** *No, my dear, he gave them to me.*
  il me les a donnés: *he gave (has given) them to me*
  The pronouns are in the same order as in **elle me les a données.**
  But, this time, **les** is masculine (it stands for **les boutons de
  manchettes** which is masculine), and **donnés** is consequently
  masculine too.

43 **Est-ce qu'elle n'est pas à tes parents?** *Doesn't it belong to your
  parents?*

44 **Si, elle est à eux. Mais ils me la prêtent.** *Yes, it is theirs. But they
  lend it to me.*
  a **elle est à eux**: *it is theirs* You have now learnt or can deduce all
  the forms of this idiomatic phrase used to express ownership:
  elle est à moi/à toi/à lui/à elle/à nous/à vous/à eux/à elles.
  b **ils me la prêtent**: *they lend it to me* (for word order cf. N38b above).

The language you have learnt

I'd like to . . . , I could . . .

Je voudrais *Je pourrais*	partir téléphoner	maintenant.

138

Aller, venir + infinitive

Il *va*	part*ir*.
Il *vient*	dîn*er* ce soir.

Ne pas used together in front of an infinitive

Il m'a	demandé dit	de	*ne pas*	regarder. sortir.

Past participles behave like adjectives, after être

Le dîner	*est*	serv*i*.
La salade niçoise		serv*ie*.
Mes parents	*sont*	mari*és* depuis vingt ans.
Marie-Claire et Valérie		oblig*ées* de partir.

Past participles do not change after avoir (exception: see Note 8)

Mme Martin	*a*	décid*é* de partir.
Nous	*avons*	donn*é* un litre de whisky à M. Delon.
Vous	*avez*	adopt*é* un enfant.
Ils	*ont*	invit*é* plusieurs amis à dîner.

Order of Pronouns

Ce disque, Paul	*me*	*le*	
Cette pendule, grand-père	*te* *nous*	*la*	*donne.*
Ces fauteuils, il	*vous*	*les*	

Ce disque, je veux	*le*		
Cette pendule, je veux	*la*	*lui* *leur*	donner.
Ces fauteuils, je veux	*les*		

14 Celui, ceux, celle, celles de

Ce	rond de serviette	est à vous? Non; c'est	*celui de*	mon frère.
Ces	ronds de serviette	sont à vous? Non; ce sont	*ceux de*	
Cette	serviette	est à vous? Non; c'est	*celle de*	ma sœur.
Ces	serviettes	sont à vous? Non; ce sont	*celles de*	

Much, not much, a lot

Je	mange	*beaucoup.*
Je *ne*	sors	*guère.*

Much more

Cette carte postale est	*beaucoup plus*	amusante.
Il voyage		souvent que Guy.

So . . . that . . .

Je suis	*tellement*	occupé fatigué	*que*	je vais rester chez moi.

Together

Nous sortons rarement Nous allons dîner Nous partons	*ensemble.* *tous les deux.* *toutes les deux.*

Marie-Claire va en ville.   Marie-Claire goes to town.

What happens

PART ONE
Marie-Claire a des courses à faire.: *Marie-Claire has some shopping to do.*
Monsieur Houbé, a business associate of Guy's, is coming to dinner;
so Marie-Claire has to shop.

PART TWO
À la blanchisserie teinturerie: *At the drycleaner's*
The drycleaner and Marie-Claire sort out her laundry and drycleaning.

PART THREE
Au marché: *At the market*
The apples will not grow bigger, but they may ripen.

New words in this lesson

à la main by hand
à rayures striped
les affaires (*f*) things
les affaires (*f*) business
ailleurs elsewhere, anywhere else
attention be careful
ne . . . aucun no, not any
avant before, first
avoir l'air to look, to appear (to be)
avoir la gentillesse (de) to be kind
   enough (to)
le blanchissage laundry
la blanchisserie laundry (the place)
la blanchisserie teinturerie laundry/
   cleaner's
bleu marine navy blue
bon teint fast (colour)
le bouton button
le cachet stamp
celle-ci this one
celle-là that one, this one
celui-ci this one
(un) certain (M. Houbé) (a) certain
   (M. Houbé)

ces . . . -ci these ones
ces . . . -là those ones, these ones
ceux . . . -ci these ones
ceux . . . -là those ones, these ones
la chaussette sock
la chemise shirt
le col collar
le complet suit
le complet d'homme man's suit
je conseille (de) I advise (to)
conseiller (de) to advise
le côté side
la couleur colour
les courses (*f*) shopping
couvert (de) covered (with)
ne craignez rien don't worry
craindre to fear, to worry
vous croyez you think
d'une minute à l'autre any minute now
le désordre mess
déteindre to run (colour)
devoir to be supposed to
le dîner d'affaires business dinner
(il) doit (he) is supposed to

15

enlever to take off
faire le blanchissage to do laundry
faire la lessive to do the washing
nous faisons le blanchissage we do
  laundry
fragile fragile
gratuitement free
la jupe skirt
la laverie automatique launderette
la lessive washing
(les) leurs theirs (their ones)
le linge washing
la liste list
mal fait badly done
la marchande stall-holder
le marché market
marqué marked
marquer to mark
(elles) se mélangent (they) get mixed
  up
se mélanger to get mixed up
(ils) mettent (they) put
nous mettons we put
moi-même myself
le mouchoir handkerchief
mûr ripe
mûrir to ripen
je nettoie I clean
nettoyer to clean
nettoyer à sec to dry clean
(les) nôtres ours (our ones)
on one
ils ont l'air they look, appear
(il) ouvre (it) opens
ouvrir to open

le pantalon trousers
le paquet parcel
peint à la main handpainted
nous perdons we lose
perdre to lose
la poche pocket
(être) pressé (to be) in a hurry
le pyjama pyjamas
qu'est-ce qu'il y a pour votre service?
  what can I do for you?
quinzième fifteenth
le reçu receipt
le repassage ironing
repasser to iron
le risque risk
(il) risque (it) risks, (it's) in danger of
risquer to be in danger of, to risk
rose pink
sale dirty
samedi Saturday
le sous-vêtement underwear
le supermarché supermarket
la tache stain
la teinturerie cleaner's
le teinturier cleaner
tellement (de) so many
la veste jacket (pyjama)
le veston jacket (of a suit)
les vêtements (*m*) clothes
je veux dire I mean
(les) vôtres yours (your ones)
j'y pense by the way, while I think
  about it
y penser to think about

Notes

PART ONE

1   **Les gens y parlent naturellement d'eux,** *Of course people talk about themselves* (lit. *them*),
    les gens y parlent d'eux: lit. *there people talk about themselves*
    You learnt **y** meaning *there* in **j'y vais** (L14, N25). This is another example of **y** used in the sense of *there* instead of **là**.

2   **de leurs affaires à eux, de leur santé.** *about their own business, their health.*

a   **leurs affaires à eux:** *their own business (affairs)*   **À eux** emphasises **leurs.**

b   **de leur santé**   Notice that **de** is repeated.

142

3   **Ce soir, un certain M. Houbé doit venir dîner.** *This evening, a certain* *M. Houbé is supposed to be coming to dinner.*
M. Houbé doit venir: *M. Houbé is supposed to come*   **Doit** followed by an infinitive here means *is supposed to.*

15

4   **Mais avant, je vais sortir pour faire des courses au marché et au supermarché.** *But first I'm going out to do some shopping at the market and at the supermarket.*
(mais) avant: *(but) before*
Before + expression of time is **avant**:
avant **mon départ**: BEFORE *my departure.*
Before + expression of place is **devant**:
Le boulevard Haussmann est là devant vous.: *The boulevard Haussmann is there in front of (before) you.*

5   **J'ai à préparer une liste des choses à faire.** *I have to prepare a list of the things I have to do.*
a   **j'ai *à*** + infinitive: *I have* TO + infinitive
b   **choses *à* faire**: *things* TO *do* (cf. **quelque chose *à* déclarer**: *something* TO *declare* L1, N52)

6   **J'ai aussi du linge à laver: des chemises et des sous-vêtements.** *I've also got some things to wash: shirts and underwear.*
J'ai du linge à laver   A pattern emerges from these examples:
J'*ai* des courses *à* faire.
J'*ai* des choses *à* faire.
J'*ai* du linge *à* laver.

7   **Alors je vais porter ce linge à la blanchisserie.** *So, I'll take these things to the laundry.*
Je vais *porter* ce linge *à* la blanchisserie.: *I shall* TAKE *these things* TO *the laundry.* We learned that **porter** can be the equivalent of *to carry*: **Je *porte* trois petits déjeuners sur trois plateaux** (L3, N15) and also to *take . . . to/into*: **Je porte les petits déjeuners dans les chambres.** Here we have **porter . . . à**: *to take . . . to.*

8   **Oh, j'y pense! Le complet bleu marine de Guy est couvert de taches.** *Oh, while I think of it (by the way!) Guy's navy suit is covered in stains.*
j'y pense!: *by the way, while I think of it!*
couvert *de* . . .: *covered* IN   Notice that **couvert** is followed by **de.** **Couvert** is the past participle of **couvrir.** (cf. App. IIC)

9   **Il est à nettoyer.** *It's to be cleaned.* (cf. N5b & 6b above)

15   **10**   Je vais porter ma petite jupe à rayures marron et blanches à la
teinturerie; *I'll take my little brown and white striped skirt to the
dry-cleaners;*
une jupe à rayures marron et blanches: *a skirt with brown and white
stripes*   Notice that marron does not agree with rayures. Marron,
the colour, cannot take an e or an s.

11   elle est à nettoyer et à repasser. *It's to be washed and pressed.*

PART TWO

12   et je suis obligé de tout faire moi-même. *and I have to do everything
myself.*
de tout faire   Notice that this sort of tout, a pronoun meaning
everything, comes before faire.

13   Ce chemisier, je le nettoie à sec, bien entendu? *I dry clean this
blouse, of course?*
nettoyer à sec: *to dry clean.*   Like payer (L11) the y of the infinitive
form becomes i in certain forms:
je nett*oie*   tu nett*oies*,
il/elle nett*oie*   ils/elles nett*oient*.
As in payer, the y remains in nous nettoyons, vous nettoyez

14   Et le marron de ma jupe ne risque pas de déteindre sur le blanc?
Is there any risk of the brown running into the white of my skirt?
(lit. *And the brown of my skirt doesn't risk running on the white?*)
a   (il) risque de: lit. *it risks* (*it's in danger of*)   Notice that il risque is
followed by de plus an infinitive. Il risque de manquer son train.
b   Déteindre: *to run* (*of colours*) is an irregular -re verb (App. IIIE).
This is the way it is used: le marron déteint *sur* le blanc.

15   Non; ne craignez rien: c'est une couleur bon teint. *No, don't worry,
it's a fast colour.*
a   ne craignez rien: lit. *fear nothing*   Craindre: *to fear* is an irregular
verb, like déteindre (App. IIIE).
b   Une couleur bon teint means *a fast colour.*

16   Mais je vous conseille d'enlever ces boutons peints. *But I advise you
to take off these painted buttons.*
conseiller de + infinitive: *to advise to* + infinitive.

17   Ils ont l'air fragiles. *They look fragile.*
Avoir l'air + adjective: *to look/seem* + adjective.

18   Surtout celui-ci. *Especially this one* (*here*).
Celui-ci: lit. *this one here*, *this one*, refers to a masculine singular
noun. You learnt celui de . . .: *that of* . . . in L14, N34.

144

19 **Il est très gros et on dirait qu'il est peint à la main.** *It's very big and it looks hand painted.*
On dirait que is a useful phrase to be learnt by heart. **On dirait qu'il est fatigué** is roughly equivalent to: *Il a l'air* (fatigué) (N17 above).

b **peint à la main**: *painted by hand* Remember that past participles behave like ordinary adjectives: *ils* sont peint*s* à la main (N16 above); *il* est pein*t* à la main.

20 **Ceux-là, sur le côté, sont très petits.** *Those, at the side, are very small.*
Ceux-là is the masculine plural of **celui-là. Celui-ci** is used for *this one*, **celui-là** for *that one.*

21 **Bon. Alors, je laisse ceux-ci** *Right. Then, I'll leave these*
Ceux-ci is the plural of **celui-ci.**

22 **—je veux dire ceux du complet d'homme.** *—I mean those on the man's suit.* (lit. *those of . . .*)

a **je veux dire**: *I mean* (lit. *I wish to say*) You can, of course, conjugate the phrase: **tu veux dire, il/elle veut dire, nous voulons dire** etc.

b **ceux du . . .**: *those of* Remember **celle de . . . celle de ton père** (cf. L14, N29) and **celui de . . . celui de ton père** (cf. L14, B4).

23 **Pas à sec; il est à laver.** *Not dry cleaned; it's to be washed.*
Pas à sec is a short way of saying **il n'est pas à nettoyer à sec.**

24 **Alors, je n'ai pas besoin d'aller ailleurs.** *So, I needn't go anywhere else.*
ailleurs: *elsewhere, somewhere else* Do not confuse **ailleurs**: *elsewhere*, with **d'ailleurs**: *besides, moreover* (cf. L.11).

25 **Quel désordre!** *What a muddle!*
quel . . .!: *what a . . .!* You learnt **quel** — and its plural and feminine forms: **quels, quelle, quelles** — in L12 (N4c, 5b, 7a, 8). This sort of **quel** was equivalent to the English interrogative *what?* The same **quel** — and its plural and feminine forms — is used in exclamations:
Quel ∧ **désordre!**: *What a muddle!*
Quelle ∧ **belle journée!**: *What a nice day!*
Note that there is no article after **quel/s/le/les.**

26 **Celle-là est toute petite; elle est à moi.** *This one is very small; it's mine.*

a **Celle-là**: lit. *this one*, is feminine singular, referring to **veste.**

b **toute petite**: *quite small* You will be surprised that **tout**, which is here equivalent to the adverb *quite* and is an adverb, agrees with **veste**, and with **petite.** This is a grammatical oddity: normally

15

adverbs are invariable. The rule is that **tout** agrees with the adjective when the adjective is FEMININE (singular or plural):

La veste est tout*e* petit*e*.

Elles sont tout*es* blanch*es*.

It follows from this that **tout** does not change and behaves like any other adverb in front of a MASCULINE adjective:

Il est *tout* blanc.

Ils sont *tout* blancs.

The rule is made more complicated by the fact that what we said (**tout** agrees when the adjective is feminine) does not apply if the feminine adjective begins with a VOWEL or a SILENT H:

Elle est *tout* aimable.

Elles sont *tout* heureuses.

27 **Ce pyjama-ci est à vous, Mademoiselle?** *Is this pair of pyjamas yours?*

a In note **18** you saw **celui-ci,** which was translated by *this one.* In this sentence you have a similar construction: **ce . . . -ci,** plus an adjective: **ce pyjama-ci:** *this pair of pyjamas.*

b **(le) pyjama:** *(the) pyjamas* Unlike the English words *pyjamas* and *trousers,* the French words **pyjama,** and **pantalon,** have a singular form: **un pyjama:** *pyjamas* **un pantalon:** *trousers.*

28 **Oui. Mon frère ne porte pas de pyjama rose!** *Yes. My brother doesn't wear pink pyjamas!*

Notice once more that **de** and not **un** is used after a negative:

Mon frère porte un pyjama rose.

Mon frère *ne* porte *pas de* pyjama rose.

29 **Ah, oui, en effet. M.C. . . . Alors, ces mouchoirs-ci sont à vous?**
. . . et ces mouchoirs-là sont à votre frère. *Oh yes, you're right. M.C. . . . So, these handkerchiefs are yours? . . . and these are your brother's.*

a In note 27 you saw **ce pyjama-ci:** *this pair of pyjamas.* Here you have: **ces mouchoirs-ci:** *these handkerchiefs.* **ce . . . -ci:** *this;* **ces . . . -ci:** *these.*

b **ces mouchoirs-là:** *these handkerchiefs, those handkerchiefs* (cf. note above)

30 **Attendez . . . je ne vois pas d'initiales sur ceux-là.** *Just a moment, I can't see any initials on these/those.*

a **je ne vois pas de . . .** *I cannot see any* (lit. *I see no*). The French do not use **peux:** *can* in front of **vois:** *see,* as we do in English. Again **de** is used after the negative **ne . . . pas.**

b **Les initiales** are, in French, the initial of one Christian name and the initial of the surname (never the initials of two or three Christian names as can be the case in English).

146

146

31 **Vous croyez . . .? Il y a des initiales; mais elles sont toutes petites.**
Is that so . . .? (lit. *You believe?*) *There are some initials; but they are very small.*
toutes petites See N26b above.

32 **Ce sont les vôtres.** *They're yours.*
les vôtres: *yours* (plural) If it referred to a single object it would be:
C'est *le* **vôtre.**: *It's* (*m.*) *yours.*
C'est *la* **vôtre.**: *It's* (*f.*) *yours.*

33 **. . . Vous avez beaucoup de clients et si nos affaires se mélangent avec les leurs . . . . . .** *You've got lots of customers, if our things get mixed up with theirs . . .*
a **(Ils, elles) se mélangent avec**: *they get mixed up with . . .* is a phrase of the same type as **ils s'appellent, ils s'ennuient,** etc.
b **les leurs**: *theirs*

34 **Nous mettons un cachet sur leurs affaires et sur les nôtres.** *We put a stamp on their things and on ours.*
a **nous mettons**: *we put,* the **nous** form of **mettre** (L14, 4b and App. IIIB)
b **les nôtres**: *ours*

SUMMARY
mine: **le mien, la mienne, les miens, les miennes** (L14, N5b, 29)
yours: **le tien, la tienne, les tiens, les tiennes** (L14, N29)
his/hers: **le sien, la sienne, les siens, les siennes** (L14, N32)
ours: **le nôtre, la nôtre, les nôtres** (N34b above)
yours: **le vôtre, la vôtre, les vôtres** (N32 above)
theirs: **le leur, la leur, les leurs**

35 **Alors, il n'y a aucun risque.** *So, there's no risk.*
ne . . . aucun (+ masc): *no, . . . not any* The feminine is **ne . . . aucune, il** *n'***y a** *aucune* **initiale.**

36 **Nous n'avons jamais rien perdu; voilà votre reçu.** *We have never lost anything; there's your receipt.*
Perdu is the past participle of **perdre**: *to lose.*

37 **Tellement de clients mettent leur reçu dans une poche et le perdent . . .!** *So many customers put their receipt in their pocket and lose it!*
(ils) mettent: *they put* You now know all the forms of the present tense of the irregular **-re** verb **mettre**: *to put*:

je mets	**nous mettons**
tu mets	**vous mettez**
il met	**ils mettent.**

15

You also know the past participle, **mis** (App. IIIE).

(ils) perdent: *they lose* You now know all the forms of the present tense of **perdre**: *to lose*:

je perds	**nous perdons**
tu perds	**vous perdez**
il perd	**ils perdent.**

You also know the past participle, **perdu.** (See App. IIIB)

The language you have learnt

To have something to do

J'ai	du travail	*à*	faire.
	des chemises		laver.

To look tired, etc.

Ils *ont l'air*	fatigués.
	sympathiques.

He, she, it looks as if . . .

On dirait qu'	*il*	est fatigué.
	elle	va rester.

To need

J'ai besoin de	chaussures.
Je n'ai pas besoin de	prendre un bain.

Aucun, aucune

Il *n'*y a	*aucun*	risque.
Il *ne* m'a donné		document.
Il *n'*y a	*aucune*	place.
Il *ne* m'a donné		réponse.

	celui-ci.		celui-là.
Je ne veux pas	celle-ci.	**Je voudrais**	celle-là.
	ceux-ci.		ceux-là.
	celles-ci.		celles-là.

This . . . that
These . . . those

Je préfère	ce	bouton-fauteuil-	ci.	Moi, je préfère	ce	bouton-fauteuil-	là.
	ces	boutons-fauteuils-		Moi, je préfère	ces	boutons-fauteuils-	
	cette	carte-cigarette-		Moi, je préfère	cette	carte-cigarette-	
	ces	cartes-cigarettes-		Moi, je préfère	ces	cartes-cigarettes-	

Tout (meaning quite, very)

Il est	tout	heureux.
Ils sont		heureux.

Toute/s

Elle est	tou*te*	sale.
Elles sont	tou*tes*	sales.

How . . . is, are!

	ce fauteuil	est	confortable!
Comme	cette personne		ennuyeuse!
	ces fauteuils	sont	confortables!
	ces personnes		ennuyeuses!

15 **Here, there with a verb**

J'y	mange.
	vais.

Une journée à l'agence Martin et Dassié
A day at the Martin et Dassié agency

What happens

PART ONE
Guy arrive à l'agence.: *Guy arrives at the agency.*
Guy talks about his office and his staff. He has a part-time shorthand typist, a secretary, Chantal, and an assistant, but none of them are as conscientious as he is.

PART TWO
Chantal, la secrétaire particulière de Guy: *Chantal, Guy's private secretary*
Guy is looking for the key to his filing cabinet when Chantal arrives.

PART THREE
Monique, une lettre: *Monique, a letter*
Guy dictates a business letter to Monique.

New words in this lesson

à cause de because of
à fond at full blast
à l'heure on time
à la ligne new paragraph
à quoi bon . . .? what's the use of . . .? (good of . . .)
à temps partiel part time
à plein-temps full time
à tue-tête at the top of her voice
il a chaud he's hot
il a faim he's hungry
il a froid he's cold
il a mal à la tête he's got a headache
il a soif he's thirsty
absent absent
l'adjoint (*m*) assistant
adressé (à) addressed (to)
adresser (une lettre) to address a letter)
au maximum at the most

avant l'heure early
avoir chaud to be hot
avoir faim to be hungry
avoir froid to be cold
avoir mal à la tête to have a headache
avoir soif to be thirsty
la boîte box
la boîte à pansements bandage box
la boîte à pharmacie first-aid box
le bruit noise
le bureau desk
cacher to hide
la cachette hiding place
le cambrioleur burglar
elle chante she sings
chanter to sing
le chef de la publicité head of advertising
le chiffon cloth, rag
elle claque she slams

16

claquer to slam, to bang
le classeur filing cabinet
comment ça? what?
le congé notice
consciencieux conscientious
le contrat contract
le crayon pencil
dernier last
dessous underneath
dessus on top
devoir to have to
le devis estimate
dicter to dictate
discuter (de) to talk (about), to discuss
(elle) disparaît (it) disappears, vanishes
disparaître to disappear, to vanish
distingué distinguished
elle doit she has to, she must
donner congé to give (s'one) notice
le dossier file
(celui) du bas bottom (one)
du dessus from above
(celui) du haut top (one)
j'emploie I employ
employer to employ
il a emporté he took away
emporter to take away
je m'empresse (de) I waste no time
  in, I hurry to
s'empresser (de) to waste no time in,
  to hurry to
en dessous underneath
en sténo in shorthand
l'époque (f) time
j'ai essayé I've tried
essayer to try
étudier to study
l'expression (f) expression
faire marcher to play
elle fait marcher she plays
il est fermé à clef it's locked
fermer à clef to lock
vous avez fini you've finished
finir to finish
heureusement fortunately
hier soir last night, yesterday evening
huit jours a week
impossible (de) I couldn't, impossible
  (to)

incapable (de) unable (to)
je vous prie d'agréer l'expression de
  mes sentiments distingués yours truly
lentement slowly
la machine à écrire typewriter
la maison firm
malade ill
(le) mal à la gorge sore throat
le mal à la tête headache
le malheur misfortune
où diable . . . ? where in heaven's
  name . . . ?
oublier to forget
les paperasses (f) papers
le papier paper
par-dessus on top, on the top
par-dessus le marché added to which
pareil such (a)
le plaisir pleasure
le point stop, full stop
le point d'interrogation question mark
le point final final full stop
pourtant but, however
elle prend she takes
je prie I beg
prier to beg
le projet project
quinze jours fortnight
je remercie I thank
remercier to thank
la secrétaire particulière personal
  secretary
seize sixteen
seizième sixteenth
le sentiment feeling
je serais I should be, I would be
le stylo à bille ballpoint pen
je suggère I suggest
suggérer to suggest
je suppose I suppose
supposer to suppose
la tête head
le transistor transistor
un jour sur deux every other day
la virgule comma
il vit he lives
le voisin neighbour
j'ai voulu I wanted to

PART ONE

1   Quel malheur de vivre à une époque pareille! *What misfortune to live at such a time!*
a   quel malheur de vivre . . . ! Remember quel désordre! (L15, N25). Note that de precedes the infinitive introduced by quel malheur.
b   Vivre: *to live* is an irregular -re verb (App. IIIE).

2   Ce matin, je suis arrivé quelques minutes avant l'heure. *This morning I arrived a few minutes early.*
je suis arrivé: *I arrived, I have arrived*   Arriver is one of the verbs whose past tenses are conjugated with être and not with avoir.

3   J'ai voulu ouvrir mon classeur: impossible de trouver la clef! *I wanted to open my filing cabinet: I couldn't find the key!* (lit. *impossible to . . .*)
J'ai voulu: *I wanted* is the past tense of je veux: *I want*. The past participle of vouloir: *to want* is voulu (App. IVB).

4   Ma secrétaire, Chantal, l'a emportée chez elle, je suppose. *I suppose Chantal, my secretary, has taken it home.*
Emportée agrees with l' which stands for la clef; it is consequently feminine.

5   Sa machine à écrire disparaît sous les papiers; *You can't see her typewriter for papers;* (lit. *Her typewriter disappears under papers;*)
il/elle disparaît: *he/it disappears*   Disparaît is the il form of a verb which is conjugated like connaître: *to know* (L4, N25b and App. IIIC).

6   il y a des crayons et des stylos à bille dessous, *there are pencils and ballpoint pens underneath,*
dessous: *underneath*   Sous, which you saw in the previous sentence (*sous* les papiers) is used for *under* when a word follows it: *sous* le bureau. Dessous is not followed by another word. La machine à écrire est *dessous*.

7   J'emploie une sténodactylo à temps partiel *I employ a shorthand typist part time*
a   J'emploie: *I employ, I use*, comes from the verb employer. Like envoyer (L9, N31), appuyer (L10), payer (L11), and nettoyer (L15, N13) the y of employer becomes i in the following forms,

j'emploie   tu emploies
il/elle emploie   ils/elles emploient.
(App. IBe)

b **une sténodactylo**: *a shorthand typist*   **La sténo** — short for **la sténographie** — stands for *shorthand* and **la dactylo(graphie)** for *typing*.

8 **Monique, la sténodactylo, travaille un jour sur deux** *Monique, the shorthand typist, works every other day*
un jour sur deux: *every other day, one day out of two*
un jour sur trois: *one day in three*, etc.

9 **elle est incapable de la relire.** *she can't read it back.*
Être incapable de . . . + infinitive: *to be unable to . . .* implies a greater inability to read back than just **ne peut pas.**

10 **Les voisins du dessus se plaignent.** *The people upstairs complain.*
a **les voisins du dessus**: *the neighbours above*   In this phrase **le dessus** is a noun. That is why it is possible to say: **les voisins du dessus.** The same construction is used for *the neighbours underneath*: **les voisins du dessous.**
b **(Ils) se plaignent**: *they complain* is part of the verb **se plaindre**: to complain (L11).

11 **Heureusement qu'il n'y a personne en dessous!** *Fortunately, there's no one below!*
a **heureusement que . . .**   Heureusement, like any other adverb, is normally used after the verb: *Il y a* **heureusement** *quelqu'un.*
                                                                             1   2
But if, for emphasis, **heureusement** is placed at the beginning of a sentence, it must be followed by **que**:
Heureusement qu'il y a quelqu'un.
                1   2
b **en dessous**: *underneath, downstairs*   Remember that **sous** requires a word after it. (N5 above). **En dessous** — like **dessous** (N6 above), does not have to be followed by a noun or a pronoun: **il y a quelqu'un en dessous.**

12 **Elle travaille ici depuis quinze jours seulement;** *She's only been working here a fortnight;*
Quinze jours: *a fortnight* (lit. *fifteen days*), is used as commonly as the English word *fortnight.*

13 **mais elle est tellement insupportable que je lui ai donné son congé.**
But she is so unbearable that I've given her her notice.
tellement insupportable que . . . : *so unbearable that . . .*   **Tellement** + adjective + **que**: *so* + adj. + *that.*

14 **Elle doit partir dans huit jours, ou, au maximum, dans quinze jours.**
She has to leave in a week (lit. *eight days*), *or at the most two.*

elle doit partir: *she has to leave* In lesson 15, note 3, you learnt the phrase: **un certain M. Houbé doit venir dîner,** in which **doit** was translated by *is supposed to*. The infinitive of this verb is **devoir**. The most usual English equivalent is the one we have in this lesson: *to have to.*

15 **Tantôt il a faim, tantôt il a soif; tantôt il a trop chaud; tantôt il a trop froid.** *First he's hungry, then he's thirsty; then he's too hot; then he's too cold.*
tantôt ... tantôt: *first ... then*

b **il a faim ...** *he is hungry* Remember that **avoir** — and not **être** — is used in French for *he is ... years* (*old*): **il a ... ans** (L5, N7). **Avoir** is also used, and not **être**, for such phrases as *He is hungry/ thirsty* and *He is hot/cold*: **Il a faim/soif. Il a chaud/froid.** **La faim** and **la soif** are nouns and they are invariable; so are **chaud** and **froid** in these particular phrases, though they are adjectives:
Il/elle a faim/soif.
Ils/elles ont faim/soif.
Il/elle a chaud/froid.
Ils/elles ont chaud/froid.

16 **Il dit qu'il vit pour son travail, mais tous les quinze jours,** *He says he lives for his work, but every fortnight,*
Il vit: *he lives* is part of **vivre:** *to live* (N16 above).

17 **tantôt il a mal à la tête, tantôt il a mal à la gorge; ou bien c'est sa femme qui est malade.** *First he's got a headache, then he's got a sore throat; or else it's his wife who's ill.*
il a mal à la tête ... il a mal à la gorge: *he's got a headache ... he's got a sore throat* To say that you have a pain in any part of your body you say, **j'ai mal à ...** plus the name of the part affected, e.g.
J'ai mal à la jambe.: *I've got a pain in my leg, my leg's hurting.*
Elle a mal aux pieds.: *She's got sore feet, her feet hurt.*

18 **Je n'ai jamais vu un homme pareil.** *I've never seen a man like him.*
a **j'ai vu:** *I have seen, I saw* The past participle of the verb **voir:** *to see*, is **vu** (L13, N7 and App. IVB).
b **Pareil** is the masculine form of **pareille.**

19 **Ah, Chantal. Où diable avez-vous mis la clef de mon classeur?** *Ah, Chantal. Where on earth have you put the key to my filing cabinet?*
Où diable ...? lit. *... where the devil ...?*

20 Attendez! Je ne suis pas encore arrivée. *Just a moment* (lit. *wait*),
I've only just arrived. (lit. *I haven't arrived yet*)
je suis arrivée You know that certain verbs — INTRANSITIVE verbs —
form their past tense with **être** rather than with **avoir**, plus the past
participle (N2 above). You will remember that in the case of these
verbs, the participle is a sort of adjective; it must therefore agree
with the noun it refers to. So, Chantal says: **je suis arriv*ée*** and
Chantal and Monique would say: **nous sommes arriv*ées*.**

21 Donnez-moi le temps d'enlever mon manteau! *Give me time to take
my coat off!* **le temps de . . .** : *time to . . .*

22 Je l'ai cherchée partout, cette clef, mais elle n'est pas ici. *I've
looked everywhere for that key, but it's not here.*
je l'ai cherchée: *I've looked for it* (*the key*) **L'** stands for **la, (la
clef)** and is feminine. **L'** is also the direct object of the verb **ai
cherchée** and, such is the rule, because it precedes this verb, **cherch*ée***
must agree with **l'** (**la**) (L14, N8b).

23 J'espère que vous ne l'avez pas perdue. *I hope (that) you haven't lost it.*
vous . . . l'avez . . . perdue For the same reasons as with **je l'ai
cherchée,** (N22 above), **perd*ue*** must be feminine.

24 Naturellement. Elle doit être cachée sous quelque chose. *Of course.
It must be hidden under something.*
elle doit être cachée: *it* MUST *be hidden* Earlier in this lesson you
learnt **elle doit partir**: *she has to leave* (N28 above). **Doit** can also be
used to express an idea of probability, rather than an idea of
obligation. The English equivalent in such a case would be *must*.
Elle doit être cachée . . . : *it must be hidden . . .*

25 J'ai pourtant essayé de l'ouvrir et je n'ai pas pu. *But I tried to open
it and I couldn't.*
a pourtant: *but*, in the sense of *however*
b Pu is the past participle of *pouvoir* (L9, and App. IVB).

26 J'ai dû oublier de le fermer à clef! *I must have forgotten to lock it!*
j'ai dû oublier **Dû** (note the circumflex on the **u**) is the past
participle of **doit** (in all its senses, *supposed to, must*, and *have to*).
Consequently the perfect tense of **doit** is: **j'ai dû** (built on the usual
pattern, **j'ai eu, j'ai aimé**, etc.)
As you know, **doit** is followed by an infinitive: **Je dois arriver à huit
heures.** So, quite naturally, the past tense of **doit** (**j'ai dû**) must also
be followed by an infinitive. Hence: **j'ai dû oublier:**

Compare the constructions: **j'ai dû** + infinitive in French; *I* MUST HAVE + past participle in English: **J'ai dû perdre mon passeport**: *I* MUST HAVE LOST *my passport*. **J'ai dû agacer mon père**: *I* MUST HAVE IRRITATED *my father*.

27 **Alors, à quoi bon cacher la clef?** *Then, what's the good of hiding the key?*

28 **Impossible. Votre adjoint l'a emporté hier soir pour l'étudier chez lui.** *I can't. Your assistant took it last night to study it at home.*

a **impossible** In English, we would be more likely to say *I can't*, than *impossible*.

b **emporter**: *to take away*. Do not confuse **emporter**: *to take away* — and **apporter**: *to bring*, which we learned in L8.

29 **Vous n'avez pas fini de préparer votre devis pour la maison Renard et Cie.** *You haven't finished preparing your estimate for the firm Renard and Co.*

a **fini** The past participle of **finir** ends in **i** (App. IIA).

b **vous n'*avez* pas *fini de* préparer** . . . : *you* HAVEN'T FINISHED *preparing* . . . . **finir**, is in this case, followed by **de** and an infinitive.

c **Renard et Cie.**: *Renard and Co.* **Cie** is the abbreviation for **compagnie**: *company* (f.).

30 **Voilà Monique. Elle va pouvoir prendre votre lettre en sténo.** *Here's Monique. She can take your letter in shorthand.*
    elle va|pouvoir|prendre . . . : lit. *she is going|to be able|to take* . . .

PART THREE

31 **Je vous remercie de votre lettre du 5 de ce mois (point).**
    Thank you for your letter of the fifth of this month (stop).

a **je vous remercie de** . . . : lit. *I thank you for* . . .

b **du 5 de ce mois** Notice again that **cinq** not **cinquième** is used.

32 **Comme vous êtes en vacances . . . du 10 au 20 (virgule), . . .**
    As you are on holiday . . . from the tenth to the twentieth (comma), . . .
    Comme vous êtes en vacances . . . : *As you are on holiday* . . . This sort of **comme** is equivalent to *as*. Do not mistake it for **comme** in an exclamatory sentence: **Comme tu es paresseux!**

33 **Je serais très heureux de faire votre connaissance et de discuter de votre projet avec vous (point).** *I should be very pleased to make your acquaintance and to discuss your project with you (stop).*

a **je serais**: *I should be, I would be*

b **je serais heureux de** . . . + infinitive: *I'd be pleased to* . . . + infinitive

34 **Pourriez-vous déjeuner avec moi (point d'interrogation)?** *Would you have lunch with me (question mark)?* (lit. *Would you be able to lunch . . .*)
Vous pourriez: *you would be able*, is from **pouvoir**.

35 **En attendant le plaisir de faire votre connaissance (virgule),** *I look forward to meeting you (comma),*
  a **en attendant le plaisir**: lit. *waiting for the pleasure* You learnt another form of the verb **attendre** in L8, N33: **Ma femme m'attend,** *My wife is waiting for me* (App. IIIA).
  b **En attendant le plaisir de** is a set phrase often used at the end of letters; like the English *I am looking forward to*:
En attendant le plaisir de vous rencontrer, je . . .
En attendant le plaisir de vous revoir, je . . .

36 **Je vous prie d'agréer (virgule), Monsieur (virgule), l'expression de mes sentiments distingués (point final).** *Yours truly, stop.* (lit. *I beg you to accept the expression of my distinguished feelings, final full stop.*)
This French phrase is the conventional ending to business letters. It is the equivalent of *yours truly* in English.

The language you have learnt

I am hot/cold/hungry/thirsty/I have a headache

J'ai	chaud.
	froid.
	faim.
	soif.
	mal à la tête.

He/she is supposed to . . .

Il	doit	arriver demain.
Elle		partir tout à l'heure.

To be able/I am able/I was able to go/come, etc.

Je voudrais *pouvoir*	partir immédiatement.
Je *peux*	parler au réceptionniste.
J'ai *pu*	venir.

I have left/arrived/come in/returned home. (*to have* **in English,** *être* **in French).**

16

Je *suis*	parti arrivé entré rentré	difficilement.

They are married/dead/invited/hidden/finished (*to be* **in English,** *être* **in French)**

Ils *sont*	mariés. morts. invités. cachés. terminés.

He thinks/hopes/says/is certain that

Il *croit* Il *espère* Il *dit* Il *est sûr*	que	l'hôtel est confortable. Valérie va venir. la nouvelle secrétaire est consciencieuse.

What (a) . . . !

Quel	dommage!
Quelle	époque!
Quels	bons vins!
Quelles	questions!

In a week's/fortnight's time

J'arrive Je pars	*dans*	*une semaine.* *huit jours.* *quinze jours.*

Such a man/house, etc.

Je n'ai jamais vu	un	homme	*pareil.*
	une	maison	*pareille.*

159

Leçon dix-sept *Lesson seventeen*
Dix-septième leçon *Seventeenth lesson*

Guy Martin reçoit   Guy Martin receives
un visiteur.   a visitor.

What happens

PART ONE
Monsieur Houbé vous parle.: *Monsieur Houbé speaks to you.*
Luc Houbé is in Paris on business. He tells us about Paris in August;
the theatres and restaurants are closed, the inhabitants are on holiday.
He has come to see Guy about an advertising campaign for his firm.

PART TWO
À l'agence: *At the agency*
Chantal announces Luc Houbé.
Dans le bureau de Guy: *In Guy's office*
Luc Houbé and Guy have an aperitif, and Luc tells Guy what he hopes
to do in Paris apart from business.

PART THREE
Maigre et gras: *Thin and fat*
Madame and Monsieur Longeais discuss which restaurant they will go
to.
Claude n'a pas besoin de voiture.: *Claude doesn't need a car.*
The businessmen decide that, for the sake of economy, Claude must
give up his car.

New words in this lesson

à part ça apart from that
l'Administration (*f*) government,
  administration
agréable nice, pleasant
améliorer to improve
l'apéritif (*m*) drink (before a meal)
  aperitif
assis seated
l'atmosphère (*f*) atmosphere
l'attrait (*m*) appeal, attraction
au cours de during
avant de before
l'avenir (*m*) future

bavarder to chat
boire to drink
je bois I drink
la boisson drink
(on) boit (one) drinks
la boîte club
la boîte de nuit nightclub
vous buvez you drink
buvons let's drink
ça n'a pas d'importance it doesn't
  matter, it's not important
la campagne de publicité advertising
  campaign

le **chiffre d'affaires** turnover
les **chiffres de vente** (*m*) sales figures
complet no vacancies, full up
le **congé** leave
le **congé payé** paid leave, paid holidays
la **dactylo** typist
de **plus en plus** more and more
démodé outdated, old fashioned
détendu relaxed
le **digestif** digestive
dix-sept seventeen
dix-septième seventeenth
un **doigt** a finger
un **doigt de** a drop of, a little
donner rendez-vous (à) to arrange a
  meeting (with), to fix an
  appointment (with)
en some, of them, about it, etc.
en baisse falling (off), on the decline
en comparaison de compared with
en été in summer
en hausse rising, on the rise
en particulier in particular
en tout cas in any case
encourager to encourage
entendre parler de to hear about
l'**enthousiasme** (*m*) enthusiasm
l'**été** (*m*) summer
l'**exposition** (*f*) exhibition
facilement freely, easily
faire mal to harm, to hurt
faire mieux to do better
faire le plaisir to do the pleasure (of)
la **fermeture annuelle** annual closing
  down (holidays)
fort strong
la **goutte** drop
hier yesterday
l'**homme d'affaires** (*m*) businessman
illustrer to illustrate
intensif intensive
l'**interphone** (*m*) intercommunications
  system
je vous en prie please
juin June
lancer to launch
la **marque** make
meilleur better
le **moyen** means
le **moyen de transport** means of
  transport

l'**objet** (*m*) purpose, object
je m'occupe de I'm in charge of, I
  deal with
s'occuper de to be in charge of, to
  deal with
offrir to offer
on one, you, they, people, etc.
ordonné tidy
la **pancarte** sign
par ci . . . par là here . . . there
par ici this way
par là there
par mois a month, per month
parler affaires to talk business
pas tellement not very
la **pellicule** film
personne nobody
la **photo** photo
la **plupart (de)** most (of)
plus ou moins more or less
la **porte d'entrée** front door
prendre le car to catch the bus
prendre un apéritif to have a drink,
  to have an apéritif
près de nearly
le **problème** problem
la **publicité** advertising
quelque chose something
nous recevons we receive
recevoir to receive
la **réclame** advertisement
(il) **reçoit** (hè) receives
(elles) **reçoivent** (they) receive
rempli (de) full (of)
remplir to fill
résolvons let's solve
résoudre to solve
septembre September
seule single, only one
simplement merely
le **touriste** tourist
le **transport** transport
trépidant hectic
j'utilise I use
utiliser to use
vaguement vaguely
la **vente** sales
la **visite** visit
le **visiteur** visitor
nous voulons we want

17 Notes

1 **Il est difficile de trouver une seule chambre à Paris en été,** *It is difficult to find a single room in Paris in summer,*
une seule chambre: *a single room* — in the sense of *one room, one only.*

2 **parce que les hôtels sont remplis de touristes.** *because the hotels are full of tourists.*

3 **on voit la pancarte: 'complet'.**: *you see the sign 'No vacancies'.*
on voit: *one sees* **On** is frequently used in French for *you, we, they, one, everyone, people,* i.e. when talking about an indefinable person or group of persons. *You* would be used in English in this context. (cf. **on dirait que . . .** L15, N19)

4 **La plupart des théâtres et beaucoup de restaurants sont fermés.** *Most theatres and many restaurants are shut.*
la plupart de: *most,* lit. *the greatest number of* . . . CAREFUL: **la plupart *des* théâtres**: *most ∧ theatres*; **la plupart *des* restaurants**: *most ∧ restaurants*; but **beaucoup de restaurants**: *many ∧ restaurants.* **Des** after **la plupart, de** after **beaucoup.**

5 **C'est le mois de la fermeture annuelle, le mois des congés payés.** *It's the annual closing down month, the paid holiday month.*
le congé In L16, N13b, you learnt that **donner son congé** meant *to give notice.* **Congé** can be used also to mean *holiday.*

6 **Je m'occupe de la publicité.** *I'm in charge of advertising.*

7 **En 1967, nous avons vendu 6.000 bicyclettes.** *In 1967, we sold 6,000 bicycles.*

a **En 1967 (en dix-neuf cent soixante-sept)**: *in nineteen hundred and sixty-seven* **Nineteen**: **dix-neuf**; *nineteen hundred*: **dix-neuf cent**; *sixty-seven*: **soixante-sept**; *nineteen hundred* AND *sixty-seven*: **dix-neuf cent ∧ soixante-sept.** It is possible to read 1967 as *one thousand nine hundred and sixty-seven. A thousand* is **mille**; *one hundred* is **cent**; *sixty* is **soixante.** So 1967 is **mille neuf cent soixante-sept.** Note that **neuf cent ∧ soixante-sept** corresponds to *nine hundred* AND *sixty-seven.* No word for *and* in the French.

b **6.000** If this figure were written out it would be **six mille.** Note that there is no **s** on **mille**: *thousand.* As a rule, numerals do not take an **s** in the plural. **Vingt** is an exception (L9, N26). Note also that in French there is a full-stop, not a comma, in **6.000**

8 **L'année dernière, nous en avons vendu seulement 4.000.** *Last year we only sold 4.000.*
Nous en avons vendu 4.000.: lit. *We have sold four thousand of them.*
You can see that **en** corresponds to *of them* in the English sentence.
Vendu is the past participle of **vendre** (App. IVA).

9 **Je ne dis pas que les résultats sont bons; ils sont simplement meilleurs.** *I'm not saying that the results are good; they are merely better.*
les résultats sont bons . . . ils sont meilleurs.: *the results are* GOOD *. . . they are* BETTER.

10 **Mais nous voulons essayer de faire mieux.** *But we want to try to do better.*
faire mieux . . .: *to do better*   **Mieux**: *better* is the adverb corresponding to **bien.**
Il va bien.: *He is* WELL.
Il va mieux.: *He is* BETTER.
Do not confuse **meilleur** and **mieux. Meilleur** refers to a noun:
les *résultats* sont *meilleurs* (N9 above). **Mieux** is used with a verb:
il *va* mieux.

11 **Il m'en a parlé avec beaucoup d'enthousiasme.** *He spoke to me about it with great enthusiasm.*
il m'en a parlé: *he spoke to me about it*   This time **en** stands for *about it.*
Notice that **me** comes before **en**. In fact **en** comes last when it is used together with another pronoun object.

12 **Il est agréable de parler affaires, assis à une bonne table!** *It's nice to talk business, over a good meal.* (lit. *It is pleasant to talk business seated/sitting at a good table.*)
Assis à . . .: *seated at* is a past participle.

13 **On peut bavarder plus facilement qu'au restaurant.** *You can chat more freely than in a restaurant.*
on peut bavarder . . . *you/one can chat . . .*   Here is another example of the very useful French word **on.**

PART TWO
14 **Avant de parler affaires, vous allez me faire le plaisir de prendre un apéritif.** *Before talking business, you'll do me the pleasure of having a drink (with me)* (lit. *. . . of taking an aperitif*).
Avant de is always followed by an infinitive:
before leaving: **avant de partir**

17

15 **Qu'est-ce que je peux vous offrir?** *What will you have?* (Lit. *What can I offer you?*)
Offrir: *to offer* is conjugated like ouvrir (App. 11C).

16 **Non. Mais, dans mon métier, on vous invite sans arrêt à boire.** *No. But in my job people are always offering you drinks.* (lit. *one invites you continuously to drink.*)
a **on** See N3. The equivalent here is *people.*
b **Boire:** *to drink,* is the infinitive form of **je bois** and **on boit.**
c **à** You have met verbs which take **de** before an infinitive (**L5, N25**). There are others which take **à** — **inviter à:** *to invite (to do something).*

17 **Vous buvez un apéritif par ci, un digestif par là . . .** *You drink an aperitif here, a digestive there . . .*
Vous buvez: *you drink* is the **vous** form of **boire.**

18 **Oui, je sais. Mais il y a des boissons plus ou moins fortes.** *Yes, I know. But some drinks are stronger than others* (lit. . . . *there are drinks which are more or less strong.*)

19 **Un doigt de Byrrh ou de St. Raphaël n'a jamais fait de mal à personne.** *A little Byrrh or St. Raphaël never harmed anyone.*
a **un doigt de** (lit. *a finger of*), is the equivalent of *a drop of,* or *a little.*
b **Byrrh and St. Raphaël** are aperitifs.

20 **J'y viens souvent, vous savez.** *I come here often, you know.*
j'y viens Y stands for *here;* in this case meaning *Paris.*

21 **Non. Mais j'en ai vaguement entendu parler.** *No. But I've heard something* (lit. *I've vaguely heard*) *about it.*
a **J'ai entendu parler de . . . :** *I have heard about . . .*
b **en,** in **j'en ai entendu parler,** stands for *the hotel,* i.e. *about it.*

22 **Je veux en prendre beaucoup:** *I want to take lots of them:*
Here **en** means *of them,* as it did in N8 above.

23 **J'en ai acheté cinq!** *I bought five* (lit. *of them*)*!*

24 **Oui. J'ai reçu votre lettre du premier.** *Yes. I received your letter of the first.*
a **j'ai reçu:** *I received, I have received* **Reçu** is the past participle of the verb **recevoir.**
b **votre lettre du premier:** *your letter of the first* (i.e. *the first of this month*) Remember that this is an exception to the rule. *The second third, fourth,* etc. *of July* (or any month) becomes **le deux, le trois, le quatre,** etc juillet. But the FIRST *of July* is always **le *premier* juillet.**

25 **Ah . . . nous recevons tellement de lettres!** *Oh . . . we receive so many letters!*
Nous recevons: *we receive* is the **nous** form of **recevoir**.

26 **Elles reçoivent les lettres et elles les égarent.** *They receive (the) letters and they mislay them.*
Elles reçoivent: is another form of **recevoir**. (App. IVA)

27 **Mais comment donner à la bicyclette, ce moyen de transport démodé, un attrait nouveau?'** *But how can we give the bicycle, this old fashioned means of transport, a new appeal?'*
comment donner . . . ?: lit. *how to give . . . ?* The English equivalent is *how do you give, how can we give, how does one give.*
Comment may be used in this way, immediately before an infinitive:
Comment le consoler?: *How can we console him?*

28 **Eh bien, résolvons ce problème . . .** *Right, let's solve the problem . . .*
Résolvons: *let's solve* is part of a very irregular verb, **résoudre**.

29 **Alors, buvons à l'avenir de votre usine!** *Let's drink to the future of your factory then!*
buvons à . . . : *let's drink to . . .*

The language you have learnt

Before . . . -ing

Je voudrais	prendre un apéritif prendre quelques photos	*avant de*	part*ir.* rentr*er.*

How . . . ?

Comment est-ce que	*vous pouvez* travailler ici? *vous préférez* voyager? En avion ou par le train?
Comment	*pouvez-vous* travailler ici? *préférez-vous* voyager? En avion ou par le train?

En: about it

Il m' Elle Guy	*en*	a parlé. a entendu parler. a discuté avec M. Houbé.

17 **Most people**

La plupart des	Français employés	ont un mois de congé en été.

On: you, they, people

En France,		boit beaucoup de vin.
Dans les usines,		encourage les gens à travailler.
Dans les banques,	*on*	ne travaille pas le lundi.
Vous voyez, d'ici,		voit tout le jardin.

En: some (of it/of them)

J'		ai.
Nous		avons.
Vous	*en*	voulez.
Ils		ont vendu.
Elles		voudraient.

Good, better

Le	poisson café		*bon/meilleur.*
La	truite salade	*est*	*bonne/meilleure.*

Better

Il	va parle	*mieux.*

Standing/sitting

Je suis	*debout*	près de la fenêtre.
	assis	dans le fauteuil.

Les trois coups   The three knocks

What happens

PART ONE
M. Levoisin a téléphoné.: *M. Levoisin has phoned.*
Monsieur Delon tells us that Monsieur Levoisin has just invited them
to the theatre. He had difficulty getting any seats at all, but Monsieur
Delon doesn't mind sitting in the balcony. Besides he loves the
atmosphere of the theatre: the people, the lights, the scenery.

PART TWO
Une soirée au théâtre: *An evening at the theatre*
Madame Delon tells her husband that they have all been invited to
the theatre that very evening. She makes him guess which theatre.
Valérie will probably be free because Georges is working, but Monsieur
Delon is more worried about what to wear than about his daughter.

PART THREE
Pas de robes: *No dresses*
Louise's mother cannot find anything to wear.

Jean et Jeanne prennent rendez-vous par téléphone.: *Jean and Jeanne
arrange a meeting on the telephone.*
Jeanne is not very positive.

New words in this lesson

tu as accepté you accepted
accepter to accept
amener to bring
applaudi applauded
applaudir to applaud
après tout after all
auquel to which
le balcon balcony seat
brillant outstanding, brilliant
ça m'est égal I don't mind
ce que what
clair light

classique classical
la comédie comedy
la comédie musicale musical
le comédien actor
la comédienne actress
complet sold out
le coup knock, blow
de service on duty
le décor set
elle est devenue she's become
devenir to become
devine! guess!

167

18

deviner to guess
dix-huitième eighteenth
le drame drama
elle-même herself
emprunte borrow
emprunter to borrow
être de service to work
faire la queue to queue
il a fait la queue he queued
les fauteuils d'orchestre (*m*) stalls
le foyer foyer
frénétiquement wildly
le garçon boy
le guichet box-office
habillé dressed
l'idée (*f*) idea
(ça) inquiète (that) worries
inquiéter to worry
le lever rise
la lumière light
malgré in spite of
mauve mauve
le meilleur the best
n'importe no matter . . .
n'importe comment anyhow
n'importe où anywhere (no matter where)
n'importe quand anytime, (no matter when)
n'importe quel any (no matter what)
n'importe qui anyone (no matter who)
n'importe quoi anything (no matter what)
l'ouvreuse (*f*) usherette

par téléphone by telephone
pas plus no more
la pièce play
pire worse
plaire to please
plein de full of
le poulailler gods
se procurer to get, to obtain, to get hold of
le programme programme
la queue queue
rapporté brought back
rapporter to bring back
(j'en suis) ravi (I'm) delighted (about it)
le répertoire repertoire
retenir to book
il a retenu he's booked
le rideau curtain
la salle auditorium
la scène stage
sèchement curtly
soigné carefully done
le spectacle theatre, show, play
le spectacle de variétés variety show
les spectateurs (*m*) audience
timide shy
tous les quatre all four of us
tout de même all the same
la tragédie tragedy
une fois ou deux once or twice
(me) va très bien really suits (me)
il vaut mieux it's better (to)
vert green

Notes

PART ONE

1 **Les trois coups**: lit. *The three knocks*
In French theatres immediately before the curtain rises, you hear a series of quick knocks followed by three slow deliberate knocks. These three knocks — **les trois coups** — mean that the play is about to begin.

2 **Il a réussi à se procurer des billets pour le Français.** *He's managed to get hold of tickets for 'Le Français.'*
a **Il a réussi à . . .** is from **réussir à . . .** : *to succeed in . . . , to manage.*
Réussir is conjugated like **finir** (App. IIA). Note that the French for to *succeed* IN is **réussir à.**

b **Se procurer**: lit. *to get* (*hold of*), *to obtain with difficulty* is a verb of the same type as **il s'appelle,** and **il s'ennuie.**

c **Le Français** is short for **Le Théâtre Français,** another name for **la Comédie Française,** the famous national theatre founded by Louis XIV. It specializes in French classical plays.

3 **On joue 'le Médecin malgré lui,' de Molière.** *They're doing Molière's 'le Médecin malgré lui.'*

a **on joue**: lit. *one plays* (*they're playing*)   Like *to play*: **jouer** is used both in connection with the theatre and with sport. Remember **Je joue au tennis tous les jours** (L2, N15).

b **'le Médecin malgré lui'** (lit. *The doctor in spite of himself*) is the title of one of Molière's most famous comedies. Molière was a seventeenth-century dramatist.

4 **Il y a longtemps qu'il veut nous inviter à aller au théâtre.** *He's been wanting to invite us to the theatre for a long time.*
Il y a longtemps que . . . is equivalent to the phrase **depuis longtemps** which you learnt in L4: **Je suis chauffeur de taxi** *depuis longtemps* (N6). The two following sentences mean exactly the same. Compare them carefully:
Il y a longtemps **que j'attends.**
J'attends *depuis longtemps.*
The present tense is used in both cases and is the equivalent of an English past tense: I HAVE BEEN WAITING *a long time.*

5 **Il a fait la queue devant le théâtre pendant une heure pour louer des places pour la semaine prochaine.** *He queued for an hour in front of the theatre to book seats for next week.*
Il *a fait* **la queue** *pendant* **une heure.**: *He* QUEUED FOR *one hour.*

6 **Quand il est arrivé au guichet, l'employée lui a dit sèchement: 'Complet.'** *When he reached the box office, the woman said curtly (to him): 'sold out.'*
complet: *sold out* (*full*)   You learnt the same word, **complet,** in lesson 17, (N3); in that context, speaking of a hotel, it was the equivalent of *no vacancies* in English.

7 **M. Levoisin a immédiatement offert de les lui acheter.** *M. Levoisin immediately offered to buy them from him.*

a **(il) a offert**: (*he*) *offered*   **Offert** is the past participle of the verb **offrir** (L17, N15 and App. IIC).

b **Il a offert de** *les lui* **acheter.**: *He offered to buy them from him.* Remember that **les** precedes **lui** (cf. L14 N36).

8 Naturellement, ce ne sont pas les meilleures places. *Of course they are not the best seats.*
les meilleures places: *the best seats* Meilleures is the feminine plural of meilleur (L17, N9).

9 Après tout, il y a pire. *After all, there are worse.*
pire: *worse* Mal: *bad*; pire: *worse*

10 Il vaut mieux avoir des balcons qu'aller au poulailler! *It's better to have seats in the balcony than in* (lit. *to go to*) *the gods!*
Vaut comes from the verb valoir *to be worth*, but remember il vaut mieux as a set expression meaning *it's better to.*

11 Il faut dire que j'adore les spectacles *I must say I love the theatre*
a il faut dire que . . . : lit. *it must be said that . . .*
b Le spectacle is a useful word in French because it can apply to any type of performance: a straight play, a musical, a circus, etc.

12 Quelle atmosphère! *What an atmosphere!*
Quelle . . . ! is the form used in an exclamation before a feminine noun (cf. quel désordre! L15, N25).

13 Les lumières du foyer, les ouvreuses vendant leurs programmes, la salle pleine de monde, *The lights in the foyer, the usherettes selling their programmes, the auditorium full of people,*
a Vendant: *selling* is a form of vendre: *to sell.* You learnt a part of a verb with the same ending in L16, N35, (en) attendant: lit. *awaiting.* Vendant and attendant are called PRESENT PARTICIPLES.
b La salle is normally used for a large public room/hall/auditorium.
c pleine de monde: *full of people* Pleine is the feminine form of plein.

14 — les meilleurs de toute la France, peut-être. — *the best in all France/the whole of France perhaps.*
le meilleur *de*: *the best* IN

15 Et je sais qu'ils vont être frénétiquement applaudis par les spectateurs à la fin du spectacle. *And I know they'll be wildly applauded by the audience* (lit. *the spectators*) *at the end of the performance.*
être applaudi(s) par: *to be applauded/clapped by* Applaudi is the past participle of applaudir: *to clap.* Par is used for *by* in a phrase like this. You may remember être caché, which you learnt in L16, N24 — elle doit être cachée sous quelque chose. Chantal could have said, La boîte *est cachée par* le chiffon.

16 **Non, tous les quatre. Et il va amener sa femme.** *No, all four of us. And he's bringing his wife.*

a **tous les quatre**: lit. *all the four*   Remember, **tous les deux**: *both* (L6, N25)

b **amener**: *to bring*   In L8, you saw **La femme de chambre** *apporte* **les petits déjeuners.**: *The chambermaid* BRINGS *the breakfasts.* The French equivalent of *to bring* is **apporter** when the object of the verb is a thing (e.g. **le petit déjeuner**), but **amener** when it is a person.

17 **Il a retenu les places?** *Has he booked seats?*
Retenir les places is another way of saying *to book.* You learnt **louer** and **réserver** for *to book* a seat on a train (L12).
Louer, réserver and **retenir,** are all roughly equivalent. **Retenir** is conjugated like **venir** (App. IID).

18 **Pour quand? Malheureusement, pour ce soir.** *When for?* (lit. *For when?*) *This evening, unfortunately.* Note that **pour** is repeated.

19 **Tu sais que les comédies de Molière me plaisent beaucoup.** *You know I like Molière's comedies very much.* (lit. *please me a lot*).
Les comédies de Molière me plaisent beaucoup.: *I like/enjoy Molière's comedies very much.* This is one way to say that something or someone appeals to you; that you like something or someone.

20 **Ça doit être au Français, à Chaillot, peut-être au Théâtre de la Ville . . . Alors, auquel?** *It must be the Français, or* (lit. *to*) *Chaillot, or perhaps* (*to*) *the 'Théâtre de la Ville' . . . Which one then?*

a **Chaillot** is short for **le Palais de Chaillot,** a large building which houses three museums and the **Théâtre National Populaire.**

b **auquel?**: *to which* (*are we going?*)   Remember **lequel**: *which* (L12, N40). *To which* is **auquel,** when it refers to a masculine singular noun — in this case **théâtre.**

21 **Les pièces du répertoire classique m'ont toujours plu.** *I've always liked* (*the*) *classical plays.*

a **Les pièces du répertoire classique** are the best known plays of the classical period (the seventeenth and eighteenth century).

b (**Elles**) **m'ont** (**toujours**) **plu.**: lit. *They have* (*always*) *pleased me.* **Elles/ils m'ont plu** is the past tense of **elles/ils me plaisent** (N19 above).

22 **À propos, Valérie n'est pas sortie?** *By the way, Valérie hasn't gone out?*

18

Elle est sortie.: *She has gone out.* **Sortir** is another of the verbs that form their past tense with **être** (cf. L16, N2). The past participle of **sortir** is **sorti**, and here, of course, it agrees with Valérie.

23 **D'habitude, Valérie est assez timide.** *Usually Valérie is quite shy.*

24 **Depuis quelque temps, elle est devenue sûre d'elle-même.** *For some time now she's become sure of herself.*

  a **elle est devenue**: *she has become* **Devenu** is the past participle of **devenir,** a verb which is conjugated like **venir** (cf. App. IID). Like **venir** it forms its past tenses with **être.**

  b **sûre d'elle-même**: *sure of herself* **elle-même**: *herself* You learnt **moi-même**: *myself* in L15, N12.

25 **Et j'en suis ravie.** *And I'm delighted about it.*
Here again **en** corresponds to *about it.* (cf. L17, N11, **il m'***en* **a parlé**: *he spoke to me* ABOUT IT.)

26 **Il me plaît, ce garçon.** *I like that boy.* (lit. *He pleases me, that boy*).
il me plaît: *I like him* Now you know **ils me plaisent**: *I like them*; **ils m'ont plu**: *I liked them;* and **il me plaît**: *I like him.*

27 **Je dois dire qu'il me plaît, à moi aussi.** *I must say that I like him too.*
Il me plaît, à moi aussi.: *I like him too.*
À moi aussi is added for emphasis. Notice the preposition **à**; it shows you that **plaire,** the infinitive of **il plaît,** requires **à** if it is followed by a pronoun or a noun: **ce garçon** *plaît à* **ma mère.**

28 **Je n'ai rien à me mettre.** *I've got nothing to wear* (lit. *to put on myself*).

29 **Tu en as apporté des quantités de Québec,** *You brought lots from Québec,*
tu en as apporté des quantités: lit. *you brought lots of them*

30 **Tu sais bien que je veux emporter au Canada quelques robes de Paris.** *You know very well that I want to take some dresses from Paris to Canada.*
Emporter: *to take* in the sense of *to take away.* Distinguish carefully between **apporter**: *to bring* and **emporter**: *to take (away)*:
Mme Delon a *apporté* **des robes du Canada.**
Mme Delon veut *emporter* **des robes au Canada.**

31 **Eh bien, emprunte quelque chose à Valérie.** *Well, borrow something from Valérie.*
emprunter quelque chose à quelqu'un: *to borrow something* FROM *someone*

172

32 **Elle est peut-être uh peu claire, mais elle ne fait pas trop jeune.**
Perhaps it's a bit light, but it doesn't make me look too young.
Ça fait jeune is an expression meaning *it makes one look young.*

33 **Je ne peux tout de même pas aller au théâtre** . . . *All the same
I can't go to the theatre* . . .
Adverbs such as **tout de même** and **peut-être** may be placed
between the verb and **pas**. These are adverbs which are unstressed
and which convey the attitude of the speaker rather than any
essential information.

The language you have learnt

Liking

Cette pièce Il	*me plaît.* *m'a plu.*
Ces pièces Elles	*me plaisent.* *m'ont plu.*

To borrow, lend

Est-ce que je peux Je suis ravi de	lui vous	*emprunter* *prêter*	dix francs? ce disque.

The passive

La pièce	*est*	*jouée* par les meilleurs comédiens de France.
Le spectacle		*applaudi* par les spectateurs.
Les femmes de chambre	*sont*	*choisies* par le gérant.
Les lycéens		*encouragés* par le professeur.

18

To ask someone to do something

Il *demande*	à	Valérie son père	*de*	l'aider. partir.

To ask someone for something

Je vais *demander*	de l'eau minérale	*à*	ce garçon.
	l'heure		cette dame.

Depuis . . . and il y a . . . que

Je prends mes repas ici		*depuis*	un mois.
Il y a	une semaine deux ans	*que*	je travaille ici. j'habite en France.

Inviter à, réussir à

Je *vous invite*	*à*	venir avec moi au théâtre.
J'*ai réussi*		lui parler.

Verb + that + verb

Je sais Il dit	*que*	Valérie	va venir. est chez elle.

Well, better, (the) best

Jean		*bien.*
M. Olivier	parle	*mieux* qu'eux.
Lequel des quatre		*le mieux?*

I'd rather, It's better to . . .

J'*aime mieux* Il *vaut mieux*	visiter Paris avant d'aller en province. rester ici.

174

N'importe

	parler à		qui.
Je suis prêt à	partir		quand.
	manger	*n'importe*	quoi.
	habiter		où.
	voyager		comment.

For whom? which? when?

Ce petit déjeuner, c'est	pour	*qui*? *quel* client? *quelle* chambre?
Tu as loué des places		*quand*?

19 Leçon dix-neuf *Lesson nineteen*
Dix-neuvième leçon *Nineteenth lesson*

À la rencontre de Georges Meeting Georges

What happens

PART ONE

C'est Valérie qui parle.: *It's Valerie speaking.*
Valérie is missing Georges, who is out of Paris, visiting relatives. He
has written to her every day. She has missed him terribly and realizes
that something about her life has changed. He is returning that evening
and she is going to meet him.

PART TWO

À un arrêt d'autobus: *At a bus-stop*
Valérie inquires about the buses.

Dans l'autobus: *On the bus*
She buys a ticket.

Dans le hall de la Gare d'Austerlitz: *In the hall at Austerlitz station*
A porter helps Valérie.

PART THREE

Une journée bien remplie: *A very full day*
Thérèse is feeling apathetic.

Allez chercher vos amis à la bonne gare.: *Meet your friends at the right
station.*
Trains from Toulouse don't come to the Gare du Nord.

New words in this lesson

à la fois both, at the same time
j'ai envie de I feel like
j'ai l'habitude (de) I'm used to
aller à la rencontre de to go to meet
aller chercher to meet, to fetch
l'arrêt d'autobus (*m*) bus stop
l'arrêt facultatif (*m*) request stop
l'autobus (*m*) bus
avoir envie de to feel (like)
avoir l'habitude de to be used to
avouer to admit

le billet de quai platform ticket
c'est combien? how much is it?
le carnet book (of tickets)
le chemin de fer railway
(elle) commence (it) begins
commencer to begin
comprendre to understand
j'ai compris I understood
depuis since
depuis que since
descendre to get off

176

directement directly
dix-neuf nineteen
dix-neuvième nineteenth
écrire to write
j'écris I write
il écrit he writes
il a écrit he has written
l'écriture (*f*) handwriting
(il) s'éloigne (he) moves away, goes away
s'éloigner to move away, to go away
ils ont emmené they took
emmener to take
l'émotion (*f*) emotion, feeling
en grève on strike
je m'ennuie I'm bored
s'ennuyer to be bored
les feux (*m*) lights
la file d'attente queue
le film film
la grève strike

l'indicateur (*m*) (railway) timetable
là-bas over there
la machine machine
maintenant now
ne . . . que only
le parent relative
promettre to promise
il a promis he promised
le receveur conductor (bus)
régulièrement regularly
relire to reread
je sens que I feel that
je me sens I feel
sentir to feel
se sentir to feel
le service des postes postal service
le style style
tenir parole to keep one's word
il a tenu parole he has kept his word
triste sad

Notes

PART ONE

1 **À la rencontre de Georges** *Meeting Georges*
À la rencontre de . . . is a phrase which conveys the idea of meeting.
It occurs in the phrase **aller à la rencontre de**: *to go to meet.*
Rencontrer means *to meet.* (L8).

2 **C'est Valérie qui parle.** *It's Valérie speaking.* (lit. *It's Valérie who is speaking.*) You learnt **qui** in L5, N39 in the question: **Christophe, qui est-ce?**: *Christophe,* WHO *is it?* you also saw **qui** in a statement in L16, N17: **C'est sa femme qui est malade.**: *It is his wife* WHO *is ill.* You will see more examples of **qui**: *who* in this lesson.

3 **Georges est parti lundi.** *Georges left on Monday.*
a **il est parti**: *he left, he went* **Parti** is the past participle of **partir**: *to leave* (L12). Like **arriver.** it forms its past tense with **être** (App. IIB).
b **Lundi** means, in this sentence, *on Monday.* There is no French equivalent for *on* in such phrases as *on Monday, on Tuesday,* etc. Just say **lundi, mardi,** etc. But remember that *on Monday*s, *on Tuesday*s, is *le* **lundi***, le* **mardi***,* etc. (L11, N9c).

4 **Il est allé en province voir des parents:** *He's gone to the country to see relatives:*
a **il est allé**: *he has gone, he went* **Allé** is the past participle of **aller**: *to go.* Its past tense is formed with **être** (App. ICa).

b **aller en province**: *to go to the country* **La province** is *the country* as opposed to Paris, the capital. You have already learnt the word in L5, where it was translated as *the provinces*. **La campagne**, which you have also learnt (L5, N15), describes the country as distinct from towns.

c **des parents**: *relatives, relations* As you already know, it can also mean *parents* (L2, N22).

5 des tantes et des cousins qui habitent dans une toute petite ville du Midi. *aunts and cousins who live in a very small town in the South.*

a **des cousins *qui* habitent . . .** : *cousins* WHO *live . . .*

b **une toute petite ville**: *a very small town* **Toute**, rather unexpectedly, agrees with **ville** (cf. L15, N26b).

c **Le Midi** is a general name for all the Southern provinces of France; **la Provence, le Languedoc, la Gascogne, le Béarn**, and **le Pays Basque**.

6 Quand il est parti, il a promis de m'écrire régulièrement. *When he left, he promised to write regularly to me.*
il a promis de . . . : *he promised to . . .* **Promettre**: *to promise* has the same endings as the irregular **-re** verb **mettre** (App. IIIE).

7 Et je dois dire qu'il a tenu parole: il m'a écrit tous les jours. *And I must say he's kept his word: he's written to me every day.*

a **il a tenu parole** **Tenir parole** means *to keep one's word*. **Tenir** has the same endings as **venir**, but it forms its past tense with **avoir** (App. IID).

b **il a écrit**: *he has written, he wrote* Notice the past participle of **écrire — écrit**.

8 Je dois avouer que j'ai lu ces lettres avec beaucoup d'émotion. *I must admit, I was very touched when I read these letters.*

a **je dois avouer que . . .** : lit. *I must admit that . . .* **Que** must not be left out.

b **J'ai lu**: *I read, I have read* **Lu** is the past participle of **lire**: *to read*. Remember **lisez**: *read* (L10) and **relire**: lit. *to reread* (L11, N50).

9 Il écrit de très belles lettres. *He writes very beautiful letters.*

a **Il écrit**: *he writes* is the **il** form of **écrire**.

b **de très belles lettres** **Il écrit *des* lettres**, but **Il écrit *de* belles lettres** (cf. L14, N7)

10 Moi, je n'écris pas bien. *I don't write well.*
J'écris is the **je** form of **écrire**.

11   En disant ça, je parle à la fois de mon écriture et de mon style.
When I say that, I'm talking about both my handwriting and my style.

a   **en disant ça**: lit. *while saying that*   You learnt the forms **vendant** and **attendant** (from **vendre** and **attendre**) in L8. These are present participles. **Disant** is the present participle of **dire** (App. IIIE).

12   Dans chacune de ses lettres, il me dit: *In each of his letters he says (to me)*:
Chacune de . . . is the feminine form of **chacun de** . . . (L10).

13   'Comme tu écris bien, ma chère Valérie!' *'How beautifully you write, my dear Valérie!'*

14   Je n'ai pas l'habitude d'écrire beaucoup. *I'm not used to writing a lot.*
j'ai l'habitude de . . . : *I'm used to* . . . , *I'm accustomed to* . . .
Notice that **avoir** is used in the French phrase: *avoir* **l'habitude de**: TO BE *used to*.

15   À la maison, nous n'écrivons que très rarement. *At home, we only write very rarely.*
To express *only*, **ne** is placed as usual between subject and verb, and **que** goes immediately before the words to which *only* refers. Compare earlier **ne** . . . **que trois fois**: *only three times* (i.e. not four or five).

16   En lisant les lettres de Georges, *Reading Georges' letters,*
en lisant: lit. *while reading* (cf. N11 above)

17   j'ai compris que quelque chose a changé dans ma vie. *I realized that something has changed in my life.*
j'ai compris que . . . : lit. *I have understood* . . .   **Compris** is the past participle of **comprendre**: *to understand*, which is conjugated like **prendre** (App. IIIE).

18   Depuis lundi, je m'ennuie. *Since Monday, I've been bored.*
Je m'ennuie: lit. *I'm bored* is from **s'ennuyer**. It is conjugated like **payer** (App. IBe). **Je** *m'ennuie* belongs to the same category of verbs as **je** *m'appelle*.

19   Depuis qu'il est parti, j'ai envie de ne rien faire. *Since he left, I haven't felt like doing anything.*

a   **depuis qu'il est parti**: *since he left*   You have just heard Valérie say **je** *m'ennuie depuis* **lundi**: *I* HAVE BEEN BORED SINCE *Monday*.
You know that the verb used with **depuis** is always in the present (whereas, in English, in an equivalent sentence with *since*, the verb is in the past). Valérie wants to show that she is bored while she is speaking — hence the present in French. Here now is the French

19   phrase for another kind of *since* — the *since* which introduces such a sentence as *since he left, I haven't slept*. The French equivalent of this sort of *since* is **depuis que**:

Depuis que Georges est parti, Valérie ne dort pas.
                           1   2

In this sentence, verb no. 1 (**est parti**) is in the past because Georges left some time ago, and verb no. 2 (**dort**) is in the present because Valérie is still at this moment, unable to sleep. Study these two examples and their English equivalents:

J'*habite* à Paris *depuis* l'an dernier.: *I* HAVE LIVED *in Paris* SINCE *last year.*

Depuis qu'il *a acheté* un appartement, il *est* heureux.: SINCE *he* BOUGHT *a flat, he* HAS BEEN *happy.*

b   **J'ai envie de . . .** is equivalent to *I feel like . . .*   The verb following **avoir envie de** is always in the infinitive form.

20   **Depuis qu'il n'est plus à la réception de l'hôtel,** *Since he hasn't been at the hotel reception desk,*

a   **depuis qu'il n'est plus**   Here **depuis que** is followed by a present tense, because the action is not completed — Georges is still away.

b   **il *n'est plus***: *lit. he is* NO LONGER

21   **je sens que quelque chose me manque.** *I've felt that something is missing.*

a   **je sens que . . .**: lit. *I feel that . . .*   Again a present is used in French because Valérie is describing her feelings at the moment. **Je sens** is part of the verb **sentir**, which is conjugated like **sortir** (App. IIB).

b   **quelque chose me manque**: *something is missing* (lit: *I miss something*). In L12, you saw **manquer le train**: *to miss the train.* Here **manquer** is used in a different way. When you want to say *I miss something/somebody*, start with the French for *something* (**quelque chose**) or *somebody* and add **me manque**:

I miss something.: **Quelque chose me manque.**
      1   2   1   2

I miss Valérie.: **Valérie me manque.**
   1   2   1   2

I miss Georges.: **Georges me manque.**
   1   2   1   2

22   **En passant devant son bureau, je me sens toute triste.** *When I pass his desk, I feel quite sad.*

a   **en passant devant**: lit. *while, on passing in front of* (N11 above).

b   **je me sens**: *I feel*   Do not forget **me**; it is as important as **me** in **je m'appelle** or **je m'ennuie.**

23   **Georges me manque beaucoup.** *I miss Georges a lot.* (cf. this lesson, N21b).

180

24 **J'espère que je lui manque un peu aussi.** *I hope he is missing me a little too.*
je lui manque: *he misses me* (cf. note 21b above)

25 **J'ai rencontré un de ses amis qui m'a immédiatement invitée à aller au cinéma.** *I met one of his friends who immediately invited me to go to the cinema.*
(il) m'a invitée **Invitée** agrees with **me**, in this case Valérie, and is consequently feminine (cf. L14, 8b).

26 **Je n'ai été au cinéma que deux fois** *I've only been to the cinema twice*
j'ai été Été is the past participle of **être**.

27 **depuis que je suis à Paris.** *since I've been in Paris.*
As Valérie is still in Paris when she is speaking, she uses the present after **depuis que**.

28 **pour voir un film qui m'a beaucoup plu.** *to see a film which I liked very much.*
a **un film qui m'a plu**: *a film* WHICH/THAT *I liked* **Qui** is equivalent to *which* or *that* in a sentence like this.
b **qui m'a plu**: *which I liked* (L18, N21b)

29 **On donne de bien beaux films à Paris en ce moment.** *They're showing some excellent films in Paris at the moment.*
a **On donne**: lit. *one gives*. It is equivalent to **on joue** which you learnt in L18, N3.
b **de bien beaux** See L14, N7.

PART TWO
30 **Où est-ce que vous allez, Mademoiselle?** *Where are you going, (Miss)?* You learnt **Où est Pierre?** in L5, N28. In this question
$$\text{Pierre comes after the verb.}$$
Pierre comes after the verb. In a similar way, Valérie could ask here:
Où s'arrête l'autobus?
But **l'autobus** does not go after the verb if **où est-ce que** . . . is substituted for **où**. **Où est-ce que l'autobus s'arrête?** (cf. **comment trouvez-vous Paris?** L17 and *comment est-ce que* **vous trouvez Paris?**)

31 **À la Gare d'Austerlitz.** lit. *to the Austerlitz Station.*
Austerlitz is the name of a town in Czechoslovakia, where Napoleon I defeated the Austrians and the Russians in 1805.

19

32 **Alors, vous pouvez d'abord prendre le 69 qui va directement à la Bastille. Mais il ne s'arrête pas ici.** *Well, first you can take the 69 which goes direct to la Bastille; but it doesn't stop here.*

a **qui va directement à . . .** : lit. *which goes directly to . . .*

b **La Bastille** is the famous prison in Paris which was stormed in 1789, at the beginning of the French Revolution. There is now a square by this name.

33 **Là, vous changez, et vous prenez le 89.** *There you change and take the 89.*

89: **quatre-vingt-neuf**: 80 in French is **quatre-vingts** (lit. *four twenties*). 81 is **quatre-vingt-un**; 82: **quatre-vingt-deux**, etc, 90 is **quatre-vingt-dix**; 91: **quatre-vingt-onze**; 99: **quatre-vingt-dix-neuf**. Notice that there is an s at the end of **vingt** in **quatre-vingts** and none when 80 is followed by another figure: **quatre-ving*t*-un.**

34 **Ça prend combien de temps?** *How long does that take?* **Ça prend . . .** is a phrase commonly used for *it takes . . .* when you want to indicate the time something takes.

Ça prend . . . heures pour aller de Paris à Niort.: *It takes . . . hours to go from Paris to Niort.*

You learnt **combien de temps?** in L11:

Ça prend combien de temps? *How long does it take?*

35 **Vous n'avez pas un carnet?** *Haven't you got a book of tickets?*

un carnet Books of bus tickets, from which you can detach the appropriate ticket or tickets for each journey, are sold on Paris buses. Notice that in every day speech the rule that **de** should be used, instead of **un**, after a negative (cf. L7, N26) is often waived.

36 **Non, je n'en ai pas.** *No, I haven't got one.*

37 **Voilà . . . quatre tickets . . . ça fait 4F 40.** *Here you are . . . four tickets . . . that's 4 francs 40 centimes.*

quatre tickets: *four tickets* The French for a railway, underground, cinema or theatre ticket is **billet**. **Ticket** is used for a BUS ticket.

38 **Voulez-vous me dire où je dois descendre, s'il vous plaît?** *Would you tell me where to get off, please?*

a **descendre** means *to get off*, when it refers to buses, trains, cars, etc. (lit. *to go down*). It is a regular **-re** verb (App. IIIA).

39 **(Au porteur qui s'éloigne)** (*To the porter who is going away*)

a **le porteur *qui* s'éloigne**: *the porter* WHO *is going away* This is another example of **qui**: *who*.

b **Il s'éloigne** is a phrase meaning *he is going away, moving away*.

40 Et où est-ce que je peux prendre un billet de quai? *And where can I get a platform ticket?*
prendre un billet de quai: *to get a platform ticket*

PART THREE

41 Je me suis ennuyée;: *I've been bored;*
This is the past tense of **je m'ennuie** (N18 above).

42 Comment? Vous vous êtes ennuyée? *What? You've been bored?* This is another form of the past tense.

The language you have learnt

I went, I have been

Hier,	je *suis allé* j'*ai été*	au cinéma. à Paris. visiter la Tour Eiffel.

While + present participle

Je pense à vous	*en*	visitant Paris. lisant le journal. disant ça. passant devant ce magasin.

En + present participle

Il m'a regardé	*en*	entrant. arrivant. partant.

Only + verb

Je	*ne*	vais prendre	*que*	du potage.
		mange		du poisson.
		bois		de l'eau.
		lis		le journal.
		fume		des cigarettes.
		voyage		par le train.

19 Qui

Vous avez	un oncle	qui	est très sympathique.
	une cousine		habite dans le Midi.
	des amis		partent pour le Canada.
	des boutons de manchettes		ont l'air très beaux.

De instead of des

Elle a	de	longs	cheveux.	
		très	grandes	jambes.
		jeunes	parents.	
		vieux	grands-parents.	

Since + verb

Je m'ennuie	depuis que	Georges est parti.
Je suis heureux		je ne travaille plus.
		j'habite en province.

To be used to . . . , to feel like . . .

| J'ai l'habitude | de | passer mes vacances à la campagne. |
| J'ai envie | | prendre mon petit déjeuner dans ma chambre. |

Missing someone

Georges est parti.	*Il me manque.* Je pense à lui sans arrêt.
Je suis partie sans Georges.	*Je lui manque.* Il me dit qu'il pense à moi sans arrêt.
Depuis que vous êtes parti,	*vous me manquez.* Je pense à vous sans arrêt.

184

J'ai mal à l'estomac. I've got a pain in my stomach.

What happens

PART ONE
Le docteur Soula se présente.: *Doctor Soula introduces himself.*
Doctor Soula practises medicine in Paris. He has a surgery in the
morning and does his rounds in the afternoon. He says medicine has
changed enormously since he qualified.

PART TWO
Dans le cabinet du Docteur Soula: *In Doctor Soula's surgery*
Doctor Soula examines Monsieur Levoisin and decides he has a cold.
He advises him to fast for twenty-four hours because he has stomach-
ache.

PART THREE
Chez le pharmacien: *At the chemist's*
The chemist isn't really interested.

Je veux être malade.: *I want to be ill.*
The patient is afraid of being in good health.

New words in this lesson

à peu près almost, more or less
j'ai mal (à) I have a pain (in)
aigu sharp
s'allonger to lie down
allongez-vous lie down
les amygdales (*f*) tonsils
l'appendice (*m*) appendix
en appliquant by rubbing in, by
  applying
appliquer to rub in, to apply
on attrape le rhume one catches a cold
attraper le rhume to catch a cold
au début at the beginning
au printemps in spring
nous aurons l'occasion de we'll have
  the opportunity (of)
(ils) auront (they) will have

j'ai ausculté I've sounded
ausculter to sound (the chest)
l'automne (*m*) autumn
avoir du mal (à) to have difficulty (in)
avoir l'occasion de to have the chance
  to
avoir le rhume to have a cold
avoir le temps de to have time to
avoir mal à to have a pain (in)
les bactéries (*f*) bacteria
bientôt soon
bizarre strange
la bonne chère good food
la bouche mouth
le cabinet surgery, practice
le cachet capsule
ce . . . -là that . . .

le **chercheur** research worker
la **chirurgie** surgery
la **clinique** clinic, nursing home
le **comprimé** tablet
considéré considered
considérer to consider
la **consultation** consultation
consulter to have a surgery
le **cou** neck
la **cuillerée à café** teaspoonful
le **début** beginning
on a découvert (they) have discovered
découvrir to discover
détendez-vous relax
se **détendre** to relax
la **douleur** pain
la **drogue** drug
du temps de at the time of, when
en automne in autumn
en bonne santé in good health
en clinique in a clinic, in a nursing home
en plein été in the middle of summer
énorme great, enormous
l'**estomac** (m) stomach
être enrhumé to have a cold
(**ils) sont enrhumés** (they) have colds
expliquer to explain
(**elles) ont fait des progrès** (they) have made progress
faire des progrès to make progress, to improve
faire mal to hurt
fatal fatal
la **fièvre** fever, temperature
le **foie** liver
le **fortifiant** tonic
la **gorge** throat
grave serious
guérir to cure
hélas! alas!
l'**hôpital** (m) hospital
il y a peu de temps a short while ago
inconnu unknown
incurable incurable
la **jeunesse** youth
(**le) mal à l'estomac** stomach-ache
(**le) mal au cœur** nausea, sick feeling
le **malade** patient, sick person
le **malade imaginaire** hypochondriac
la **maladie** illness
la **maladie de cœur** heart complaint

mécontent unhappy
le **médecin** doctor
la **médecine** medicine
le **médicament** medicine
se **mettre à la diète** to fast
se **mettre au régime** to go on a diet
des **milliers (de)** (m) thousands (of)
normal normal
la **nourriture** food
l'**opération** (f) operation
l'**ordonnance** (f) prescription
je pars en tournée I do my rounds
partir en tournée to do his (doctor's) rounds
le **pharmacien** chemist
la **pilule** pill
plus . . . plus the more . . . the more
la **pommade** ointment
pour le moment for the time being
prescrire to prescribe
le **printemps** spring
probablement probably
profondément deeply
qu'est-ce qui . . . ? what . . . ?
qu'est-ce qui ne va pas? what's the matter?
le **remède** remedy
se **reposer** to rest
respirer to breathe
respirez breathe
le **rhume** cold
la **saison** season
le **séjour** stay, time spent
se **sentir mal** to feel unwell
vous serez you will be
(**ils) seront** (they) will be
le **sirop** syrup
soigneusement carefully
la **sorte** kind, sort
souffrir (de) to have something wrong (with)
soulager to ease, to relieve pain
(**ils) soulageront** (they) will ease
sucer to suck
vous sucerez you will suck
suivre to follow
le **symptôme** symptom
des **tas de** heaps of, lots of
la **température** temperature
le **traitement** treatment
traiter to treat

trente-trois thirty-three
l'ulcère (*m*) ulcer
l'urgence (*f*) emergency

vingtième twentieth
vingt-quatre twenty-four
le virus virus

Notes

PART ONE

1 Le docteur Soula se présente. *Doctor Soula introduces himself.*

a **le docteur Soula** Before a title such as **docteur, le** is used. Notice that **docteur** is written with a small **d.**

b **Je suis médecin**: *I'm a doctor.*

2 Je consulte tous les matins. *I have a surgery every morning.*
When a doctor says **je consulte tous les matins** he means: *I have a surgery, I see my patients every morning.* But a patient can say: **Je consulte mon médecin quand j'ai mal à l'estomac. Consulte** (followed by the object, **médecin**) then means *consult*: *I consult my doctor* . . .

3 Un jour, vous serez probablement malades. *Probably, one day you will be ill.*
vous serez: *you will be/you'll be* This is the FUTURE tense of **être.** You already know two tenses: 1. the present tense (**je suis**: *I am*; **nous regardons**: *we look* etc.), which is used to describe things and actions which are happening at the moment. 2. The past tense (**j'ai été**: *I was*, **nous avons regardé**: *we have looked at*, etc.), which is used to describe past actions. To describe future actions and things which will happen in the future, we use the future tense, the *I shall/will* tense in English. **Vous serez** is part of this future tense.

4 Je n'en serai pas trop mécontent, parce que, ce jour-là, *I shan't be too unhappy about it, because then* (lit. *that day*),
Je serai: *I shall be, I'll be* is another form of the future tense of **être.** The future tense ending for the **je** form is always **-ai.**

5 j'aurai le plaisir de faire votre connaissance. *I'll have the pleasure of meeting you.*
j'aurai: *I shall have, I'll have* This is the **je** form of the future tense of **avoir**: *to have.*

6 Nous aurons l'occasion de parler un peu. *We'll have the opportunity of talking a little.*
Nous aurons: *we will have/we shall have, we'll have* is the **nous** form of **j'aurai.** The ending for the **nous** form of all verbs in the future tense is **-ons.**

7 Naturellement, le dimanche, je ne donne pas de consultation; j'essaie de me reposer; *On Sundays, of course, I don't have a surgery; I try to rest;*
Je ne donne pas de consultation is the same as je ne consulte pas (N2 above).

8 On a découvert des virus et des bactéries inconnus du temps de ma jeunesse. *They've discovered viruses and bacteriae (which were) unknown when I was young.*
on a découvert Découvrir: *to discover* is conjugated like ouvrir. This, of course, is the past tense.

9 On sait traiter et guérir des maladies considérées comme incurables il y a peu de temps. *They can treat and cure illnesses which were considered incurable a short time ago.* (lit. *One knows how to treat and cure illnesses considered incurable a short time ago.*)

10 Bientôt, les chercheurs trouveront des drogues qui guériront des maladies qui, pour le moment, sont encore souvent fatales. *Soon research workers will find drugs which will cure illnesses which are still often fatal.*

a (ils) trouveront: *they will find, they'll find* This is the ils form of the future tense of a regular -er verb, trouver. To make the ils form of the future tense of all regular -er verbs, simply add -ont to the infinitive: ils regarderont, ils mangeront etc.

b (Ils) guériront: *they will cure* is the ils form of the future tense of the -ir verb guérir. As in the case of -er verbs just add -ont to the infinitive, e.g. ils finiront.

11 J'en examinerai des milliers au cours des années qui viennent! *I'll examine thousands more in the coming years!* (lit. *I'll examine thousands of them, in the course of the years which are coming*).
j'examinerai: *I shall examine* This is the je form of the future tense. Remember the ending of je serai and j'aurai (N4 and 5 above). The je form of all regular verbs is obtained by adding -ai to the infinitive: je trouverai, je guérirai.

12 ceux qui croient souffrir de l'appendice, *those who think there's something wrong with their appendix,*

a (ils) croient: *(they) think, believe* You learnt je crois in L11, N49, and elle croit in L14, N13. These forms belong to the same irregular verb, croire (App. IIIE).

b Souffrir: *to suffer* is an irregular -ir verb, following the same pattern as ouvrir, offrir, découvrir, couvrir (L15).
Souffrir de means *to have something wrong with, to have a pain in.*

13 **d'un ulcère à l'estomac ou d'une maladie de cœur.** *a stomach ulcer or a heart complaint.* Notice that **de** is repeated.

14 **Il y a aussi ceux qui adorent parler de leurs opérations et de leurs séjours à l'hôpital ou en clinique.** *There are also those who love talking about their operations and the time they've spent in hospital or in a nursing home.*

15 **Plus on leur donne de cachets, de comprimés et de pilules, plus ils sont contents.** *The more capsules, tablets and pills you give them, the more pleased they are.*

   ʌ **plus . . .** ʌ **plus:** THE *more . . .* THE *more*

PART TWO

16 **Alors, qu'est-ce qui ne va pas?** *Well, what's troubling you? (what's the matter?)*

17 **Ouvrez la bouche . . . et dites 'Aaaaaah'.** *Open your* (lit. *the*) *mouth and say 'Aaaaaah'.*
   The article **le, la, les** is often used before a part of the body in French, when in English we would use a possessive adjective (*my, your, his,* etc.):
   J'ai mal à *la* gorge.
   Je souffre de *l'*estomac (N12b above).

18 **Respirez profondément . . .** *Breathe deeply . . .*
   Profondément: *deeply* comes from the feminine adjective **profonde**; an acute accent and **-ment** have been added (cf. **énorme, énormément**).

19 **On attrape le rhume en toutes saisons, vous savez: au printemps, en été, en automne et en hiver!** *You can catch a* (lit. *the*) *cold in any season (all seasons), you know. In spring, summer, autumn, and winter!*
   au **printemps,** *en* **été,** *en* **automne,** *en* **hiver.**

20 **Je vous prescris du sirop et des comprimés.** *I'll give you some syrup and tablets.* (lit. *I prescribe for you some syrup and some tablets.*)
   je prescris: *I prescribe* The infinitive of **je prescris** is **prescrire.** It is conjugated like **écrire** (App. IIIE).

21 **Prenez deux cuillerées à café de sirop trois fois par jour . . . et vous sucerez un comprimé toutes les trois heures.** *Take two teaspoonfuls of syrup three times a day . . . You must (will) also suck a tablet every three hours.*

   a **deux cuillerées à café:** lit. *two coffee spoonfuls*
   une cuillère: *a spoon*; **une cuillerée:** *a spoonful* Adding **-ée** to certain French words is like adding **-ful** in English:
   une bouche, une bouchée: *a mouth, a mouthful* (of food).

b **Vous sucerez**: *you will suck* is the **vous** form of the future tense of the verb **sucer**: *to suck*. Like **serez** (N3 above) it ends in **-ez**. The **vous** form of all regular **-er** and **-ir** verbs is made by adding **-ez** to the infinitive: **vous regarderez, vous grossirez**.

22 **Je suis à peu près sûr qu'en appliquant soigneusement cette pommade, vous n'aurez pas besoin de revenir me voir.** *I'm almost sure that if you rub this ointment in carefully, you won't need to come back and see me.*

a **En appliquant**: *by applying* is another example of **en** followed by a present participle (L19, N11). Here it is equivalent to *by* + present participle.

b **Vous aurez** is the **vous** form of the future of **avoir**: *nous* **auro***ns*, *vous* **aur***ez*.

c **revenir me voir**: lit. *to come back* TO *see me*, i.e. *to come back* AND *see me* Remember that expressions such as *to go and see* and *to come and see*, correspond to **aller voir** and **venir voir**; no word for *and* is needed in French.

23 **Vous avez des douleurs d'estomac aiguës ou simplement mal au cœur?** *Have you got sharp stomach pains or do you just feel sick?* **Avoir mal au cœur** means *to feel sick* (and NOT to have pains in the region of the heart). If you want to say you have a bad heart, you have to say **j'ai le cœur malade**, or **j'ai une maladie de cœur**.

24 **C'est votre foie qui est affreux! Vous aimez trop le vin et la bonne chère.** *It's your liver that's awful! You're too fond of wine and good food.*

25 **Mais le plus important, ce sera de vous mettre au régime.** *But the most important thing will be to go on a diet.* **Ce sera**: *it/that will be* **sera** is the **il** form of the future of **être**.

26 **Vous aurez certainement du mal à le suivre au début. Mais il le faut.** *You'll certainly have difficulty in following it at the beginning. But it is essential.*

a **avoir du mal à**: *to have difficulty in* Do not confuse the phrase **avoir *du* mal à**: *to have difficulty in, to find it difficult to*, and **avoir ∧ mal à**: *to have a pain in*: **J'ai du mal à comprendre.**: *I have difficulty in understanding.* **J'ai mal à l'estomac.**: *I have a pain in my stomach.*

b **Suivre**: *to follow*, is an irregular verb. You will learn its main forms later.

c **Il le faut** is a phrase meaning *it is essential, it is necessary, you must.* Remember **il faut dresser les hommes** (L14).

27 **Sans nourriture et sans vin, je me sentirai très mal.** *Without food and wine I shall feel very ill.*

a **sans nourriture et sans vin**   Notice that **sans** must be repeated.

b **Je me sentirai:** *I shall feel* is the **je** form of the future of an **-ir** verb (**se sentir**) (cf. N11 above).

28 **Mais votre estomac et votre foie auront le temps de se reposer** *But your stomach and liver will have time to rest*

a **votre estomac et votre foie**   Notice that **votre** is repeated.

b **Auront** is the **ils** form of the future of **avoir**.

29 **et, en quelques jours, ils seront probablement guéris.** *And, in a few days, they'll probably be cured.*

a **en quelques jours:** *in/within a few days*   Be careful not to confuse *en* **quelques jours** and *dans* **quelques jours. En quelques jours** means *in/within a few days.* **Dans quelques jours,** means *in a few days from now.*

b **ils seront guéris:** *they will be cured*   **Ils seront** is the **ils** form of the future tense of **être**; **guéri** is the past participle of **guérir**.

30 **Vous donnerez cette ordonnance au pharmacien.** *Give this prescription to the chemist.* (lit. *You'll give . . .*)

The language you have learnt.

The endings of the future tense: -er and -ir verbs

Je	poster*ai* finir*ai*	
Tu	poster*as* finir*as*	
Il Elle	poster*a* finir*a*	cette lettre demain.
Nous	poster*ons* finir*ons*	
Vous	poster*ez* finir*ez*	
Ils Elles	poster*ont* finir*ont*	

I shall, will . . .

Demain, je	termine*rai* cette lettre. partir*ai* pour la campagne.

I know how to

Je sais	jouer au football. répondre à ses questions. souffrir sans rien dire.

By + present participle

En	travaill*ant*,	vous réussirez.
	appliqu*ant* cette pommade,	vous guérirez.
	part*ant* tout de suite,	vous arriverez à l'heure.

I was born

Je suis né	en France. il y a vingt ans.

The more . . . the more

Plus	il est fatigué,	*plus*	il travaille.
	il prend des médicaments,		il est malade.
	il mange,		il est content.

In the Spring, etc.

Je voudrais aller en vacances J'aime voyager Il veut visiter Paris	*au printemps.* *en été.* *en automne.* *en hiver.*

In a few days' (etc.) time

Il arrivera Il partira	*dans*	quelques jours. deux heures.

In (within) a few hours, etc.

Il peut faire ce travail	*en*	quelques jours. deux heures.

Projets de vacances   Holiday plans

What happens

PART ONE

C'est Monsieur Louvier qui parle.: *It's Monsieur Louvier speaking.*
The Louviers are going to plan their holiday this evening. Monsieur
Louvier is annoyed because Valérie, whom he doesn't like, will probably
be there too. He knows that his wife will want to stay with her relatives,
who live on a farm, and Georges wants to buy a caravan or go camping.
All Monsieur Louvier wants is peace and comfort.

PART TWO

Entre la poire et le fromage: *Between the pears and the cheese*
Monsieur Louvier doesn't want to spend a month camping; Georges
has had enough of hotels and his mother thinks a month with her
relatives is the best idea; so they cannot agree.
Monsieur Louvier adds to the confusion by suggesting that they go to
Spain.

PART THREE

Comment dit-on . . .?: *How do you say . . .?*
Pierre complains to Jean about a Spaniard who keeps asking questions.
Aimez-vous les gens que vous ne connaissez pas?: *Do you like people
you don't know?*
Monsieur Bernard says that only after getting to know people can one
dislike them.

New words in this lesson

à l'étranger abroad
à mon âge at my age
à mon avis in my opinion
à nouveau again
l'Allemagne (*f*) Germany
aller à l'étranger to go abroad
l'Angleterre (*f*) England
j'annonce I tell, I announce
annoncer to announce
août August

au milieu de amongst, in the middle of
au moins at least
il baragouine he jabbers
baragouiner to jabber
la bête animal
ça n'a aucune importance that doesn't
   matter at all
le calme peace, quiet
camper to camp
le camping camping

21

la caravane caravan
le 'caravaning' caravaning
ce qui what
ce qui compte what counts, the
  important thing
le changement change
comme d'habitude as usual
compliquer to complicate
tu compliques you complicate
davantage more
de mauvaise foi dishonest
de votre côté your way, on your own
le dictionnaire dictionary
vous dormez you sleep
dormir to sleep
nous dormons we sleep
je dors I sleep
doué gifted
en question in question
encombré de packed with
épouser to marry
l'Espagne (f) Spain
l'espagnol (m) Spanish
l'Espagnol/e (m & f) Spaniard
elle étouffe she's suffocating
étouffer to suffocate
être censé to be supposed to
être doué pour to be good at
l'excuse (f) excuse
la ferme farm
fermer l'œil to sleep (a wink)
fort (simple) very (simple)
(il) fréquente (he) sees
fréquenter to see, to associate with
  (someone)
j'irai I'll go
l'Italie (f) Italy
joli fine, nice
la langue language
de mauvaises excuses feeble excuses

le mieux the best
le mieux c'est de the best thing is to
le mot word
organisé organised
organiser to organise
par économie for the sake of economy
le pays country
la poire pear
le Portugal Portugal
nous pourrons we shall be able to
précisément precisely
prétendre to claim
tu prétends you claim
les projets de vacances (m) holiday
  plans
puisque since, as
la question n'est pas là that's not the
  point
réfléchir to consider, to think over
réfléchissons let's consider, let's think
  over
ils ont restauré they've renovated
restaurer to renovate
retourner to go back
elle retournera she'll go back
le rêve dream
sensible sensitive
(elle) sera (she) will be
je serai I'll be
sérieusement seriously
si . . . c'est que if . . . it's because
la solution solution
le souci worry
tel et tel such and such (a)
la tente tent
le terrain de camping camping site
terriblement terribly
le trou hole
vingt et unième twenty-first
le voyage journey

Notes

PART ONE

1 **C'est Monsieur Louvier qui parle.** *It's M. Louvier* (lit. *who is*)
  speaking.
  You have seen several examples of this construction since L16;
  c'est sa femme qui est malade. It is an idiomatic way of emphasising
  a word, here **M. Louvier.**

194

2 **Valérie sera là, elle aussi, je suppose.** *Valérie will be there too,* **21**
I expect.
Valérie sera là: *Valérie will be there.* **Sera** is the **il** and **elle** form of
the future of **être.**

3 **Je dois avouer qu'elle m'agace un peu, cette jeune fille.** *I must admit*
that that girl irritates me a bit.
A more straightforward construction would have been: **cette jeune**
fille m'agace un peu. By replacing **cette jeune fille** by **elle,** and
placing it at the end of the sentence, **cette jeune fille** is emphasized
(cf. L2, N52).

4 **Je serai content quand elle retournera au Canada.** *I'll be glad when*
she goes (lit. *will go*) *back to Canada.*
When the verb which precedes **quand** is in the future, the verb that
follows should also be in the future.

5 **Ils habitent à la campagne, dans une vieille ferme qu'ils ont**
restaurée. *They live in the country, in an old farm that they've*
renovated.
a **Restaurée** is a past participle, and agrees with **ferme** because **que,**
the direct object referring to **la ferme,** is placed before it
(cf. L14, N8b).
b **habiter à:** *to live in*

6 **il a plu tous les jours, du matin jusqu'au soir.** *it rained every day,*
from morning till night.
Il a plu: *it rained* is the past tense of **il pleut:** *it is raining*
(cf. L9, N6).

7 **Je suis sûr que, si nous y retournons, il va encore pleuvoir.** *I'm sure*
that if we go back (*there*), *it will rain again.*
Pleuvoir: *to rain* is the infinitive of **il pleut** and **il a plu** (N6 above).

8 **Le camping et le 'caravaning', comme on dit maintenant, c'est très**
joli, mais moi, j'aime le confort. *Camping and caravaning, as they*
say now, is very fine, but I like comfort.
Le camping et le 'caravaning' The article must be used in front of
these two words, as it was with **sport (le sport)** and **médecine**
(la médecine). See L2, N13.

9 **Camper sur un terrain de camping encombré de voitures, de tentes**
et de caravanes, non merci! *Camping on a camping site packed with*
cars, tents, and caravans, no thank you!
Camper sur un terrain de camping This shows you that an infinitive
can be used as a noun. **Fumer est mauvais pour la santé.:** *Smoking*
is bad for health. In English we use a present participle.

10 Ce qui compte en vacances, c'est le calme et le confort, vous ne trouvez pas? *The important things on holiday are peace and comfort; don't you think so?* (lit. *What counts on holiday . . . don't you find?*)
Ce qui compte When *what* is neither interrogative (*what time is it?*) nor exclamative (*what a pity!*), and is the subject of the verb, **ce qui** is used: *What counts is . . .* : **Ce qui compte, c'est . . .** Notice that **ce** is repeated.

11 Mon rêve, c'est d'aller à l'étranger. N'importe où: en Angleterre, en Italie, en Allemagne, au Portugal, en Espagne . . . *My dream is to go abroad. Anywhere: (to) England, Italy, Germany, Portugal, Spain . . .*
en Angleterre, en Italie, en Allemagne, au Portugal, en Espagne: *in/to England, Italy, Germany, Portugal, Spain*
En is used before feminine names of countries — **l'Angleterre, l'Italie, l'Allemagne** and **l'Espagne** are all feminine; **au** is used before a masculine name of a country, such as **le Portugal. En** and **au** + the name of the *country* mean *at* or *to*, according to the context.

12 Je crois que c'est l'Espagne que je préfère. *I think I prefer Spain.* (lit. *I think it's Spain that I prefer.*)
c'est l'Espagne que je préfère This construction is similar to the one you learnt in N1 above. **Que** may not be omitted. *C'est* M. Louvier *qui* parle; *C'est* l'Espagne *que* je préfère.

13 L'Espagne est un pays que j'aime beaucoup . . . *Spain is a country (that) I like very much . . .*
L'Espagne The article is used before names of countries. In the case of **en Angleterre, en Italie, au Portugal,** etc., it is felt that the article is present in **en** and **au.**

14 Ce que je veux, c'est voyager. *What I want to do is to travel* (lit. *What I want is to travel.*)
ce que: *what* In *what I want, what* is the object of *I want.* (*I* is the subject of *want*). This type of *what* corresponds to **ce que** in French.
What counts is comfort.: **Ce qui compte, c'est le confort.**
  subj. verb   subj. verb
Tell me WHAT YOU WANT.: **Dites-moi ce que vous voulez.**
      obj. subj. verb   obj. subj. verb

15 Vous ne vous occupez de rien. *You don't have to bother about anything.* (lit. *You don't see to anything.*)
cf. **Je m'occupe de la publicité** (L17, N6).

16 **Je n'irai pas passer un mois sur un terrain de camping.** *I will not go and spend a month on a camping site.*
J'irai: *I shall/will go*, is the future of **aller**: *to go*. **Aller,** although an **-er** verb, is very irregular. Its future is not formed like the future of **trouver** or **regarder** (see App. ICa).

17 **Allons, Louise, explique à ton fils que nous voulons au moins pouvoir dormir pendant nos vacances.** *Look, Louise, explain to your son that we want at least to be able to sleep during our holiday.*
Dormir: *to sleep* You will learn more forms of this verb in this lesson.

18 **Moi, ça m'est égal. Je dors n'importe où, n'importe quand et n'importe comment.** *It's all the same to me. I can sleep anywhere, anytime and anyhow.*
Je dors: *I sleep* is the **je** form of the present tense of **dormir**. As you can see, it is an irregular verb (cf. App. IIE).

19 **Oh, ça, ce n'est pas vrai! Quand nous dormons la fenêtre ouverte, tu dis que tu ne peux pas fermer l'œil à cause du bruit!** *Oh,* THAT'S *not true! When we sleep with the window open, you say you can't sleep a wink for the noise!*
a **Ça, c'est vrai** is equivalent to *that's true.* **C'est vrai** would just be *it's true.*
b **Nous dormons**: *we sleep* is the **nous** form of the present tense of **dormir.**
c **la fenêtre ouverte**: *with the window open*

20 **Et quand vous dormez la fenêtre fermée, Maman dit qu'elle étouffe.** *And when you sleep with the window closed, Mother says she's suffocating.*
Vous dormez: *you sleep* is the **vous** form of the present tense of **dormir.**

21 **Puisque vous êtes si sensibles, il y a une solution fort simple**: *Since you are so sensitive, there's a very simple solution:*
a **Puisque**: *Since* in the sense of *as*: **Puisqu'il fait beau, sortons.** Remember that *since* can also be **depuis** or **depuis que** (cf. L4, Note 6 and L19, Note 19).
b **sensible** Careful! **Sensible** means *sensitive.*
c **fort simple**: *very simple* **Fort** is sometimes used for *very*: **c'est fort beau** = **c'est très beau**: *it's very nice.*

22 **allez passer vos vacances de votre côté; et moi, je passerai les**

miennes du mien. *go and spend your holidays your way and I'll spend mine my way.*
Du mien stands for **de mon côté**: *my way.*

23 **Je n'ai aucune envie de passer un mois dans un trou avec des paysans, au milieu des bêtes.** *I've no desire to spend a month in some hole with peasants, surrounded by animals.*
des paysans **Paysan** is used when you are talking about people who live and work in the country (*countrymen*). It is not basically derogatory, but context and tone of voice can make it so; as in this sentence.

24 **Nous sommes censés discuter de nos projets de vacances.** *We're supposed to be discussing our holiday plans.*
être censé: *to be supposed to* **Je suis censé partir maintenant**: *I'm supposed to leave now.* **Être censé** can in fact be replaced by **devoir. Ce soir, un certain M. Houbé doit venir dîner** (L15, N3).

25 **'Comment dit-on tel et tel mot en espagnol?'** '*What's the Spanish for such and such a word?*'
a **Comment dit-on?**: lit. *How does one say?*
b **tel et tel mot**: *such and such a word* The feminine is **telle et telle**: *such and such a.*
c **Comment dit-on en espagnol?** This is a useful phrase. If you want to say: *What's the French for . . .?* you say: **Comment dit-on . . . en français?** (Just insert the English word you want the French for).

26 **Si l'Espagnol en question comprend ta question, c'est qu'il connaît le français.** *If the Spaniard in question understands your question it's because* (lit. *that*) *he knows French.*
il connaît le français Notice the use of the article before names of languages.

27 **Oui; tu ne veux pas aller en Espagne parce que tu prétends que je ne sais pas l'espagnol** *Yes; you don't want to go to Spain because you claim that I don't know Spanish*
a **prétendre (que)** Be careful! **Prétendre** means *to claim.* It is a regular **-re** verb, conjugated like **descendre** (cf. App. IIIA).
b **je sais l'espagnol** Notice that the French for *I know French/Spanish*, etc. is either **Je connais le français/l'espagnol** or **Je sais le français/l'espagnol.** Otherwise **connaître** and **savoir** are not interchangeable. (For **connaître** cf. L4, N12 and for **savoir**, cf. L6, N20).

28 **Réfléchissons davantage à la question.** *Let's think the matter over a bit more.*

a **Réfléchissons** is part of **réfléchir (à)**: *to think* (*over*). It is a regular -**ir** verb, conjugated like **finir** (App. IIA).

b **davantage**: *more*, used with a verb. **Mangez davantage!**: *Eat more!*

29 **Quand nous aurons une idée, nous pourrons en discuter à nouveau.**
When we have an idea, we can talk about it again. (See N4 above).

The language you have learnt

It's raining, it rained

Il pleut *Il a plu*	tous les jours. cet été.

Future forms of vouloir, aller, pouvoir, voir

	voudra	retourner au Canada.
Il	*ira*	au Canada.
	pourra	partir en vacances.
	verra	le gérant de l'hôtel.

Verbs in the future + quand

Je *serai* content		elle *partira* au Canada.
Il *partira*		j'*arriverai*.
Nous *irons* vous voir	*quand*	nous *serons* à Paris.
Ils *dormiront*		nous *arriverons*.
Vous *pourrez* téléphoner		vous *serez* à la gare.

Doing something is . . .

Camper	en été est très agréable.
Trouver	un hôtel pendant les vacances n'est guère facile.
Voyager	en avion est très rapide.
Aller	à l'étranger, c'est mon rêve.

21 Ce qui

Ce qui	compte, c'est le confort. coûte cher ne l'intéresse pas. m'agace, c'est le bruit.

Ce que

Le garçon me sert toujours	*ce que*	j'aime. je préfère.
Les guides ne montrent jamais		je veux voir. j'aimerais pouvoir admirer.

It is . . . who/whom

C'est	M. Louvier	*qui*	parle. arrive.
	Georges	*que*	je cherche. nous voudrions voir.

Whom, which

Voilà	la jeune fille	*que*	Georges fréquente.
	le jeune homme		Valérie fréquente.
	la dame		vous avez vue hier.
	la voiture		je préfère.
	le pays		je veux visiter.

What's the English/Spanish for . . . ?

Comment dit-on	dictionnaire hôtel caravane	en	anglais? espagnol?

Since (because)

Puisque	vous avez faim,	mangez.
	vous êtes fatigué,	ne faites rien.

Vive le sport! Up with sport!

What happens

PART ONE
Paul en a assez.: *Paul's had enough.*
Paul is fed up because he feels he is being neglected by his parents;
and his sister Valérie does nothing but talk about Georges Louvier.
What's more, he's got no money. The boy from the next room tried
to borrow some from him yesterday.

PART TWO
Au café du coin: *At the corner café*
Paul is anxious to see a sports programme on television, and arrives
out of breath. The owner says his television doesn't work very well.
He switches it on but it breaks down. Monsieur Levoisin assures
Paul that he can read the results in the paper.

PART THREE
La retraite est faite pour travailler.: *Retirement is for working.*
Monsieur Bonenfant is going to look for work when he retires.

New words in this lesson

elle a tendance à it tends to
l'adulte (*m & f*) adult
je n'ai aucune chance de I've no
  chance of
l'allemand (*m*) German
allumer le poste to switch on the set
l'anglais (*m*) English
l'appareil (*m*) set
l'argent de poche (*m*) pocket money
assister à to be present at, to witness
avancer to gain, to be fast
avant-hier the day before yesterday
n'avoir aucune chance de to have no
  chance of
avoir tendance à to tend to
ça alors! Oh no!, what next!
ça chauffe it's warming up

ça ne m'étonne pas that doesn't
  surprise me
le café café
célèbre famous
la chaîne channel
chauffer to warm up
comment faire what to do
la coupe cup
courir to run
j'ai couru I ran
la couverture cover
la défaite defeat
devoir to owe
ils doivent they owe
dont of which, of whom
éducatif educational
l'émission (*f*) programme, broadcast

j'en ai par-dessus la tête I'm fed up
en avoir par-dessus la tête to be fed up
en direct live
en fait in fact
en noir et blanc black and white
en panne broken, out of order
je m'ennuie à mourir I'm bored to
  death
s'ennuyer à mourir to be bored to
  death
l'équipe (f) team
essoufflé out of breath
et . . .? what about . . .?
étonnant surprising
étonner to surprise
vous faites you do
je ferai I'll do
vous ferez you'll do
frapper to knock
il est grand temps (de) it's high time
  (to)
laquelle who, whom, which
vous lirez you'll read
le match match
le match de football football match
les mathématiques (f) mathematics
mettre la télé to switch on the
  television
je meurs de soif I'm dying of thirst
la mi-temps half
mourir to die
mourir de soif to die of thirst
opposer to oppose, to confront
parler de la pluie et du beau temps to
  talk about nothing in particular
se passer to happen

elle pense (à) she thinks (of)
penser to think
penser à to think of, about
la personne person
le pire worst
le pire c'est que the worst of it is
la pluie rain
le poste set
qu'est-ce qui se passe? what's
  happening?
je rendrai I'll give back
rendre to give back
le résumé summary
retarder to be slow, to lose
vous retardez you're slow
sauter to jump
sautez skip, jump
sélectionné selected
la speakerine announcer
supporter to stand, to bear
surpris surprised
la télé T.V.
le téléviseur television set
la télévision television
le téléspectateur viewer
le temps weather
le temps passe time flies
le terrain pitch
il tombe en panne it breaks down
tomber en panne to break down
la touche push button
la valeur quality
la victoire victory
vingt-deux twenty-two
vingt-deuxième twenty-second
vive le sport! long live sport!

Notes

PART ONE

1 **Mon père et ma mère sont allés voir un film dont tout le monde
   parle.** *My father and my mother have gone to see a film which
   everyone is talking about.*
   un film dont tout le monde parle: lit. *a film of which everyone is
   talking*

2 **En fait, ils sont partis sans me le dire.** *As a matter of fact, they
   left without telling me.*

a **ils sont partis** Notice the agreement of the past participle, **partis**, with the subject, **ils.**

b **sans me le dire**: lit. *without telling me it*

3 **Valérie, elle, me parle de la pluie et du beau temps,** *Valérie talks to me about nothing in particular*,
parler de la pluie et du beau temps: lit. *to talk about the rain and the fine weather*, an idiomatic expression meaning *to talk about nothing in particular*. **Temps** is used here in the sense of *weather*.

4 **et d'une personne à laquelle elle pense sans arrêt.** *and someone she thinks about all the time.* (lit. *and about a person of whom she thinks without stopping.*)
à laquelle elle pense: *of whom she thinks* **Penser** (**à**) is *to think* (*of*). **Laquelle** is the feminine of **lequel** (L12, N40).

5 **Vous avez deviné que la personne dont elle me parle, c'est Georges Louvier.** *You've guessed that the person whom she talks to me about, is Georges Louvier.*
dont cf. N1 above.

6 **C'est la seule chose dont je suis sûr!** *It's the only thing I'm sure of!* (lit. *It's the only thing of which I am sure.*)

7 **Je ne sais pas comment faire pour me procurer l'argent dont j'ai besoin.** *I don't know what to do to get the money I need.*

a **comment faire**: *what to do, what's to be done* In L11 you learnt a similar phrase: **Que faire?**: *What shall I do?*

b **pour me procurer**: *to get* (lit. *to obtain for myself*) Again **procurer** suggests there is difficulty in getting something (L18, N2b).

c **l'argent dont j'ai besoin**: lit. *the money of which I have need* Remember the phrase **avoir besoin** takes **de** (as the English phrase *to be in need* takes *of*).

8 **Quand je pense que le garçon dont la chambre est voisine de la mienne** *When I think that the boy whose room is next to mine*
le garçon dont la chambre: lit. *the boy of whom the room* Here **dont** is equivalent to *whose*. Be careful not to leave out the article **la** before **chambre.**

9 **est venu hier frapper à ma porte pour m'emprunter de l'argent!** *came and knocked on my door yesterday to borrow some money from me!*

a **(il) est venu**: (*he*) *came*, (*he*) *has come* **Venu** is the past participle of the irregular verb **venir.** As you can see, it is one of the verbs which form their past tense with **être** (App. IID).

b **pour emprunter de l'argent:** lit. *in order to borrow some money*
You learnt **emprunter** in L18, N31. Notice the construction:
emprunter quelque chose *à* **quelqu'un:** *to borrow something* FROM
someone.

10 **'Je te le rendrai quand mes parents m'auront donné l'argent de
poche qu'ils me doivent,' m'a-t-il dit.** *'I'll give it back to you when
my parents have given me the pocket money they owe me,' he said.*

a **je te le rendrai:** *I shall give it back to you* This is the **je** form of
the future tense of **rendre,** an **-re** verb. The endings you learnt
for the future of an **-er** verb are also used with regular **-re** verbs.
They are added to the infinitive of the **-re** verb after removing
the final **e:**
infinitive: **rendre**
future: **je rendrai.**

b **quand ils m'auront donné** Just as we had the future before and after
quand in the sentence: **Je ser*ai* content quand elle retourner*a*,** so we
have here: **Je te le rendr*ai* quand ils m'aur*ont* donné de l'argent.**
In fact, the second future is a future perfect, meaning literally,
they will have given.

11 **Moi, mes parents ne me donnent pas d'argent de poche régulièrement.**
MY *parents don't give* ME *pocket money regularly.*

12 **Et ils se sauvent** . . . *And off they go* . . .

PART TWO

13 **J'ai couru pour être à l'heure.** *I ran so that I'd be on time.* (lit. *I
ran in order to be on time.*)
J'ai couru: *I ran, I have run* is the perfect of a new irregular verb.
You will learn the main parts of it in this lesson.

14 **J'ai eu peur de manquer Sports-Dimanche.** *I was afraid of missing
Sports-Dimanche.*

a **j'ai eu peur de:** *I was afraid of* Remember **avoir peur de:** *to be
afraid of* (L6, N38). **Eu** is the past participle of **avoir.**

b **Sports-Dimanche** is a television sports programme screened on
Sundays.

15 **Quelle heure avez-vous à votre montre?** *What time is it by your
watch?/What time do you make it?*

16 **Vous retardez.** *You're slow.*
Retarder means *to be slow.* You can use the same verb for **ma
montre retarde:** *my watch is slow* or **je retarde:** *I am slow*; as you
can in English.

17 **Il y a un Télé 7 Jours sur la table là-bas. Allez le chercher.** *There is a Télé 7 Jours on the table over there. Go and* (lit. *to*) *get it.* **Télé 7 Jours** is a kind of Radio and TV Times, giving details of television programmes. It is not published by the state-run television service but by a publishing firm.

18 **C'est le bon numéro?** *Is it the current* (lit. *right*) *issue?* **Le numéro** means *the issue,* when it refers to a newspaper, a magazine etc. Remember **la bonne date**: *the right date* (L7, N11b).

19 **Du deux au huit août.** *August the second to the eighth.* **du deux au huit août**: lit. *from the two to the eight August* Notice again that cardinal numbers (**deux, huit**) are used in dates, not ordinal numbers as in English (*second, eighth*). Remember that there is an exception: **le premier**: *the first* (**le premier août**).

20 **Nous vous invitons maintenant à assister au match de football qui va opposer le Red Star aux Girondins,** *We invite you now to be present at the football match between The Red Star and the Girondins,*
a **assister à** Careful! **Assister à** means *to be present* (*at*), *to attend.*
b **qui va opposer le Red Star aux Girondins**: *which is between the Red Star and the Girondins*
opposer: lit. *to oppose, to set against*

21 **en direct du Parc des Princes.** *live from the Parc des Princes.* **Le Parc des Princes** is a well-known Paris sports ground.

22 **Allons-nous assister à la victoire ou à la défaite de la célèbre équipe de Bordeaux, dont tout le monde connaît la valeur?** *Are we going to witness the victory or the defeat of the famous team from Bordeaux, whose high standard is known by everybody?*
a **la célèbre équipe de Bordeaux**: *the famous Bordeaux team* (the Girondins).
b **dont tout le monde connaît la valeur**: lit. *whose quality everybody knows* Here again, **dont** equals *whose.*

23 **Le téléviseur**: *The television set.* This is the more technical term for a TV set, the one used in catalogues. **Poste** or **appareil de télévision** are more colloquial.

24 **Et le match?** *What about the match?* **Et** corresponds here to *what about . . . ?*

25 **Bah, vous lirez les résultats dans le journal de demain.** *Oh, you'll read the results in tomorrow's paper.* **Vous lirez**: *you will read* is the future of **lire**: *to read* (App. IIIE).

26 **je meurs de soif.** *I'm dying of thirst.*

Je meurs: *I am dying, I die* is the **je** form of the present tense of **mourir** (App. IIE).

PART THREE

27 **Ça fait quarante ans que je ne fais rien.** *I've been doing nothing for forty years.*

Ça fait . . . que je + verb in the present is another way of saying either **je** + verb in the present **depuis . . .** (L4, N6), or **Il y a . . . que je** + verb in the present.

Je suis **chauffeur de taxi** *depuis* **longtemps.**

Il y a **longtemps** *que je suis* **chauffeur de taxi.**

Ça fait **longtemps** *que je suis* **chauffeur de taxi.**

The language you have learnt

Future forms of -re verbs

J'attend*rai* Tu attend*ras*, etc.	jusqu'à demain. son arrivée.
Je prend*rai* Tu prend*ras*, etc.	ses affaires. un bain.
Je rend*rai* Tu rend*ras*, etc.	ce qu'il a acheté. sa clef à la réception.

About whom, of which

C'est	une personne un comédien	*dont*	tout le monde parle. je ne veux pas parler.
	un film un restaurant		

Whose, of which

Le professeur	*dont*	je connais la sœur,	est très sympathique.
La chambre		la porte est ouverte,	est très confortable.

Quand with future tenses

Je serai content		elle sera partie.
Il partira	*quand*	je serai arrivé.
Je voyagerai beaucoup		j'aurai pris ma retraite.

Your clock is fast, slow

Allons, il n'est pas encore midi!	Cette pendule	*avance.*
Vite, c'est l'heure de partir!	Cette pendule	*retarde.*

Perhaps

Peut-être qu'	il va partir. elle est déjà arrivée. il a raison.

I'm going

J'ai fini mon travail. Il est tard.	*Je m'en vaiș.* *Je pars.*

Dont with avoir besoin, envie, peur de

Mon mari va m'acheter	la robe le manteau	*dont*	*j'ai besoin* *j'ai envie.*
C'est	un homme une femme		*j'ai peur.*

Ce dont . . . c'est de

Ce dont	je suis sûr, je suis certain, j'ai peur,	*c'est de* ne pas aimer habiter en province.

Leçon vingt-trois   *Lesson twenty-three*
Vingt-troisième leçon   *Twenty-third lesson*

Le dernier film de Jacques Duhamel

Jacques Duhamel's latest film

What happens

PART ONE

Les Delon vont au cinéma.: *The Delons go to the cinema.*
Monsieur and Madame Delon are getting ready to go to the cinema,
when Monsieur Levoisin phones. Madame Delon is looking for her
hairbrush, which she accuses her husband of having taken. He tells her
she loses everything — but he has to admit he has mislaid his belt.

PART TWO

Dans la chambre des Delon: *In the Delons' room*
Monsieur Delon helps his wife to fasten her bracelet.

Au cinéma Rex: *At the Rex cinema*
Outside the cinema, they read the poster. They go in and make their
way to two seats in the third row.

PART THREE

À la sortie du cinéma: *Leaving the cinema*
Monsieur and Madame Delon discuss the film. Madame Delon reads
a summary of it on a poster.

New words in this lesson

à la sortie de on the way out of
à quoi sert? what's (something) for?
abandonné deserted, abandoned
abandonner to desert, to abandon
accroché caught, hooked
accrocher to catch, to hook
les actualités (*f*) **de la semaine**
  newsreel, news of the week
l'affiche (*f*) poster
affiché posted up
afficher to post up
l'amour (*m*) love
l'ange (*m*) angel
après Jésus-Christ A.D.
s'arranger to be settled, to be all right

avant Jésus-Christ B.C.
le bord edge
le bracelet bracelet
le bras arm
tu brossais you were brushing
la brosse brush
la brosse à cheveux hairbrush
brosser to brush
ça revient au même it's the same thing
ça suffit! that's enough!
ça tient it's fast, it'll hold
c'est trop fort it's too bad, it's too
  much
la ceinture belt
la chaîne chain

la chaînette de sûreté safety chain
le chat cat
la colère anger
je comparais I was comparing
comparer to compare
complètement completely
la corbeille à papier wastepaper basket
le coup de téléphone telephone call
court short
de court métrage short (footage)
la cravate tie
le crime crime
le crochet hook
de quoi (boire) enough (to buy a drink)
décroche-le! unhook it!
décrocher to unhook
nous dérangeons we're disturbing
déranger to disturb
dernier latest
le dessin animé cartoon
la direction management
la discussion argument, discussion
le dossier back
droit straight
elles durent they last
durer to last
elle égorge she cuts the throats
égorger to cut (someone's) throat
(être) en train de (to be) in the middle of
s'enfuir to flee, to run away
(elle) s'enfuit (she) flees, she runs away
l'entracte (m) interval
j'étais I was
le far west wild west
être en train de to be in the middle of doing something
la fermeture clasp
finir par to end up by
finir par s'arranger to turn out all right
le foulard scarf
il gênait it was bothering
gêner to bother, to get in the way
le grand film main film
l'héroïne (f) heroine
le héros hero
(elle) a inspiré (it) inspired
inspirer to inspire

invraisemblable unbelievable
la légende legend
lorsque when
les lunettes (f) spectacles
malin mischievous
la merveille wonder
la meurtrière murderess
on verra bien we'll soon see
par amour for love, out of love,
par dépit from, for spite, out of spite
par vengeance for revenge, out of revenge
le Pays des Merveilles Wonderland
le peigne comb
pendant que while
permanent continuous
elle poignarde she stabs
poignarder to stab
porter plainte à to complain to
j'ai posé I put
poser to put
possible possible
le pourboire tip
pratique practical
prendre quelque chose to have a drink
la querelle quarrel
le rang row
nous avons ri we laughed
nous rions we laugh
rire to laugh
rire de to laugh at, about
je ris I laugh
(elle) rit (she) laughs
la seule the only one
le siège seat
(il) a sonné (it) rang
sonner to ring
la sortie way out
suffisant sufficient, enough
se taire to be quiet
taisez-vous! be quiet!
la tasse cup
tiens hold
tenir to hold
tenir droit to hold straight
il est tombé it fell
tomber to fall
vingt-troisième twenty-third
voir clair to see clearly
je ne vois pas bien clair I can't see very well
le western western, cowboy film

23 Notes

1 J'étais en train de choisir une cravate pour sortir avec ma femme.
I was in the middle of choosing a tie, so that I could go out with my wife.

a **j'étais**: *I was* This is part of another verb tense, called the IMPERFECT tense. It is a past tense. You already know one past tense, the PERFECT. The perfect of **choisir** is, as you know, **j'ai choisi.** Broadly speaking, the PERFECT tense is used to REPORT an action which took place at a SPECIFIC time. **Hier je *suis allé* dans un grand magasin et j'*ai choisi* une cravate.**: *Yesterday I WENT to a large store and a CHOSE a tie.* The IMPERFECT, this new tense, DESCRIBES an action which was going on at some UNSPECIFIED time in the past. We are not told — because it does not matter in the context — when the action began and/or when it ended. It is often equivalent to the verbal phrase *I/you/he* etc., *was/were . . . ing.* In fact, you can assume that when you mean to say *I was . . . ing, I was in the middle of . . . ing,* you must use the imperfect. *I AM in the middle of . . .* is **je *suis* en train de . . .** so *I WAS in the middle of . . .* is **j'*étais* en train de . . .** Étais comes from **être** and is the je form of this new past tense. When M. Delon says: **j'*étais* en train de choisir une cravate** he is DESCRIBING what he WAS DOING at some UNSPECIFIED time.

b **En train de . . .** *in the middle of . . .* is followed by a verb in the infinitive.

2 Je lui parlais du film que nous allons voir lorsque le téléphone a sonné. *I was talking to her about the film we're going to see when the telephone rang.*

a **je parlais**: *I was talking* This is part of the imperfect tense of **parler.** M. Delon tells us what he WAS DOING when the phone rang: hence the imperfect. Looking at the ending of **j'ét*ais*** and **parl*ais*** you can deduce that the je form of the imperfect always ends in **-ais.**

b **lorsque** You already know **quand**: *when.* **Lorsque** also means *when.*

c **(Il) a sonné** is from **sonner**: *to ring* Here the other past tense — the perfect — must be used because M. Delon is REPORTING a particular event.

3 C'est moi qui ai répondu. *I answered.* (lit. *It is I who answered.*)
moi qui ai répondu **ai** répondu because *qui* refers to **moi.**

4 Vous en avez de la chance!' *You're lucky!'*

You learnt **elle a de la chance** in L9. By adding **en** to the phrase, **de la chance** is emphasized.

5 **Vous parliez de moi?'** *Were you talking about me?'*
   vous parl*iez***:** *you* WERE *talk*ING This, too, is the imperfect tense.
   Notice that the ending for the **vous** form of the imperfect is **-iez**.

6 **'Parce que tu parlais d'anges.'** *'Because you were talking about angles.'*
   tu parlais: *you were talking* The ending for the **tu** form of the imperfect is **-ais**; the same as the **je** form (N2a above).

7 **'Sa femme et lui pensaient nous inviter ce soir et je lui ai dit que nous sortons.'** *'He and his wife were thinking of inviting us out this evening, and I told him that we are going out.'*
a **sa femme et lui** Notice the word order.
b **(ils) pensaient**: *(they) were thinking* The ending of the **ils** form of the imperfect tense is always **-aient**.

8 **Quelques instants plus tard, Yvonne cherchait sa brosse à cheveux.** *A few minutes later, Yvonne was looking for her hairbrush.*
   (elle) cherchait: *(she) was looking for* Notice the **-ait** ending of the **il** and **elle** form of the imperfect.

9 **Et je me rappelle que tu brossais ta perruque un peu avant le coup de téléphone de M. Levoisin.'** *And I remember that you were brushing your wig a little while before M. Levoisin's phone call.'*
   Tu brossais is again an imperfect: it means *you were brushing*.

10 **Pendant que tu parlais à M. Levoisin,** *While you were talking to M. Levoisin,*
   pendant que: *while* You learnt **pendant**: *during* used in front of a noun in L10:
   Pendant les vacances, je travaille avec Guy.
   Pendant que is *while* and introduces a sentence with a verb:
   Pendant que je travaille, Marie-Claire ne fait rien.

11 **je comparais la couleur de mon rouge à lèvres et celle de mon foulard.** *I was comparing the colour of my lipstick and the colour of my scarf.*
   je comparais is the imperfect of **comparer**. Mme Delon DESCRIBES what she WAS DOING while her husband WAS TALKING to M. Levoisin. So the imperfect is used twice.

12 **Malheureusement, pendant que nous discutions,** *Unfortunately, while we were arguing,*
   nous discutions *we were arguing* The **nous** form of the imperfect tense always ends in **-ions**.

13 Et nous avons ri tous les deux. *And we both laughed.*
nous avons ri: *we laughed* **Ri**: *laughed* is the past participle of a
verb you will learn in some detail in this lesson.

14 Mais elles ne durent pas, et nous rions de nos colères. *But they don't
last, and we laugh about our tempers.*
nous rions: *we laugh* **Nous avons ri** is the **nous** form of the perfect
tense; **nous rions** is the **nous** form of the present tense.

15 D'habitude, c'est Yvonne qui rit la première. *Usually it's Yvonne who
laughs first.*
(elle) rit la première: *(she) laughs first* Notice the **il/elle** form: **rit**.
Do not omit **la**.
He went ∧ *first.*: **Il est parti** *le* **premier.**
He went ∧ *last.*: **Il est parti** *le* **dernier.**
She went ∧ *last.*: **Elle est partie** *la* **dernière.**

16 Alors, moi aussi, je ris . . . et tout finit par s'arranger. *Then I laugh
too, and everything turns out all right.*
a **je ris**: *I laugh* You now know, **je ris, tu ris, il rit, nous rions, vous
riez.** All these belong to the present tense of **rire.**
b **tout finit par s'arranger**: *everything turns out all right* **Finir par**
conveys the same idea as *eventually.* **J'ai fini par comprendre**:
Eventually I understood.

PART TWO
**17 Je l'ai posé au bord de la table et il est tombé dans la corbeille à
papier.** *I put it on the edge of the table and it fell into the waste
paper basket.*
il est tombé **Tomber** means *to fall.* Like **arriver, tomber** forms its
past tenses with **être,** not with **avoir.**

18 Oui, mais ne bouge pas . . . tiens ton bras droit. *Yes, but don't
move . . . hold your arm straight.*
tiens: *hold,* a familiar command. This is from the verb **tenir,** which
has the same forms as **venir.** We came across the same word,
tenir, in L19, N7a, in the phrase **tenir parole.** (App. IID).

19 À quoi sert cette petite chaîne? *What is this little chain for?*
à quoi sert . . . ?: *what is . . . for?* FOR *what purpose is . . . ?*

20 Cette petite chaîne, c'est pour quoi faire? *What is this little chain
supposed to do?*
C'est pour quoi faire?: *What is it for?* *What* used in connection
with *for* is **quoi.** As you saw in N19 above, **quoi** is also used in
connection with **à:**
À *quoi* **sert cette chaîne?**: WHAT *is this chain* FOR?

21 **Oui, oui, ça tient.** *Yes, it holds.*
    (Il) tient: *it holds* is the **il** form of **tenir** (cf. **il vient**).

22 **Qu'est-ce qu'il y a au programme?** *What's on the programme?*

23 **On verra bien.** *We'll soon see.* (lit. *We'll see well.*)
    on verra: lit. *we shall see, one will see*   This is a form of the future
    tense of **voir** (cf. App. IVB).

24 **Vous ne pouvez pas vous taire?** *Can't you be quiet?*
    Try to learn the whole sentence by heart. We shall explain
    vous taire later in the course.

25 **Même pas de quoi boire une tasse de café!** *Not even enough to get a*
    cup of coffee!
    pas de quoi + infinitive: *not enough to* + infinitive

26 **Nous dérangeons tout le monde.** *We are disturbing everyone.*
    Nous dérangeons: *we are disturbing* is from the verb **déranger.**
    -Er verbs ending in **-ger** end in **-eons** in the **nous** form, e.g. **nous**
    mangeons: *we eat* (App. IBc).

27 **Ça, vous pouvez le dire!** *You can say that again!* (cf. App. IBc)
    lit. *That you can say.*

PART THREE

28 **'La légende de Médée a inspiré une tragédie à Euripide près de**
    cinq siècles avant Jésus-Christ, '*The legend of Medea inspired*
    Euripides to write a tragedy almost 500 years B.C., (lit. . . .
    inspired a tragedy to Euripides)
    avant Jésus-Christ: *B.C.* (lit. *before Jesus Christ*)

29 **et une autre à Sénèque, pendant le premier siècle après Jésus-Christ.**
    and Seneca to write another during the first century A.D.
    après Jésus-Christ: *A.D.* (lit. *after Jesus Christ*)

30 **On sait comment Médée s'enfuit avec Jason et comment, Jason**
    l'ayant abandonnée, elle égorge ses enfants.' *Everyone knows how*
    Medea runs away with Jason and, how, when Jason has deserted
    her, she cuts her children's throats.'
 a **(Elle) s'enfuit:** (*she*) *runs away*, is part of an irregular **-ir** verb
    (App. IIE).
 b **Jason, l'ayant abandonnée:** lit. *Jason having abandoned her:*
    L'ayant abandonné is the equivalent of *having abandoned.* **Ayant:**
    having, is the present participle of **avoir.**

23 The language you have learnt

You're lucky

Vous en avez de la chance!	Vous avez gagné à la loterie! Vous avez de longues vacances!

Hooking and unhooking

Votre manteau	*est accroché*	à la porte.	*Décrochez-le!*
Votre serviette	*est accrochée*	au mur.	*Décrochez-la!*

The imperfect tense

J'*étais en train de*	travaill*er* parl*er*	quand il est parti.
Je	travaill*ais* parl*ais*	quand il est entré.

While with the imperfect

Je	travaill*ais* bavard*ais*	*pendant qu'*	il parl*ait*. il téléphon*ait*.

The endings of the imperfect

Je   discut*ais*.
Tu   discut*ais*.
Il
Elle } discut*ait*.
Nous discut*ions*.
Vous discut*iez*.
Ils
Elles } discut*aient*.

Position of adverbs

Il vient Il téléphone		*souvent.* *quelquefois.* *rarement.*	
Il	est	*souvent* *quelquefois*	venu.
	a	*rarement*	téléphoné.

Il l'a tuée	par	amour. dépit. vengeance.

Monsieur Houbé est de   Monsieur Houbé on a
     sortie à Paris.   trip to Paris.

What happens

PART ONE

Quand j'étais jeune . . . : *When I was young . . .*
Luc Houbé tells us about how he used to behave when he was on
a business trip to Paris, when he was younger. He used to economise
as much as possible, to keep his expenses low. Now he spends more,
and allows himself more time for relaxation and amusement.

PART TWO

Luc Houbé et Marie-Claire Martin hèlent un taxi. : *Luc Houbé and
Marie-Claire Martin hail a táxi.*
Luc wants to take a taxi, Marie-Claire says they should go by
underground. Luc doesn't like the underground so they take a taxi.

À l'intérieur du Petit Palais: *Inside the Petit Palais*
They buy tickets for an exhibition.

À l'exposition Cézanne: *At the Cézanne exhibition*
Luc is a little disturbed by the self-portrait of Cézanne.

PART THREE

Exposition d'art celte: *Exhibition of Celtic art*
Marie-Claire is fascinated by all she sees, and envies the
archaeologists who make such discoveries.

New words in this lesson

à l'air looking
à l'intérieur de inside
à pied on foot
à proximité de near to, close to
à travers through
elle a lieu (à) it is taking place (at),
   it is on (at)
l'antiquité (*f*) antiquity
l'arc-en-ciel (*m*) rainbow
l'archéologue (*m*) archaeologist
l'art (*m*) art

l'assiette (*f*) plate
au compteur on the meter
austère austere, severe
avoir à to have to
avoir lieu (à) to take place (at)
le bâtiment building
le bijou jewel
le billet (bank) note
le bronze bronze
le caoutchouc rubber
celte celtic

le **cerf** reindeer
le **chef-d'œuvre** masterpiece
chic smart, fashionable
le **cil** eyelash
le **compteur** meter
consciencieusement conscientiously
le **couteau** knife
la **cuillère** spoon
je **débutais** I was starting out
débuter to start out, to start one's career
la **découverte** discovery
la **démarche** step
je me **déplaçais** I went about
se **déplacer** to go about (to go from place to place)
je **descendais (dans)** I stayed (at)
descendre dans to stay at
direct direct
élevé large, high
émouvant moving
en autobus by bus
en caoutchouc rubber
en déplacement travelling
entier whole
envier to envy, to be envious of
vous enviez you envy, you are envious of
l'**escalier roulant** (*m*) escalator
être de sortie to be on a trip
faire des folies to be rash
fameux famous
la **figure** face
la **flèche** arrow
(**elles**) se **fondent** (they) melt
se **fondre** to melt
la **fourchette** fork
les **frais** (*m*) expenses
le **front** forehead
la **galerie** gallery
le **gardien de service** keeper on duty
grec(que) Greek
le **gros billet** large note
(**ils**) **hèlent** (they) hail, call
héler to hail, call
jamais never
(**le**) **jaune** yellow
la **joue** cheek
là-dedans inside, in there
latin latin
lui-même himself
le **manche** handle

le **mélange** mixture
le **métro** metro
le **miroir** mirror
le **musée** museum
nécessaire necessary
le **nez** nose
ni . . . nor . . .
la **note de frais** expenses (bill)
l'**œuvre** (*f*) work
on n'a pas idée de . . . fancy . . .
l'**orange** (*m*) orange
l'**os** (*m*) bone
des **ossements** (*m*) bones, old bones
l'**outil** (*m*) tool
le **parquet ciré** polished floor
la **peau** skin
peindre to paint
pendant une journée entière for a whole day
se **permettre (de)** to allow oneself (to), to afford (to)
la **petite monnaie** change
la **pièce de monnaie** coin
le **pneu** tyre
poli polished
le **portillon automatique** automatic gate
pour cent per cent
le **quai** bank (of river)
le **quartier** quarter
qu'est-ce que c'est? what is it?
la **rame (de métro)** train
je **regrette** I'm sorry
regretter to be sorry
remboursé paid back, reimbursed
rembourser to pay back, to reimburse
sculpté carved, sculpted
sculpter to carve, to sculpt
soupçonneux suspicious
la **station de métro** metro station
le **tableau** picture
tout juste just
le **tunnel** tunnel
la **vallée** valley
le **vase** vase
le **verre** glass
vous verrez you will see
vingt-quatrième twenty-fourth
le **violet** violet
la **vitrine** show-case
la **voiture** tube, train, carriage
vous voulez rire! you're joking!
les **yeux** (*m*) eyes

24 Notes

PART ONE

1 Quand j'étais jeune ... *When I was young ...*
We said in L23, N1a, that the imperfect is the past tense used
to DESCRIBE a past action which happened at some unspecified
time. The same tense is also used to refer to a STATE OF AFFAIRS
existing at an unspecified time in the past.

**2 Il y a quelques années, j'avais l'habitude de venir à Paris tous
les mois.** *A few years ago, I used to come to Paris every month.*
j'avais l'habitude de: lit. *I had the habit of*
J'avais is an imperfect form of **avoir**. When you want to DESCRIBE
what you USED TO DO in the past, or what USED TO BE, you use
the imperfect.

3 J'arrivais de Bordeaux le matin au premier train. *I used to come
from Bordeaux in the morning on the first train.*
Again **j'arrivais** describes what Luc Houbé USED TO do a few
years ago.

4 Je prenais le métro; j'allais à mon hôtel. *I used to take the tube and
go to my hotel.*
je prenais ... j'allais: *I used to* (or *I would*) *take ... I used to*
(*I would*) *go.*

5 Je descends dans un hôtel beaucoup plus chic. *I stay in a much
more fashionable hotel.*
Chic: *fashionable, smart* is masculine here. This adjective is unusual
because it does not take an **e** in the feminine:
Un homme chic, une femme chic.
It does take an **s** in the masculine and feminine plural:
des hommes chics, des femmes chics.

6 Il y a longtemps que je ne suis allé visiter un musée. *I haven't been
to visit a museum for a long time.*
Il y a longtemps que je *ne* suis allé literally means *there is (a)
long time that I have not gone.* Notice that French omits the **pas**
here. There are a number of occasions when such omission of
pas can occur.

7 Elle a lieu au Petit Palais. *It's on* (lit. *it has place*) *at the Petit Palais.*
Le Petit Palais is a well-known building in Paris near the Seine.

**8 les longues galeries aux parquets cirés, les salles remplies d'objets
de l'antiquité grecque et latine ...** *the long galleries with polished
floors, the rooms full·of Greek and Roman antiquities ...*

218

les galeries *aux* parquets cirés: *the galleries with polished floors* **24**
This construction with **aux** corresponds to an English construction
with *with*.

9 **Luc Houbé et Marie-Claire Martin hèlent un taxi.** *Luc Houbé and
   Marie-Claire Martin hail a taxi.*
   héler: *to hail* As in **préférer** (L2) the é of **héler** is replaced by **è**
   in front of an ending with silent e: **je hèle, je hélerai,** etc.

10 **Je déteste le métro, les escaliers roulants, les portillons
   automatiques, le bruit des rames dans les tunnels . . .** *I hate the
   underground, the escalators, the automatic gates, the noise of the
   trains in the tunnels . . .*
 a **les portillons automatiques**: *the automatic gates* These gates close
   automatically when a train approaches, and shut off access to the
   platform while the train is in the station.
 b **une rame (de. métro)**: *a (tube) train* **Rame** and not **train** is used for
   underground trains.

11 **D'ailleurs, en voilà un.** *Here's one now.* (lit. *Besides, here's one
   of them*) (cf. L17, N23).
   J'ai acheté cinq pellicules.
   J'en ai acheté *cinq*.
   Voilà cinq pellicules.
   ***En* voilà *cinq*.**

12 **C'est le bâtiment aux grandes fenêtres?** *Is it the building with large
   windows?* See N8 above.
   ***aux* grandes fenêtres**: WITH *large windows*

13 **Alors, je vous dois combien?** *Right, how much do I owe you?*
   In lesson 8, you learnt how to say *how much is it?*: **C'est combien?**
   (N39). In lesson 9, N25 you learnt another way of asking the same
   question, **ça fait combien?** You can also use **devoir** to ask how much
   you owe:
   Je vous dois combien?: lit. *I owe you how much?*
   This is still more colloquial than **combien est-ce que je vous dois?**
   (for **combien est-ce que . . . ?** see L8, N19).

14 **Combien voulez-vous?** *How much do you want?*
   This is another possible way of asking *how much?* Marie-Claire
   could have used the more colloquial construction: **Combien
   est-ce que vous voulez?**

15   Les billets sont à combien? *How much are the tickets?*
This is yet another way of asking the price:
Les billets *sont à combien*?
Ce foulard *est à combien*? Compare this with the construction
you saw in L8, N39.
L'entrée, c'est combien?
Les billets, c'est combien?

16   Je regrette, je n'ai que de gros billets. *I'm sorry, I haven't got*
anything smaller. (lit. *I've only got large notes.*)
(le) billet: bank note   As well as meaning *ticket*, **billet** can mean
a *bank note*. **Un gros billet**, lit. *a big note*, a note of high
denomination.

17   L'exposition Cézanne, c'est où? *Where's the Cézanne exhibition?*
This is a colloquial way of asking where something is. This
phrase is obviously constructed on the same pattern as the phrase
L'entrée, *c'est combien*? (cf. L8, N39 and N15 above).

18   Vous n'avez qu'à suivre les flèches. *Just follow the arrows.* (lit.
You have only to follow the arrows.)
vous *n'avez qu'*à   Remember ne . . . que is equivalent to *only*
(L19, N26). **Vous n'avez qu'à** is a useful idiomatic phrase equivalent
to *you just*, or *why don't you, let him/her . . .*
Vous êtes fatigué? Vous *n'avez qu'*à vous reposer. It can of course
also be used with the **je/tu/il** etc. forms.

19   La fameuse Montagne Sainte-Victoire! C'est un chef-d'œuvre!
The famous Sainte-Victoire Mountain! It's a masterpiece!
a   **La Montagne Sainte-Victoire** is a mountain near Aix-en-Provence,
shown in several of Cézanne's paintings.
b   **un chef-d'œuvre**: *a masterpiece*   The plural is **des chefs-d'œuvre.**
As in **des hors-d'œuvre** (L4, N19), **œuvre** does not take an **s** in
the plural.
c   **J'adore la Provence. Pas vous?** *I love Provence, don't you?*
la Provence is an area in South East France.

20   J'y allais en vacances quand j'étais petit. *I used to go there on*
holiday when I was little.
j'y allais: *I used to go there*   Notice the imperfect form of **aller.**

21   Cet homme aux yeux noirs et à l'air soupçonneux, c'est qui?
Who's that man with dark eyes and with a suspicious look?
cet homme aux yeux noirs: *that man with black eyes* (*that black-*
eyed man)   See N8, and 12 above.

22 **Quelle idée d'aller mettre de l'orange et du violet sur sa figure!**
What a strange idea to put orange and violet on his face!
quelle idée de: *what a strange idea to*

23 **Il a même le blanc des yeux bleu!** *Even the whites of his eyes
are blue!*
Le blanc is used in the singular here. Remember, in French you
don't have to use **ses** (L16, N17).

24 **Enfin, tout de même!** *Well really!*

PART THREE

25 **Que dit la pancarte?** *What does the card say?*
You learnt the construction **qu'est-ce que vous prenez?** in L4, N43.
Here, Marie-Claire could equally well have asked: **Qu'est-ce
que la pancarte dit?** Equally in L4, she could have said:
que prenez-vous? instead of **qu'est-ce que vous prenez?**

26 **Objets découverts dans la vallée de la Marne.** *Objects discovered
in the valley of the Marne.*
la Marne: *the River Marne*, a river in North-East France, a
tributary of the Seine

27 **Regardez ces outils dans la vitrine** . . . *Look at those tools in the
show-case* . . .
la vitrine: *the show-case* (in a museum)   Otherwise **vitrine** means
a *shop window*.

28 **À cette époque-là, je crois qu'on mangeait avec ses doigts.** *In those
days, I think they ate with their fingers.*
a **on mangeait**   Remember, an **e** is added after the **g** in **-ger** verbs
in front of **a** and **o** (cf. L23, N26 and also App. IIBc).
b **avec ses doigts**   We saw in L12, N32 the sentence: **il est sage de
louer *sa* place**: *it is wise to book* ONE'S *seat*. We had said that after
an impersonal phrase such as **il est sage de** . . . *it is wise to* . . .
son, sa, ses are used (**son, sa, ses** which normally stand for *his*
and *her*) where we use *one's* in English. This is another example
of an impersonal phrase, **on mangeait**, which calls for **son/sa/ses**.
On **mangeait avec *ses* doigts.**: ONE *used to eat with* ONE'S *fingers*.

29 **Regardez tous ces bijoux.** *Look at all these jewels.*
Des bijoux is the plural of **un bijou**. The plural of a few words
ending in **-ou** is **-oux**.

30 **Des ossements?** *Bones?*
Des ossements: *bones, old bones* is always used in the plural.

31 **Des os de cerfs sculptés. Vous n'enviez pas les archéologues qui font de telles découvertes?** *Sculpted reindeer bones. Don't you envy the archaeologists who make such discoveries?*

a **des os**: *bones* If you listen carefully to Luc's pronunciation of **des ossements** and Marie-Claire's of **des os,** you will notice the sounds of **o** in **ossements** is not the same as that in **des os.** For some strange reason, **o** in **un os** (sing.) and **o** in **des ossements** (pl.) have the same pronunciation (the mouth is quite open); but **o** in **des os** (pl.) is different (the lips are closely rounded).

b **de telles découvertes**: *such discoveries* Note that **de** and not **des** is used, because **telles,** an adjective, comes before the noun (cf. L14, N7).

The language you have learnt

I can't afford to . . .

Je ne peux pas me permettre	*d'*acheter ce manteau.
	de faire des folies.

Another use of the imperfect tense I used to

L'année dernière,	je pren*ais* le métro pour aller à mon travail. j'arriv*ais* à mon bureau à huit heures. je mang*eais* avec des amis. je finiss*ais* mon travail à sept heures.

For a long time

Il y a longtemps que je ne	suis allé dans le Midi. lui ai rendu visite.

Où? qui? combien?

C'est Il est Vous allez	*où?*
C'est C'est pour C'est à	*qui?*
Je vous dois Ça fait Ces chaussures sont à	*combien?*

Blue-eyed, dark-haired, etc.

Vous voyez cette maison	*aux*	grandes fenêtres? murs blancs?
J'aime les femmes		yeux bleus. cheveux noirs.
Vous voyez cet homme	*à l'air*	triste? heureux?

Made of

La façade est	*en*	pierre.
Les pneus sont		caoutchouc.
Cette bouteille n'est pas		verre.
Cette pièce est		bronze.
Ce peigne est		os.

Le, la, les with parts of the body

Elle a	*le*	nez rouge.
	les	yeux bleus.
Il a du noir sur	*la*	joue.
J'ai mal à	*la*	tête. gorge.

Such a, an, such

Je n'ai jamais vu	*un tel* homme.
	une telle femme.
	de tels hommes.
	de telles femmes.

Leçon vingt-cinq   *Lesson twenty-five*
Vingt-cinquième leçon   *Twenty-fifth lesson*

Le lendemain   The next day

What happens

PART ONE
Marie-Claire pense à sa journée d'hier.: *Marie-Claire thinks about what she did yesterday.*
Marie-Claire is exhausted. She and Luc went to a night-club and stayed until five o'clock in the morning dancing, drinking and laughing. After they had visited the Petit Palais they went on a pleasure boat on the Seine. Afterwards Luc took Marie-Claire to **Chez Loulou,** a fashionable club, where she saw well-known politicians, and one minister from the present government.

PART TWO
Marie-Claire répond au téléphone.: *Marie-Claire answers the phone.*
Paul phones Marie-Claire and complains because he is always alone. Now his mother has asked him to buy flowers and he wants Marie-Claire to help him. His father wants him to hire a car and send a telegram to Canada.
Au bureau de poste: *At the post office*
Paul and Marie-Claire send a telegram and post letters.

PART THREE
La vaisselle: *The washing up*
Monsieur Sade has forgotten his wallet; he suggests volunteering to do the washing up to pay for the meal.

New words in this lesson

à l'instant this minute, just now
actuel present
l'addition (*f*) bill
(les) amitiés (*f*) regards
l'annuaire (*m*) directory
approcher (de) to get near (to)
après avoir after having
au fait by the way
au lit in bed
au petit bonheur la chance on the off chance

bâiller to yawn
le bar bar
le bateau-mouche pleasure boat
c'est à toi de it's up to you to
c'est bien le cas! that's just how it is!
c'est fait that's done
c'est un peu fort! it's a bit much!
c'est une question de principe it's a matter of principle
ça non! certainly not!
ça s'épelle that's spelt

connu known, well-known
continuer to continue, to go on
le dancing dancing
nous avons dansé we danced
danser to dance
de ma vie in my life
débarquer to land, to return
le destinataire addressee
détestable detestable
la discothèque discotheque
(il) (m)'a donné chaud (it) made (me) warm
donner chaud to make warm
nous avons embarqué we set out
embarquer to set out
en majuscules in capital letters
en vogue in fashion
l'ennui c'est que the annoying thing is that
s'épeler to be spelt
être de retour to be back
faire des achats to shop, to buy things
faire les démarches to take steps, to make arrangements
faire la vaisselle to do the washing-up
faire le tour (de) to go round
faire une excursion to take a trip
(je) fais la vaisselle I wash up
je ne fais que bâiller I can't stop yawning
après avoir fait le tour having gone round
le fleuriste florist
le formulaire form
fuir to flee, to avoid
gémir to complain, to moan
tu gémis you complain, you moan
la glace ice
le gouvernement government
heureusement que luckily
(elle) s'intéresse (à) (she's) interested (in)
s'intéresser (à) to be interested (in)
le jus de fruit(s) fruit juice
le jus de tomate tomato juice
laisser tomber to leave, to drop
le lendemain following day

je me lève I get up
se lever to get up
le lilas lilac
louer to hire
la manie mania
mettre à la poste to post
le ministre minister
le modèle model
le muguet lily of the valley
navré very sorry
nulle part nowhere, not . . . anywhere
le palais palace
par hasard by chance
parler politique to talk politics
le politicien politician
le portefeuille wallet
la poste post office
prière de please
(nous) prolongeons we're prolonging
prolonger to prolong, to extend
la propriété place, property
quelqu'un d'autre someone else
il avait quitté he had left
quitter to leave
(elle) a rafraîchi (it) refreshed
rafraîchir to refresh
rejoindre to join
la rose rose
soigner to look after
soit . . . soit either . . . or
spécial special
le tarif normal normal rate, first class
le tarif réduit reduced rate, second class
terrible! dreadful!
le texte text
tout le temps all the time, always
toutes sortes de all kinds of
une fois de plus once again
elles valent they cost
valoir to cost, to be worth
le vélo bike
ving-cinq twenty-five
vingt-cinquième twenty-fifth
le week-end week-end
je n'y connais rien en fleurs I don't know anything about flowers

25

25 Notes

1 **Marie-Claire pense à sa journée d'hier.** *Marie-Claire thinks about what she did yesterday.*
sa journée d'hier cf. **une journée de travail, une semaine de vacances.**

2 **Nous avons dansé, nous avons ri, nous avons bu.** *We danced, we laughed, we drank.*
Dansé, ri, bu are respectively the past participles of **danser, rire** and **boire.**

3 **mais il était déjà parti.** *but he had already left.*
Il était parti is the **il** form of a new tense — the PLUPERFECT.
Il était parti corresponds to *he had gone.*
As you know, the perfect tense of **partir** is made up of the present of **être** and the past participle **parti.** The PLUPERFECT tense of **partir** is composed of the imperfect of **être** followed by the past participle **parti.** All verbs which are conjugated with **être** in the perfect also use the imperfect of **être** to make the pluperfect tense: **il était arrivé, il était venu,** etc. *he had arrived, he had come etc.*

4 **Comme par hasard, il avait quitté le bureau plus tôt que d'habitude.**
As it happened, he had left the office earlier than usual.
il avait quitté: *he had left* This is another example of the pluperfect.
Quitter is conjugated with **avoir** in the past tenses, so we use the IMPERFECT of **avoir** — **avait** — followed by the past participle.

5 **J'oubliais de dire qu'après avoir visité le Petit Palais, Luc et moi, nous avons eu l'idée de faire une excursion sur la Seine en bateau-mouche.** *I was forgetting to say that after we had visited (having visited) the Petit Palais, Luc and I fancied a trip on the Seine in a pleasure boat.*
après avoir visité: lit. *after having visited/after visiting*
Remember that prepositions such as **avant de**: *before* are followed by an infinitive in French (L17, N14). **Après**: *after* is also followed by an infinitive, this time in the past — **avoir** or **être** + past participle, lit. *after having . . .*:
après avoir mangé: *after having eaten, after eating*
après être parti: *after having left, after leaving*

6 **Nous avons embarqué au Pont de l'Alma pour débarquer au même endroit, après avoir fait le tour de l'Île de la Cité.** *We got on at the Pont de l'Alma and got off (lit. only to get off) in the same place when we'd gone round the Île de la Cité.*

a **Le Pont de L'Alma** is one of the most famous bridges on the
  Seine in Paris.
b **pour débarquer . . .:** *only to get off . . .*

7 **Il a acheté l'annuaire des spectacles.** *He bought a 'What's on in Paris'.*
  L'annuaire des spectacles: lit. *the directory of shows* is a pamphlet
  listing what is showing at theatres, cinemas, etc. in Paris.

8 **Il a cherché une boîte où il était allé quelques années plus tôt.**
  He looked for a club where he had been some years earlier.
  Il était allé: *he had been* is another example of the pluperfect.
  Était is used — not **avait** — because **aller** is conjugated with
  être (N3 above).

9 **Je n'avais jamais eu si chaud de ma vie.** *I'd never felt so hot
  in my life.*
  je n'avais jamais eu si chaud: Remember **avoir chaud:** *to be,
  feel warm, hot.*
  J'avais eu chaud.: *I* HAD BEEN *hot* is the pluperfect of **avoir chaud.**

10 **Après ça, j'ai seulement bu des jus de fruit et des jus de tomate.**
   After that, I only drank fruit juices and tomato juice.
   Marie-Claire could also have said: **Je n'ai bu que des jus de fruit**
   (L19).
   Jus ends in s even in the singular: **des jus de fruit, un jus de fruit.**

PART TWO
11 **et je me lève à l'instant.** *and I've just got up.*
a **Je me lève:** lit. *I get up, I'm getting up* is a phrase built on the same
  pattern as **je m'appelle, je m'ennuie.** Do not omit **me.**
b **À l'instant:** *a moment ago* can also mean *immediately, at once.*

12 **Je ne fais que bâiller.** *I do nothing but yawn.*
   je ne fais que: *I do nothing but*

13 **tout le monde va te fuir.** *everyone will run away from you.*
   Fuir is an irregular -ir verb (App. IIE).

14 **Si seulement ils m'emmenaient avec eux!** *If only they took me
   with them!*
   Si seulement is always followed by the imperfect or the pluperfect:
   Si seulement il venait! *If only he came!*
   Si seulement il avait écrit!: *If only he had written!*

15 Ne te plains pas! *Don't moan!*
Continue to treat phrases of this type as phrases to be learnt by heart. This type of construction will be explained in L28.

16 L'ennui, c'est que je n'y connais rien en fleurs. *The trouble is I know nothing about flowers.*
Je n'y connais rien en . . . means *I know nothing about.*
He knows nothing about sport.: **Il n'y connaît rien en sport.**

17 Elles ne valent pas cher en ce moment. *They're not expensive at the moment.*
The singular of **ils/elles valent** is **il/elle vaut.**
Il vaut 10F.: *It is worth 10F.*

18 C'est à ton père de faire ça. *It's up to your father to do that.*
C'est *à* vous *de* dire ça.: *It's up to you to say that.*
C'est *à* moi *de* le faire.: *It's up to me to do it.*

19 Il n'y a pas un formulaire spécial? *Isn't there a special form?*
Remember that in everyday speech the rule that **de** should be used instead of **un** after a negative is often waived (L19, N35).

20 'Prolongeons': ça s'épelle avec un 'e'? ʹPROLONGEONSʹ: *is that spelt with an 'e'?*
Paul has deliberately left out **nous** because he is writing a telegram. Remember that **-er** verbs ending in **-ger** end in **-eons** in the **nous** form (L23, N26).

21 "Prolongeons séjour en France quinze jours. Serons de retour fin du mois. *"Prolonging stay in France a fortnight. Returning end of month.* Paul is using telegraphic style. The conversational equivalent would be:
Nous prolongeons notre séjour en France de quinze jours. Nous serons de retour à la fin du mois.

22 Prière de continuer soigner chat. *Please carry on looking after cat.*
 a Prière de is not often used in conversation, but is often seen on signs.
Prière de ne pas fumer.: *Please don't smoke.*
Prière de fermer la porte.: *Please close the door.*
 b continuer: lit. *to continue   To continue* TO *do something* is **continuer à faire quelque chose. À** has been left out because it is a telegram.

23 Alors, je l'envoie au tarif normal. *Then I'll send it at the normal rate.*
Le tarif normal is the more expensive of the two rates (the other one is called **tarif réduit**: *the reduced rate*) and corresponds to *first class* in England.

24 **J'écris à l'usine pour leur demander des renseignements sur un nouveau modèle de vélo.** *I'm writing to the factory to ask them for information about a new model of bicycle.*

(**Un**) **vélo** is a word for **bicyclette**, equivalent to *bike*. (It is short for **vélocipède** which is never used.)

25

The language you have learnt

The pluperfect

		dit	bonjour.
	avait	*pris*	son sac.
		eu	le rhume.
Je croyais qu'il		*quitté*	sa femme.
	était	*allé*	en France.
		parti	pour le Canada.
		resté	chez lui.

After . . . -ing

	visité	la Tour Eiffel,	
Après avoir	*dîné,*		nous irons au cinéma.
	fait	les courses,	
	mangé,		

I am continually . . . -ing

Je ne fais que	*bâiller.* *boire.* *perdre* mon sac. *courir.*

If only . . . !

Si seulement	je gagn*ais* à la loterie nationale! je pouv*ais* partir! il décid*ait* de rester! mes parents m'emmen*aient*!

	est content			je lui rends visite.
	sera content			j'arriverai.
Il	vous téléphonera	*quand lorsque*		Valérie sera partie.
	partira en vacances			son travail sera terminé.
	achète des roses			c'est la saison.

Another way of saying where

J'aime camper		il y a des arbres.
Il est allé	*là où*	vous lui avez dit d'aller.
Je suis retourné(e)		j'ai perdu mon sac.

It's . . . 's turn to . . .

C'est à	Paul moi toi lui elle nous vous eux elles ton père	*de*	faire ça. jouer. porter les valises.

Savez-vous conduire? Can you drive?

What happens

PART ONE
Madame Louvier apprend à conduire.: *Madame Louvier is learning to drive.*
Madame Louvier would like to live out of Paris. In the capital she has to travel by public transport — or ask her husband to drive her.
If she could drive, she could go where she pleased, even abroad.
So she is having driving lessons. Monsieur Levoisin is helping her.

PART TWO
Dans la voiture de Monsieur Levoisin: *In Monsieur Levoisin's car*
Monsieur Levoisin reassures Madame Louvier and gives her some sound advice as they drive along. The engine gets hot and they stop.
A policeman comes up and tells them they are parked illegally.
However, Monsieur Levoisin and the policeman are old friends and all three go off for a drink together.

PART THREE
Naturellement: *Of course*
A motorist has to change his habits.

New words in this lesson

l'agent de service (*m*) officer on duty
ancien former, ex-
arrêté stopped
arrêter to stop
arriver à faire quelque chose to manage to do something
je m'attends à I'm expecting to
au volant at the wheel, driving
l'auto-école (*f*) driving school
l'automobiliste (*m*) driver
autrefois formerly, before
bloqué stuck
bouillir to boil
bousculé hurried
elle, il bout (it) is boiling
brûler les feux to jump the lights

ça fait des années for years, it's years since
le capot bonnet
car for
changer de vitesse to change gear
le chant song
chaque fois (que) every time (that)
la circulation traffic
le clignotant indicator
le coffre boot
comme leur poche like the back of their hand
conduire to drive
la contravention ticket
la crevaison puncture
crever to get a puncture

231

26

dans tout ça with all that
de ma faute my fault
de mal en pis worse and worse, from bad to worse
de mauvaise humeur in a bad temper
de mieux en mieux better and better
de notre faute our fault
se débrouiller to cope, to manage
dresser une contravention to charge someone
échouer to fail
emprunter to make use of
en sens interdit the wrong way
être pressé to be in a hurry
l'examen (m) exam, test
faire attention to pay attention
ne pas faire excès de vitesse not to speed, not to exceed the speed limit
faire le plein d'eau to fill up on water
faisant attention paying attention
la faute fault
fêter to celebrate
les feux rouges (m) traffic lights
figure-toi imagine
se figurer to imagine
freiner to brake
la fumée smoke
le gardien de la paix policeman
garer to park
se garer to park
griller les feux to jump the lights
vous grillez les feux you jump the lights
ininterrompu non-stop
s'inscrire (à) to enroll (at)
je me suis inscrite (à) I've enrolled (at)
interdit (de) forbidden (to)
on ira we'll go
j'irais I'd go
le long de alongside, beside
mais si yes (you will)
méchant nasty
le ménage housework
merveilleux marvellous
le miracle miracle
miraculeux miraculous
le moniteur instructor
le moteur engine
l'objection (f) objection

l'obsession (f) obsession
l'oiseau (m) bird
le panneau sign
le panneau de signalisation road sign
passer le permis to take the driving test
le permis de conduire driving licence
petit à petit little by little
la pompe à essence petrol pump
pratiquement practically, more or less
prendre un verre to have a drink
la priorité à droite priority to traffic on the right
je proteste I protest
protester to protest
prudent wise, prudent
le radiateur radiator
je recommande I recommend
recommander to recommend
vous serez reçu you'll pass
être reçu to pass
le règlement rule
réparer to repair
le retrait du permis withdrawal of the licence
le rétroviseur driving mirror
la roue de secours spare wheel
le roulement rumbling (of cars)
rouler to drive
la route road
savoir (conduire) to know how to (drive)
(rouler en) sens interdit (to drive) the wrong way
si jamais if ever
la station service service station
stationnement interdit no parking
stationner to park
tomber en panne d'essence to run out of petrol
tous ensemble all together
tout en at the same time
tranquillement calmly, peacefully, quietly
les transports en commun (m) public transport
le trottoir pavement
vous verriez you'd see
vingt-six twenty-six
vingt-sixième twenty-sixth

Notes

26

PART ONE

1 **Savez-vous conduire?** *Can you* (lit. *Do you know how to) drive?*

2 **J'ai cru ne pas pouvoir rentrer:** *I thought I wouldn't be able to get home*
J'ai cru: *I thought, I believed* — is the perfect from **croire** (the past participle is **cru**). See App. IIIE.
Croire can be constructed with an infinitive, but only if the subject of **croire** and the subject of the following verb are the same:
j'ai cru pouvoir: *I thought I could*
Je crois pouvoir: *I think I can.*

3 **Comme j'aimerais habiter une petite ville!** *How I'd like to live in a small town!*
j'aimerais: *I should like to* (cf. L13, N3)
Just as *I should like* is the conditional of *to like*, so **j'aimerais** is the conditional of **aimer.** The conditional is easy to form in French. The **je** form is obtained by adding **-ais** to the infinitive if the verb is a regular verb.

4 **J'adorerais pouvoir faire mes courses sans être pressée.** *I'd love to be able to go shopping without being in a hurry.*
a **J'adorerais:** *I should love* is another example of the conditional of a regular -er verb.
b **Sans être pressée** is another example of a preposition — **sans** — which has to be followed by an infinitive.

5 **Je me lèverais tranquillement le matin.** *I'd get up calmly every morning.*
Je me lèverais is the conditional tense of **je me lève** (cf. L25, N11).

6 **Nous déjeunerions, les fenêtres ouvertes, et nous entendrions le chant des oiseaux,** *We'd have lunch with the windows open, and we'd hear the singing of the birds.*
a **nous déjeunerions:** *we would/should have lunch* The **nous** form of the conditional of regular -er verbs is made by adding **-ions** to the infinitive: **nous aimerions, nous adorerions.**
b **nous entendrions:** *we would/should hear* To make the **nous** form of the conditional of regular -re verbs the final **e** of the infinitive is dropped and replaced by the ending **-ions: nous descendrions, nous attendrions.**

7 **Je finirais mon petit ménage tranquillement, et j'irais faire mes courses sans être bousculée.** *I'd finish my housework peacefully and I'd go and do my shopping without being hustled.*

26

a **je finirais**: *I would/should finish*   Again the ending -ais has been added to the infinitive.

b **mon petit ménage**: *my bit of housework*   This is an idiomatic use of **petit**. Note — **le ménage**: *housework*, **faire le ménage**: *to do the housework*.

c **j'irais**: *I would/should go*   Notice the -ais ending of the conditional tense. **J'irais** is the conditional of **aller,** which as you already know, is irregular. The conditional **j'irais** looks similar to the future, **j'irai.** If you listen carefully to the ending of **j'irai** (L21, N16) and to the ending of **j'irais** here you will realize that they do not sound exactly the same.

8 **Ah! Ce serait merveilleux!** *Oh! It would be wonderful!*
Il serait is the **il** form of the conditional of **être.** Again you can see the similarity between the future of **être, il** *sera* and the conditional, **il** *serait*.

9 **Comme je ne sais pas conduire, je suis obligée d'emprunter les transports en commun chaque fois que je veux sortir.** *Since I can't drive I have to go by public transport every time I want to go out.*
Emprunter which you learnt in the sense of *to borrow* (L18, N31) can be used in connection with travelling, as it is here, and in such phrases as: **emprunter une route**: *to take a certain road.*

10 **Si je savais conduire, je pourrais aller me promener quand je veux et là où je veux.** *If I could drive, I'd be able to go for a drive when I want and where I want.*

a **Je savais** is the **je** form of the imperfect tense of the irregular -**oir** verb **savoir** (App. IVB).

b **si je savais . . . je pourrais . . .** : *if I could . . . I would be able to . . .*
An imperfect after **si** is followed by a conditional tense here. This is a common combination of tenses.

11 **Je me verrais même très bien aller à l'étranger au volant de ma voiture** *I could even see myself going abroad at the wheel of my car*
Je verrais, the **je** form of the conditional tense of **voir** (App. IVB).

12 **— car je m'achèterais une voiture si j'avais mon permis de conduire.**
— for I'd buy myself a car, if I had my driving licence.
je m'achèterais . . . si j'avais . . .   This is the same combination of tenses that you saw in N10 above; this time the conditional comes first, the **si** + imperfect second.

13 **'Tout le monde dirait que tu as quitté ton mari,' me dit-il.**
'Everyone would say that you've left your husband,' he tells me.
(II) dirait is the **il** form of the conditional of **dire.**

14 **Un vieil ami des Delon, M. Levoisin, m'aide aussi: c'est un ancien chauffeur de taxi.** *An old friend of the Delons, M. Levoisin helps me too: he's an ex-taxi-driver.*
un ancien: *a former, an ex* The feminine is **une ancienne.**

PART TWO
15 **Il m'en faudra des leçons avant de pouvoir passer mon permis de conduire!** *I'll need some lessons before I'm able to take my driving test!*
Il faudra is the future of **il faut. Il m'en faudra** literally means *it will be necessary for me.* **En** reinforces **des leçons** as it reinforced **de la chance** in **vous en avez de la chance** (L23, N4).

16 **Petit à petit, vous ferez des progrès . . . vous conduirez de mieux en mieux et . . . vous serez reçue à l'examen!** *Little by little, you'll improve . . . you'll drive better and better and . . . you'll pass the exam!*
a **Vous ferez** is the **vous** form of the future of **faire** (App. IIIE).
b **Vous conduirez**: *you will drive*, is the **vous** form of the future of **conduire.**

17 **Mon mari me dit que l'examen est plus difficile qu'il ne l'était autrefois.** *My husband tells me that the test is more difficult than it was in the past.*
plus difficile qu'il ne l'était autrefois: *more difficult than it was in the past* After a comparative like this (**plus difficile que**), **ne** has no meaning. It is very much the same **ne** as in the sentence:
Il y a longtemps que je ne suis allé visiter un musée (L24, N6).
Note also **l'** in front of **était. L'** stands for **difficile** and has no equivalent in the corresponding English sentence.

18 **Et il dit que si je réussis à l'examen, ce sera un miracle.** *And he says if I pass the test it will be a miracle.*

19 **Jamais je ne pourrai me débrouiller dans tout ça.** *I shall never be able to cope with all that.*
Jamais je ne pourrai is an alternative to **je ne pourrai jamais.**

20 **Si vous connaissiez le quartier, vous verriez, c'est facile.** *If you knew the area, you'd see, it's easy.*

21 **Si j'y arrive jamais, ce sera miraculeux.** *If I ever manage to, it will be a miracle.*
Jamais used in connection with **ne** means *never.* **Si jamais** means *if ever.*

22 **Ce que je vous recommande, c'est de ne pas faire d'excès de vitesse, de ne pas rouler en sens interdit et de ne pas brûler les feux rouges.** *My advice is* (lit. *what I recommend to you is) not to exceed the speed limit, not to drive into a road marked 'no entry' and not to go through red lights.*

23 **Et puis il y a la priorité à droite, les passages cloutés . . .** *And then there is priority on the right, the pedestrian crossings . . .*
la priorité à droite: lit. *the priority to the right* In France drivers coming from the right have the right of way, even if the car is coming from the right on a secondary road. There are however, halt signs on many secondary roads to protect the traffic on the main road.

24 **Il y a une ligne blanche.** *There's a white line.*
In France a white line means no parking.

25 **Non, Monsieur l'agent, mais . . .** *No constable, but . . .*
Monsieur l'agent is the phrase to use when you address a policeman — the equivalent of *constable* or *officer* in English.

26 **Ça fait des années qu'on ne s'est vu!** *It's been years since we saw each other!*
This sentence is equivalent to **Il y a des années qu'on ne s'est vu.** Remember also **ça fait quarante ans que je ne fais rien** (L22, N27). Notice the **ne**: it is superfluous (L24, N6).

27 **Rendez-vous au café dans cinq minutes.** *See you in the café in five minutes.*

The language you have learnt

The endings of the conditional tense (-er and -ir verbs)

Je porter*ais* Tu porter*ais* Il Elle } porter*ait* Nous porter*ions* Vous porter*iez* Ils Elles } porter*aient*	cette lettre,	si la poste était ouverte.

The conditional; si and the imperfect tense

Je déjeuner*ais*	au Ritz tous les jours,	si c'*était* possible.
Je partir*ais*	en avion,	

Si and the imperfect tense; the conditional

Si	vous *connaissiez* Valérie,	vous *comprendriez*.
	je *pouvais* partir,	j'*irais* vous rendre visite.

... more ... than

Il est	*plus*	grand	*que*	je	*ne*	le croyais.
C'est		difficile		vous		le diriez.

Whenever

Il est ravi	*chaque fois qu'*	elle téléphone.
Elle perd son carnet de chèques		elle va dans un grand magasin.

I'm learning, I know how to

J'apprends à	conduire.
Je sais	parler espagnol.

It's not my, your, his, etc., fault

Nous avons crevé.	*Ce n'est pas de*	*ma* *ta* *sa* *notre* *votre* *leur*	*faute.*
La pendule ne marche pas.			
Le verre est tombé			

Week-end à la campagne   A weekend in the country

What happens

PART ONE

Guy Martin parle de sa voiture de sport.: *Guy Martin talks about his sports car.*
Guy has a secondhand sports car of which he is very proud. He takes good care of it. He has found a garage which he feels he can trust with repairs and servicing — even with the cleaning. His sister, Marie-Claire, is nervous when he drives; this is not really surprising since their parents died in a road accident. They are going with Paul and Luc Houbé to stay with an uncle in the country.

PART TWO

Guy Martin prépare sa voiture.: *Guy Martin prepares his car.*
Marie-Claire has made sandwiches for a picnic but Guy is not very pleased. Luc and Paul arrive, and after chatting they set off.

PART THREE

Vous n'êtes pas mort?: *You're not dead?*
Monsieur Dulac lost his spare wheel.

New words in this lesson

à bord in, on board
à l'ombre in the shade
à la radio on the radio
l'accident (*m*) accident
l'accident de voiture (*m*) car accident
l'affaire (*f*) bargain
j'ai beau dire although I tell
au soleil in the sun
l'autoroute (*f*) motorway
avoir beau dire to say in vain
la brume mist
la brume matinale early-morning mist
ça fait combien? how much is that?
ça me convient that suits me
ça ne valait pas la peine it wasn't
   really worth it

cent cinquante a hundred and fifty
la chaleur heat
conduire to take
convenir to suit
d'occasion second-hand
décapotable convertible
déçu disappointed
le degré degree
les degrés centigrade degrees
   centigrade
les degrés fahrenheit degrees
   fahrenheit
dès que as soon as
en cours de route on the way
en osier wicker
en voiture by car

238

environ about
la façon manner, way
j'ai failli I nearly
faillir to nearly (do something)
faire bonne impression to make a good
   impression
faire confiance à to trust
faire de la place to make room
faire de la vitesse to go fast, to speed
faire du cent to do 100 km an hour
faire faire to have done
faire une tête pareille to look like that
je fais faire I have done
il a fait bonne impression he made a
   good impression
fameux precious
fier proud
(qui) fonctionne (which) works
fonctionner to work
furieux furious
le garagiste garage owner
honnête honest
(il) s'impatiente (he)'s getting
   impatient
s'impatienter to get impatient
l'imperméable (m) raincoat
intelligent intelligent
le kilomètre kilometre
l'autre jour the other day
la météo weather forecast
mort de peur scared stiff
naturel natural
neuf new
l'ombre (f) shade
le panier basket
le panier à provisions shopping basket
le panier en osier wicker basket
la personnalité personality, character
pique-niquer to picnic

plaindre to pity
je plains I pity
la portière car door
pour ainsi dire to speak of
prendre soin to take care
je prends soin I take care
les prévisions météorologiques (f)
   weather forecast
quatre cents four hundred
rassurée reassured
rassurer to reassure
(ça) rend (it) makes
(elle) (me) rend malade (it) makes
   (me) ill
rendre to make
rendre malade to make ill
la réparation repair
répéter to repeat
réviser to service
revoilà here's . . . again
la roue wheel
sain et sauf safe and sound
le sandwich sandwich
si . . . que ça as . . . as that
le soleil sun
le thermomètre thermometer
je tiens à I intend
je ne tiens pas à mourir I don't want
   to die
tenir à to intend to, to wish to
trembler to shake, to tremble
il a trompé he deceived
tromper to deceive
tué killed
tuer to kill
vingt-sept twenty-seven
ving-septième twenty-seventh
la vitesse speed
la voiture de sport sports car

27

Notes

PART ONE
1 **J'aurais aimé acheter une voiture neuve.** *I would have liked to buy
   a new car.*
a **j'aurais aimé**: *I should (would) have liked* This is the **je** form of
   the PAST conditional tense of **aimer**. The **je** form of the PRESENT
   conditional of **avoir** (or **être**) is followed by the past participle
   of the verb.

27 b **une voiture neuve**: *a new car* **Neuve** is the feminine of **neuf**.
Neuf/neuve are used AFTER the noun and it means *new* in the sense of *brand new*. When *new* means *another, a different one* the French for it is **nouveau/nouvel/nouvelle**:
Nous venons d'engager un nouveau dessinateur (L10, N10).

2 **Mais, neuve, elle valait 20.000 francs.** *But it was worth (it cost) 20,000 francs new.*
Elle valait is the imperfect of **vaut** (in **ça vaut la peine**: *it's worth it*) See App. IVB.

3 **et je n'ai pour ainsi dire pas eu d'ennuis avec.** *and I haven't had any bother worth speaking of.* (lit. *so to speak*)
a **pour ainsi dire**: *so to speak*
b **avoir des ennuis avec**: *to have bother/trouble with*
Avec stands alone at the end of this sentence. The pronoun **elle**: *it* is understood. This is a colloquial construction:
J'ai un manteau noir, mais je ne sors jamais avec.

4 **Je la fais réviser régulièrement.** *I have it serviced regularly.*
faire réviser une voiture: *to have a car serviced*
Compare the French and the English constructions:
Je fais réviser ma voiture tous les trois mois.: *I have my car serviced every three months.*
French: **faire,** infinitive, noun.
English: *to have,* noun, past participle.

5 **Dès qu'il y a quelque chose qui ne fonctionne pas bien, je la conduis au garage,** *As soon as something goes wrong,* (lit. *something which doesn't work well*), *I take it to the garage,*
Conduire can mean *to take* as well as *to drive*.

6 **et je fais réparer ce qui ne va pas.** *and I have whatever is wrong mended.*

7 **Je croyais pouvoir faire confiance au garagiste qui m'avait vendu la voiture.** *I thought I could trust the garage owner who had sold me the car.*

8 **Il m'a fait payer une réparation qu'il n'avait pas faite.** *He made me pay for a repair that he hadn't done.*
il m'a fait payer: *he made me pay*
payer ∧ **une réparation**: *to pay* FOR *a repair*

9 **J'ai été très déçu et, naturellement, j'ai changé de garage.** *I was very disappointed and, naturally, I changed garages.*

Déçu: *disappointed*, is the past participle of **décevoir**. It is conjugated like **recevoir** (App. IVA). Careful! **Décevoir** means *to disappoint; to deceive* is **tromper**.

10 **Depuis, j'ai fait tous les garages du quartier.** *Since then I've tried* (lit. *done*) *all the garages in the area.*

11 **Je lui fais faire tout ce qui est à faire.** *I get him to do all there is to be done.*
je lui fais faire: lit. *I make him do* This shows you that **faire** can mean either *to make* or *to do*. Note the use of **lui** in this sentence.

12 **J'ai beau lui dire qu'il n'y a rien à craindre, elle a peur.** *I've told her that there's nothing to fear, but it's no use, she's afraid.*
j'ai beau lui dire When **avoir beau** (+ an infinitive) is incorporated into a sentence, it introduces the idea of *in vain*:
Il a eu beau chercher, il n'a rien trouvé.: *He looked, but it was no use, he did not find anything.*

13 **Mais nos parents ont été tués dans un accident de voiture;** *But our parents were* (lit. *have been*) *killed in a car accident;*

14 **Dès que je fais du cent, elle commence à trembler.** *As soon as I do a hundred, she begins to tremble.*
faire du cent: *to do 100 kilometres an hour* One kilometre, a thousand metres = ⅝th of a mile.

15 **Si je bavarde en conduisant, elle ne fait que répéter: 'Fais attention! Tu ferais mieux de te taire!'** *If I chat while I'm driving, she keeps on saying: 'Pay attention! You'd do better to keep quiet!'*
a **tu ferais mieux de**: lit. *you would do better to*
b **te taire**: *to keep quiet* Remember **taisez-vous** (L23).

16 **Ça me rend furieux.** *That makes me mad.*
The French for *to make* + an adjective is **rendre** + an adjective:
Le café me rend malade.: *Coffee makes me ill.*
Rendre is conjugated like **descendre** (App. IIIA).

17 **J'aurais préféré avoir une sœur un peu moins intelligente.** *I'd rather have had a sister a little less intelligent.*
J'aurais préféré: (lit.) *I should* (*would*) *have preferred* See N1a above.

18 **une propriété à quatre cents kilomètres de Paris.** *a farm* (*a property*) (lit. *at*) *four hundred kilometres from Paris.*
À may not be left out in front of a phrase indicating a distance:
J'habite à dix kilomètres de Paris.
Notice that **cents** in **quatre cents** has an s.

19 Allons, va chercher ton fameux panier . . . Cours! *Well, go and get your precious basket . . . Run!*

a **ton fameux panier** **Fameux** is used here sarcastically to mean *precious*.

b **Cours!**: *Run!* You learnt **j'ai couru**: *I have run* in L22, N13. From this form you can deduce the **tu** form of the present: **tu cours**. The infinitive is **courir** (App. IIE).

20 Ah, c'est pour ça; parce qu'on doit pouvoir faire 400 Km en trois heures avec une voiture comme ça. *Oh, that's the reason; because you should be able to do 400 Km in three hours with a car like that.*

a **c'est pour ça**: lit. *it's for that*

b **en trois heures** Take care to distinguish between **Nous arriverons** *dans* **quatre heures.**: *We shall arrive* IN *four hours.* (*from now*) and **On peut faire 400 Km** *en* **trois heures.**: *We/you can do 400 Km* IN *three hours.*

21 Tu penses bien que j'ai choisi le plus petit des deux. *Well naturally I've chosen the smaller of the two.*

a **tu penses bien que**: *naturally* — an idiomatic expression: **Tu penses bien qu'il va venir.**: *Naturally he'll come.*

b **le plus petit des deux**: lit. *the smallest of the two* Remember **petit**: *small*, **plus petit**: *smaller*, **le plus petit**: *the smallest* (L12, N7b).

22 Fais-le-moi passer, veux-tu? *Pass it to me, will you?*
faire passer: *to pass*
Faites-moi passer le sel, s'il vous plaît.: *Pass me the salt, please.*

23 Oh! J'ai failli le laisser tomber! *Oh, I almost dropped it!*
J'ai failli: *I almost* is followed by an infinitive:
J'ai failli manquer le train.: *I almost missed the train.*

23 J'avoue que je n'aurais pas cru que mon coffre pouvait tenir tant de choses. *I admit I wouldn't have believed my boot could hold so many things.*
je n'aurais pas cru: *I should/would not have believed* See N1a above.

24 Ce n'est pas la peine d'en prendre. *It's not worth taking them.*
This is a shortened form of **Ce n'est pas la peine d'en prendre un.**: *It is not worth taking one of them.*

25 Ça va faire combien au soleil? *How much will that be in the sun?*
Ça fait combien? *How much is that?* can be used when asking about temperature or distance, as well as price.

26 **La voiture me rend malade.** *Cars* (lit. *the car*) *make me ill.* Remember **rendre** + an adjective: *to make* + an adjective (N16 above).

27 **J'aimerais mille fois mieux aller chez mon oncle par le train — ou même à bicyclette — plutôt que d'y aller en voiture.** *I'd be a thousand times happier going to uncle's by train — or even on a bicycle — rather than going (there) by car.*

a **j'aimerais mille fois mieux**: lit. *I would like a thousand times more*

b **par le train, à bicyclette, en voiture** — Notice the different prepositions used in these three phrases.

28 **Pourquoi pas à pied, pendant que tu y es?** *Why not on foot, while you're at it?*
Pendant que tu y es is an idiom corresponding to *while you're at it.*

29 **Si nous devons mourir, nous mourrons tous ensemble!** *If we must die, we'll all die together!*

a **Nous devons**: *we must* is the **nous** form of the present tense of **devoir.**

b **Nous mourrons**: *we will die* is the **nous** form of the future tense of **mourir** (App. IIE).

The language you have learnt

The past conditional

J'aurais	aimé préféré adoré	aller en France avec vous. visiter Paris.

If + pluperfect + conditional

Si vous	aviez	*terminé* votre travail, *téléphoné,*	vous *auriez pu* aller au théâtre.
	étiez	*sorti,* *allé* faire vos courses,	vous *auriez rencontré* Valérie.

To have something done

Je vais	*faire*	*réviser* ma voiture. nettoyer mon complet. *faire* une robe.

27   To have had something done

J'ai fait	répar**er** ma montre. lav**er** mon linge. *faire* une robe.

I'd better, I'd rather

Je ferais mieux de *J'aimerais mieux*	partir. faire laver mon linge. ne rien faire.

Rendre + adjective

Cette histoire me	*rend*	furieux.
Cette robe vous		ridicule.

As soon as

Je partirai Je viendrai	*dès que*	je pourrai. Georges sera parti.

It's no use

	essayer,	je ne réussis pas.
J'ai beau	demander,	personne ne me répond.

It wasn't worth it

J'ai	cherché pendant des heures, risqué ma vie,	*mais ça ne valait pas* *la peine.*

I almost

J'ai failli	tomb**er** en panne. *avoir* un accident.

244

Not as . . . as all that

	grand	
Il n'est pas si	sympathique	*que ça.*
	difficile	

By train, bicycle, car, on foot

	par le train.
J'aime mieux y aller	*à* bicyclette.
	en voiture.
	à pied.

Leçon vingt-huit   *Lesson twenty-eight*
Vingt-huitième leçon   *Twenty-eighth lesson*

Chez l'oncle André   At Uncle André's

What happens

PART ONE

Monsieur André Julliard se présente.: *Monsieur André Julliard introduces himself.*
Monsieur Julliard is Guy's and Marie-Claire's uncle. He has a farm in Auvergne where he lives alone, except for his animals. Loneliness sometimes gets him down and he thinks back to the serious road accident fifteen years ago in which his sister – Guy's and Marie-Claire's mother – and her husband were involved.

PART TWO

Soyez les bienvenus!: *Welcome!*
Guy and Marie-Claire tell their uncle about the journey. He then tells them that he does almost everything on the farm himself, odd jobs, gardening, carpentry, cooking – he even makes his own bread.
Suddenly Paul spots an old bicycle outside. It has been there for over fifty years but is still in working order.

PART THREE

Quelle occasion!: *What a bargain!*
The husband has bought a second-hand car. The garage has told him it would be cheaper to replace the engine than to have it completely overhauled.

New words in this lesson

à moitié chemin half-way
abattre to cut down
ancien old
(il) appartenait (it) belonged
appartenir to belong
il m'arrive de sometimes I . . .
atroce terrible
au bord de beside, on the side of
elles se battent they fight
se battre to fight
le beau-frère brother-in-law
bordé (de) lined (with)
le boulanger baker

bricoler to do odd jobs, to potter
ça doit être it/that must be
le champ field
le chemin way
le chien dog
la cinquantaine fifty (years old)
se comprendre to understand each other
nous nous comprenons we understand each other
le compteur speedometer
le conducteur driver

convaincu convinced
je cueille I pick
cueillir to pick
le cultivateur cultivator
dans tous les cas in any case
dehors outside
ils ont déménagé they moved
déménager to move (house)
en détail in detail
se disputer to quarrel
la dizaine ten
le doute doubt
je me doutais I thought
se douter to think
je m'endors I fall asleep
s'endormir to fall asleep
j'en doute I doubt it
s'en douter to doubt
en douter to doubt (it)
en état de marche in working order
en sens inverse in the opposite direction
je m'en suis servi I have used it
s'en servir to use
entouré (de) surrounded (by)
l'être humain (m) human (being)
faire du vélo to cycle
se faire la cour to woo each other
faire les honneurs to do the honours
je faisais du vélo I used to cycle
les fondations (f) foundations
elles se font la cour they woo each other
le fruit fruit
la glace mirror
installé installed, settled in
inutile (de) no point (in), (it's) useless (to)
le jardinier gardener
l'un à l'autre one to the other
ce matin même this very morning
(elles) menaçaient (they) were threatening
menacer to threaten
mentir to lie
le menuisier carpenter
je me mets à I start to
se mettre à to start to, to begin to

le meuble piece of furniture
montrer le chemin show the way
le nom name
où ça? where?
j'ouvre la marche (I open the march), I lead the way
ouvrir la marche (to open the march), to lead the way
je me pardonne I forgive myself
se pardonner to forgive oneself
passer to exceed
la passion passion
(elle) pèse (it) weighs
peser to weigh
le pont bridge
quand même even so, all the same
quelle occasion! what a bargain!
la racine root
raconter to tell
je raconterai I'll tell
se rafraîchir to freshen up
(qui) se reflètent (which) are reflected
se refléter to be reflected
la rivière river
sans doute doubtless, without doubt, probably
le saule pleureur weeping willow
(il) serrait (he) was keeping to
serrer to keep to
serrer sa droite to keep to his right
servez-vous! help yourselves!
se servir to help oneself
se servir de to use
soi-même oneself
la solitude solitude
sportif sporting
à tempérament by instalments
le tournant bend
usé worn
(elles) se vendent (they) are selling
se vendre to sell
le vent wind
le verger orchard
la vieillesse old age
vingt-huit twenty-eight
vingt-huitième twenty-eighth
je vis I live
la volaille poultry

28 Notes

PART ONE

1 **M. André Julliard se présente.** *M. André Julliard introduces himself.* In this sort of phrase, **se** stands for *himself.* You have already learnt the phrase **se présente** (L10). You have also heard Mme. Delon say **Je me maquille.**: *I am making myself up* (L7). From now on, we shall call **me** and **se** REFLEXIVE PRONOUNS when they stand for *myself* and *himself* or *herself.*

2 **Ma ferme est entourée de champs que traverse une petite rivière.** *My farm is surrounded by fields with a little river running through.*

a **Ma ferme *est entourée de* champs.** We came across this sort of construction in L14: **Je *suis invitée* chez les Louvier.**: *I* AM INVITED *to the Louviers.* As you can see, the French construction is the same as the English one, a part of the verb **être**: *to be* + a past participle.

b **que traverse une petite rivière** means the same as **qu'une petite rivière traverse.**

3 **La rivière est bordée d'arbres qui se reflètent dans l'eau.** *The river is lined with trees which are reflected in the water.*

a **la rivière est bordée d'arbres**: *the river is lined with trees.*

b **qui se reflètent**: *which are reflected* or literally *which reflect themselves* **Se,** in **se reflètent** can, in this sentence, be equated with *reflect themselves* but the real meaning is *are reflected.* You have met this sort of construction (a verb preceded by **se**) several times, for example: **ils s'appellent**, which is equivalent to *they are called.* In L25, N20 you saw the sentence: **'Prolongeons': ça s'épelle avec un 'e'.**: *'Prolongeons' is spelt with an e.* **S'épelle** equals *is spelt.* So remember that, in some cases, a verb preceded by **se** is equivalent to *is* or *are* and a past participle. **Refléter** is conjugated like **inquiéter** (See App. 1Bg).

4 **Je l'ai fait abattre; mais je ne me le pardonne pas.** *I had it cut down but I can't forgive myself (for it).*

a **je l'ai fait abattre**: *I had it cut down* Remember: **je la fais réviser**: *I have it serviced* (L27, N4).

b **je ne me le pardonne pas**: *I do not forgive myself* This is the same sort of construction as in N1 above, **je me présente.** You can see that, in the negative, **ne** comes before **me.**

5 **J'approche de la cinquantaine.** *I'm nearly fifty.* (lit. *I'm approaching fifty.*)
la cinquantaine (c.f. "Encore une dizaine d'années") **aine** added to

a figure gives the idea of ABOUT. **Il a la trentaine/la quarantaine/la cinquantaine/la soixantaine** means *He is about thirty/forty/fifty/sixty.* Note the definite article in each of the four phrases. Note also that there is no corresponding ready-made phrase for *he is about twenty/ seventy/eighty* or *ninety*. In these cases you have to say **il a environ vingt ans/soixante-dix ans/quatre-vingts ans/quatre-vingt-dix ans.**

6 **Quand je me regarde dans la glace, je me dis**: *When I look at myself in the mirror, I say to myself*:
je me regarde . . . je me dis: *I look at myself . . . I say to myself*
Here are two more examples of the **je me . . . il se . . .** type of construction you learnt in N1 and 4b above.

7 **Je vis seul, mais j'ai de bons voisins.** *I live alone, but I've got good neighbours.*
de bons voisins Remember that when an adjective precedes the noun, in most cases **de** is used — not **des**.

8 **Naturellement, quand la solitude me pèse un peu, je me parle à moi-même, ou à mes bêtes, en particulier à mon chien.** *Naturally when loneliness gets me down, I talk to myself or to my animals, especially to my dog.*
a **la solitude me pèse** Peser means *to weigh.* Notice the accent: **(il) pèse.**
Peser behaves like **acheter**: its first **e** becomes **è** when there is a silent **e** in the following syllable: **je pèse, je pèserai**; but **nous pesons, vous pesez** (App. 1Bf).
b **je me parle à moi-même**: *I talk to myself*
Moi-même reinforces the reflexive pronoun **me**.
Remember **parler** is constructed with **à** (e.g. **Georges parle à Valérie**). That is why M. Julliard has to say: **Je me parle *à* moi-même.**

9 **Médor et moi, nous nous parlons l'un à l'autre, et nous nous comprenons.** *Médor and I, (we) talk to each other, and (we) understand each other.*
a **nous nous parlons . . . nous nous comprenons** This is another interesting type of construction.
Nous nous . . . -ons stands for *we . . . each other.*
nous nous comprenons: *we understand each other*
nous nous parlons: *we talk to each other*
From this you can deduce that *you . . . each other* is **vous vous . . . -ez.**
vous vous comprenez: *you understand each other*
vous vous parlez: *you talk to each other*

28

249

b **l'un à l'autre**: *the one to the other*, in fact *each other*. This phrase reinforces **nous nous**. It can also be used to reinforce **vous vous**.

10 **Je suis convaincu qu'un homme et une bête peuvent se comprendre.**
I'm convinced that a man and an animal can understand each other.
(ils) peuvent se comprendre: *they can understand each other*
Ils se . . . -ent is the **ils** form corresponding to **nous nous . . . -ons** and **vous vous . . . -ez.**

11 **Dans tous les cas, il ne fait aucun doute que les bêtes se comprennent**: *In any case, there's no doubt that animals understand one another*:
ils se **comprennent**: *they understand one another*
This shows you that **ils se . . . -ent** is also equivalent to *they . . . one another.*
ils se **comprennent**: THEY *understand* EACH OTHER (Guy and Paul)
ils se **comprennent**: THEY *understand* ONE ANOTHER (Guy, Paul and Luc)

12 **elles se parlent, elles s'appellent, comme le font des êtres humains.**
they speak to one another, they call one another, as human beings do.
a **elles se parlent, elles s'appellent**: *they speak to one another, they call each other/one another*
The context will show whether the English for **elles/ils *se* parlent** is *they speak to* EACH OTHER or ONE ANOTHER.
Ils s'appellent could, of course, also mean *they are called.* Again, the context will make the meaning clear.
b **comme le font des êtres humains**: *as human beings do*
Compare the word order in the French and the English sentence (N2b above). Do not omit the idiomatic **le** in front of **font.**

13 **En ce moment, les légumes se vendent pour presque rien.** *At the moment, vegetables are being sold for almost nothing.*
les légumes se vendent: *vegetables are being sold, vegetables are sold*
This is another example of the type of **se** verb we described in N3b above: **Les arbres se reflètent dans l'eau.**: *The trees* ARE REFLECTED *in the water.*

14 **Mais ça m'est égal. Je vais quand même au marché.** *But I don't mind. I still go to the market.*
quand même: *still, all the same* **Tout de même**, which you learnt in L24, has the same meaning. M. Julliard could have said: **Je vais tout de même au marché.**

15 Il m'arrive de m'ennuyer. *I get fed up sometimes.*
The **me** which precedes **ennuyer** is a REFLEXIVE PRONOUN. The **je**
form of the present tense is **je m'ennuie.** This is obviously not the
same type of verb as **je m'appelle:** *I am called;* **je me présente:** *I
introduce myself;* **nous nous battons:** *we fight each other, one
another.* **S'ennuyer** belongs to a large group of verbs constructed
with a MEANINGLESS reflexive pronoun.
You have seen many examples of these during the course. Here
are a few of them:
je *me* **sauve:** *I'm off* (L10)
il *se* **plaint:** *he complains* (L11, N5)
il *s'***arrête:** *it/he stops* (L12, 14a)
je *me* **rappelle:** *I remember* (L13)
il *s'***impatiente:** *he is getting impatient* (L27), etc.
If you left the reflexive pronoun out, the verb would have a different
meaning. **Je** *me* **sauve** means *I'm off, I am going* but **Je sauve
quelqu'un** means *I save someone.*

16 Si je m'arrête de travailler, si je m'assois et si je me mets à penser . . .
If I stop working, if I sit down and I start to think . . .
Je m'arrête, je m'assois, je me mets à These three verbs must
have a reflexive pronoun when they are used in these senses.

17 alors, je me rappelle l'atroce accident d'il y a quinze ans. *then I
remember the dreadful accident fifteen years ago.*
je me rappelle: *I remember* This verb, which you learnt in L13,
must be conjugated with a meaningless reflexive pronoun, like
je m'ennuie, je m'arrête, je m'assois, etc.

18 Ma sœur, son mari, et moi étions dans ma voiture. *My sister, her
husband and I were in my car.*
The **nous** form, **-étions,** has to be used because the sentence
actually stands for: **Ma sœur, son mari et moi,** *nous étions* **dans ma
voiture.**

19 Nous nous promenions. *We were out for a drive.*
This is another example of the type of verb which must be
conjugated with a meaningless reflexive pronoun like **je** *m'***ennuie** (*I get
bored*), **je** *m'***arrête** (*I stop*), **je** *me* **rappelle** (*I remember*).

20 Ma sœur et mon beau-frère, c'étaient M. et Mme Martin, *My sister
and brother-in-law were Mr. and Mrs. Martin,*
(le) beau-frère: (*the*) *brother-in-law* This gives you the pattern
which will enable you to say *sister-in-law, son-in-law, daughter-in-
law,* etc.: **la belle-sœur, le beau-fils, la belle-fille, le beau-père, la**

28

belle-mère, les beau*x*-parent*s*. As you can see, in the plural, both words take the signs of the plural (**les beau*x*-frère*s*, les belle*s*-sœur*s*,** etc.).

PART TWO

21 Nous n'avons pas passé le cent. *We didn't do more than a hundred.*
Passer is used here in the sense of *to exceed, to go beyond.*
You could say: **Il a passé la soixantaine**: *He is over sixty.*

22 Allons, vous n'allez pas vous disputer! Vos amis veulent certainement se laver et se rafraîchir un peu. *Come on, you're not going to quarrel! Your friends certainly want to have a wash and something to drink.*
a Vous n'allez pas *vous* disputer.: *You are not going to quarrel.*
Vous must be used here, in front of **disputer**, in the same way as **me** had to be used in front of **ennuyer** in **il m'arrive de *m*'ennuyer** (cf. N15 above). It is a meaningless reflexive pronoun.
b (ils) veulent se laver: (*they*) *want to have a wash* (lit. *to wash themselves*). As you can see, **se** is the reflexive pronoun used with the infinitive in connection with the **ils** form: **Ils veulent se laver.**
Se is also used with **il** and **elle**:
Il/elle veut *se* laver.
Study the reflexive pronouns in the following:

Je me **lave**	*Je* **veux** *me* **laver**
Tu te **laves**	*Tu* **veux** *te* **laver**
Il/elle se **lave**	*Il/elle* **veut** *se* **laver**
Nous nous **lavons**	*Nous* **voulons** *nous* **laver**
Vous vous **lavez**	*Vous* **voulez** *vous* **laver**
Ils/elles se **lavent**	*Ils/elles* **veulent** *se* **laver**

23 Mais non, c'est à toi de leur faire les honneurs de ta maison. *Oh no, it's up to you to do* (lit. *to them*) *the honours of your house.*

24 Vous vous êtes arrêtés, j'espère. *I hope you stopped.*
Note that the past tense of all reflexive verbs is conjugated with **être**:
Je me suis lavé.: *I washed myself.*
Ils se sont compris.: *They understood each other/one another.*
Elles se sont ennuyées.: *They got bored.*
Naturally the past participle agrees with the subject.

25 Nous nous sommes arrêtés à moitié chemin et . . . *We stopped halfway and . . .*
You know that *I stop* is **je m'arrête**; *we stop* is **nous nous arrêtons**. The perfect is conjugated with **être**, so *we stopped* is **nous nous sommes arrêtés.**

252

26 **Mais, vous savez, quand on veut faire tout soi-même, on n'a pas le temps de tout faire.** *But you know, when you want to do everything yourself, you haven't got the time to do everything.*
soi-même: lit. *oneself*
You know that **moi-même**: *myself* is used to reinforce the reflexive pronoun **me**: **je me parle à *moi-même*** (N8b above). In other words, **moi-même** is used in connection with the **je** form of the verb. From this you cán deduce the other forms: **toi-même, lui-même, elle-même, nous-mêmes, vous-mêmes, eux-mêmes, elles-mêmes.**
Soi-même is the form used in connection with **on.**

27 **Mangez des bons fruits de mon verger, cueillis par moi, ce matin même.** *Eat some good fruit from my orchard, gathered by me this very morning.*
a **des bons fruits** Notice that here, contrary to the general principle you learnt in L14 (N7), **des** is used even though an adjective precedes the noun.
b **ce matin même**: *this very morning* Careful! You learnt that **même** used with a noun means *same*: **le même restaurant** (L4, N28). This is so when **même** is used BEFORE the noun:
le *même* matin: *the* SAME *morning*
But when **même** is used AFTER the noun, it is equivalent to *very*:
le matin même: *the* VERY *morning*.

28 **Ça doit être merveilleux de cueillir ses fruits soi-même.** *It must be marvellous to pick your fruit yourself.*
a **Cueillir**: *to pick, gather, pluck* is an irregular verb (App. IIE).
b **ses fruits soi-même.** The **ses** form of the possessive adjective is used in an impersonal sentence. Compare:
***Je* cueille *mes* fruits *moi-même*.**: *I pick* MY *fruit* MYSELF.
***Il* cueille *ses* fruits *lui-même*.**: HE *picks* HIS *fruit* HIMSELF.
Il est merveilleux de cueillir *ses* fruits *soi-même*.: *It is marvellous to pick* ONE'S *fruit* ONESELF.
You saw this use of **ses** (with the impersonal **on**) in (L24, N28):
À cette époque-là, je crois qu'on mangeait avec *ses* doigts.

29 **Oui; mais je ne m'en suis jamais servi!** *Yes, but I've never used it!*
se servir de In the sense of *to make use of*, **servir** is always conjugated with a reflexive pronoun and followed by **de**; without a reflexive pronoun it has a different meaning — *to serve* — (App. IIE).

30 **Mais ce vieux vélo appartenait sans doute aux anciens propriétaires.** *But this old bike probably belonged to the former owners.*
les anciens propriétaires: *the former, previous owners* Note that **ancien** is, in this phrase, used in front of this noun.

28

31 **Ils ont même laissé des quantités de meubles anciens dont certains ont, sans aucun doute, beaucoup de valeur.** *They even left a lot of old furniture some of which is undoubtedly valuable.* (lit. *They even left quantities of old furniture, of which certain ones have without any doubt, much value.*)

a **des meubles anciens**: *old furniture* Here **ancien** is used AFTER the noun. It then means *old*.

b **sans aucun doute**: lit. *without any doubt* Sans doute means *probably*.

32 **J'en doute.** *I doubt it. To doubt something* is **douter** *de* quelque chose. So *I doubt* is **j'en** doute. *I doubt that* . . . is **je doute que** . . .

33 **Je me doutais bien que tu voudrais aller le voir.** *I felt sure you'd want to go and see it.*
Take care to distinguish between **je doute que** . . .: *I doubt that* . . . and **je** *me* **doute que**: *I feel sure that.*

The language you have learnt

The passive

Mon jardin	*est*	entouré de murs.
La rivière		bordée d'arbres.
Mes vacances	*sont*	finies.

Verbs with reflexive pronouns and passive meanings

Ma ferme	*se trouve*	dans un petit village de province.
Le tabac	*se vend*	facilement.
Mon frère	*s'appelle*	Paul.

Verbs which take a "useless" reflexive pronoun

Je	*m'*	arrête assois	ici.
	me	mets à travailler. promène tous les soirs.	

Je me		regarde dans la glace.
Tu te		regardes dans la glace.
Il Elle	se	regarde dans la glace.
Nous nous		regardons dans la glace.
Vous vous		regardez dans la glace.
Ils Elles	se	regardent dans la glace.

Myself, yourself, etc.

Je fais mes courses		moi-même.
Tu fais tes courses		toi-même.
Il	fait ses courses	lui-même.
Elle		elle-même.
Nous faisons nos courses		nous-mêmes.
Vous faites vos courses		vous-mêmes.
Ils	font leurs courses	eux-mêmes.
Elles		elles-mêmes.

Each other, one another

Nous nous		comprenons querellons	l'un/l'une l'autre. les uns/les unes les autres.
Vous vous		comprenez querellez	
Ils	se	comprennent querellent	l'un l'autre. les uns les autres.
Elles			l'une l'autre. les unes les autres.

28 Doubting, supposing

Il a dit qu'il	viendrait, partirait,	mais *j'en doute.*
Je me doutais (*bien*) *qu'*il		viendrait. partirait.

Le quatorze juillet The fourteenth of July

What happens

PART ONE
Demain c'est la fête.: *Tomorrow's the national holiday.*
Marie-Claire enjoyed her weekend in Auvergne, but is glad to be back
in Paris. She was determined not to stay longer even though her uncle
tried hard to persuade her. She must write and thank him for his
hospitality. Luc and Paul enjoyed themselves on the farm; Paul with the
bicycle he found. Marie-Claire would hate to live in the country.
Tomorrow is the fourteenth of July — Bastille day, a national holiday.

PART TWO
Sur les Champs-Elysées: *On the Champs-Elysées*
Monsieur and Madame Delon are on the crowded Champs-Elysées.
Monsieur Delon and Paul quarrel; Paul goes off, saying he can see
Marie-Claire. Monsieur Delon complains about Paul, about Valérie
and then about his wife; but she is diplomatic. They decide to go for
a stroll.

PART THREE
Pourquoi se fatiguer?: *Why bother?*
Pierre thinks the solution is obvious.

Qui paiera le marchand de journaux?: *Who'll pay the newsagent?*
The little boy has lost two francs.

New words in this lesson

l'accueil (*m*) welcome, hospitality
accuser to accuse
tu accuses you accuse
admettre to admit
j'ai hâte de I can't wait to, I'm in a
  hurry to
l'air (*m*) air
alors que when, while
l'argument (*m*) argument
attaquer to attack

(ils) attaquèrent (they) attacked
au besoin if necessary
au grand air in the open air
avoir hâte de to be in a hurry to
le bal dance
ça, par exemple! well!
c'est bien ça that's right
changer d'avis to change one's mind
il cherchait à he tried to
chercher à to try to

29

chic nice, kind
la compagnie company
le compliment compliment
contre against
curieux curious
de plus more
je me suis décidée à I decided to
se décider à to decide to
le défilé procession
désolé very sorry
dire bonjour to say hello
se distraire to amuse oneself
je me suis distraite I amused myself
s'emparer de to take hold of
l'étranger (m) stranger
se fatiguer to tire oneself
la fête holiday
la fête nationale national holiday
les feux d'artifice (m) fireworks
la foule crowd
grandir to grow (big)
il grandit he grows (big)
il n'y a pas de mal that's alright
le jour de fête holiday
le livre book
le marchand de journaux newspaper
  seller
marcher to walk
marcher sur le pied to step on
  someone's foot
le mariage wedding
le monument monument
l'occupation (f) occupation
le Parisien Parisian
la patience patience

se perdre to lose oneself
persuader to persuade
le peuple people
la plainte complaint
se plaire to enjoy oneself
il s'est plu he enjoyed himself
profiter de to take advantage of
profitons de let's take advantage of
se promener au hasard to wander
  (around)
quant à as for
les remerciements (m) thanks
se rendre compte to realise
je me rends compte I realise
repartir to go away again
reprendre to take up again
repris (par) taken up (by)
retrouver to find again
(il) se révolta (it) revolted
se révolter (contre) to revolt (against)
la Révolution Française French
  Revolution
royal royal
saisir to seize
(il) saisit (he) seizes
je souhaite I hope
souhaiter to hope
tant mieux! thank goodness!
tenir bon to insist
la tyrannie tyranny
nous verrons we'll see
vicié evil
vieillir to grow old
vingt-neuf twenty-nine
vingt-neuvième twenty-ninth

Notes

PART ONE

1 **Guy aurait voulu rester un jour de plus.** *Guy would have liked to stay one more day.*

2 **Alors, je me suis décidée à employer les grands arguments.** *So I decided to put forward a strong case.*
Je me suis décidée à You learnt the verb **décider** in L14: **Nous avons décidé de vivre chacun notre vie.** As you can see, **décider** is constructed with **de** and means *to decide, to make up one's mind*. *Se* **décider** is constructed with **à** and implies that the decision was not reached at once; it followed some hesitation:

258

J'ai décidé de partir.: *I made up my mind to go.*
Je me suis décidé à partir.: *I eventually decided to go.*
Of course, as *se décider à* is a reflexive verb, its past tenses have
to be conjugated with **être**.

3 **J'ai dit tout simplement: 'Je suis désolée, mais je dois absolument
rentrer à Paris demain.** *I simply said: 'I'm sorry, but I absolutely
must return to Paris tomorrow'.*
Je dois is the **je** form of a verb you will study more systematically
in this lesson. You saw it first in L15, N3 where it meant *is
supposed to*. Here, in **je dois rentrer à Paris, je dois** is the equivalent
of *I must, I have to, it is my duty to*. The infinitive of **je dois** is
devoir (cf. App. IVB).

4 **J'ai dû tenir bon.** *I had to stand firm.*
Dû is the past participle of **devoir** (notice the circumflex which
helps to distinguish it from **du** meaning *some* or *of the*). So, the
je form of the past tense of **devoir** is **j'ai dû.**

5 **Mais, il a fini par admettre qu'il devait, lui aussi, rentrer aujourd'hui.**
But he ended up by admitting that he had to return home today too.
Il devait is part of the imperfect tense of **devoir**.

6 **En ce moment, il doit penser à nous.** *At this moment, he must be
thinking of us.*
il doit penser à nous: *he must be thinking of us, he is bound/likely
to be thinking of us* As you can see from this example, **il doit** can
mean *he must* in the sense of *he is bound/likely to . . .*

7 **Je devrais lui écrire aujourd'hui pour le remercier de son bon accueil.**
I ought to write to him today to thank him for his hospitality.
Je devrais is the **je** form of the conditional tense of **devoir**.

8 **J'aurais dû l'inviter à venir nous voir.** *I should have invited him to
come and see us.*
J'aurais dû l'inviter: *I should have invited him* **J'aurais dû** is the **je**
form of the conditional in the past of **devoir,** in the same way as
j'aurais aimé is the conditional in the past of **aimer** (L27, N1a).

9 **Je le ferai par lettre.** *I'll do it in a* (lit. *by*) *letter.*

10 **Inutile de dire que Luc s'est plu à Plainchamp et que Paul s'est
bien amusé avec le vieux vélo qu'il a trouvé.** *No need to say that
Luc liked it at Plainchamp and Paul enjoyed himself immensely
with the old bike he found.*
Se plaire is a reflexive verb meaning *to be happy*. The reflexive
pronoun, which is in fact meaningless, cannot be omitted. As with

29 all reflexive verbs, the past tenses of **se plaire** have to be conjugated with **être**. Its past participle is **plu**, so the perfect of **se plaire** is: **je *me* suis plu** (cf. App. IIIE).

11 **Moi, je me suis distraite comme j'ai pu.** *I amused myself as much as I could.*
se distraire: *to amuse oneself* The past participle is **distrait**. It is an irregular verb (cf. App. IIIE).

12 **Je pourrais peut-être, au besoin, vivre dans une ville de province, Oh . . . et encore . . .** *Perhaps I could, if necessary, live in a country town — Oh . . . even that . . .*
Je pourrais: *I should be able to, I could* is the conditional tense of **pouvoir**: *to be able to*; (cf. App. IVB).

13 **Demain, c'est le quartorze juillet, jour de la fête nationale!**
Tomorrow is the fourteenth of July, the national holiday!

14 **'Ce jour-là,' disent les livres d'histoire, 'le peuple de Paris se révolta contre la tyrannie royale.** *'That day,' say the history books, 'the people of Paris rebelled against the royal tyranny.*
Il se révolta is an example of a tense grammarians call the past historic. It has exactly the same meaning as the past tense you already know. **Il se révolta** is therefore equivalent to **il s'est révolté**. The only difference is one of style: the past historic is a tense which is never used in conversation, only in writing.

15 **Les Parisiens attaquèrent la Bastille et finirent par s'en emparer.**
The Parisians attacked the Bastille and ended up taking it over.
a **(Ils) attaquèrent**: *they attacked* is the **ils** form of the past historic of **attaquer**. As you now know, **ils attaquèrent** means the same as **ils ont attaqué**. The author of a history book would use this tense to report historical events.
b **(Ils) finirent** is the **ils** form of the past historic of **finir**.

16 **Le 14 Juillet 1789 marqua le début de la Révolution Française.'**
The 14th July, 1789 marked the beginning of the French Revolution.'
1789: **dix-sept cent quatre-vingt-neuf**
(il) marqua: *it marked* (cf. N14b above)

PART TWO

17 **Je vous demande pardon, Madame, je vous ai marché sur le pied.**
I beg your pardon, I stepped on your foot.

18 **Faites, je vous en prie . . .** *Please, do . . .*
Je vous en prie is commonly used to invite someone to do something.

19 **Il n'y a plus moyen d'avancer.** *It's no longer possible to move forward.*

20 **Je t'en prie, Paul; tu ne vas pas te mettre à te plaindre!** *Please, Paul, don't start complaining!*

21 **Si j'avais su, je serais resté à la campagne.** *If I'd known, I would have stayed in the country.*
a **si j'avais su** for **savoir**, see App. IVB.
b **je serais resté**: *I would have stayed*
Rester forms its past tenses with **être**.

22 **Tu as raison, tu aurais dû terminer tes vacances tout seul.** *You're right — you should have finished your holiday alone.*

23 **J'aurais pu, tu sais!** *I could have done, you know!*
je peux rester: *I am able to stay/I can stay*
je pourrais rester: *I should be able to stay/I could stay*
j'aurais pu rester: *I should have been able to stay/I could have stayed*

24 **Ouf! Tant mieux!** *Phew! Thank goodness for that!*
Tant mieux! is the opposite of **tant pis!**: *too bad!*

25 **C'est curieux, plus il grandit, plus il devient insupportable!**
It's strange, the bigger he gets, the more unbearable he becomes!

26 **Non seulement je dois supporter ce garçon mais je dois te supporter, toi!** *Not only must I put up with that boy, but I have to put up with you!*

27 **Mais . . . je n'ai rien dit de mal . . .** *But . . . I said nothing bad . . .*
De is made necessary by **rien**.

28 **Quant à ta fille, elle préfère passer la journée avec un étranger plutôt qu'avec ses parents.** *As for your daughter, she prefers to spend the day with a stranger rather than with her parents.*
un étranger: *a stranger*
You learnt the phrase **à l'étranger**: *abroad* in L21 (N11). The word **étranger**: *stranger* can also be used in the sense of *foreigner*.

29 **Nous verrons bien.** *We'll soon see.*
Bien reinforces **nous verrons**.

30 **J'en suis sûre. Et je souhaite que ma fille trouve un aussi bon mari que le mien.** *I'm sure of it. And I hope my daughter finds a husband as good as mine.*
un aussi bon mari que le mien   Notice the word order carefully:
a good husband: **un bon mari**
1   2   3   1   2   3
as good a husband as: **un aussi bon mari que**
1   2   3   1   2   3

261

29

31 **Merci du compliment.** *Thank you for the compliment.*
merci du Both **merci** and the verb **remercier** are followed by **de**.

32 **Promenons-nous au hasard dans Paris.** *Let's wander around Paris.*
promenons-nous Notice the command forms of reflexive verbs.
Nous nous promenons.: *We are having a walk.* **Promenons-nous.**:
Let's have a walk.
Vous vous taisez.: *You are keeping quiet.*
Taisez-vous.: *Be quiet.*

The language you have learnt

Must = probably

Je suppose qu'en ce moment	*il doit*	penser à moi. travailler.

I ought to

Je devrais	travailler; m'en aller;	mais, tant pis, je reste.

I should, could have

J'aurais dû *J'aurais pu*	chercher. partir.

Se plaire, se distraire, s'amuser

J'espère que vous allez	*vous plaire* *vous distraire* *vous amuser*	à Paris. au bord de la mer. en France.

The past tense of se plaire, s'amuser

Je	*me suis plu* *me suis amusé*	au bord de la mer. en France.

The more + verb

Plus	je travaille,	*plus*	je dors.
	je voyage,		je m'ennuie.

The more + adjective and noun

29

Plus	un meuble est ancien,	*plus*	il est cher.
	j'ai de clients,		je gagne d'argent,

Whereas, while

Vous travaillez, Vous êtes à votre bureau,	*alors que* *pendant que*	je m'amuse. moi, je me distrais. je ne fais rien.

I'm sorry

Je suis	*désolé* *navré*	mais	j'ai oublié. je ne peux pas venir.

It doesn't matter

Excusez-moi.	*Je vous en prie.*
Je vous demande pardon.	*Il n'y a pas de mal.*

263

Le départ   The departure

What happens

PART ONE

Il faut que les Delon retournent au Canada.: *The Delons must go back to Canada.*
The holiday is over. Monsieur Delon is rather sorry but he knows Paul will be overjoyed at the thought of going back to Canada. They are going back via London. Monsieur Delon is going to the travel agency to check their bookings. He is afraid that there might be a strike.

PART TWO

Préparatifs de départ: *Preparations for departure*
Madame Delon has bought so many dresses that she needs a new trunk to put them all in. Paul looks in the classified advertisements in the paper but finds nothing suitable. Monsieur Delon tells Paul he should write to Monsieur Julliard — and to watch his spelling.

La lettre de Paul: *Paul's letter*
Paul writes to thank Monsieur Julliard for having him to stay.

Le dénouement: *The end of the story*
Monsieur and Madame Delon are thinking about the bill when Georges and Valérie burst in and announce that they want to get married. They order some champagne to celebrate and Monsieur Delon says he will get a teaching post in Paris to be near them. Paul, whose new bicycle is already on its way to Canada, is not so pleased.

PART THREE

Ici on parle toutes les langues.: *All languages spoken here.*
The customer thinks there must be lots of interpreters.

Épilogue: *Epilogue*
The Delon family says goodbye to you.

New words in this lesson

à louer to let
à moins que unless
à vendre for sale
s'adresser (à) to apply (to)

adressez-vous (à) apply (to)
l'agence de voyages (*f*) travel agency
attention à . . . be careful of
aveugle blind

boire à la santé de to drink the health of
bon souvenir regards
la bouteille bottle
le champagne champagne
d'après ce que according to what
de si tôt in a hurry
la demande d'emploi post wanted
le dénouement the ending
dépensier extravagant
embrasser to kiss
s'empêcher de to stop oneself, to prevent oneself
t'empêcher de to stop yourself, to prevent yourself
encore une fois once again
l'épilogue (m) epilogue
l'étiquette (f) etiquette
faire cadeau de to make a gift of
tu fasses cadeau de you make a gift of
il faut que it is necessary that . . .
les félicitations (f) congratulations
le fiancé fiancé
la guitare guitar
l'hôtesse de l'air (f) air hostess
l'interprète (m & f) interpreter
jouer de to play
le malheur c'est que the unfortunate thing is
la malle trunk
le moment moment
nommer to appoint
la note bill
les nouvelles (f) news
obtenir to get, to gain

les occasions diverses (f) general bargains
l'offre d'emploi (f) post vacant
l'orthographe (f) spelling
la page page
il paraît que it appears that
paraître to appear
passer par to go via
la permission permission
les petites annonces (f) advertisements
la poste restante poste restante
pour que tu dises for you to say
pourvu que . . . as long as . . .
le préparatif preparation
prévenir to warn
prévenu warned
(elles) réclament (they) are demanding, claiming
réclamer to demand, to claim
la règle rule
respecter to respect
le salaire salary
(elles) se mettent en grève (they're) going on strike
se mettre en grève to go on strike
ils se prononcent they are pronounced
se prononcer to be pronounced
la situation job
le souvenir memory
le Syndicat d'Initiative information office
trentième thirtieth
trop de too many
valable valid
vérifier to check
la villa villa
le vol flight

30

Notes

PART ONE

1 **Il faut que les Delon retournent au Canada.** *The Delons must go back to Canada.*

il faut que . . . : lit. *it is necessary that . . .* In French, certain phrases and verbs are followed by a special form of the verb, which we shall refer to as the SUBJUNCTIVE. You will learn the most common of these phrases and verbs in this lesson. **Il faut que . . .** which corresponds to *must* is one of these. It so happens that the **ils** form of the subjunctive of **retourner** is **retournent** and looks exactly

265

30

like the **ils** form of the ordinary present (this remark is true of all regular **-er** verbs).

2 **Je regrette qu'il ne nous soit pas possible de rester plus longtemps.** *I'm sorry that it is not possible for us to stay any longer.*
je regrette qu'il soit: *I'm sorry that it is* This is another phrase — a verb expressing an emotion — which is followed by the subjunctive.
The **il** form of the subjunctive of **être** is required because **regretter que** precedes.
Notice the il form of the subjunctive of **être: il soit** (See Appendix).

3 **C'est dommage que le temps passe si vite en vacances!** *It's a pity that time passes so quickly on holiday!*
C'est dommage que le temps passe.: *It's a pity that time passes.*
C'est dommage que, which also expresses an emotion, is another phrase which must be followed by a verb in the subjunctive. The **il** form of the subjunctive of **passer** — an **-er** verb — is **il passe.**
You can see that the **il** form of the subjunctive of **passer** — and of all **-er** verbs — looks the same as the ordinary form.

4 **J'ai peur qu'il ne veuille pas revenir en France de si tôt.** *I'm afraid that he won't want to come back to France in a hurry.*
j'ai peur qu'il ne veuille pas **J'ai peur que** is another phrase expressing emotion — fear this time — which is followed by a subjunctive. **Veuille** is the **il** form of the subjunctive of **vouloir.**

5˙ **Mais, je crains qu'il ne remporte un mauvais souvenir de son séjour ici.** *But I'm afraid he'll take away a bad memory of his stay here.*
Je crains que . . . , like **j'ai peur que . . .** (both phrases mean roughly the same) must be followed by a subjunctive:
Je *crains*/*j'ai peur* qu'il ne *retourne* au Canada.
Je *crains*/*j'ai peur* qu'il ne *soit* là.
Note that, in the sentence **je crains qu'il *ne* remporte un mauvais souvenir, ne** is not a negative (the negative is normally **ne . . . pas**).
Ne must be incorporated into a sentence introduced by **craindre que** (and by **avoir peur que**). It is the same **ne** as in: **Il y a longtemps que je *ne* suis allé visiter un musée** (L24, N6).

6 **Je suis content qu'il se soit quand même fait des amis.** *All the same, I'm glad he's made himself some friends.*
Je suis content que . . . : *I'm glad that . . .* is another phrase expressing an emotion — satisfaction — which must be followed by a verb in the subjunctive.

266

7 **Je voudrais que Paul voie un peu la capitale anglaise et qu'il puisse** **30**
la comparer avec Paris. *I'd like Paul to see a little of the English
capital, and for him to be able to compare it with Paris.*

a **Je voudrais que Paul voie la capitale:** lit. *I would like that Paul should
see the capital*
Vouloir que is another phrase which must be followed by a subjunctive.
Voie is the **je** form of the subjunctive of **voir** (App. IVB).

b **et qu'il puisse comparer** **Puisse** is the **il** form of the subjunctive of
pouvoir (App. IVB).

8 **Je veux aussi qu'Yvonne fasse connaissance avec Londres.** *I also
want Yvonne to get to know London.*
Fasse is the **je**, as well as the **il/elle** form of the subjunctive of **faire**.

9 **Je vais aller à l'agence de voyages pour vérifier que nos places sont
bien louées sur le vol 742 mardi matin.** *I'm going to go to the travel
agent's to check that our seats are in fact booked on flight 742
Tuesday morning.*
742: sept cent quarante-deux

10 **Je doute que l'employé à qui j'ai parlé ait fait tout ce que je lui ai
demandé.** *I doubt if the clerk to whom I spoke has done all I asked
him (to do).*
je doute que l'employé ... *ait fait* **Je doute que** is another phrase
— it expresses doubt — which must be followed by a subjunctive.
In this sentence, **je doute que** is followed by the **il** form of the
subjunctive of **avoir**: **il ait** (See Appendix).
To be more accurate, we should say that **il *ait fait*** is in fact the
PAST tense of the subjunctive of **faire**. Compare these two
examples:
ORDINARY PAST:
Il *a fait* son travail.: *He has done his work.*
PAST SUBJUNCTIVE:
Je *doute qu'*il *ait fait* son travail.: *I doubt whether he has done his
work.*
Compare also the present and the past tense of the subjunctive of
faire:
Je *doute qu'*il *fasse* son travail. (present)
Je *doute qu'*il *ait fait* son travail. (past)

11 **Il est possible qu'elles se mettent en grève après-demain.** *It's possible
that they are going on strike the day after tomorrow.*
Il est possible que is another expression of doubt which, like **je
doute que ...** must be followed by a subjunctive. **Se mettent** is here
the **elles** form of the subjunctive of **se mettre** (App. IIIE).

30 12 D'après ce que j'ai lu dans le journal, je ne crois pas que les hôtesses de l'air réussissent à obtenir une augmentation. *According to what I read in the newspaper, I don't think the air hostesses will succeed in getting an increase.*
Je ne crois pas que . . . is another verbal phrase which must be followed by a subjunctive. Though **elles réussissent** looks like an ordinary present, it is here the **elles** form of the subjunctive of **réussir** (App. IIA).

13 Valérie, elle, croit qu'elles réussiront. *Valérie thinks they'll succeed.*
elle croit qu'elles réussiront Notice that, rather unexpectedly, **elle croit que** is followed by an ordinary future. It is felt that the negative form: **je/tu**, etc. **ne crois pas** is loaded with more doubt than the positive form **je/tu**, etc. **crois**. So **je ne crois pas que** is usually followed by the verb in the subjunctive, **je crois que** is never. Compare:
Je *crois qu'*elles *réussiront.* (ordinary future)
Je *ne crois pas qu'*elles *réussissent.* (subjunctive)

14 À propos . . . il faut que j'aille à la poste voir si j'ai des lettres en poste restante. *By the way, I must go to the post office to see if I have any letters poste restante.*
J'aille is the **je** form of the subjunctive of **aller** (App. ICa).

PART TWO
15 Pour que tu dises ça, il faut vraiment que tu en aies beaucoup! *For you to say that, you really must have a lot!*
a pour que tu dises ça: lit. *in order that you should say that* **Pour que** is followed by the subjunctive — here **tu dises** which is the **tu** form of the subjunctive of **dire** (cf. App. IIIE).
b il faut que tu aies Tu aies is the **tu** form of the subjunctive of **avoir**.

16 Tu sais bien que je n'avais rien à me mettre. *You KNOW I had nothing to put on.*
All the phrases you have so far learnt which take the subjunctive include **que**: **il faut que, je regrette que, c'est dommage que, j'ai peur que, je crains que, je suis content que, je veux que, je doute que, il est possible que, je ne crois pas que, pour que**. But do not jump to the conclusion that any phrase including **que** must be followed by a subjunctive. **Je sais que** is followed, as you can see, by the ordinary form.

17 Tu es la femme la plus dépensière que je connaisse. *You are the most extravagant woman I know.*
La femme la plus dépensière que je connaisse: Verbs which follow

phrases built on the pattern of **le plus dépensier que . . . , le plus grand que . . .** etc., are usually in the subjunctive.

18 **Il va falloir que nous achetions une malle.** *We are going to have to buy a trunk.*
Nous achetions is the **nous** form of the subjunctive of **acheter.**

19 **À moins que tu ne fasses cadeau de tes robes à Mme Louvier . . .**
Unless you give your dresses to Madame Louvier . . .
À moins que . . . : *unless* is yet another phrase which must be followed by a subjunctive. Here it is followed by the **tu** form of the subjunctive of **faire.**
Note that **ne** in this sentence is not negative. It is the same sort of superfluous **ne** that you saw in N5 above.

20 **Apprenez à jouer de la guitare en vingt leçons . . .** *Learn to play the guitar in twenty lessons . . .*
jouer *de* **la guitare**: *to play the guitar*   Remember that you learnt the verb **jouer** in Lesson 2. Paul said: **je joue** *au* **tennis tous les jours** (N15).
When **jouer** is used in connection with a game, it must be followed by **à**: **je joue** *au* **football.** But *to play an instrument* — here a guitar — is **jouer** *de* **la guitare.**

21 **Adressez-vous au Syndicat d'Initiative de Nice.** *Write to the Nice 'Syndicat d'Initiative.'*
Le Syndicat d'Initiative is an organisation run by local people in holiday resorts or cultural centres, whose job is to provide information concerning the town.

22 **Les mots ne s'écrivent pas toujours comme ils se prononcent.**
Words are not always written as they are pronounced.

23 **Tu as demandé à l'hôtel de préparer la note?** *Have you asked the hotel to prepare the bill?*
la note: *the bill*   A *hotel bill* is **une note** but a *restaurant bill* is **une addition** (L25).

24 **Oui, pourvu qu'elle ne soit pas trop élevée!** *Yes, let's hope that it's not too high!*
pourvu qu'elle ne soit pas . . .   When the sentence introduced by **pourvu que . . .** ends with an exclamation mark, **pourvu que** means *let's hope that.* It is a phrase which has to be followed by a subjunctive.

25 Excusez-moi de vous déranger . . . et . . . de ne pas vous avoir prévenus . . . *Excuse me for disturbing you, and . . . for not having told you before . . .*

Excusez-moi de . . . + an infinitive: *excuse me for . . .*

26 Il faut que vous sachiez que j'aime votre fille et que je voudrais l'épouser. *I want you to know that I love your daughter and I would like to marry her.*

Il faut que vous sachiez Sachiez is the **vous** form of the subjunctive of **savoir**. It is introduced by **il faut que** (N1 above and App. IVB).

27 Venez que je vous embrasse tous les deux. *Come here, so I can kiss you both.* **Venez que** is a phrase which has to be followed by the subjunctive.

28 Et . . . pour pouvoir rester à Paris avec vous, je vais demander au Ministre de l'Éducation Nationale de me nommer professeur à Paris. *And, to be able to stay in Paris with you, I'm going to ask the Ministry of Education to appoint me as a teacher in Paris.*

The language you have learnt

Il faut que + subjunctive

Il faut que	j'*aille* à la poste. je *sois* à la gare à huit heures.

Verbs that take the subjunctive

Je regrette que		*parte*	demain.
C'est dommage que		*soit*	à la gare en ce moment.
Je suis content que	M. Delon	*ne voie pas*	les égouts.
J'ai peur que		*n'ait*	le rhume.
Je crains que		*ne soit*	fatigué.

The subjunctive after vouloir que

Je veux que *Je voudrais que*	Valérie *fasse* la connaissance de Georges. Paul *mette* son manteau.

French—English

a (il/elle) *2* has (he, she)
à *1* at, to, *2* in
à bientôt *8* see you soon
à bord *27* in, on board
à cause de *16* because of
à côté de *8* near, beside
à droite *6* (on, to the) right
à elle *14* hers
à eux *14* theirs
à fond *16* at full blast
à gauche *6* (on, to the) left
à l'air *24* looking
à l'étranger *21* abroad
à l'heure *16* on time
à l'instant *25* this minute, just now
à l'intérieur (de) *24* inside
à l'ombre *27* in the shade
à la campagne *5* in the country
à la droite *14* on, at the right
à la fin de *13* at the end of
à la fois *19* both, at the same time
à la gauche *14* on, at the left
à la ligne *16* new paragraph
à la main *15* by hand
à la maison *8* at home
à la radio *27* on the radio
à la réflexion *12* on reflexion, come to think of it
à louer *30* to let
à ma taille *6* my size
à moi *14* mine
à moins que *30* unless
à moitié chemin *28* half-way
à mon âge *21* at my age
à mon avis *21* in my opinion
à nouveau *21* again
à part *5* apart from
à part ça *17* apart from that
à peu près *20* almost, more or less
à pied *24* on foot
à plein-temps *16* full-time
à propos *7* by the way
à proximité de *24* near to, close to
à quoi bon? *16* what's the use of?

à quoi sert? *23* what's (something) for?
à rayures *15* striped
à table! *4* come and eat!, let's eat!
à tempérament *28* by instalments
à temps partiel *16* part-time
à toi *14* yours
à tout à l'heure *7* see you later
à travers *24* through
à tue-tête *16* at the top of her voice
à vendre *30* for sale
à votre service *7* at your service
à vrai dire *10* really, to tell the truth
abandonner *23* to desert, to abandon
abattre *28* to cut down
absent *16* absent
absolument *12* definitely
accepter *18* to accept
l' accident (*m*) *27* accident
l' accident de voiture (*m*) *27* car accident
accompagner *6* to go with, accompany
accrocher *23* to catch (on something), to hook
l' accueil (*m*) *29* welcome, hospitality
accuser *29* to accuse
acheter *6* to buy
l' acier-inox (*m*) *13* stainless steel
les actualités (de la semaine) (*f*) *23* news (of the week)
actuel *25* present
l' addition (*f*) *25* bill
l' adjoint (*m*) *16* assistant
l' Administration (*f*) *17* Government, administration
admettre *29* to admit
admirer *1* to admire
adopter *14* to adopt
adorable *5* gorgeous
adorer *2* to love
l' adresse (*f*) *7* address
adresser (une lettre) *16* to address (a letter)

s' **adresser** (à) *30* to apply (to)
l' **adulte** (*m*) *22* adult
l' **aéroport** (*m*) *1* airport
l' **affaire** (*f*) *27* bargain
les **affaires** (*f*) *15* things, business
l' **affiche** (*f*) *23* poster
   afficher *23* to post up
   affreux *7* terrible
l' **after-shave** (*m*) *1* after-shave
   agacer *14* to annoy
l' **agence** (*f*) *10* agency
l' **agence de publicité** (*f*)
   10 advertising agency
l' **agence de voyages** (*f*) *30* travel
   agency
i' **agent de police** (*m*) *6* policeman
l' **agent de service** (*m*) *26* officer on
   duty
   agréable *17* pleasant, nice
   aider *6* to help
   aigu *20* sharp
   ailleurs *15* elsewhere
   aimable *3* nice
   aimablement *12* politely
   aimer *2* to like, to love
   aimer bien *9* to like very much
l' **air** (*m*) *29* air
   ajouter *8* to add
l' **Allemagne** (*f*) *21* Germany
   allemand *22* German
   aller *4* to be going to, *6* to go,
   18 to suit
l' **aller** (*m*) *12* single ticket
   aller à la rencontre de *19* to go
   to meet
   aller à l'étranger *21* to go abroad
   aller chercher *19* to meet, to fetch
l' **aller et retour** (*m*) *12* return
   ticket
   allez-vous-en *6* go away
   allô *10* hello
s' **allonger** *20* to lie down
   allons *2* well, come on
   allons bon *7* there now
   allumer (la radio) *13* to turn on
   (the radio)
   allumer le poste *22* to switch on
   the set
   alors *2* so, then
   alors que *29* when, while
   améliorer *17* to improve
   amener *18* to bring

l' **ami** (*m*) *1* friend
les **amitiés** (*f*) *25* regards
l' **amour** (*m*) *23* love
l' **ampoule** (*f*) *3* bulb
   amusant *4* funny
s' **amuser** *8* to enjoy oneself
les **amygdales** (*f*) *20* tonsils
l' **an** (*m*) *5* year
   ancien *26* former, ex-, *28* old
l' **âne** (*m*) *5* donkey
l' **ange** (*m*) *23* angel
   anglais *22* English
l' **Angleterre** (*f*) *21* England
l' **année** (*f*) *2* year
   annoncer *21* to announce, to tell
l' **annuaire** (*m*) *25* directory
l' **antiquité** (*f*) *24* antiquity
   août *21* August
l' **apéritif** (*m*) *17* drink, apéritif
l' **appareil** (*m*) *22* set (TV or radio)
l' **appartement** (*m*) *5* flat
   appartenir *28* to belong
   appeler *10* to phone
s' **appeler** *1* to be called
l' **appendice** (*m*) *20* appendix
   applaudir *18* to applaud
   appliquer *20* to apply, to rub in
   apporter *8* to bring
   apprendre *11* to learn
   approcher (de) *25* to get near (to)
   approuver *7* to endorse
   appuyer *10* to press
   après *9* after
   après avoir *25* after having
   après-demain *12* day after
   tomorrow
   après Jésus-Christ *23* A.D.
l' **après-midi** (*m*) *8* afternoon
   après tout *18* after all
l' **arbre** (*m*) *8* tree
l' **arc-en-ciel** (*m*) *24* rainbow
l' **archéologue** (*m*) *24* archaeologist
l' **argent** (*m*) *4* money
l' **argent de poche** (*m*) *22* pocket
   money
l' **argument** (*m*) *29* argument
s' **arranger** *23* to be settled
l' **arrêt d'autobus** (*m*) *19* bus-stop
l' **arrêt facultatif** (*m*) *19* request
   stop
   arrêté *26* stopped
   arrêter *26* to stop

s' **arrêter** *12* to stop
l' **arrivée** (*f*) *12* arrival
arriver *1* to arrive
arriver à faire quelque chose *26* to manage to do something
l' **art** (*m*) *24* art
l' **ascenseur** (*m*) *2* lift
s' **asseoir** *11* to sit down
assez *4* enough, *8* rather
assez de *8* enough
l' **assiette** (*f*) *24* plate
assis *17* seated
assister (à) *22* to be present at, to witness
l' **atmosphère** (*f*) *17* atmosphere
atroce *28* terrible
attaquer *29* to attack
attendre *8* to wait for
s' **attendre à** *26* to expect to
l' **attente** (*f*) *12* wait
attention! *15* be careful!
attention à *30* be careful of
l' **attrait** (*m*) *17* appeal
attraper le rhume *20* to catch a cold
au *1* at (the), *17* to (the)
au besoin *29* if necessary
au bon endroit *7* in the right place
au bord (de) *28* beside, on the side of
au coin *6* on the corner
au compteur *24* on the meter
au contraire *13* on the contrary
au cours de *17* during
au début *20* at the beginning
au fait *25* by the way
au grand air *29* in the open air
au lieu de *11* instead of
au lit *25* in bed
au mauvais endroit *7* in the wrong place
au maximum *16* at the most
au milieu de *21* amongst, in the middle of
au moins *21* at least
au petit bonheur la chance *25* on the offchance
au pied de *8* at the foot of
au printemps *20* in spring
au régime *11* on a diet
au revoir *1* good-bye

au soleil *27* in the sun
au volant *26* at the wheel, driving
aucun *15* no
l' **augmentation** (*f*) *11* rise
aujourd'hui *3* today
auquel *18* to which
ausculter *20* to sound
aussi *1* also, too, *25* so
aussi . . . que *11* as . . . as
austère *24* austere, severe
autant que *11* as much as
l' **auto-école** (*f*) *26* driving school
l' **autobus** (*m*) *19* bus
l' **automne** (*m*) *20* autumn
l' **automobiliste** (*m*) *26* driver
autoritaire *10* bossy
l' **autoroute** (*f*) *27* motorway
un **autre** *8* another
autrefois *26* formerly, before
aux *3* at (the)
avancer *22* to gain, to be fast
avant *15* before, first
avant de *17* before
avant-hier *22* day before yesterday
avant Jésus-Christ *23* B.C.
avant l'heure *16* early
avec *1* with
avec plaisir *4* with pleasure
l' **avenir** (*m*) *17* future
l' **avenue** (*f*) *6* avenue
aveugle *30* blind
l' **avion** (*m*) *1* aeroplane
avoir *1* to have
avoir à *24* to have to
n' **avoir aucune chance de** *22* to have no chance of
avoir beau dire *27* to say in vain
avoir besoin de *8* to need
avoir bonne mine *14* to look well
avoid chaud *16* to be hot
avoir de la chance *9* to be lucky
avoir de la visite *13* to have visitors
avoir du mal à *20* to have difficulty in
avoir envie de *19* to feel (like), to want to
avoir faim *16* to be hungry

avoir froid *16* to be cold
avoir hâte de *29* to be in a hurry to
avoir l'air *15* to look, to appear (to be)
avoir l'habitude de *19* to be used to
avoir l'occasion de *20* to have the opportunity (of), to have the chance (to)
avoir la gentillesse de *15* to be kind enough (to)
avoir le rhume *20* to have a cold
avoir le temps de *20* to have time to
avoir lieu (à) *24* to take place (at), to be on (at)
avoir mal à *20* to have a pain (in)
avoir mal à la tête *16* to have a headache
avoir peur *6* to be afraid
avoir raison *10* to be right
avoir soif *16* to be thirsty
avoir tendance à *22* to tend to
avoir tort *14* to be wrong
avouer *19* to admit

B

le bac *10* 'bac' (Baccalauréat examination)
les bactéries (*f*) *20* bacteria
les bagages (*m*) *1* luggage
la baignoire *3* bath (tub)
bâiller *25* to yawn
le bain *3* bath
le bal *29* dance
le balcon *18* balcony
la bande magnétique *Intro.* tape
la banlieue *4* suburbs
la banque *7* bank
le baptême *5* christening
le bar *25* bar
baragouiner *21* to jabber
barrer *7* to cross out
le bateau-mouche *25* pleasure boat
le bâtiment *24* building
le batteur électrique *13* electric food mixer
se battre *28* to fight
bavarder *17* to chat
beau *5* beautiful, handsome
le beau-frère *28* brother-in-law

beaucoup (elle aime beaucoup) *4* very much
beaucoup de *4* many
beaucoup de monde *9* a lot of people
beaucoup de place *5* plenty of room
beaucoup trop *5* much too much
le bébé *5* baby
beige *13* beige
bel *14* beautiful
belle *6* lovely, beautiful
la bête *21* animal
le beurre *2* butter
la bicyclette *2* cycling, bicycle
le bidet *3* bidet
bien *1* well, *12* very
bien cuit *4* well done (cooked)
bien entendu *8* of course
bien sûr *9* certainly
bientôt *20* soon
le bijou *24* jewel
bilingue *6* bilingual
le billet *8* ticket, *24* note
bizarre *20* strange
blanc *6* white
le blanchissage *15* laundry
la blanchisserie *15* laundry (the place)
la blanchisserie teinturerie *15* laundry, cleaner's
la blanquette de veau *11* 'blanquette' of veal
bleu *13* blue
bleu clair *13* light blue
bleu foncé *13* dark blue
bleu marine *15* navy blue
bloqué *26* stuck
boire *17* to drink
boire à la santé de *30* to drink the health of
la boiserie *13* woodwork
la boisson *17* drink
la boîte *16* box
la boîte *17* club
la boîte à lettres *9* letter box
la boîte à pansements *16* bandage box
la boîte à pharmacie *16* first aid box
la boîte de nuit *17* nightclub

bon *1* good, *7* right
bon appétit *4* enjoy your meal
bon souvenir *30* regards
bon teint *15* fast (colour)
le **bonbon** *9* sweet
bonjour *1* hello
la **bonne chère** *20* good food
bonsoir *13* hello, good evening
le **bord** *23* edge
bordé (de) *28* lined (with)
la **bouche** *20* mouth
la **boucle d'oreilles** *14* ear-ring
bouger *7* to move
bouillir *26* to boil
le **boulanger** *28* baker
le **boulevard** *6* boulevard
bousculé *26* hurried
la **bouteille** *30* bottle
le **bouton** *3* switch, *10* button
le **bouton de manchettes** *14* cuff-link
le **bracelet** *23* bracelet
le **bras** *23* arm
bref *13* in short
bricoler *28* to do odd jobs, to potter
brillant *18* outstanding, brilliant
le **bronze** *24* bronze
la **brosse** *23* brush
la **brosse à cheveux** *23* hairbrush
brosser *23* to brush
le **bruit** *16* noise
brûler les feux *26* to jump the lights
la **brume** *27* mist
la **brume matinale** *27* early-morning mist
le **buffet** *14* sideboard
le **buraliste** *9* tobacconist
le **bureau** *13* office, *16* desk
le **bureau de poste** *9* post office
le **bureau de tabac** *8* tobacconist's

C

ça *4* that
ça alors! *22* oh no!, what next!
ça chauffe *22* it's warming up
ça doit être *28* it/that must be
ça fait *2* that's, that comes to
ça fait combien? *27* how much is that?
ça fait des années (que) *26* for years, it's years since

ça m'est égal *18* I don't mind
ça me convient *27* that suits me
ça n'a pas d'importance *17* it doesn't matter, it's not important
ça ne fait rien *8* that doesn't matter
ça ne m'étonne pas *22* that doesn't surprise me
ça ne m'intéresse pas *8* that doesn't interest me
ça ne valait pas la peine *27* it wasn't really worth it
ça non *25* certainly not
ça par exemple..! *29* well really!
ça revient au même *23* it's the same thing, it's all the same
ça s'épelle *25* that's spelt
ça suffit *23* that's enough
ça tient *23* it'll hold, it's fast
ça va *1* all right
ça y est *7* right, that's it
la **cabine téléphonique** *10* telephone booth
le **cabinet** *20* surgery, practice
cacher *16* to hide
le **cachet** *15* stamp, *20* capsule
la **cachette** *16* hiding place
le **cadeau** *8* present
le **café** *4* coffee, *22* café
la **caisse** *9* till
le **caissier** *7* cashier
calme *13* calm, peaceful
le **calme** *21* peace, quiet
le **cambrioleur** *16* burglar
la **campagne** *4* country
la **campagne de publicité** *17* advertising campaign
camper *21* to camp
le **camping** *21* camping
le **Canada** *1* Canada
canadien *1* Canadian
le **canapé** *5* settee
le **caoutchouc** *24* rubber
la **capitale** *8* capital
le **capot** *26* bonnet
le **car** *1* bus
car *26* for
la **carafe** *11* carafe
la **caravane** *21* caravan
le **caravaning** *21* caravaning

le **carnet** *7* cheque book, *19* book of tickets
le **carrefour** *6* crossroads
le **carrelage** *13* tiles
la **carrière** *10* career
la **carte postale** *9* postcard
la **cassette** *Intro.* cassette
ce *2* it, *6* that, this
ce . . . -là *20* that
ce matin même *28* this very morning
c'est *2* it's, that's, is this?
c'est-à-dire (que) *10* that is, that's to say
c'est à toi de *25* it's up to you to
c'est bien ça *29* that's right
c'est bien le cas *25* that's just how it is
c'est bien simple *10* it's quite simple
c'est combien? *19* how much is it?
c'est ça *4* that's right
c'est dommage *9* it's a pity, that's a pity
c'est fait *25* that's done
c'est la vie *9* that's life
c'est parfait *2* that's good, fine
c'est pour ça *27* that's why
c'est tout *2* that's all
c'est trop fort *23* it's too bad
c'est un peu fort *25* it's a bit much
c'est une question de principe *25* it's a matter of principle
c'est vrai *2* it's true, that's true
ce n'est pas la peine *12* it's not worth it
ce que *18* what
ce qui *21* what
ce qui compte . . . c'est *21* the important thing is
ce sont *8* they are
la **ceinture** *23* belt
célèbre *22* famous
celle *14* that, the one
celle-là *15* that one
celles *14* those, the ones
celte *24* celtic
celui *14* that, the one
celui-ci *15* this one
le **cendrier** *9* ash tray

censé *21* supposed
cent *2* hundred
cent cinquante *27* a hundred and fifty
le **centime** *8* centime
le **cerf** *24* reindeer
certain (c'est certain) *6* certain, sure
certain (un certain M. Houbé) *15* certain
certains (certains voyageurs) *12* some
certainement *3* certainly
ces *6* these, those
ces . . . -ci *15* these ones
ces . . . -là *15* those ones, these ones
cet *6* this, that
cette *6* this, that
ceux *14* those, the ones
ceux-ci *15* these ones
ceux-là *15* those ones, these ones
chacun *10* each one
la **chaîne** *22* channel, *23* chain
la **chaînette de sûreté** *23* safety chain
la **chaise** *2* chair
la **chaleur** *27* heat
la **chambre** *2* room
la **chambre d'amis** *13* guest room
le **champ** *28* field
le **champagne** *30* champagne
le **champignon** *4* mushroom
le **changement** *21* change
changer *7* to change
changer d'avis *29* to change one's mind
changer de vitesse *26* to change gear
le **chant** *26* song
chanter *16* to sing
chaque *3* each
chaque fois *26* every time
charmant *3* lovely
le **chat** *23* cat
chaud *3* hot
le **chauffage** *3* heating
le **chauffage central** *3* central heating
chauffer *22* to warm up
le **chauffeur** *4* driver
le **chauffeur de taxi** *4* taxi driver

chausser (je chausse du 35) *6* to wear, to take (size shoes)

la **chaussette** *15* sock

la **chaussure** *6* shoe

le **chef-d'œuvre** *24* masterpiece

le **chef de la publicité** *16* head of advertising

le **chemin** *28* way

le **chemin de fer** *19* railway

la **chemise** *15* shirt

le **chemisier** *6* blouse

le **chèque** *7* cheque

le **chèque de voyage** *7* traveller's cheque

cher (c'est cher) *2* expensive

cher (mon cher Olivier) *4* dear

chercher *6* to look for, *14* to fetch

chercher à *29* to try to

le **chercheur** *20* research worker

chéri *3* dear, darling

les **cheveux** (*m*) *7* hair

chez *7* at, to (the shop of, etc.)

chic *24* smart, fashionable, *29* nice, kind

le **chien** *28* dog

le **chiffon** *16* cloth

le **chiffre d'affaires** *17* turnover

les **chiffres de ventes** (*m*) *17* sales figures

la **chirurgie** *20* surgery

le **chocolat** *9* chocolate

choisir *10* to choose

la **chose** *8* thing

la **cigarette** *9* cigarette

le **cil** *24* eyelash

le **ciment armé** *13* reinforced concrete

le **cinéma** *6* cinema

cinq *2* five

cinquante *9* fifty

la **cinquantaine** *28* fifty (years old)

cinquième *2* fifth

le **cintre** *3* coathanger

la **circulation** *26* traffic

clair *18* light

claquer *16* to slam

le **classeur** *16* filing cabinet

classique *18* classical

la **clef** *2* key

le **client** *3* guest, *7* customer

le **clignotant** *26* indicator

la **clinique** *20* clinic

la **cocotte minute** *13* pressure cooker

le **coffre** *26* boot (of car)

le **coiffeur** *7* hairdresser

le **coin** *6* corner

le **col** *15* collar

la **colère** *23* anger

combien? *8* how much?

combien de temps? *11* how long?

le **combiné** *10* receiver

la **comédie** *18* comedy

la **comédie musicale** *18* musical

le **comédien** *18* actor

la **comédienne** *18* actress

comme *4* like, *8* how

comme d'habitude *21* as usual

comme leur poche *26* like the back of their hand

comme toujours *13* as always

commencer (à) *19* to begin

comment *1* how

comment allez-vous? *1* how are are you?

comment ça! *16* what!

comment ça va? *4* how are you?

comment est-ce que? *7* how?

comment faire *22* what to do

la **commode** *3* chest of drawers

la **compagnie** *29* company

comparer *23* to compare

le **compartiment** *12* compartment

complet *17* no vacancies, full up, *18* sold out

le **complet** *15* suit

le **complet d'homme** *15* man's suit

complètement *23* completely

le **compliment** *29* compliment

compliquer *21* to complicate

comprendre *19* to understand

se **comprendre** *28* to understand each other

le **comprimé** *20* tablet

compris *2* included

compter *13* to count

le **compteur** *24* meter, *28* speedometer

le **comptoir** *9* counter

le **concierge** *9* concierge

le **conducteur** *28* driver

conduire *26* to drive

la **confiture** *2* jam

le **confort** *13* comfort
confortable 3 comfortable
le **congé** *16* notice, *17* leave
le **congé payé** *17* paid leave, paid
  holidays
connaître *4* to know
connu *25* known, well-known
consciencieusement
  24 conscientiously
consciencieux *16* conscientious
conseiller (de) *15* to advise
conserver *10* to keep
considérer *20* to consider
consoler *9* to console
la **consultation** *20* consultation
consulter *4* to consult, *20* to
  have a surgery
content *4* pleased
continuer *25* to continue, to go on
le **contrat** *16* contract
la **contravention** *26* ticket
contre *29* against
le **contrôle des passeports**
  1 passport control
convaincu *28* convinced
convenable *2* nice
convenir *27* to suit
la **conversation** *14* conversation
la **corbeille à papier** *23* wastepaper
  basket
la **correspondance** *12* connection
le **correspondant** *10* the person
  I'm calling
le **côté** *15* side
le **cou** *20* neck
la **couleur** *15* colour
le **coup** *18* knock, blow
le **coup de téléphone** *23* telephone
  call
la **coupe** *22* cup
la **cour** *8* courtyard
courir *22* to run
le **cours** *Intro.* course
court *23* short
le **courrier** *10* post
les **courses** (*f*) *15* shopping
le **cousin** *5* cousin (male)
la **cousine** *5* cousin (female)
le **couteau** *24* knife
coûter *9* to cost
couvert (de) *15* covered (with)
la **couverture** *3* blanket, *22* cover

craindre *15* to fear, to worry
la **cravate** *23* tie
le **crayon** *16* pencil
la **crevaison** *26* puncture
crever *26* to (get a) puncture
le **crime** *23* crime
le **crochet** *23* hook
croire *14* to think
je **crois que non** *11* I don't think
  so, I think not
le **croissant** *2* croissant
cueillir *28* to pick
la **cuillère** *24* spoon
la **cuillerée à café** *20* teaspoonful
la **cuisine** *2* kitchen
le **cuisinier** *11* cook
la **cuisinière** cook (*f*)
la **cuisinière électrique** *13* electric
  cooker
cuit *4* cooked
le **cultivateur** *28* farmer
curieux *29* curious

D

d'abord *7* first
d'accord *9* all right
d'ailleurs *11* moreover
d'après ce que *30* according to
  what
d'autres *11* others
d'habitude *10* usually
d'occasion *27* second-hand
d'un certain âge *10* middle-aged
d'une minute à l'autre *15* any
  minute now
la **dactylo** *17* typist
la **dame** *4* lady
le **dancing** *25* dance hall
dans *1* in
dans tous les cas *28* in any case
dans tout ça *26* with all that
danser *25* to dance
la **date** *7* date
davantage *21* more
de *1* of, from
de (la) *2* some
de court métrage *23* short (film)
de la journée *13* all day
de ma faute *26* my fault
de ma vie *25* in my life
de mal en pis *26* worse and
  worse, from bad to worse
de mauvaise foi *21* dishonest

de mauvaise humeur *26* in a bad temper
de mieux en mieux *26* better and better
de notre faute *26* our fault
de plus *29* more
de plus en plus *17* more and more
de quoi (boire) *23* enough (to buy a drink)
de rien *6* not at all, don't mention it
de service *18* on duty
de si tôt *30* for a while yet, in a hurry
de temps à autre *14* from time to time
de temps en temps *9* from time to time
de votre côté *21* your way
débarquer *25* to land, to return
debout *12* standing
se débrouiller *26* to cope, to manage
le début *20* beginning
débuter *24* to start out, to start one's career
décapotable *27* convertible
décider (de) *11* to decide
se décider à *29* to decide to
déclarer *1* to declare
le décor *18* set
la découverte *24* discovery
découvrir *20* to discover
décrocher *23* to unhook
décrocher (le combiné) *10* to pick up (the receiver)
déçu *27* disappointed
la défaite *22* defeat
le défilé *29* procession
le degré *27* degree
les degrés centigrade *27* degrees centigrade
les degrés fahrenheit *27* degrees fahrenheit
dehors *28* outside
déjà *6* already
déjeuner *4* to have lunch
délicieux *8* delicious
demain *4* tomorrow
la demande d'emploi *30* post wanted
demander *3* to ask for
la démarche *24* step

déménager *28* to move (house)
la demi-heure *12* half-hour
le demi-litre *1* half-litre
démodé *17* outdated, old-fashioned
le dénouement *30* dénouement
le dentiste *13* dentist
le départ *12* departure
dépenser *14* to spend
dépensier *30* extravagant
se déplacer *24* to go from place to place, to go about
depuis *4* for, *19* since
depuis longtemps *4* for a long time
depuis que *19* since
déranger *23* to disturb
dernier *16* last, *23* latest
des *1* of (the), some
des quantités de *9* lots of
dès que *27* as soon as
désagréable *10* unpleasant
descendre *6* to go down, *19* to get off
descendre (dans) *24* to stay (at)
désirer *4* to want
désolé *29* very sorry
le désordre *15* mess
le dessert *4* dessert
le dessin animé *23* cartoon
le dessinateur *10* designer
dessous *16* underneath, below
dessus *16* on top
le destinataire *25* addressee
le détail *28* detail
déteindre *15* to run (of colours)
se détendre *20* to relax
détendu *17* relaxed
le détergent *11* detergent
détestable *25* detestable
détester *8* to hate
deux *1* two
deuxième *1* second
devant *6* in front of
devenir *18* to become
deviner *18* to guess
le devis *16* estimate
devoir *15* to be supposed to, to have to, *22* to owe
dicter *16* to dictate
le dictionnaire *21* dictionary
la diète *20* diet
difficile *3* difficult

le **digestif** *17* digestive
le **dimanche** *11* Sunday
dîner *13* to have dinner
le **dîner** *13* dinner
le **dîner d'affaires** *15* business
   dinner
dire *8* to say
dire bonjour *29* to say hello
direct *24* direct
directement *19* directly
le **directeur** *10* director
la **direction** *23* management
la **discothèque** *25* discotheque
la **discussion** *23* discussion,
   argument
discuter (de) *16* to discuss, to
   talk (about)
disparaître *16* to disappear
se **disputer** *28* to quarrel
le **disque** *1* record
distingué *16* distinguished
se **distraire** *29* to amuse oneself
distrait *7* absent-minded
dix *2* ten
dix-huit *12* eighteen
dix-huitième *18* eighteenth
dixième *10* tenth
dix-neuf *19* nineteen
dix-neuvième *19* nineteenth
dix-sept *17* seventeen
dix-septième *17* seventeenth
la **dizaine** *28* ten
le **docteur** *5* doctor
le **document** *13* document
un **doigt de** *17* a drop of, finger of
le **dollar** *7* dollar
donc (venez donc) *8* then (come
   on)
donner *7* to give
donner chaud *25* to make warm
donner congé *16* to give
   (someone) notice
donner rendez-vous (à) *17* to
   arrange a meeting (with), to
   fix an appointment
dont *22* of which, of whom
dormir *21* to sleep
le **dossier** *16* file, *23* back
le **douanier** *1* customs officer
la **douche** *2* shower
doué *21* gifted, good at
la **douleur** *20* pain

le **doute** *28* doubt
se **douter** *28* to think
s'en **douter** *28* to doubt
douze *12* twelve
douzième *12* twelfth
le **drame** *18* drama
le **drapeau** *12* flag
dresser *14* to train
dresser une contravention
   26 to charge someone
la **drogue** *20* drug
droit *23* straight
drôle de *5* (a) strange
du *1* of (the), from, *2* some
(celui) **du bas** *16* the bottom
   (one)
du dessus *16* from above
(celui) **du haut** *16* the top (one)
du moins *11* at least
du temps de *20* when
du tout *8* at all
dur *4* hard (boiled), *10* hard
durer *23* to last

E

l' **eau** (*f*) *3* water
l' **eau minérale** (*f*) *4* mineral water
échouer *26* to fail
écouter *5* to listen to
écrire *19* to write
l' **écriture** (*f*) *19* handwriting
l' **écrivain** (*m*) *5* writer
éducatif *22* educational
l' **éducation** (*f*) *30* education
égarer *7* to mislay
égorger *23* to cut someone's
   throat
les **égouts** (*m*) *8* sewers
eh bien *1* well
électrique *3* electric
élevé *24* large, high
elle *2* she, it, *9* her
elle-même *18* herself
elles (aussi) *2* they (too)
s' **éloigner** *19* to move away, to go
   away
embarquer *25* to set out
embrasser *30* to kiss
l' **émission** (*f*) *22* programme,
   broadcast
emmener *19* to take

l' **émotion** (*f*) *19* emotion
émouvant *24* moving
s' **emparer (de)** *29* to·take hold of
s' **empêcher de** *30* to stop oneself,
to prevent oneself
l' **employé** (*m*) *7* clerk, employee
employer *16* to employ
emporter *16* to take away
s' **empresser (de)** *16* to waste no
time (in)
emprunter *18* to borrow, *26* to
make use of
en (France) *6* in (France)
en (nous en avons vendu) *17* of
them
s' **en aller** *6* to go away
en autobus *24* by bus
en automne *20* in autumn
en avance *7* early
en avoir assez *13* to have had
enough
en avoir par-dessus la tête *22* to
be fed up
en baisse *17* falling off, on the
decline
en bonne santé *20* in good
health
en caoutchouc *24* rubber
en ce moment *8* at the moment
en clinique *20* in a clinic
en comparaison de *17* compared
with
en couleurs *9* (in) colour
en cours de route *27* on the way
en déplacement *24* travelling
en dessous *16* underneath
en détail *28* in detail
en direct *22* live
en douter *28* to doubt (it)
en effet *5* indeed
en état de marche *28* in working
order
en été *17* in summer
en fait *22* in fact
en général *3* generally
en grève *19* on strike
en hausse *17* rising, on the rise
en hiver *13* in winter
en majuscules *25* in capital
letters
en noir et blanc *22* in black and
white

en osier *27* wicker
en panne *22* broken
en particulier *17* in particular
en pierre *13* stone
en plein cœur de *13* right in the
heart of
en plein été *20* in the middle of
summer
en pleine nuit *12* in the middle
of the night
en première *12* first class
en provenance de *12* coming from
en province *5* in the provinces
en question *21* in question
en réalité *11* in fact
en retard *7* late
en route pour *1* off to
en seconde *12* second class
en sens interdit *26* the wrong
way
en sens inverse *28* in the opposite
direction
s' **en servir** *28* to use
en somme *14* more or less
en sténo *16* in shorthand
en tout *11* in all, all together
en tout cas *17* in any case
en vacances *6* on holiday
en ville *11* into town
en vogue *25* in fashion
en voiture *27* by car
enchanté *5* delighted, pleased
encombré de *21* packed (with)
encore une fois *30* once again
encourager *17* to encourage
s' **endormir** *28* to fall asleep
l' **endroit** (*m*) *7* place
l' **enfant** (*m*) *1* child
enfin *2* well, *4* finally
s' **enfuir** *23* to flee, to run away
engager *10* to take on, to
employ
enlever *15* to take off
l' **ennui c'est que . . .** *25* the
annoying thing is that . . .
s' **ennuyer** *19* to be bored
s' **ennuyer à mourir** *22* to be bored
to death
ennuyeux *8* annoying
énorme *20* great, enormous
énormément (de) *13* enormous
amount of

ensemble *4* together
ensuite *4* next, then
entendre *10* to hear
l' enthousiasme (*m*) *17* enthusiasm
entier *24* whole
entouré (de) *28* surrounded (by)
l' entracte (*m*) *23* interval
entre *13* between
l' entrée (*f*) *8* entrance, admission charge
entrer *13* to come in
envier *24* to envy, to be envious of
environ *27* about
les environs (*m*) *5* outskirts
envoyer *9* to send
s' épeler *25* to be spelt
l' épilogue (*m*) *30* epilogue
l' époque (*f*) *16* time
épouser *21* to marry
épuisé *11* exhausted
l' équipe (*f*) *22* team
l' escalier (*m*) *2* staircase
l' escalier roulant (*m*) *24* escalator
les escaliers (*m*) *2* stairs
l' Espagne (*f*) *21* Spain
l' Espagnol/e (*m & f*) *21* Spaniard
espagnol *21* Spanish
une espèce de (*f*) *14* (a) kind of
j' espère que oui *11* I hope so
espérer *10* to hope
essayer (de) *16* to try (to)
essoufflé *22* out of breath
est-ce qu'il y a? *3* is there?
l' estomac (*m*) *20* stomach
et *1* and
et . . ? *22* what about . . ?
l' étage (*m*) *2* floor
l' étagère (*f*) *3* shelf
l' été (*m*) *17* summer
l' étiquette (*f*) *30* etiquette
étonnant *22* suprising
étonner *22* to surprise
étouffer *21* to suffocate
l' étranger (*m*) *29* stranger
être *1* to be
être censé de *21* to be supposed to
être de retour *25* to be back
être de service *18* to work
être de sortie *24* to be on a trip
être en train de *23* to be in the middle of

être enrhumé *20* to have a cold
l' être humain (*m*) *28* human (being)
être obligé de *10* to have to
être pressé *26* to be in a hurry
être quitte *14* to be even
être reçu *26* to pass (test)
les études (*f*) *10* studies
l' étudiant (*m*) *5* student
étudier *16* to study
eux *4* them
l' évier (*m*) *13* sink unit
exactement *6* exactly
exagérer *7* to exaggerate
l' examen (*m*) *26* test, exam
examiner *1* to examine
excellent *3* excellent
l' excuse (*f*) *21* excuse
excuser *5* to excuse
s' excuser *6* to be sorry, to excuse oneself
excusez-moi *6* I'm sorry, excuse me
l' expert comptable (*m*) *10* accountant
expliquer *20* to explain
l' exposition (*f*) *17* exhibition
l' express (*m*) *12* express train
l' expression (*f*) *16* expression

F

la façade *13* front
se fâcher *14* to get angry
facile *3* easy
facilement *17* easily, freely
la façon *27* manner, way
la Faculté *10* university (faculty)
faillir *27* to nearly (do something)
faire *6* to do
faire attention *26* to pay attention
faire beau *8* to be fine
faire bonne impression *27* to make a good impression
faire cadeau de *30* to make a gift of
faire chaud *8* to be warm
faire confiance à *27* to trust
faire de la place *27* to make room

faire de la vitesse *27* to speed, to go fast
faire des achats *25* to shop, to buy things
faire des courses *6* to go shopping
ne pas faire d'excès de vitesse *26* not to speed, not to exceed the speed limit
faire des folies *24* to be rash
faire des progrès *20* to make progress, to improve
faire du cent *27* to do a hundred
faire du vélo *28* to cycle
faire faire *27* to have . . . done
faire froid *8* to be cold
se faire la cour *28* to woo each other
faire la navette (entre) *13* to commute (between)
faire la queue *18* to queue
faire la vaisselle *25* to do the washing-up
faire le blanchissage *15* to do laundry
faire le plaisir *17* to do the pleasure (of)
faire le plein d'eau *26* to fill up on water
faire le tour (de) *25* to go round
faire les démarches *25* to make arrangements
faire les honneurs *28* to do the honours
faire mal *17* to harm, *20* to hurt
faire marcher *16* to play
faire mieux *17* to do better
faire noir *8* to be dark
faire pousser *13* to grow
faire une excursion *25* to take a trip
faire une tête pareille *27* to look like that
faire (votre) connaissance *5* to meet (you)
falloir *14* to be necessary
fameux *24* famous, *27* precious
la famille *2* family
le far west *23* wild west
fatal *20* fatal
fatigué *1* tired
se fatiguer *29* to tire oneself

la faute *26* fault
le fauteuil *13* armchair
les fauteuils d'orchestre *18* stalls
favorable *7* favourable
les félicitations (*f*) *30* congratulations
la femme *4* wife, *6* woman
la femme de chambre *3* chambermaid
la fenêtre *8* window
la fente *10* slot
la ferme *21* farm
fermer *6* to close, to shut
fermer à clef *16* to lock
fermer l'œil *21* to sleep (a wink)
la fermeture *23* clasp, catch
la fermeture annuelle *17* annual holiday
la fête *29* holiday
la fête nationale *29* national holiday
fêter *26* to celebrate
les feux (*m*) *19* lights
les feux d'artifice (*m*) *29* fireworks
les feux rouges (*m*) *26* traffic lights
le fiancé *30* fiancé
la fiche *2* form
fidèle *9* loyal
fier *27* proud
la fièvre *20* fever, temperature
la figure *24* face
se figurer *26* to imagine
la file d'attente *19* queue
la fille *5* daughter, *10* girl
le film *19* film
le fils *4* son
la fin *13* end
finalement *13* finally
finir *16* to finish
finir par *23* to end up by
le flacon *1* bottle
la flèche *24* arrow
la fleur *2* flower
le fleuriste *25* florist
le foie *20* liver
la fois *6* time
fonctionner *27* to work
les fondations (*f*) *28* foundations
fonder *10* to start, to found
se fondre *24* to melt
le football *2* football
former *10* to dial
formidable! *8* wonderful!

le **formulaire** *25* form
fort *17* strong, *21* very
le **fortifiant** *20* tonic
le **foulard** *23* scarf
la **foule** *29* crowd
le **four** *13* oven
la **fourchette** *24* fork
le **foyer** *18* foyer
fragile *15* fragile
les **frais** (*m*) *24* expenses
le **franc** *2* franc
français *1* French
le **Français** *4* Frenchman
la **Française** *2* French girl, French
   woman
la **France** *6* France
frapper *22* to knock
freiner *26* to brake
frénétiquement *18* wildly
fréquenter (quelqu'un) *21* to see,
   to associate with
le **frère** *2* brother
le **frigidaire** *13* fridge
les **frites** (*f*) *4* chips, fried potatoes
froid *3* cold
le **fromage** *4* cheese
le **front** *24* forehead
le **fruit** *28* fruit
fuir *25* to avoid, to flee
la **fumée** *26* smoke
fumer *9* to smoke
furieux *27* furious

G

le **gadget** *13* gadget
le **gagnant** *9* winner
gagner *8* to win, *11* to earn
gai *13* gay
la **galerie** *24* gallery
le **garage** *2* garage
le **garagiste** *27* garage owner
le **garçon** *4* waiter, *18* boy
garder *4* to keep
garder la ligne *4* to keep one's
   figure
le **gardien de la paix** *26* police-
   constable
le **gardien de service** *24* keeper on
   duty
la **gare** *12* station
garer *26* to park
se **garer** *26* to park

le **gâteau** *4* cake, pastry
gâter *13* to spoil
gémir *25* to complain, to moan
gêner *23* to bother, to get in the
   way
généralement *12* generally
le **genre** *6* kind
les **gens** (*m*) *12* people
gentil *6* nice
le **gérant (d'hôtel)** *3* (hotel)
   manager
gérer *11* to manage
la **glace** *25* ice, *28* mirror
la **gorge** *20* throat
le **gouvernement** *25* government
la **goutte** *17* drop
grand *1* large
le **grand film** *23* main film
le **grand lit** *2* double bed
le **grand magasin** *4* department
   store
la **grand-mère** *5* grandmother
le **grand-père** *5* grandfather
les **grands-parents** *5* grandparents
grandir *29* to grow (big)
gras *11* rich
gratuit *3* free
gratuitement *15* free
grave *20* serious
grec *24* Greek
la **grève** *19* strike
le **grille-pain** *13* toaster
griller les feux *26* to jump the
   lights
gris *13* grey
gros *4* fat, big
les **gros** *14* fat people
le **gros billet** *24* large note
le **gros lot** *9* big prize
grossier *12* rude
grossir *14* to put on weight
le **gruyère** *4* gruyère
guérir *20* to cure
le **guichet** *18* box office
le **guide** *8* guide
la **guitare** *30* guitar
la **gymnastique** *2* gymnastics

H

habillé *18* dressed
l' **habitant** (*m*) *8* inhabitant
habiter *1* to live (in)

le **hall** *1* hall
les **haricots verts** (*m*) *11* French beans
hélas *20* alas
héler *24* to hail, to call
l' **héroïne** (*f*) *23* heroine
le **héros** *23* hero
l' **heure** (*f*) *12* time, o'clock, hour
heureusement *16* fortunately
heureusement que *25* luckily
heureux *5* happy
hier *17* yesterday
hier soir *16* last night, yesterday evening
l' **histoire** (*f*) *6* story, *8* history
l' **homme** (*m*) *6* man
l' **homme d'affaires** (*m*) *17* business man
honnête *27* honest
l' **hôpital** *20* hospital
l' **horaire** (*m*) *12* timetable
l' **horloge parlante** (*f*) *12* speaking clock
le **hors-d'œuvre** (*m*) *4* hors d'oeuvres
l' **hôtel** *1* hotel
l' **hôtel particulier** (*m*) *13* private house, large old town house
l' **hôtellerie** (*f*) *11* hotel management
l' **hôtesse de l'air** (*f*) *30* air hostess
huit *8* eight
huit jours *16* week
huitième *8* eighth

I

ici *3* here
l' **idée** (*f*) *18* idea
idiot (**de**) *13* idiot
il *1* he, it
il est grand temps de *22* it's high time to
il y a *2* there is, (there's), there are, *9* ago
il n'y a pas de mal *29* that's all right
il vaut mieux *18* it's better
illustrer *17* to illustrate
ils *1* they
immédiatement *11* immediately

immense *13* enormous
l' **immeuble** (*m*) *13* block (of flats)
impatient *12* impatient
s' **impatienter** *27* to get impatient
l' **imperméable** (*m*) *27* rain coat
impoli *12* impolite
l' **importance** (*f*) *8* importance
important *13* important
impossible *11* impossible
impossible de *16* I couldn't
incapable (**de**) *16* unable (to)
inconnu *20* unknown
incurable *20* incurable
l' **indicateur** (*m*) *19* (railway) timetable
l' **infirmière** (*f*) *2* nurse
l' **ingénieur** (*m*) *5* engineer
ininterrompu *26* non-stop
l' **initiale** (*f*) *14* initial
inquiéter *18* to worry
s' **inquiéter** *11* to worry
s' **inscrire** (**à**) *26* to enroll (at)
inspirer *23* to inspire
installé *28* installed, settled in
l' **instruction** (*f*) *10* instruction
insupportable *13* unbearable
intelligent *27* intelligent
intensif *17* intensive
interdit (**de**) *26* forbidden (to)
intéressant *11* interesting
intéresser *8* to interest
s' **intéresser** (**à**) *25* to be interested (in)
l' **intérieur** (*m*) *13* interior
l' **interphone** (*m*) *17* intercommunication system
l' **interprète** (*m* or *f*) *30* interpreter
introduire *10* to put in
inutile (**de**) *28* no point (in), (it's) useless (to)
l' **invitation** (*f*) *14* invitation
l' **invité** (*m*) *5* guest
inviter *6* to invite
invraisemblable *23* unbelievable
l' **Italie** (*f*) *21* Italy

J

jamais *24* never
la **jambe** *5* leg
le **jambon** *2* ham
le **jardin** *2* garden

le jardinier *28* gardener
jaune *24* yellow
je *1* I
je vous en prie *17* please, I beg you
je vous prie d'agréer l'expression de mes sentiments distingués *16* yours truly
jeter un coup d'œil *3* to have a look (at), to glance at
le jeton *9* 'jeton'
jeune *2* young
la jeune fille *10* (young) girl
le jeune homme *6* young man
les jeunes *13* young people
la jeunesse *20* youth
joli *3* pretty
la joue *24* cheek
jouer (à) *2* to play
jouer (de) *30* to play
le jour *2* day
le jour de fête *29* holiday
le journal *9* newspaper
le journaliste *5* journalist
la journée *12* day
juillet (*m*) *12* July
juin (*m*) *17* June
la jupe *15* skirt
le jus de fruit(s) *25* fruit juice
le jus de tomate *25* tomato juice
jusqu'à *6* as far as

K
le kilomètre *27* kilometer

L
l'autre jour *27* the other day
l'un à l'autre *28* one to the other
l'un . . . l'autre *11* one . . . another
la *2* the
la (voilà) *7* (here) it (is), (there) it (is)
là *3* there
là-bas *19* over there
là-dedans *24* inside, in there
laid *8* ugly
laisser *9* to leave

laisser tomber *25* to leave, to drop
laisser tranquille *13* to leave alone, to let be
le lait *11* milk
la laitue *4* lettuce
la lampe *3* lamp
lancer *17* to launch
la langue *21* language
laquelle *22* who, whom, which
latin *24* latin
le lavabo *2* wash-basin
laver *11* to wash
se laver les mains *14* to wash one's hands
la laverie automatique *15* launderette
le *1* the
le (voilà) *7* (here) it (is), (there) it (is)
la leçon *1* lesson
la légende *23* legend
léger *11* light
le légume *4* vegetable
le lendemain *25* following day
lentement *16* slowly
lequel *12* which (one)
les *1* the, *6* them
les (voilà) *7* (here, there) they (are)
la lessive *15* washing
la lettre *9* letter
leur *6* their, *9* to them
les leurs *15* theirs, their ones
le lever *18* rise
se lever *25* to get up
libre *11* free
le lilas *25* lilac
le linge *15* washing
lire *10* to read
la liste *15* list
le lit *2* bed
le livre *29* book
le locataire *13* tenant
loin *7* far, a long way
long *5* long (time)
le long de *26* alongside, beside
longtemps *4* a long time
lorsque *23* when
la loterie *8* lottery
louer *12* to book, *25* to hire
le loyer *13* rent

lui *9* to her, him
lui (aussi) *4* he (too)
lui-même *24* himself
la lumière *18* light
lundi *4* Monday
les lunettes (*f*) *23* spectacles
le lycéen *2* schoolboy

M

M. *1* Mr.
ma *2* my
la machine *19* machine
la machine à écrire *16* typewriter
la machine à laver la vaisselle
  13 dishwasher
Madame *1* Mrs., madam
Mademoiselle *1* miss
le magasin *4* shop
magnifique *2* marvellous
maigre *14* thin
maigrir *14* to lose weight
la main *7* hand
maintenant *19* now
mais *1* but
mais si *26* yes
la maison *4* house, *16* firm
la maison d'édition *6* publishing
  house
la maîtresse de maison *13* housewife
le mal à l'estomac *20* stomach-ache
le mal à la gorge *16* sore throat
le mal à la tête *16* headache
le mal au cœur *20* nausea, sick
  feeling
mal fait *15* badly done
malade *16* ill
le malade *20* patient, sick person
le malade imaginaire
  20 hypochondriac
la maladie *20* illness
la maladie de cœur *20* heart
  complaint
malgré *18* in spite of
le malheur *16* misfortune
le malheur c'est que *30* the
  unfortunate thing is
malheureusement
  10 unfortunately
malin *23* mischievous
la malle *30* trunk
maman *5* mother, mummy
le manche *24* handle

manger *4* to eat
la manie *25* mania
manquer *12* to miss
le manteau *6* coat.
se maquiller *7* to make oneself up
le marchand de journaux
  29 newspaper seller
le marchand de tabac *6* tobacconist
la marchande *15* stall-holder
le marché *15* market
marcher *3* to work, *29* to walk
marcher sur le pied *29* to step on
  someone's foot
mardi *11* Tuesday
le mari *5* husband
le mariage *29* wedding
marié *4* married
se marier *14* to get married
la marque *17* make
marqué *15* marked
marquer *15* to mark
marron *13* brown
le match *22* match
le match de football *22* football
  match
les mathématiques (*f*) *22* maths
le matin *3* morning
ce matin même *28* this very
  morning
mauvais *7* wrong
mauve *18* mauve
me *6* me
méchant *26* nasty
mécontent *20* unhappy
le médecin *20* doctor
la médecine *20* medicine
le médicament *20* medicine
meilleur *17* better
le meilleur *18* the best
le mélange *24* mixture
se mélanger *15* to get mixed up
même *3* even, *4* same
même pas *13* not even
menacer *28* to threaten
le ménage *26* housework
mentir *28* to lie
le menu *4* menu
le menuisier *28* carpenter
merci *1* thank you
la mère *2* mother
la merveille *23* wonder
merveilleux *26* marvellous

mes *1* my
Mesdames *6* ladies
Messieurs *4* gentlemen
Messieurs-Dames *1* ladies and
  gentlemen, sir and madam
la météo *27* weather forecast
le métier *11* job, career
le métrage *23* footage, length of
  film
le mètre *13* metre
le métro *24* metro
mettre *7* to put
mettre (l'omnibus met) *12* to take
se mettre à *28* to start to, to begin
  to
mettre à la poste *25* to post
se mettre à la diète *20* to fast
se mettre au régime *20* to go on a
  diet
se mettre en grève *30* to go on
  strike
mettre la télé *22* to switch on the
  T.V.
le meuble *28* piece of furniture
la meurtrière *23* murderess
le microsillon *1* L.P.
mien *14* mine, my one
mieux *21* best
le mieux, c'est de . . . *21* the best
  thing is to
des milliers (de) *20* thousands (of)
le ministre *25* minister
minuit *12* midnight
minuscule *13* minute
la minute *6* minute
le miracle *26* miracle
miraculeux *26* miraculous
le miroir *24* mirror
la mi-temps *22* half
le mixer *13* foodmixer
Mme *1* Mrs.
la mode *6* fashion
le modèle *25* model
moderne *13* modern
moi *1* me
moi, je . . . *1* I
moi-même *15* myself
moins *9* minus, *10* less
moins . . . que *11* less . . . than
le mois *10* month
le moment *30* moment
mon *1* my
mon Dieu . . ! *10* good heavens . . !

le moniteur *26* instructor
monsieur *1* Mr., sir
monsieur l'agent *6* officer
monter *2* to go up
monter (dans) *1* to get into
la montre *14* watch
montrer *11* to show
montrer le chemin *28* to show the
  way
le monument *29* monument
mort *10* dead
la mort *14* death
mort de peur *27* scared stiff
le mot *21* word
le moteur *26* engine
le mouchoir (*m*) *15* handkerchief
mourir *22* to die
mourir de soif *22* to die of thirst
le moyen *17* means
le moyen de transport *27* means of
  transport
le muguet *25* lily of the valley
le mur *13* wall
mûr *15* ripe
mûrir *15* to ripen
le musée *24* museum

N

n'est-ce pas? *2* isn't it? aren't
  they? etc.
n'importe *18* no matter
n'importe comment *18* anyhow
n'importe où *18* anywhere
n'importe quand *18* any time
n'importe quel *18* any, no matter
  what
n'importe qui *18* anyone
n'importe quoi *18* anything
national *8* national
naturel *27* natural
naturellement *3* of course
navré *25* very sorry
ne guère *14* hardly (ever)
ne . . . jamais *9* never, not ever
ne . . . pas *1* not
ne . . . pas assez *8* not enough
ne . . . pas encore *11* not yet
ne . . . personne *11* no one
ne . . . plus *11* no more
ne . . . que *19* only
ne . . . rien *1* nothing

ne vous en faites pas *14* don't
  worry
nécessaire *24* necessary
nerveux *12* nervous
nettoyer *15* to clean
nettoyer à sec *15* to dry clean
neuf *9* nine
neuf *27* new
le neveu *5* nephew
neuvième *9* ninth
le nez *24* nose
ni *24* nor
la nièce *5* niece
noir *6* black
le nom *28* name
nommer *30* to appoint
non *1* no
non alors! *2* oh no!
non-fumeur *12* non-smoker
non plus *11* neither
normal *20* normal
nos *4* our
la note *30* bill
la note de frais *24* expenses (bill)
notre *4* our
le nôtre *15* ours (our one)
la nourriture *20* food
nous *3* we, *9* us
nouveau *10* new
nouvel *10* new
nouvelle *10* new
les nouvelles (*f*) *30* news
la nuit *12* night
nulle part *25* nowhere, not . . .
  anywhere
le numéro *2* number

O

l' objection (*f*) *26* objection
l' objet (*m*) *17* purpose
obliger *13* to make, force, oblige
observer *1* to watch
l' obsession (*f*) *26* obsession
obtenir *30* to get, gain
d' occasion *27* second-hand
(les) occasions diverses (*f*) *30* general
  bargains
l' occupation (*f*) *29* occupation
occupé *10* engaged, *14* busy
s' occuper de *17* to deal with, to
  be in charge of

l' odeur (*f*) *8* smell
l' œuf (*m*) *2* egg
l' œuf dur mayonnaise (*m*) *4* egg
  mayonnaise
l' œuvre (*f*) *24* work
l' oignon *4* onion
l' offre d'emploi (*f*) *30* post vacant
offrir *17* to offer
l' oiseau (*m*) *26* bird
l' ombre (*f*) *27* shade
l' omnibus (*m*) *12* stopping train
on *15* one
on n'a pas idée de . . ! *24*
  fancy . . !
on verra bien *23* we'll soon see
l' oncle (*m*) *5* uncle
onze *11* eleven
onzième *11* eleventh
l' opération (*f*) *20* operation
l' opératrice (*f*) *10* operator
opposer *22* to oppose
optimiste *12* optimistic
l' orange (*m*) *24* orange
ordinaire *8* ordinary
l' ordonnance (*f*) *20* prescription
ordonné *17* tidy
l' oreiller (*m*) *3* pillow
organisé *21* organized
organiser *21* to organize
l' orthographe (*f*) *30* spelling
l' os (*m*) *24* bone
oser *14* to dare
des ossements (*m*) *24* bones, old
  bones
ou *4* or
où *5* where
ou bien *6* or (rather)
où ça? *28* where?
où diable? *16* where in heaven's
  name?
oublier *16* to forget
oui *1* yes
l' outil (*m*) *24* tool
ouvert *8* open
ouvrir *15* to open
ouvrir la marche *28* to lead the
  way
l' ouvreuse (*f*) *18* usherette

P

la page *30* page
le pain *2* bread

la **paire** *6* pair
le **palais** *25* palace
la **pancarte** *17* sign
le **panier** *27* basket
le **panier à provisions** *27* shopping basket
le **panier en osier** *27* wicker basket
le **panneau** *26* sign
le **panneau de signalisation** *26* road sign
le **pantalon** *15* trousers
papa *7* father, daddy
les **paperasses** (*f*) *16* papers
le **papier** *16* paper
le **paquet** *15* parcel
par *5* by, *8* out of
par alliance *5* by marriage
par amour *23* for love, out of love
par ci *17* here
par cœur *12* by heart
par dépit *23* for spite, out of spite
par-dessus *16* on top, on the top
par-dessus le marché *16* added to which
par économie *21* for the sake of economy
par exemple *9* for instance, for example
par hasard *25* by chance
par ici *17* this way
par jour *2* per day
par là *17* there
par mois *17* per month
par téléphone *18* by telephone
par terre *13* on the floor
par vengeance *23* for revenge
il **paraît que** *30* it appears that
paraître *30* to appear
parce que *7* because
pardon *2* sorry
se **pardonner** *28* to forgive oneself
pareil *16* such (a)
le **parent** *2* parent, *19* relative
paresseux *8* lazy
parfait *2* perfect
parfois *12* sometimes
le **parfum** *1* perfume
le **Parisien** *29* Parisian

parler *7* to talk
parler affaires *17* to talk business
parler de la pluie et du beau temps *22* to talk about nothing in particular
parler politique *25* to talk politics
le **parquet ciré** *24* polished floor
particulièrement *14* particularly
la **partie** *1* part
partir *12* to leave
partir en tournée *20* to do one's rounds (doctor)
partout *8* everywhere
pas (des) *1* not
pas de *8* no
pas du tout *8* not at all
pas encore *11* not yet
pas mal *5* not bad
pas plus *18* no more
pas tellement *17* not very
le **passage clouté** *6* pedestrian crossing
le **passeport** *1* passport
passer *10* to sit, to take (an exam), *11* to spend (time), *14* to pass, *28* to do more than
se **passer** *22* to happen
passer le permis *26* to take the driving test
passer par *30* to go via
passer une bonne journée *13* to have a good day
la **passion** *28* passion
passionnant *11* fascinating
la **patience** *29* patience
patient *13* patient
le **patron** *11* boss
pauvre *13* poor
payer *11* to pay
le **pays** *21* country
le **paysan** *4* peasant
la **peau** *24* skin
le **peigne** *23* comb
peindre *24* to paint
la **peine** *12* bother, trouble
peint *13* painted
peint à la main *15* handpainted
la **pellicule** *17* film
pendant *10* during
pendant que *23* while
pendant une journée entière *24* for a whole day

la **pendule** *13* clock
penser *22* to think
penser à *22* to think of, about
perdre *15* to lose
se **perdre** *29* to lose oneself
le **père** *2* father
permanent *23* continuous
permettre *11* to allow
se **permettre (de)** *24* to afford (to), to allow oneself (to)
le **permis de conduire** *26* driving licence
la **permission** *30* permission
la **perruque** *7* wig
la **personnalité** *27* personality, character
personne *17* nobody
la **personne** *22* person
le **personnel** *10* staff
persuader *29* to persuade
peser *28* to weigh
pessimiste *12* pessimistic
petit *1* small
petit à petit *26* little by little
le **petit déjeuner** *2* breakfast
le **petit-fils** *5* grandson
la **petite amie** *13* girl-friend
la **petite monnaie** *24* change (money)
les **petites annonces** (*f*) *30* advertisements
les **petits pois** (*m*) *4* peas
un **peu** *9* a little **peu** *11* little
peu de *9* few
le **peuple** *29* people
peut-être *6* perhaps
le **pharmacien** *20* chemist
la **photo** *17* photograph
la **pièce** *13* room, *18* play
la **pièce de monnaie** *24* coin
le **pied** *8* foot
la **pilule** *20* pill
la **pipe** *9* pipe
pique-niquer *27* to picnic
pire *18* worse
le **pire** *22* the worst
le **pire, c'est que . . .** *22* the worst of it is . . .
le **placard** *3* wardrobe
la **place** *12* seat
le **plafond** *13* ceiling

plaindre *27* to pity
se **plaindre** *11* to complain
la **plainte** *29* complaint
plaire *18* to please
se **plaire** *29* to enjoy oneself
le **plaisir** *16* pleasure
le **plan** *6* map
le **plat** *14* plate, dish
le **plat principal** *4* main course
le **plateau** *3* tray
le **plein air** *8* open air
plein de *18* full of
pleuvoir *9* to rain
la **pluie** *22* rain
la **plupart (de)** *17* most (of)
plus *9* more
plus ou moins *17* more or less
plus . . . plus *20* the more . . . the more
plus . . . que *11* more . . . than
plusieurs *6* several
plutôt *10* rather
plutôt que (de) *13* rather than
le **pneu** *24* tyre
la **poche** *15* pocket
poignarder *23* to stab
le **point** *16* stop, full stop
le **point d'interrogation** *16* question mark
le **point final** *16* last full stop
la **pointure** *6* size
la **poire** *21* pear
le **poisson** *4* fish
poli *12* polite, *24* polished
le **policier** *1* immigration officer
le **politicien** *25* politician
la **pommade** *20* ointment
la **pomme** *4* apple, potato
la **pompe à essence** *26* petrol pump
ponctuel *13* punctual
le **pont** *28* bridge
le **portail** *13* doorway
la **porte** *6* door
la **porte d'entrée** *17* front door
le **portefeuille** *25* wallet
porter *3* to carry
porter (une robe) *14* to wear
porter plainte à *23* to complain to
la **portière** *27* car door
le **portillon automatique** *24* automatic gate

le **Portugal** *21* Portugal
poser *23* to put, to place
poser (des questions) *12* to ask
  (questions)
possible *23* possible
le **poste** *22* set
la **poste** *25* post office
la **poste restante** *30* poste restante
poster *9* to post
le **potage aux légumes** *4* vegetable
  soup
la **poubelle** *2* dustbin
la **poudre de riz** *7* (face) powder
le **poulailler** *18* gods (in theatre)
le **poulet** *4* chicken
le **poulet rôti** *4* roast chicken
pour *1* for, *6* in order to
pour ainsi dire *27* to speak of
pour cent *24* per cent
pour le moment *20* for the time
  being
pour que (tu dises) *30* for you
  (to say)
le **pourboire** *23* tip
pourquoi? *7* why?
pourquoi est-ce que? *7* why?
pourquoi pas? *7* why not?
pourtant *16* but, however
pourvu que *30* as long as
pouvoir *6* can, to be able
pratique *23* practical, convenient
pratiquement *26* practically,
  more or less
précis *12* exactly
précisément *21* precisely
préférer *2* to prefer
premier *1* first
prendre *3* to take
prendre à la légère *13* to take
  lightly
prendre au sérieux *13* to take
  seriously
prendre la retraite *4* to retire
prendre le car *17* to catch the bus
prendre quelque chose *23* to have
  a drink
prendre rendez-vous *13* to make
  an appointment
prendre soin *27* to take care
prendre un apéritif *17* to have a
  drink (aperitif)
prendre un verre *26* to have a
  drink

le **préparatif** *30* preparation
préparer *13* to prepare
près (de) *8* near
près de *17* nearly
prescrire *20* to prescribe
présenter *5* to introduce
se **présenter** *10* to introduce
  oneself
presque *2* almost
(être) **pressé** *15* (to be) in a hurry
prêt *7* ready
prétendre *21* to claim
prêter *14* to lend
prévenir *30* to warn
prévenu *30* warned
les **prévisions météorologiques** (*f*)
  27 weather forecast
prier *16* to beg
prière de . . . *25* please . . .
le **printemps** *20* spring
la **priorité à droite** *26* priority to
  traffic on the right
la **prise de courant** *3* socket
le **prix** *9* price
probablement *20* probably
le **problème** *17* problem
prochain *10* next
se **procurer** *18* to get hold of
le **professeur** *Intro.* teacher
profiter (de) *29* to take
  advantage (of)
profondément *20* deeply
le **programme** *18* programme
le **projet** *16* project
les **projets de vacances** (*m*)
  21 holiday plans
prolonger *25* to prolong, to
  extend
se **promener** *6* to go for a walk
se **promener au hasard** *29* to
  wander
promettre *19* to promise
se **prononcer** *30* to be pronounced
propre *11* clean
le **propriétaire** *9* owner
la **propriété** *25* place, property
protester *26* to protest
prudent *26* wise, prudent
la **publicité** *17* advertising
puis *6* then
puisque *21* since, as
le **pyjama** *15* pyjamas

Q

qu'est-ce que? *4* what?
qu'est-ce que c'est? *24* what is it?
qu'est-ce que c'est que ça? *14* what on earth's that?
qu'est-ce qui? *20* what?
qu'est-ce qui ne va pas? *20* what's the matter?
qu'est-ce qui se passe? *22* what's happening?
qu'est-ce qu'ils veulent encore? *13* now what do they want?
qu'est-ce qu'il y a? *7* what's the matter?
qu'est-ce qu' il y a pour votre service? *15* what can I do for you?
le quai *12* platform, *24* bank (of river)
quand *8* when
quand même *28* even so, all the same
quant à *29* as for
quarante *9* forty
quarante-deux *Intro.* forty-two
le quart *12* quarter
le quart d'heure *1* quarter of an hour
le quartier *13* area, *24* quarter
quatorze *14* fourteen
quatorzième *14* fourteenth
quatre *2* four
quatre-vingts *9* eighty
quatre cents *27* four hundred
quatrième *4* fourth
que *10* that
que faire? *11* what can you do?
quel *12* which, what
quelle *12* which, what
quelle heure est-il? *12* what time is it?
quelle occasion! *28* what a bargain!
quelqu'un *11* someone
quelqu'un d'autre *25* someone else
quelques *11* some
quelque chose *1* anything, *17* something
quelquefois *3* sometimes
quelques-uns *12* some

la querelle *23* quarrel
la question *12* question
une question de principe *25* a matter of principle
la queue *18* queue
qui *5* who
qui est-ce? *5* who's that?, who is it?
quinze *12* fifteen
quinze jours *16* fortnight
quinzième *15* fifteenth
quitter *25* to leave
quoi? *7* what?

R

raccrocher *10* to hang up
la racine *28* root
raconter *28* to tell
le radiateur *26* radiator
la radio *13* radio
rafraîchir *25* to refresh
se rafraîchir *28* to freshen up
la rame *24* train (on metro)
le rang *23* row (of seats)
rapide *12* fast
le rapide *12* fast train
se rappeler *13* to remember
rapporter *18* to bring back
rare *12* rare
rarement *14* rarely
le rasoir électrique *3* electric razor
rassurer *27* to reassure
le rat *8* rat
ravi *18* delighted
la réception *2* reception (desk)
le réceptionniste *2* receptionist
le receveur *19* (bus) conductor
recevoir *17* to receive
les réclamations (*f*) *10* complaints
la réclame *17* advertisement
réclamer *30* to demand, to claim
recommander *26* to recommend
recommencer *10* to begin again
reconnaître *6* to recognize
le reçu *15* receipt
refaire *11* to make (a bed)
refait *11* made, remade
la référence *10* reference
réfléchir *21* to think over, to consider

se **refléter** *28* to be reflected
refuser *5* to refuse
regarder *1* to look at
regardez-moi ça! *8* just look at that!
le **régime** *11* diet
la **règle** *30* rule
le **règlement** *26* rule
regretter *24* to be sorry
régulièrement *19* regularly
rejoindre *25* to join
relire *11* to read back, *19* to reread
rembourser *24* to pay back, to reimburse
le **remède** *20* remedy
les **remerciements** (*m*) *29* thanks
remercier *16* to thank
remplacer *2* to replace
rempli (de) *17* full of
remplir *17* to fill
rencontrer *8* to meet
le **rendez-vous** *1* meeting
rendre *22* to give back, *27* to make
se **rendre compte** *29* to realise
rendre malade *27* to make ill
rendre visite à *6* to visit
les **renseignements** (*m*) *12* enquiries
rentrer *14* to come in, to come back
renverser *13* to spill
la **réparation** *27* repair
réparer *26* to repair
repartir *29* to go away again
le **repas** *13* meal
le **repassage** *15* ironing
repasser *15* to iron
le **répertoire** *18* repertoire
répéter *27* to repeat
répondre *12* to answer
le **repos** *15* rest
reposant *14* relaxing, restful
se **reposer** *20* to rest
reprendre *29* to take up again
repris (par) *29* taken up (by)
la **réservation** *12* reservation
réserver *12* to reserve
résoudre *17* to resolve
respecter *30* to respect
respirer *20* to breathe
le **restaurant** *4* restaurant

restaurer *21* to renovate
rester *11* to stay (remain)
le **résultat** *10* result
le **résumé** *22* summary
retarder *22* to lose, to be slow
retéléphoner *12* to phone back
retenir *18* to book
retourner *21* to go back
le **retrait du permis** *26* disqualification (driving)
la **retraite** *4* retirement
retrouver *29* to find again
le **rétroviseur** *26* driving mirror
réussir *10* to succeed
le **rêve** *21* dream
revenir *6* to come back
réviser *27* to service
revoilà *27* here's . . . again
se **révolter (contre)** *29* to revolt (against)
la **Révolution Française** *29* French Revolution
la **revue** *9* magazine
les **rhumatismes** (*m*) *5* rheumatism
le **rhume** *20* cold
le **rideau** *18* curtain
ridicule *12* ridiculous
rien *8* nothing
rien de spécial *11* nothing special
rire *23* to laugh, to laugh at, about
le **risque** *15* risk
risquer *15* to risk
la **rivière** *28* river
la **robe** *6* dress
le **rond de serviette** *14* serviette ring
rose *15* pink
la **rose** *25* rose
la **roue** *27* wheel
la **roue de secours** *26* spare wheel
rouge *4* red
le **rouge à lèvres** *7* lipstick
le **roulement** *26* roar, rumbling
rouler *26* to drive
rouler en sens interdit *26* to drive the wrong way
la **route** *26* road
royal *29* royal
la **rue** *5* street

S

s'il te plaît *7* please
s'il vous plaît *1* please
sa *5* his, her, its
le sac *1* bag
le sac à main *1* handbag
sage *12* wise
saignant *4* rare
sain et sauf *27* safe and sound
saisir *29* to seize
la saison *20* season
la salade *4* salad
la salade niçoise *4* niçoise salad
le salaire *30* salary
sale *15* dirty
la salle *18* auditorium
la salle à manger *13* dining-room
la salle de bains *2* bathroom
le salon *13* sitting-room
le salon de coiffure *7* hairdresser's
le samedi *15* Saturday
le sandwich *27* sandwich
sans *3* without
sans arrêt *14* continuously
sans doute *28* doubtless, without
doubt
la santé *9* health
sauf *13* except
le saule pleureur *28* weeping willow
sauter *22* to jump, to skip
se sauver *10* to hurry away, to
be off
savoir *6* to know
savoir (conduire) *26* to know
how to (drive)
la scène *18* stage
sculpté *24* sculpted, carved
sculpter *24* to sculpt, to carve
sèchement *18* curtly
la secrétaire *2* secretary
la secrétaire particulière
16 personal secretary
seize *16* sixteen
seizième *16* sixteenth
le séjour *20* stay (time spent)
le sel *14* salt
selectionné *22* selected
la semaine *2* week
sembler *13* to seem
(en) sens interdit *26* wrong way
sensible *21* sensitive
le sentiment *16* feeling

sentir *19* to feel
se sentir *19* to feel
se sentir mal *20* to feel unwell
sept *3* seven
septembre *17* September
septième *7* seventh
sérieusement *21* seriously
serrer *28* to keep to
serrer sa droite *28* to keep to his
right
le service *2* service charge
le services des postes *19* postal
service
le service des renseignements
12 enquiries
la serviette *3* towel, *14* serviette
servir *11* to serve
se servir *28* to help oneself
se servir de *28* to use
ses *5* his, her, its
seul *8* alone
la seule *23* the only one
seulement *2* only
si *8* if, *9* yes, *13* so
si ... c'est que *21* if ... it's
because
si jamais *26* if ever
si ... que ça *27* as ... as that
le siècle *8* century
le siège *23* seat
le sien *14* his (one), hers
la sienne *14* his (one), hers
la signature *7* signature
signer *2* to sign
simple *10* simple
simplement *17* merely
le singe *5* monkey
le sirop *20* syrup
la situation *30* job
situé *13* placed, situated
six *3* six
six heures et demie *12* half-past
six
sixième *6* sixth
snob *11* snobbish
la sœur *2* sister
le sofa *5* sofa
soi-même *28* oneself
soigné *18* carefully done
soigner *25* to look after
soigneusement *20* carefully
le soir *9* evening

295

la **soirée** *14* evening
soit ... soit *25* either ... or
soixante-dix *9* seventy
la **sole meunière** *11* sole meunière
le **soleil** *27* sun
solennel *11* solemn, formal
la **solitude** *28* solitude
la **solution** *21* solution
son *5* her, his, its
le **son** *Appendix* sound
sonner *23* to ring
la **sorte** *20* kind, sort
à la **sortie de** *23* on the way out of
sortir *6* to go out
le **souci** *21* worry
souffrir (de) *20* to have
something wrong (with)
souhaiter *29* to hope
soulager *20* to ease, to relieve
pain
soupçonneux *24* suspicious
la **soupe** *4* soup
la **soupe à l'oignon** *4* onion soup
la **soupe du jour** *4* soup of the day
sous *7* under
le **sous-vêtement** *15* underwear
le **souvenir** *30* memory
souvent *9* often
soyez les bienvenus! *9* welcome!
la **speakerine** *22* announcer
spécial *25* special
le **spectacle** *8* sight
le **spectacle** *18* theatre, show
le **spectacle de variétés** *18* variety
show
les **spectateurs** *(m)* *18* audience
le **sport** *2* sport
sportif *28* sporty
la **station de métro** *24* metro station
la **station service** *26* service station
stationnement interdit *26* no
parking
stationner *26* to park
la **statue** *8* statue
le **steak** *4* steak
le **steak aux pommes** *4* steak and
chips
la **sténo** *11* shorthand
la **sténo-dactylo** *10* shorthand
typist
le **style** *19* style
le **stylo à bille** *16* ballpoint pen

sucer *20* to suck
suffisant *23* sufficient, enough
suggérer *16* to suggest
suivre *20* to follow
le **supermarché** *15* the supermarket
supporter *22* to stand, to bear
supposer *16* to suppose
sur *2* on, on to, *13* by
sûr *11* sure
surpris *22* surprised
surtout *3* especially
surveiller *10* to supervise
sympathique *3* nice
le **symptôme** *20* symptom
le **Syndicat d'Initiative** *30* tourists'
information centre

T

ta *14* your
le **tabac** *6* tobacco
la **table** *4* table
le **tableau** *24* picture
la **tablette** *9* bar
la **tache** *15* stain
la **taille** *6* size
se **taire** *23* to be quiet
tant de *11* so many
tant mieux *29* thank goodness
tant pis *4* too bad
la **tante** *5* aunt
tantôt ... tantôt *11* first ... then
taper à la machine *10* to type
tard *12* late
le **tarif normal** *25* normal rate
le **tarif réduit** *25* reduced rate
des **tas de** *20* heaps of, lots of
la **tasse** *23* cup
le **taux de change** *7* rate of exchange
la **taxe** *2* tax
le **taxi** *4* taxi
te *7* you, to you
la **teinturerie** *15* cleaners
le **teinturier** *15* cleaner
tel et tel *21* such and such (a)
la **télé** *22* T.V.
le **télégramme** *9* telegram
le **téléphone** *3* telephone
téléphoner (à) *3* to telephone
le **téléspectateur** *22* viewer
le **téléviseur** *22* television set
la **télévision** *22* television
tellement *8* so much

tellement de *15* so many
tellement . . . que *14* so . . . that
la température *20* temperature
le temps *11* time, *22* weather
le temps passe *22* time flies
tenez *8* here you are
tenir *23* to hold
tenir à *27* to wish, to intend to
tenir bon *29* to insist
tenir parole *19* to keep one's word
le tennis *2* tennis
la tente *21* tent
terminer *10* to finish
le terminus *12* terminus
le terrain (de football) *22* (football) pitch
le terrain de camping *21* camping site
la terrasse *11* terrace
terrible! *25* wonderful!
terriblement *21* terribly
tes *5* your
la tête *16* head
têtu *5* stubborn
têtu comme un âne *5* stubborn as a mule
le texte *25* text
le théâtre *13* theatre
le thermomètre *27* thermometer
le ticket *7* slip, ticket
le tien *14* yours, your one
la tienne *14* yours, your one
tiens! *5* look!
je ne tiens pas à mourir *27* I don't want to die
le timbre *9* stamp
le timbre-poste *9* postage stamp
timide *18* shy
le tiroir *14* drawer
toi *5* you
tomber *23* to fall
tomber en panne *22* to break down
tomber en panne d'essence *26* to run out of petrol
ton *5* your
la tonalité *10* dialling tone
tôt *12* early
la touche *22* push button
toujours *6* always
la tour *8* tower

le touriste *17* tourist
le tournant *28* bend
tourner *6* to turn
tous *5* all
tous ensemble *26* all together
tous les deux *4* both
tous les deux ans *6* every two years
tous les jours *2* every day
tous les quatre *18* all four of us
tout *2* everything, all
tout à l'heure *12* in a minute
tout de même *18* all the same
tout de suite *9* immediately
tout droit *6* straight on
tout en *26* at the same time
tout juste *24* just
tout le monde *2* everyone
tout le temps *25* all the time, always
tout petit *13* very small
tout près *8* quite near, very near
tout seul *9* all alone
tout va bien *5* everything's fine
toute l'année *2* all the year round
toute la famille *2* the whole family
toute la journée *12* all day long
toutes les chambres *2* all the rooms
toutes les semaines *2* every week
toutes sortes de *25* all kinds of
la tragédie *18* tragedy
le train *12* train
le train direct *12* through train
le traitement *20* treatment
traiter *20* to treat
la tranche *2* slice
tranquille *13* quiet
tranquillement *26* calmly, peacefully, quietly
le transistor *16* transistor (radio)
le transport *17* transport
les transports en commun (*m*) *26* public transport
le travail *9* work
travailler *5* to work
travailleur *11* hardworking
traverser *6* to cross
le traversin *3* bolster
treize *12* thirteen
treizième *13* thirteenth

trembler *27* to tremble, to shake
trente *9* thirty
trente-cinq *6* thirty-five
trente-huit *6* thirty-eight
trente mille *20* thirty thousand
trente-trois *20* thirty-three
trentième *30* thirtieth
trépidant *17* hectic
très *1* very
le trimestre *13* term
triste *19* sad
trois *2* three
troisième *1* third
tromper *27* to deceive
se tromper *5* to be wrong, to make
  a mistake
trop *5* too much
trop de *30* too many
le trottoir *26* pavement
le trou *21* hole
trouver *6* to find
se trouver *6* to be (situated)
la truite *4* trout
tu *5* you
tué *27* killed
tuer *27* to kill
le tunnel *24* tunnel
la tyrannie *29* tyranny

U

l' ulcère (*m*) *20* ulcer
un *1* a, one
un instant *1* just a moment
un jour sur deux *16* every other
  day
une *2* a, one
une fois *13* once
une fois de plus *25* once again
une fois ou deux *18* once or twice
l' uniforme (*m*) *1* uniform
l' urgence (*f*) *20* emergency
urgent *7* urgent
usé *28* worn
l' usine (*f*) *5* factory
utiliser *17* to use

V

va-t-en *8* go away
les vacances (*f*) *6* holidays
vaguement *17* vaguely

la vaisselle *11* washing-up
valable *30* valid
la valeur *22* quality, value
la valise *2* suitcase
la vallée *24* valley
valoir *25* to cost, to be worth
valoir la peine *27* to be worth
  the trouble
varié *4* mixed
le vase *24* vase
il vaut mieux *18* it's better
le veau *11* veal
le veilleur de nuit *11* night porter
le vélo *25* bike
la vendeuse *4* (shop) assistant
vendre *9* to sell
se vendre *28* to sell
(le) vendredi *12* Friday
venez *2* come
venir *2* to come
venir de *10* to have just
le vent *28* wind
la vente *17* sale
le verger *28* orchard
vérifier *30* to check
le verre *24* glass
vert *18* green
la veste *15* jacket
le vestibule *13* hall
le veston *15* jacket (of a suit)
les vêtements (*m*) *15* clothes
vicié *29* evil
la victoire *22* victory
vider *3* to unpack, to empty
la vie *14* life
vieil *8* old
vieille *8* old
la vieillesse *28* old age
vieillir *29* to grow old
vieux *8* old
vilain *5* ugly
la villa *30* villa
la ville *2* city, town
le vin *4* wine
le vin blanc *11* white wine
le vin rouge ordinaire *4* (ordinary)
  red wine
vingt *3* twenty
vingtième *20* twentieth
vingt-cinq *25* twenty-five
vingt-cinquième *25* twenty-fifth
vingt-deux *22* twenty-two

vingt-deuxième *22* twenty-second
vingt et un *5* twenty-one
vingt et unième *21* twenty-first
vingt-huit *28* twenty-eight
vingt-huitième *28* twenty-eighth
vingt-neuf *29* twenty-nine
vingt-neuvième *29* twenty-ninth
vingt-quatre *5* twenty-four
vingt-quatrième *24* twenty-fourth
vingt-sept *27* twenty-seven
vingt-septième *27* twenty-seventh
vingt-six *26* twenty-six
vingt-sixième *26* twenty-sixth
vingt-trois *5* twenty-three
vingt-troisième *23* twenty-third
le violet *24* violet
la virgule *16* comma
le virus *20* virus
la visite *17* visit
visiter *8* to visit
le visiteur *17* visitor
vite *14* quickly
la vitesse *27* speed
la vitrine *24* show case
vive (le sport)! *22* long live (sport)!
vivre *14* to live
voilà *1* there is, there are, here
   is, here are
voir *4* to see
voir clair *23* to see clearly, well
voisin *4* next (neighbouring)
le voisin *16* neighbour
la voiture *14* car, *24* carriage, train,
   tube
la voiture de sport *27* sports car

la voix *10* voice
le vol *30* flight
la volaille *28* poultry
vos *1* your
votre *1* your
le vôtre *15* yours (your one)
vouloir *2* to want to
vouloir dire *15* to mean
vous *1* you
vous (aussi) *4* you (too)
vous voulez rire! *24* you're joking!
le voyage *21* journey
voyager *11* to travel
le voyageur *1* passenger
voyons *4* let's see
vrai *2* true
vraiment *7* really
la vue *2* view

W

le wagon-restaurant *12* dining-car
les waters (*m*) *13* toilet
le week-end *25* week-end
le western *23* western, cowboy film
le whisky *1* whisky

Y

y (j'y vais) *14* I'm going
y (j'y pense) *15* by the way,
   while I think about it
je n' y connais rien en fleurs *25* I
   don't know anything about
   flowers
les yeux (*m*) *24* eyes

English—French

A

a un, une
A.D. après Jésus-Christ
a little un peu
a long time longtemps
a lot of people beaucoup de
   monde
to abandon abandonner
to be able pouvoir
about environ
(from) above du dessus
abroad à l'étranger
absent absent
absent-minded distrait
absolutely absolument
to accept accepter
accident l'accident (m)
to accompany accompagner
according to what d'après
   ce que
accountant l'expert
   comptable (m)
to accuse accuser
actor le comédien
actress la comédienne
to add ajouter
added to which par-dessus
   le marché
address l'adresse (f)
to address (a letter) adresser
   (une lettre)
addressee le destinataire
administration
   l'administration (f)
to admire admirer
admission charge l'entrée (f)
to admit admettre, avouer
to adopt adopter
adult l'adulte (m)
advertisement la réclame
advertisements (classified)
   les petites annonces (f)
advertising la publicité
advertising agency l'agence
   de publicité (f)
advertising campaign la
   campagne de publicité
to advise conseiller (de)
aeroplane l'avion (m)

to afford (to) se permettre (de)
to be afraid avoir peur
after après
after all après tout
after having . . . après
   avoir . . .
after-shave l'after-shave (m)
afternoon l'après-midi (m)
again à nouveau
against contre
agency l'agence (f)
ago il y a
air l'air (m)
air hostess l'hôtesse de
   l'air (f)
airport l'aéroport (m)
alas hélas
all tout, tous
all alone tout seul
all day de la journée
all day long toute la journée
all four (of us) tous les
   quatre
all kinds of toutes sortes de
all right ça va, d'accord
all the rooms toutes les
   chambres
all the same quand même,
   tout de même
all the time tout le temps
all the year round toute
   l'année
all together en tout, tous
   ensemble
to allow permettre
to allow oneself (to) se
   permettre (de)
almost à peu près, presque
alone seul
alongside le long le
already déjà
also aussi
always toujours, tout le
   temps
amongst au milieu de
to amuse oneself se distraire
and et
angel l'ange (m)
to get angry se fâcher

animal la bête
to announce annoncer
announcer la speakerine
to annoy agacer
annoying ennuyeux
the annoying thing is that . . .
l'ennui c'est que . . .
annual closing-down la
fermeture annuelle
another un autre
to answer répondre
antiquity l'antiquité (*f*)
any n'importe quel
any minute now d'une
minute à l'autre
anyhow n'importe
comment
any time n'importe quand
anyone n'importe qui
anything quelque chose,
n'importe quoi
anywhere n'importe où
apart from à part
apart from that à part ça
aperitif l'apéritif (*m*)
appeal l'attrait (*m*)
to appear paraître
to appear (to be) avoir l'air
appendix l'appendice (*m*)
to applaud applaudir
apple la pomme
to apply appliquer
to apply (to) s'adresser (à)
to appoint nommer
archaeologist l'archéologue
(*m*)
area quartier (*m*)
aren't they? n'est-ce pas?
argument la discussion,
l'argument (*m*)
arm le bras
armchair le fauteuil
to arrange a meeting (with)
donner rendez-vous (à)
arrival l'arrivée (*f*)
to arrive arriver
arrow la flèche
art l'art (*m*)
as puisque
as a matter of fact en fait
as always comme toujours
as . . . as aussi . . . que

as . . . as that si . . . que ça
as far as jusqu'à
as for quant à
as long as pourvu que
as much as autant que
as soon as dès que
as usual comme d'habitude
ash-tray le cendrier
to ask (questions) poser (des
questions)
to ask for demander
assistant l'adjoint (*m*)
to associate with (someone)
fréquenter (quelqu'un)
at à
at (the shop of etc.) chez
at all du tout
at first d'abord
at full blast à fond
at home à la maison
at least au moins, du moins
at my age à mon âge
at the beginning au début
at the end of à la fin de
at the foot of au pied de
at the left à la gauche
at the moment en ce moment
at the most au maximum
at the right à la droite
at the same time à la fois,
tout en . . .
at the top of her voice à tue-
tête
at the wheel au volant
at your service à votre
service
atmosphere l'atmosphère (*f*)
to attack attaquer
audience les spectateurs (*m*)
auditorium la salle
August août (*m*)
aunt la tante
austere austère
automatic gate le portillon
automatique
autumn l'automne (*m*)
avenue l'avenue (*f*)
to avoid fuir

B

back le dossier
to be back être de retour

bacteria les bactéries (*f*)
badly done mal fait
bag le sac
baker le boulanger
balcony le balcon
ballpoint pen le stylo à bille
bandage box la boîte à
  pansements
bank la banque
bank (of a river) le quai
bar le bar, la tablette
bargain l'affaire (*f*)
basket le panier
bath le bain
bathroom la salle de bains
bath (tub) la baignoire
B.C. avant Jésus-Christ
to be être
to be able pouvoir
to be afraid avoir peur
to be back être de retour
to be bored s'ennuyer
to be bored to death s'ennuyer
  à mourir
to be called s'appeler
be careful! attention!
be careful of . . . attention
  à . . .
to be cold avoir froid, faire
  froid
to be dark faire noir
to be envious of envier
to be even être quitte
to be fast avancer
to be fed up en avoir par-
  dessus la tête
to be fine faire beau
to be going to aller
to be hot avoir chaud
to be hungry avoir faim
to be in a hurry être pressé
to be in a hurry to avoir hâte
  de
to be in charge of s'occuper de
to be in the middle of être en
  train de
to be interested in s'intéresser à
to be kind enough to avoir la
  gentillesse (de)
to be lucky avoir de la chance
to be necessary falloir
to be off se sauver

to be on (at) avoir lieu (à)
to be on a trip être de sortie
to be present (at) assister (à)
to be pronounced se prononcer
to be quiet se taire
to be rash faire des folies
to be reflected se refléter
to be right avoir raison
to be settled s'arranger
to be situated se trouver
to be slow retarder
to be sorry regretter, s'excuser
to be spelt s'épeler
to be supposed to être censé de,
  devoir
to be thirsty avoir soif
to be used to avoir l'habitude
  de
to be warm faire chaud
to be worth valoir
to be wrong avoir tort, se
  tromper
to bear supporter
beautiful beau, bel, belle,
  beaux, belles
because parce que
because of à cause de
to become devenir
bed le lit
before autrefois, avant,
  avant de
to beg prier
to begin commencer (à)
to begin again recommencer
to begin to se mettre à
beginning le début
beige beige
to belong appartenir
below dessous
belt la ceinture
bend le tournant
beside à côté, au bord de,
  le long de
best mieux
the best le meilleur
the best thing is to . . . le mieux
  c'est de . . .
better meilleur
to do better faire mieux
better and better de mieux
  en mieux
between entre

bicycle la bicyclette
bidet le bidet
big gros, grosse
big prize le gros lot
bike le vélo
bilingual bilingue
bill l'addition (*f*), la note
bird l'oiseau (*m*)
black noir
blanket la couverture
'blanquette' of veal la blanquette de veau
blind aveugle
block (of flats) l'immeuble (*m*)
blouse le chemisier
blow le coup
blue bleu
to boil bouillir
bolster le traversin
bone l'os (*m*)
bones des ossements (*m*)
bonnet le capot
book le livre
to book retenir, louer
book of tickets le carnet
boot (of car) le coffre
to be bored s'ennuyer
to be bored to death s'ennuyer à mourir
to borrow emprunter
boss le patron
bossy autoritaire
both à la fois, tous les deux
bother la peine
to bother gêner
bottle la bouteille, le flacon
the bottom (one) (celui) du bas
boulevard le boulevard
box la boîte
box-office le guichet
boy le garçon
bracelet le bracelet
to brake freiner
bread le pain
to break down tomber en panne
breakfast le petit déjeuner
to breathe respirer
bridge le pont
brilliant brillant
to bring amener, apporter

to bring back rapporter
broadcast l'émission (*f*)
broken en panne
bronze le bronze
brother le frère
brother-in-law le beau-frère
brown marron
brush la brosse
to brush brosser
building le bâtiment
bulb l'ampoule (*f*)
burglar le cambrioleur
bus l'autobus (*m*), le car
bus conductor le receveur
bus-stop l'arrêt d'autobus (*m*)
business les affaires (*f*)
business dinner le dîner d'affaires
business man l'homme d'affaires (*m*)
busy occupé
but mais, pourtant
butter le beurre
button le bouton
to buy acheter
to buy things faire des achats
by par, sur
by bus en autobus
by car en voiture
by chance par hasard
by hand à la main
by heart par cœur
by instalments à tempérament
by marriage par alliance
by telephone par téléphone
by the way à propos, au fait, j'y pense

C

café le café
cake le gâteau
to call héler
calm calme
calmly tranquillement
to camp camper
camping le camping
camping site le terrain de camping
can pouvoir
Cánada le Canada

Canadian canadien
capital la capitale
capsule le cachet
car la voiture
car accident l'accident de
voiture (*m*)
car door la portière
carafe la carafe
caravan la caravane
caravaning le caravaning
career la carrière, le métier
carefully soigneusement
carefully done soigné
carpenter le menuisier
carriage la voiture
to carry porter
cartoon le dessin animé
to carve sculpter
carved sculpté
cashier le caissier
cassette la cassette
cat le chat
catch la fermeture
to catch (on something)
accrocher
to catch a cold attraper le rhume
to catch the bus prendre le car
ceiling le plafond
to celebrate fêter
Celtic celte
centime le centime
central heating le chauffage
central
century le siècle
certain certain
certainly bien sûr,
certainement
certainly not! ça non!
chain la chaîne
chair la chaise
chambermaid la femme de
chambre
champagne le champagne
change la petite monnaie, le
changement
to change changer
to change gear changer de
vitesse
to change one's mind changer
d'avis
channel la chaîne
character la personnalité

to charge someone dresser une
contravention
to chat bavarder
to check vérifier
cheek la joue
cheese le fromage
chemist le pharmacien
cheque le chèque
cheque book le carnet
(de chèques)
chest of drawers la commode
chicken le poulet
child l'enfant (*m*)
chips les frites (*f*)
chocolate le chocolat
to choose choisir
christening le baptême
cigarette la cigarette
cinema le cinéma
city la ville
to claim prétendre, réclamer
clasp la fermeture
classical classique
clean propre
to clean nettoyer
cleaner le teinturier
cleaner's la teinturerie
clerk l'employé (*m*)
clinic la clinique
clock la pendule
to close ·fermer
close to à proximité de
cloth le chiffon
clothes les vêtements (*m*)
club la boîte
coat le manteau
coathanger le cintre
coffee le café
coin la pièce de monnaie
cold froid
cold le rhume
collar le col
colour la couleur
comb le peigne
come venez
to come venir
come and eat! à table!
to come back rentrer, revenir
to come in entrer, rentrer
come on . . . allons . . .
come to think of it . . . à la
réflexion . . .

comedy la comédie
comfort le confort
comfortable confortable
coming from en provenance de
comma virgule
to commute (between) faire la navette (entre)
company la compagnie
to compare comparer
compared with en comparaison de
compartment le compartiment
to complain gémir, se plaindre
to complain to porter plainte à
complaint la plainte
complaints les réclamations (f)
completely complètement
complicate compliquer
compliment le compliment
concierge le concierge
congratulations les félicitations (f)
connection la correspondance
conscientious consciencieux
conscientiously consciencieusement
to consider considérer, réfléchir
to console consoler
to consult consulter
consultation la consultation
to continue continuer
continuous permanent
continuously sans arrêt
contract le contrat
convenient pratique
conversation la conversation
convertible décapotable
convinced convaincu
cook le cuisinier (m), or la cuisinière (f)
cooked cuit
to cope se débrouiller
corner le coin
to cost coûter, valoir
to count compter
counter le comptoir
country la campagne, le pays
course le cours

courtyard la cour
cousin le cousin, la cousine
cover la couverture
covered (with) couvert (de)
cowboy film le western
crime le crime
croissant le croissant
to cross traverser
to cross out barrer
crossroads le carrefour
crowd la foule
cuff-link le bouton de manchettes
cup la coupe, la tasse
to cure guérir
curious curieux
curtain le rideau
curtly sèchement
customer le client
customs officer le douanier
to cut down abattre
to cut someone's throat égorger
to cycle faire du vélo
cycling la bicyclette

D

daddy papa
dance le bal
to dance danser
dance hall le dancing
to dare oser
dark blue bleu foncé
darling chéri
date la date
daughter la fille
day le jour, la journée
day after tomorrow après-demain
day before yesterday avant-hier
dead mort
to deal with s'occuper de
dear cher, chère, chéri
death la mort
to deceive tromper
to decide décider (de)
to decide to se décider à
to declare déclarer
deeply profondément
defeat la défaite
degree le degré

degrees centigrade les degrés centigrade
degrees fahrenheit les degrés fahrenheit
delicious délicieux
delighted enchanté, ravi
to **demand** réclamer
dénouement le dénouement
dentist le dentiste
department store le grand magasin
departure le départ
to **desert** abandonner
designer le dessinateur
desk le bureau
dessert le dessert
detail le détail
detergent lè détergent
detestable détestable
to **dial** former
dialling tone la tonalité
to **dictate** dicter
dictionary le dictionnaire
to **die** mourir
to **die of thirst** mourir de soif
diet le regime, la diète
difficult difficile
digestive le digestif
dining-car le wagon-restaurant
dining-room la salle à manger
dinner le dîner
direct direct
directly directement
director le directeur
directory l'annuaire (*m*)
dirty sale
to **disappear** disparaître
disappointed déçu
discotheque la discothèque
to **discover** découvrir
discovery la découverte
to **discuss** discuter (de)
discussion la discussion
dish le plat
dishonest de mauvaise foi
dishwasher la machine à laver la vaisselle
disqualification (driving) le retrait du permis
distinguished distingué

to **disturb** déranger
to **do** faire
to **do a hundred (Km per hour)** faire du cent
to **do better** faire mieux
to **do laundry** faire le blanchissage
to **do more than ...** passer
to **do odd jobs** bricoler
to **do one's rounds** partir en tournée
to **do the honours** faire les honneurs
to **do the pleasure (of)** faire le plaisir (de)
to **do the washing-up** faire la vaisselle
doctor le docteur, le médecin
document le document
dog le chien
dollar le dollar
donkey l'âne (*m*)
don't mention it de rien
I **don't want to die** je ne tiens pas à mourir
don't worry ne vous en faites pas
door la porte
doorway le portail
double bed le grand lit
doubt le doute
I **doubt (it)** j'en doute
doubtless sans doute
drama le drame
drawer le tiroir
dream le rêve
dress la robe
dressed habillé
drink la boisson, l'apéritif (*m*)
to **drink** boire
to **drink the health of** boire à la santé de
to **drive** conduire, rouler
to **drive the wrong way** rouler en sens interdit
driver l'automobiliste (*m*), le chauffeur, le conducteur
driving au volant
driving licence le permis de conduire

driving mirror le rétroviseur
driving school
  l'auto-école (*f*)
drop la goutte
to drop laisser tomber
a drop of un doigt de
drug la drogue
to dry clean nettoyer à sec
during au cours de, pendant
dustbin la poubelle

E

each chaque
each (one) chacun, chacune
early avant l'heure, en
  avance, tôt
early morning mist la brume
  matinale
to earn gagner
ear-ring la boucle d'oreilles
to ease soulager
easily facilement
easy facile
to eat manger
edge le bord
education l'éducation (*f*)
educational éducatif
egg l'œuf (*m*)
egg mayonnaise l'œuf dur
  mayonnaise (*m*)
eight huit
eighteen dix-huit
eighteenth dix-huitième
eighth huitième
eighty quatre-vingts
either . . . or soit . . . soit
electric électrique
electric razor le rasoir
  électrique
electric cooker la cuisinière
  électrique
electric food mixer le
  batteur électrique
eleven onze
eleventh onzième
elsewhere ailleurs
emergency l'urgence (*f*)
emotion l'émotion (*f*)
to employ employer, engager
employee l'employé (*m*)

to empty vider
to encourage encourager
end la fin
to end up by finir par
to endorse approuver
engaged occupé
engine le moteur
engineer l'ingénieur (*m*)
England l'Angleterre (*f*)
English anglais
to enjoy oneself s'amuser, se
  plaire
enjoy your meal! bon
  appétit!
enormous énorme, immense
enormous amount of
  énormément de
enough assez, assez de,
  suffisant
enough to buy a drink de
  quoi boire
enquiries les
  renseignements (*m*), le
  service des renseignements
to enrol (at) s'inscrire (à)
enthusiasm l'enthousiasme
  (*m*)
entrance l'entrée (*f*)
to envy envier
epilogue l'épilogue (*m*)
escalator l'escalier roulant
  (*m*)
especially surtout
estimate le devis
etiquette l'étiquette (*f*)
even même
even so quand même
evening le soir, la soirée
every day tous les jours
every other day un jour sur
  deux
every time chaque fois
every two years tous les
  deux ans
every week toutes les
  semaines
everyone tout le monde
everything tout
everything's fine tout va
  bien
everywhere partout
evil vicié

ex- ancien
exactly exactement, précis
to **exaggerate** exagérer
exam l'examen (*m*)
to **examine** examiner
not to **exceed the speed limit** ne
    pas faire d'excès de
    vitesse
excellent excellent
except sauf
excuse l'excuse (*f*)
to **excuse** excuser
excuse me excusez-moi
to **excuse oneself** s'excuser
exhausted épuisé
exhibition l'exposition (*f*)
to **expect to** s'attendre à
expenses les frais (*m*)
expenses (bill) la note de
    frais
expensive cher, chère
to **explain** expliquer
express train l'express (*m*),
    le rapide
expression l'expression (*f*)
to **extend** prolonger
extravagant dépensier
eyelash le cil
eyes les yeux (*m*)

F

face la figure
face powder la poudre de riz
factory l'usine (*f*)
faculty (of university) la
    Faculté
to **fail** échouer
to **fall** tomber
to **fall asleep** s'endormir
falling off en baisse
family la famille
famous célèbre, fameux
fancy . . . on n'a pas idée
    de . . .
far loin
farm la ferme
farmer le cultivateur
fascinating passionnant
fashion la mode
fashionable chic

fast rapide
fast (of colours) bon teint
to **fast** se mettre à la diète
fat gros
fat people les gros
fatal fatal
father papa, le père
fault la faute
favourable favorable
to **fear** craindre
to **feel** sentir, se sentir
to **feel (like)** avoir envie de
to **feel unwell** se sentir mal
feeling le sentiment
to **fetch** aller chercher, chercher
fever la fièvre
few peu de
fiancé le fiancé
field le champ
fifteen quinze
fifteenth quinzième
fifth cinquième
fifty cinquante
fifty (years old) la
    cinquantaine
to **fight** se battre
file le dossier
filing cabinet le classeur
to **fill** remplir
to **fill up on water** faire le
    plein d'eau
film le film, la pellicule
finally enfin, finalement
to **find** trouver
to **find again** retrouver
fine c'est parfait
a **finger of** un doigt de
to **finish** finir, terminer
fireworks les feux d'artifice
    (*m*)
firm la maison
first avant, premier
first-aid box la boîte à
    pharmacie
first class en première
first . . . then tantôt . . .
    tantôt
fish le poisson
five cinq
to **fix an appointment** donner
    rendez-vous (à)
flag le drapeau

flat l'appartement (*m*)
to flee fuir, s'enfuir
flight le vol
floor l'étage (*m*)
florist le fleuriste
flower la fleur
to follow suivre
following day le lendemain
food la nourriture
food mixer le mixer
foot le pied
football le football
football match le match de
football
for depuis, pour, car
for a long time depuis
longtemps
for a whole day pendant une
journée entière
for example par exemple
for instance par exemple
for love par amour
for revenge par vengeance
for sale à vendre
for spite par dépit
for the sake of economy par
économie
for the time being pour le
moment
for years ça fait des années
for (you to say) pour que
(tu dises)
forbidden (to) interdit (de)
to force obliger
forehead le front
to forget oublier
to forgive oneself se pardonner
fork la fourchette
form le formulaire, la fiche
formal solennel
former ancien
formerly autrefois
fortnight quinze jours
fortunately heureusement
forty quarante
forty-two quarante-deux
to found fonder
foundations les fondations (*f*)
four quatre
fourteen quatorze
four hundred quatre cents
fourteenth quatorzième

fourth quatrième
foyer le foyer
fragile fragile
franc le franc
France la France
free gratuit, gratuitement,
libre
freely facilement
French français
French beans les haricots
verts (*m*)
French girl la Française
French Revolution
la Révolution Française
Frenchman le Français
to freshen up se rafraîchir
Friday le vendredi
fridge le frigidaire
fried potatoes les frites (*f*)
friend l'ami (*m*)
from de, du
from above du dessus
from bad to worse de mal
en pis
from time to time de temps
en temps, de temps à autre
front la façade
front door la porte d'entrée
fruit le fruit
fruit juice le jus de fruit(s)
full of plein de, rempli (de)
full stop le point
full-time à plein-temps
full up complet
funny amusant
furious furieux
furniture (piece of) le meuble
future l'avenir (*m*)

G

gadget le gadget
to gain obtenir
to gain (of clocks, etc.)
avancer
gallery la galerie
garage le garage
garage owner le garagiste
garden le jardin
gardener le jardinier
gay gai

general bargains les occasions diverses (*f*)
generally en général, généralement
Gentlemen Messieurs
German allemand
Germany l'Allemagne
to get obtenir
to get angry se fâcher
to get hold of se procurer
to get impatient s'impatienter
to get in the way gêner
to get into monter (dans)
to get married se marier
to get mixed up se mélanger
to get near (to) approcher (de)
to get off descendre
to get up se lever
gifted doué
girl la fille
girl (young) la jeune fille
girl-friend la petite amie
to give donner
to give back rendre
to give (someone) notice donner congé
to glance at jeter un coup d'œil (à)
glass le verre
to go aller
to go about se déplacer
to go abroad aller à l'étranger
go away! allez-vous-en, va-t-en!
to go away s'en aller, s'éloigner
to go away again repartir
to go back retourner
to go down descendre
to go fast faire de la vitesse
to go for a walk se promener
to go from place to place se déplacer
to go on continuer
to go on a diet se mettre au régime
to go on strike se mettre en grève
to go out sortir
to go round faire le tour (de)
to go shopping faire des courses

to go and meet aller à la rencontre de
to go up monter
to go via passer par
to go with accompagner
gods (theatre) le poulailler
to be going to aller
good bon
good at doué
good-bye au revoir
good evening bonsoir
good food la bonne chère
good heavens! mon Dieu!
gorgeous adorable
government l'Administration (*f*), le gouvernement
grandfather le grand-père
grandmother la grand-mère
grandparents les grands-parents (*m*)
grandson le petit-fils
great énorme
Greek grec
green vert
grey gris
to grow faire pousser
to grow (big) grandir
to grow old vieillir
gruyère le gruyère
to guess deviner
guest le client, l'invité (*m*)
guest room la chambre d'amis
guide le guide
guitar la guitare
gymnastics la gymnastique

H

to hail héler
hair les cheveux (*m*)
hairbrush la brosse à cheveux
hairdresser le coiffeur
hairdresser's le salon de coiffure
half-hour la demi-heure
half-litre le demi-litre
half-past six six heures et demie
half-time la mi-temps

half-way à moitié chemin
hall le hall, le vestibule
ham le jambon
hand la main
handpainted peint à la
  main
handbag le sac à main
handkerchief le mouchoir
handle le manche
handsome beau
hàndwriting l'écriture (f)
to hang up raccrocher
to happen se passer
happy heureux
hard dur
hard (boiled) dur
hardly (ever) ne . . . guère
hardworking travailleur
to harm faire mal
(he, she) has (il, elle) a
to hate détester
to have avoir
to have a cold avoir le rhume,
  être enrhumé
to have a drink (aperitif)
  prendre quelque chose,
  prendre un apéritif,
  prendre un verre
to have a good day passer une
  bonne journée
to have a headache avoir mal
  à la tête
to have a look at jeter un
  coup d'œil (à)
to have a pain in avoir mal à
to have a surgery consulter
to have difficulty in avoir du
  mal à
to have dinner dîner
to have . . . done faire faire
to have had enough en avoir
  ássez
to have just venir de
to have lunch déjeuner
to have no chance of n'avoir
  aucune chance de
to have something wrong (with)
  souffrir (de)
to have the chance to avoir
  l'occasion de
to have the opportunity of
  avoir l'occasion de

to have time to avoir le temps
  de
to have to être obligé de,
  falloir, avoir à
to have visitors avoir de la
  visite
he il
he (too) lui (aussi)
head la tête
head of advertising le chef
  de la publicité
headache le mal à la tête
to have a headache avoir mal
  à la tête
health la santé
heaps of des tas de
to hear entendre
heart complaint la maladie
  de cœur
heat la chaleur
heating le chauffage
hectic trépidant
hello allô, bonjour, bonsoir
to help aider
to help oneself se servir
her elle, son, sa, ses
(to) her lui
here ici, par ici
here are voilà
here is voilà
here it is la voilà, le voilà
here they are les voilà
here you are tenez
here's . . . again revoilà
hero le héros
heroine l'héroïne (f)
hers à elle, le sien
herself elle-même
to hide cacher
hiding place la cachette
high élevé
(to) him lui
himself lui-même
to hire louer
his son, sa, ses
his (one) le sien
history l'histoire (f)
to hold tenir
hole le trou
holiday le jour de fête,
  la fête
holiday plans les projets de
  vacances

holidays les vacances (*f*)
honest honnête
hook le crochet
to hook accrocher
to hope espérer, souhaiter
hors-d'œuvre hors
d'œuvre (*m*)
hospital l'hôpital (*m*)
hotel l'hôtel (*m*)
hotel management
l'hôtellerie (*f*)
hour l'heure (*f*)
house la maison
housewife la maîtresse de
maison
housework le ménage
how comme, comment
est-ce que . . . ?,
comment . . . ?
how are things? comment
ça va ?
how are you? comment
allez-vous ?
how long? combien de
temps ?
how much? combien ?
how much is it? c'est
combien ?
how much is that? ça fait
combien ?
however pourtant
human being l'être humain
(*m*)
hundred cent
a hundred and fifty cent
cinquante
hurried bousculé
to hurry away se sauver
to hurt faire mal
husband le mari
hypochondriac le malade
imaginaire

I

I je, moi je . . .
I couldn't . . . impossible
de . . .
I don't know anything about
flowers je n'y connais
rien en fleurs
I don't mind ça m'est égal

I don't think so je crois que
non
I hope so j'espère que oui
I think not je crois que non
I'm going j'y vais
I'm sorry excusez-moi
ice la glace
idea l'idée (*f*)
idiot idiot (de)
if si
if ever si jamais
if . . . it's because si . . .
c'est que
if necessary au besoin
ill malade
illness la maladie
to illustrate illustrer
to imagine se figurer
immediately immédiatement,
tout de suite
immigration officer le
policier
impatient impatient
impolite impoli
importance l'importance (*f*)
important important
the important thing is . . . ce qui
compte . . . c'est . . .
impossible impossible
to improve améliorer, faire des
progrès
in en, dans, à bord
in a bad temper de
mauvaise humeur
in a clinic en clinique
in a minute tout à l'heure
in all en tout
in any case dans tous les
cas, en tout cas
in autumn en automne
in bed au lit
in black and white en noir
et blanc
in capital letters en
majuscules
in colour en couleur
in detail en détail
in fact en fait, en réalité
in fashion en vogue
in front of devant
in good health en bonne
santé

in my life de ma vie
in my opinion à mon avis
in order to pour
in particular en particulier
in question en question
in short bref
in shorthand en sténo
in spite of malgré
in spring au printemps
in summer en été
in the country à la
campagne
in the middle of au milieu
de
in the middle of summer en
plein été
in the middle of the night en
pleine nuit
in the open air au grand air
in the opposite direction en
sens inverse
in the provinces en province
in the right place au bon
endroit
in the shade à l'ombre
in the sun au soleil
in the wrong place au
mauvais endroit
in there là-dedans
in winter en hiver
in working order en état de
marche
included compris
incurable incurable
indeed en effet
indicator le clignotant
inhabitant l'habitant (m)
initial l'initiale (f)
inside à l'intérieur (de),
là-dedans
to insist tenir bon
to inspire inspirer
instead of au lieu de
installed installé
instructions les instructions
(f)
instructor le moniteur
intelligent intelligent
to intend to tenir à
intensive intensif
intercommunication system
l'interphone (m)

interesting intéressant
interior l'intérieur (m)
interpreter l'interprète (m
or f)
interval l'entracte (m)
into town en ville
to introduce présenter
to introduce oneself se
présenter
invitation l'invitation (f)
to invite inviter
to iron repasser
ironing le repassage
is there . . . ? est-ce qu'il
y a . . . ?
is this . . . ? c'est . . . ?
isn't it? n'est-ce pas?
it elle, il, ce
(here, there) it (is), etc. le (voilà)
la (voilà)
it appears that il paraît que
it doesn't matter ça n'a pas
d'importance
it must be ça doit être
it wasn't really worth it ça
ne valait pas la peine
it'll hold ça tient
it's c'est
it's a bit much c'est un
peu fort
it's a matter of principle
c'est une question de
principe
it's a pity c'est dommage
it's all the same ça revient
au même
it's better il vaut mieux
it's fast ça tient
it's high time to il est grand
temps de
it's quite simple c'est bien
simple
it's not important ça n'a
pas d'importance
it's not worth the trouble
ce n'est pas la peine
it's the same thing ça
revient au même
it's too bad c'est trop fort
it's true c'est vrai
it's up to you . . . c'est à
toi de . . .

it's **warming up** ça chauffe
it's **been years since** ça fait
  des années (que)
Italy l'Italie (*f*)
its sa, ses, son

J

to **jabber** baragouiner
jacket la veste, le veston
jam la confiture
'jeton' le jeton
jewel le bijou
job le métier, la situation
to **join** rejoindre
journalist le journaliste
journey le voyage
July juillet (*m*)
to **jump** sauter
to **jump the lights** brûler les
  feux, griller les feux
June juin (*m*)
just tout juste
just a moment un instant
just look at that! regardez-
  moi ça!
just now à l'instant

K

to **keep** conserver, garder
to **keep one's figure** garder la
  ligne
to **keep one's word** tenir
  parole
to **keep to** serrer
to **keep to his right** serrer sa
  droite
keeper on duty le gardien
  de service
key la clef
to **kill** tuer
killed tué
kilometer le kilomètre
kind chic
kind le genre, la sorte
(a) **kind of** une espèce de
to **kiss** embrasser
kitchen la cuisine
knife le couteau
knock le coup
to **knock** frapper

to **know** connaître, savoir
to **know how to** savoir
known connu

L

Ladies Mesdames
Ladies and Gentlemen
  Messieurs-Dames
lady la dame
lamp la lampe
to **land** débarquer
language la langue
large grand, élevé
large note le gros billet
last dernier
to **last** durer
last full stop le point final
last night hier soir
late en retard, tard
latest dernier
latin latin
to **laugh** rire
to **laugh at, about** rire de
to **launch** lancer
launderette la laverie
  automatique
laundry (the place) la
  blanchisserie
laundry/cleaners la
  blanchisserie teinturerie
laundry le blanchissage
lazy paresseux
to **lead the way** ouvrir la
  marche
to **learn** apprendre
leave le congé
to **leave** laisser, laisser tomber,
  quitter, partir
to **leave alone** laisser tranquille
to **lend** prêter
(on, to the) **left** à gauche
leg la jambe
legend la légende
less moins
less . . . than moins . . . que
lesson la leçon
to **let be** laisser tranquille
let's eat! à table!
let's see voyons
letter la lettre
letter box la boîte à lettres

314

lettuce la laitue
to lie mentir
to lie down s'allonger
life la vie
lift l'ascenseur (m)
light clair, léger
light la lumière
light blue bleu clair
lights les feux (m)
like comme
to like aimer
like the back of their hand
comme leur poche
to like very much aimer bien
lilac le lilas
lily of the valley le muguet
lined (with) bordé (de)
lipstick le rouge à lèvres
list la liste
to listen to écouter
a little un peu
little by little petit à petit
little (not much) peu
live en direct
to live vivre
to live (in) habiter
liver le foie
to lock fermer à clef
long (time) long
long live (sport)! vive (le sport)!
a long way loin
look! tiens!
to look avoir l'air
to look after soigner
to look at regarder
to look for chercher
to look like that faire une
tête pareille
to look well avoir bonne mine
looking à l'air
to lose retarder, perdre
to lose oneself se perdre
to lose weight maigrir
lots of des quantités de,
des tas de
lottery la loterie
love l'amour (m)
to love adorer, aimer
lovely belle, charmant
loyal fidèle
L.P. le microsillon
luckily heureusement que

luggage les bagages (m)

M

machine la machine
Madam Madame
made refait
magazine la revue
main course le plat principal
main film le grand film
make la marque
to make rendre, obliger
to make (a bed) refaire
to make a gift of faire cadeau de
to make a good impression
faire bonne impression
to make a mistake se tromper
to make a trip faire une
excursion
to make an appointment
prendre rendez-vous
to make arrangements faire
les démarches
to make ill rendre malade
to make oneself up se maquiller
to make progress faire des
progrès
to make room faire de la place
to make use of emprunter
to make warm donner chaud
man l'homme (m)
to manage gérer, se débrouiller
to manage to do something
arriver à faire quelque-
chose
management la direction
(hotel) manager le gérant (d'hôtel)
mania la manie
many beaucoup de
map le plan
to mark marquer
marked marqué
market le marché
married marié
to marry épouser
marvellous magnifique,
merveilleux
masterpiece le chef-d'œuvre
match le match
maths les mathématiques (f)
a matter of principle une
question de principe
mauve mauve
me me, moi

meal le repas
to mean vouloir dire
means le moyen
means of transport le
moyen de transport
medicine la médecine, le
médicament
to meet (you) faire (votre)
connaissance
to meet aller chercher,
rencontrer
meeting le rendez-vous
to melt se fondre
memory le souvenir
menu le menu
merely simplement
mess le désordre
meter le compteur
metre le mètre
metro le métro
metro station la station de
métro
middle-aged d'un certain
âge
midnight minuit
milk le lait
mine à moi, le mien
mineral water l'eau
minérale (f)
minister le ministre
minus moins
minute (tiny) minuscule
minute la minute
miracle le miracle
miraculous miraculeux
mirror la glace, le miroir
mischievous malin
misfortune le malheur
to mislay égarer
miss Mademoiselle
to miss manquer
mist la brume
mixed varié
mixture le mélange
to moan gémir
model le modèle
modern moderne
moment le moment
Monday lundi
money l'argent (m)
monkey le singe
month le mois

monument le monument
more davantage, de plus,
plus
more and more de plus en
plus
more or less à peu près, en
somme, plus ou moins,
pratiquement
more . . . than plus . . . que
the more . . . the more
plus . . . plus
moreover d'ailleurs
morning le matin
most (of) la plupart (de)
mother maman, la mère
motorway l'autoroute (f)
mouth la bouche
to move bouger
to move away s'éloigner
to move (house) déménager
moving émouvant
Mr. Monsieur, M.
Mrs. Madame, Mme
much too much beaucoup
trop
mummy maman
murderess la meurtrière
museum le musée
mushroom le champignon
musical la comédie
musicale
my mon, ma, mes
my fault de ma faute
my size à ma taille
myself moi-même

N

name le nom
nasty méchant
national national
national holiday la fête
nationale
natural naturel
nausea le mal au cœur
navy blue bleu marine
near à côté de, près de
near to à proximité de
nearly près de
to nearly (do something) faillir
necessary nécessaire
to be necessary falloir

neck le cou
to **need** avoir besoin de
neighbour le voisin
neighbouring voisin
neither non plus
nephew le neveu
never jamais, ne . . . jamais
nervous nerveux
new neuf, nouveau, nouvel,
  nouvelle, nouveaux,
  nouvelles
new paragraph à la ligne
news les nouvelles (*f*),
  les actualités (*f*)
newspaper le journal
newspaper seller le
  marchand de journaux
next ensuite, prochain
next, neighbouring voisin
nice agréable, aimable,
  chic, convenable, gentil,
  sympathique
niçoise salad la salade
  niçoise
niece la nièce
night la nuit
night porter le veilleur de
  nuit
night club la boîte de nuit
nine neuf
nineteen dix-neuf
nineteenth dix-neuvième
ninth neuvième
no non
no (not any) aucun, pas de
no matter n'importe
no matter what n'importe
  quel
no more ne . . . plus, pas
  plus
no one ne . . . personne
no parking stationnement
  interdit
no point in inutile (de)
no vacancies complet
nobody personne
noise le bruit
non-smoker non-fumeur
non-stop ininterrompu
nor ni
normal normal
normal rate le tarif normal

nose le nez
not ne . . . pas, pas
not . . . anywhere nulle part
not at all de rien, pas du
  tout
not bad pas mal
not enough ne . . . pas assez
not even même pas
not much peu
not very pas tellement
not yet pas encore
note le billet
nothing rien, ne . . . rien
nothing special rien de
  spécial
notice le congé
now maintenant
now what do they want?
  qu'est-ce qu'ils veulent
  encore?
nowhere nulle part
number le numéro
nurse l'infirmière (*f*)

O

objection l'objection (*f*)
to **oblige** obliger
obsession l'obsession (*f*)
occupation l'occupation (*f*)
o'clock l'heure (*f*)
of de
of course bien entendu,
  naturellement
of the des, du, de la
of them en
of which dont
of whom dont
off to en route pour
to **offer** offrir
office le bureau
officer monsieur l'agent,
  l'agent de service (*m*)
often souvent
oh no! ça alors! non alors!
ointment la pommade
old vieux, vieil, vieille,
  vieilles
old age la vieillesse
old bones des ossements (*m*)
old-fashioned démodé
on sur
on a diet au régime

on board à bord
on duty de service
on foot à pied
on holiday en vacances
on reflection à la réflexion
on strike en grève
on the contrary au contraire
on the corner au coin
on the decline en baisse
on the floor par terre
on the left à la gauche
on the meter au compteur
on the offchance au petit
  bonheur la chance
on the radio à la radio
on the right à la droite
on the rise en hausse
on the side of au bord (de)
on the top par-dessus
on the way en cours de route
on the way out of à la sortie
  de
on time à l'heure
on to sur
on top dessus, par-dessus
once une fois
once again encore une fois,
  une fois de plus
one on, un, une
the one celui, celle
one . . . another l'un . . .
  l'autre
one to the other l'un à
  l'autre
the ones ceux, celles
oneself soi-même
onion l'oignon
onion soup la soupe à l'oignon
only ne . . . que, seulement
the only one la seule
open ouvert
to open ouvrir
open air le plein air
operation l'opération (f)
operator l'opératrice (f)
to oppose opposer
optimistic optimiste
or ou
or (rather) ou bien
orange l'orange (m)
orchard le verger
ordinary ordinaire

to organize organiser
organized organisé
the other day l'autre jour
others d'autres
our notre, nos
our fault de notre faute
ours, our one le nôtre
outdated démodé
out of par
out of breath essoufflé
out of love par amour
out of spite par dépit
outside dehors
outskirts les environs (m)
outstanding brillant
oven le four
over there là-bas
to owe devoir
owner le propriétaire

P

page la page
paid holidays le congé payé
paid leave le congé payé
pain la douleur
to paint peindre
painted peint
pair la paire
packed (with) encombré
  (de)
palace le palais
paper le papier
papers les paperasses (f)
parcel le paquet
parent le parent
Parisian le Parisien
to park garer, se garer,
  stationner
part la partie
part-time à temps partiel
particularly particulièrement
to pass passer
to pass (test) être reçu
to pass (an examination)
  réussir
passenger le voyageur
passion la passion
passport le passeport
passport control le contrôle
  des passeports
pastry le gâteau
patient patient

patient le malade
patience la patience
pavement le trottoir
to pay payer
to pay attention faire attention
to pay back rembourser
peace le calme
peaceful calme
peacefully tranquillement
pear la poire
peas les petits pois (*m*)
peasant le paysan
pedestrian crossing le
    passage clouté
pencil le crayon
people les gens (*m*), le
    peuple
per cent pour cent
per day par jour
per month par mois
perfect parfait
perfume le parfum
perhaps peut-être
permission la permission
person la personne
the person I'm calling le
    correspondant
personal secretary la
    secrétaire particulière
personality la personnalité
to persuade persuader
pessimistic pessimiste
petrol pump la pompe à
    essence
to phone appeler
to phone back retéléphoner
photograph la photo
to pick cueillir
to pick up (the receiver)
    décrocher (le combiné)
to picnic pique-niquer
picture le tableau
piece of furniture le meuble
pill la pilule
pillow l'oreiller (*m*)
pink rose
pipe la pipe
pitch (football) le terrain (de
    football)
to pity plaindre
place l'endroit (*m*), la
    propriété

to place poser
placed situé
plate l'assiette (*f*), le plat
platform le quai
play la pièce
to play faire marcher, jouer à,
    jouer de
pleasant agréable
please je vous en prie,
    prière de, s'il te plaît,
    s'il vous plaît
to please plaire
pleased content, enchanté
pleasure le plaisir
pleasure boat le bateau-
    mouche
plenty of room beaucoup de
    place
pocket la poche
pocket money l'argent de
    poche (*m*)
policeman l'agent de police
    (*m*), le gardien de la paix
polished poli
polished floor le parquet
    ciré
polite poli
politely aimablement
politician le politicien
poor pauvre
Portugal le Portugal
possible possible
post le courrier
to post poster, mettre à la
    poste
post office le bureau de
    poste, la poste
to post up afficher
post vacant l'offre d'emploi
    (*f*)
post wanted la demande
    d'emploi
postage stamp le
    timbre-poste
postal service le service des
    postes
postcard la carte postale
poste restante la poste
    restante
poster l'affiche (*f*)
potato la pomme (de
    terre)

to **potter** bricoler
poultry la volaille
practical pratique
practically pratiquement
practice le cabinet
precisely précisément
to **prefer** préférer
preparation le préparatif
to **prepare** préparer
to **prescribe** prescrire
prescription l'ordonnance (*f*)
present actuel
present le cadeau
to **press** appuyer
pressure cooker la cocotte
minute
pretty joli
to **prevent oneself** s'empêcher
de
price le prix
principle le principe
**priority to traffic on the
right** la priorité à droite
(*f*)
private house l'hôtel
particulier
probably probablement
problem le problème
procession le défilé
programme l'émission (*f*),
le programme
project le projet
to **prolong** prolonger
to **promise** promettre
to be **pronounced** se prononcer
property la propriété
to **protest** protester
proud fier
prudent prudent
public transport les
transports en commun (*m*)
publishing house la maison
d'édition
punctual ponctuel
puncture la crevaison
to get a **puncture** crever
purpose l'objet (*m*)
push button la touche
to **put** mettre, poser
to **put in** introduire
to **put on weight** grossir
pyjamas le pyjama

Q

quality la valeur
quarrel la querelle
to **quarrel** se disputer
quarter le quart, le quartier
quarter of an hour le quart
d'heure
question la question
question mark le point
d'interrogation
queue la file d'attente, la
queue
to **queue** faire la queue
quickly vite
quiet tranquille
quiet le calme
to be **quiet** se taire
quietly tranquillement
quite near tout près

R

radiator le radiateur
radio la radio
railway le chemin de fer
rain la pluie
to **rain** pleuvoir
rainbow l'arc-en-ciel (*m*)
raincoat l'imperméable (*m*)
rare rare
rare (underdone) saignant
rarely rarement
rat le rat
rate of exchange le taux de
change
rather assez, plutôt
rather than plutôt que (de)
to **read** lire
to **read back** relire
ready prêt
to **realize** se rendre compte
really à vrai dire, vraiment
to **reassure** rassurer
receipt le reçu
to **receive** recevoir
receiver le combiné
reception (desk) la
réception
receptionist le réceptionniste
to **recognize** reconnaître
to **recommend** recommander
record le disque
red rouge

red wine le vin rouge	**rich (of food)** gras
(ordinary) red wine le vin rouge ordinaire	**ridiculous** ridicule
reduced rate le tarif réduit	**right** bon, ça y est
reference la référence	**(on, to the) right** à droite
to be reflected se refléter	**right in the heart of** en plein cœur de
to refresh rafraîchir	**to ring** sonner
to refuse refuser	**ripe** mûr
regards les amitiés, bon souvenir	**to ripen** mûrir
regularly régulièrement	**rise** l'augmentation (f), le lever
to reimburse rembourser	**rising** en hausse
reindeer le cerf	**risk** le risque
reinforced concrete le ciment armé	**to risk** risquer
relative le parent	**river** la rivière
to relax se détendre	**road** la route
relaxed détendu	**road sign** le panneau de signalisation
relaxing reposant	**roar (of traffic)** le roulement
to relieve pain soulager	**roast chicken** le poulet rôti
remade refait	**room** la chambre, la pièce
remedy le remède	**root** la racine
to remember se rappeler	**rose** la rose
to renovate restaurer	**row (of seats)** le rang
rent le loyer	**royal** royal
repair la réparation	**to rub in** appliquer
to repair réparer	**rubber** le caoutchouc
to repeat répéter	**rude** grossier
repertoire le répertoire	**rule** la règle, le règlement
to replace remplacer	**rumbling (of traffic)** le roulement
request stop l'arrêt facultatif (m)	**to run** courir
to reread relire	**to run (of colours)** déteindre
research worker le chercheur	**to run away** s'enfuir
reservation la réservation	**to run out of petrol** tomber en panne d'essence
to reserve réserver	
to resolve résoudre	
respect respecter	**S**
rest le repos	
to rest se reposer	**sad** triste
restaurant le restaurant	**safe and sound** sain et sauf
restful reposant	**safety chain** la chaînette de sûreté
result le résultat	**salad** la salade
to retire prendre la retraite	**salary** le salaire
retirement la retraite	**sale** la vente
to return débarquer	**sales figures** les chiffres de ventes
return ticket l'aller et retour (m)	**salt** le sel
to revolt (against) se révolter (contre)	**same** même
rheumatism les rhumatismes (m)	**sandwich** le sandwich
	Saturday le samedi

to say dire
to say hello dire bonjour
to say in vain avoir beau dire
scared stiff mort de peur
scarf le foulard
schoolboy le lycéen
to sculpt sculpter
sculpted sculpté
season la saison
seat la place, le siège
seated assis
second deuxième
second class en seconde
second-hand d'occasion
secretary la secrétaire
to see voir
to see clearly voir clair
to see (someone) fréquenter (quelqu'un)
to see well voir clair
see you later à tout à l'heure
see you soon à bientôt
to seem sembler
to seize saisir
selected selectionné
to sell vendre, se vendre
to send envoyer
sensitive sensible
September septembre
serious grave
seriously sérieusement
to serve servir
to service réviser
service charge le service
service station la station-service
serviette la serviette
serviette ring le rond de serviette
set (TV or radio) l'appareil (m), le poste
set (theatre) le décor
to set out embarquer
settee le canapé
to be settled s'arranger
settled in installé
seven sept
seventeen dix-sept
seventeenth dix-septième
seventh septième
seventy soixante-dix

several plusieurs
severe austère
sewers les égouts (m)
shade l'ombre (f)
to shake trembler
sharp aigu
she elle
shelf l'étagère (f)
shirt la chemise
shoe la chaussure
shop le magasin
to shop faire des achats
shop assistant la vendeuse
shopping les courses (f)
shopping basket le panier à provisions
short court
short (film) de court métrage
shorthand la sténo
shorthand typist la sténo-dactylo
show le spectacle
to show montrer
to show the way montrer le chemin
show case la vitrine
shower la douche
to shut fermer
shy timide
sick feeling le mal au cœur
sick person le malade
side le côté
sideboard le buffet
sight le spectacle
sign la pancarte, le panneau
to sign signer
signature la signature
simple simple
since depuis, depuis que
since (because) puisque
to sing chanter
single ticket l'aller (m)
sink unit l'évier (m)
sir monsieur
sister la sœur
sit (an exam) passer
to sit down s'asseoir
sitting-room le salon
situated situé
six six
sixteen seize
sixteenth seizième

sixth sixième
size la pointure, la taille
skin la peau
to **skip** sauter
skirt la jupe
to **slam** claquer
to **sleep** dormir
to **sleep (a wink)** fermer l'œil
slice la tranche
slot la fente
slip le ticket
slowly lentement
small petit
smart chic
smell l'odeur (f)
smoke la fumée
to **smoke** fumer
snobbish snob
so alors
so (so big, etc.) si
so many tant de, tellement de
so much tellement
so . . . that tellement . . . que
sock la chaussette
socket la prise de courant
sofa le sofa
sold out complet
solemn solennel
solitude la solitude
solution la solution
some certains, de (la), des, du, quelques, quelques-uns
someone quelqu'un
someone else quelqu'un d'autre
something quelque chose
sometimes parfois, quelquefois
son le fils
song le chant
soon bientôt
sore throat le mal à la gorge
sorry pardon
sort la sorte
sound le son
to **sound (chest)** ausculter
soup la soupe
soup of the day la soupe du jour

Spain l'Espagne (f)
Spaniard l'Espagnol/e (m & f)
Spanish espagnol
spare wheel la roue de secours
to **speak of** pour ainsi dire
speaking clock l'horloge parlante (f)
special spécial
spectacles les lunettes (f)
speed la vitesse
to **speed** faire de la vitesse
speedometer le compteur
spelling l'orthographe (f)
to be **spelt** s'épeler
to **spend** dépenser
to **spend (time)** passer
to **spill** renverser
to **spoil** gâter
spoon la cuillère
sport le sport
sports car la voiture de sport
sporty sportif
spring le printemps
to **stab** poignarder
staff le personnel
stage la scène
stain la tache
stainless steel l'acier inox (m)
staircase l'escalier (m)
stairs les escaliers (m)
stall-holder la marchande
stalls les fauteuils d'orchestre (m)
stamp le timbre, le cachet
to **stand** supporter
standing debout
to **start (found)** fonder
to **start one's career** débuter
to **start out** débuter
to **start to** se mettre à
station la gare
statue la statue
stay (time spent) le séjour
to **stay (remain)** rester
to **stay (at)** descendre dans
steak le steak
steak and chips le steak aux pommes
step la démarche
to **step on someone's foot** marcher sur le pied

stomach l'estomac (*m*)
stomach ache le mal à l'estomac
stone (made of) en pierre
stop (punctuation) le point
to **stop** arrêter, s'arrêter
to **stop oneself** s'empêcher de
stopped arrêté
stopping train l'omnibus (*m*)
store (department) le grand magasin
story l'histoire (*f*)
straight droit
straight on tout droit
strange bizarre
(a) **strange** drôle de
stranger l'étranger (*m*)
street la rue
strike la grève
striped à rayures
strong fort
stubborn têtu
stubborn as a mule têtu comme un âne
stuck bloqué
student l'étudiant (*m*)
studies les études (*f*)
to **study** étudier
style le style
suburbs la banlieue
to **succeed** réussir
such (a) pareil
such and such (a) tel et tel
to **suck** sucer
sufficient suffisant
to **suffocate** étouffer
to **suggest** suggérer
suit le complet
to **suit** aller, convenir
suitcase la valise
summary le résumé
summer l'été (*m*)
sun le soleil
Sunday le dimanche
supermarket le supermarché
to **supervise** surveiller
to **suppose** supposer
supposed censé
sure certain, sûr
surgery le cabinet, la chirurgie
to **surprise** étonner

surprised surpris
surprising étonnant
surrounded (by) entouré (de)
suspicious soupçonneux
sweet le bonbon
switch le bouton
to **switch on the set** allumer le poste
to **switch on the T.V.** mettre la télé
symptom le symptôme
syrup le sirop

T

table la table
tablet le comprimé
to **take** emmener, prendre
to **take (an exam)** passer
to **take (the bus takes . . .)** mettre (l'omnibus met . . .)
to **take advantage of** profiter de
to **take away** emporter
to **take care** prendre soin
to **take hold of** s'emparer de
to **take lightly** prendre à la légère
to **take off** enlever
to **take on** engager
to **take place (at)** avoir lieu (à)
to **take seriously** prendre au sérieux
to **take (size shoes)** chausser (je chausse du . . .)
to **take the driving test** passer le permis
to **take up again** reprendre
taken up (by) repris (par)
to **talk** parler
to **talk (about)** discuter (de)
to **talk about nothing in particular** parler de la pluie et du beau temps
to **talk business** parler affaires
to **talk politics** parler politique
tape la bande magnétique
tax la taxe
taxi le taxi
taxi driver le chauffeur de taxi
teacher le professeur
team l'équipe (*f*)

teaspoonful la cuillerée à café
telegram le télégramme
telephone le téléphone
to **telephone** téléphoner à
telephone booth la cabine téléphonique
telephone call le coup de téléphone
television la télévision
television set le téléviseur
to **tell** annoncer, raconter
to **tell the truth** à vrai dire
temper la colère
temperature la température
ten dix, la dizaine
tenant le locataire
to **tend to** avoir tendance à
tennis le tennis
tent la tente
tenth dixième
term le trimestre
terminus le terminus
terrace la terrasse
terrible affreux, atroce
terribly terriblement
test l'examen (*m*)
text le texte
to **thank** remercier
thank goodness tant mieux
thank you merci
thanks les remerciements (*m*)
that ça, ce, ce . . . -là, celle, celui, cet, cette, que
that comes to ça fait
that doesn't interest me ça ne m'intéresse pas
that doesn't matter ça ne fait rien
that doesn't surprise me ça ne m'étonne pas
that is c'est-à-dire (que)
that must be ça doit être
that one celle-là
that suits me ça me convient
that's ça fait, c'est
that's a pity c'est dommage
that's all c'est tout
that's all right il n'y a pas de mal
that's done c'est fait

that's enough ça suffit
that's good c'est parfait
that's it ça y est
that's just how it is c'est bien le cas
that's life c'est la vie
that's right c'est ça, c'est bien ça
that's spelt ça s'épelle
that's to say c'est-à-dire (que)
that's true c'est vrai
the le, la, les
theatre le spectacle, le théâtre
their leur
theirs, their ones à eux, leur (les)
them eux, les
(to) **them** leur
then alors, ensuite, puis
then (come on) donc (venez donc)
there là, par là
there are il y a, voilà
there is il y a, voilà
there it is la voilà, le voilà
there now! allons bon!
there they are les voilà
thermometer le thermomètre
these ces
these ones ceux-là
they ils
they are ce sont
they (too) elles (aussi)
thin maigre
thing la chose
things les affaires (*f*)
to **think** croire, se douter, penser
to **think about** penser à
to **think of** penser à
to **think over** réfléchir
third troisième
thirteen treize
thirteenth treizième
thirtieth trentième
thirty trente
thirty-eight trente-huit
thirty-five trente-cinq
thirty thousand trente mille
thirty-three trente-trois

this ce, cet, cette
this minute à l'instant
this one celui-ci, celle-ci
this very morning ce matin
même
this way par ici
those ces, ceux, celles
those ones ceux-là, celles-là
thousands (of) des milliers
(de)
to threaten menacer
three trois
throat la gorge
through à travers
through train le train direct
ticket le billet, le ticket
ticket (fine) la contravention
tidy ordonné
tie la cravate
tiles le carrelage
till la caisse
time l'époque (*f*), la fois,
l'heure (*f*), le temps
time flies le temps passe
timetable l'indicateur (*m*),
l'horaire (*m*)
tip le pourboire
to tire oneself se fatiguer
tired fatigué
to à
to (the shop of, etc.) chez
to her lui
to him lui
to let à louer
to them leur
to which auquel, auquelle
to you te, vous
toaster le grille-pain
tobacco le tabac
tobacconist le buraliste, le
marchand de tabac
tobacconist's le bureau de
tabac
today aujourd'hui
together ensemble
toilet les waters (*m*)
tomato juice le jus de
tomate
tomorrow demain
tonsils les amygdales (*f*)
too aussi
too bad! tant pis!

too many trop de
too much trop
tool l'outil (*m*)
the top one celui du haut
tourist le touriste
tourists' information centre
le Syndicat d'Initiative
towel la serviette
tower la tour
town la ville
traffic la circulation
traffic lights les feux
rouges (*m*)
tragedy la tragédie
train le train, la voiture
train (on metro) la rame
to train dresser
transistor (radio) le transistor
transport le transport
to travel voyager
travel agent l'agence de
voyages (*f*)
traveller's cheque le chèque
de voyage
travelling en déplacement
tray le plateau
to treat traiter
treatment le traitement
tree l'arbre (*m*)
to tremble trembler
trouble la peine
trousers le pantalon
trout la truite
true vrai
trunk (luggage) la malle
to trust faire confiance à
to try to essayer de, chercher à
tube (train) la voiture
Tuesday mardi
tunnel le tunnel
to turn tourner
to turn on (the radio) allumer
(la radio)
turnover le chiffre d'affaires
twelfth douzième
twelve douze
twentieth vingtième
twenty vingt
twenty-eight vingt-huit
twenty-eighth vingt-huitième
twenty-fifth vingt-cinquième
twenty-first vingt et unième

326

twenty-five vingt-cinq
twenty-four vingt-quatre
twenty-fourth vingt-quatrième
twenty-one vingt et un
twenty-nine vingt-neuf
twenty-ninth vingt-neuvième
twenty-second vingt-deuxième
twenty-seven vingt-sept
twenty-seventh vingt-septième
twenty-six vingt-six
twenty-sixth vingt-sixième
twenty-third vingt-troisième
twenty-three vingt-trois
twenty-two vingt-deux
two deux
T.V. la télé
to type taper à la machine
typewriter la machine à écrire
typist la dactylo
tyre le pneu
tyranny la tyrannie

U

ugly laid, vilain
ulcer l'ulcère (*m*)
unable (to) incapable (de)
unbearable insupportable
unbelievable invraisemblable
uncle l'oncle (*m*)
underneath dessous, en dessous
to understand comprendre
to understand each other se comprendre
underwear le sous-vêtement
the unfortunate thing is . . . le malheur c'est que . . .
unfortunately malheureusement
unhappy mécontent
to unhook décrocher
uniform l'uniforme (*m*)
university la Faculté
unknown inconnu
unless à moins que

to unpack vider
unpleasant désagréable
urgent urgent
us nous
to use s'en servir, utiliser
to be used to avoir l'habitude de
(it's) useless (to) inutile (de)
usherette l'ouvreuse (*f*)
usually d'habitude

V

vaguely vaguement
valid valable
valley la vallée
value la valeur
variety show le spectacle de variétés
vase le vase
veal le veau
vegetable le légume
vegetable soup le potage aux légumes
very bien, fort, très
very much beaucoup
very near tout près
very small tout petit
very sorry désolé, navré
victory la victoire
view la vue
viewer le téléspectateur
villa la villa
violet le violet
virus le virus
visit la visite
to visit rendre visite à, visiter
visitor le visiteur
voice la voix

W

wait l'attente (*f*)
to wait for attendre
waiter le garçon
to walk marcher
wall le mur
wallet le portefeuille
to wander se promener au hasard
to want désirer
to want to vouloir, avoir envie de

wardrobe le placard
warm chaud
to warm up chauffer
to warn prévenir
warned prévenu
to wash laver
to wash one's hands se laver
les mains
wash-basin le lavabo
washing la lessive, le linge
washing-up la vaisselle
to waste no time in
s'empresser (de)
wastepaper basket la
corbeille à papier
watch la montre
to watch observer
water l'eau (f)
way (manner) la façon
way le chemin
we nous
we'll soon see on verra
bien
to wear porter
to wear shoes chausser (je
chausse du . . .)
weather le temps
weather forecast la météo,
les prévisions
météorologiques (f)
wedding le mariage
week huit jours, la semaine
week-end le week-end
weeping willow le saule
pleureur
to weigh peser
welcome l'accueil (m)
welcome! soyez les
bienvenus!
well! allons! eh bien! enfin
well bien
well cooked bien cuit
well done bien cuit
well-known connu
well really . . ! ça par
exemple . . !
western le western
what quel, quelle, ce que,
ce qui
what! comment ça!
what . . ? qu'est-ce qui . . ?
qu'est-ce que . . ? quoi?

what a bargain! quelle
occasion!
what about . . ? et . . ?
what can I do for you?
qu'est-ce qu'il y a pour
votre service?
what can you do? que faire?
what is it? qu'est-ce que
c'est?
what next! ça alors!
what on earth's that?
qu'est-ce que c'est que ça?
what time is it? quelle heure
est-il?
what to do comment faire
what's happening? qu'est-ce
qui se passe?
what's (something) for? à
quoi sert . . . ?
what's the matter? qu'est-ce
qu'il y a? qu'est-ce qui ne
va pas?
what's the use of? à quoi
bon?
wheel la roue
when alors que
when du temps de, lorsque,
quand
where où
where? où ça?
where in heaven's name? où
diable?
which lequel, laquelle, quel,
quelle
(of) which dont
(to) which auquel, à laquelle
while alors que, pendant que
while I think about it
j'y pense
whisky le whisky
white blanc
white wine le vin blanc
who lequel, laquelle, qui
who is it? qui est-ce?
who's that? qui est-ce?
whole entier
the whole family toute la famille
whom lequel, laquelle
(of) whom dont
why? pourquoi? pourquoi
est-ce que . . ?
why not? pourquoi pas?

wicker (made of) en osier
wicker basket le panier en osier
wife la femme
wig la perruque
wild west le far-west
wildly frénétiquement
to **win** gagner
wind le vent
window la fenêtre
wine le vin
winner le gagnant
wise prudent, sage
to **wish to** tenir à
with avec
with all that dans tout ça
with pleasure avec plaisir
without sans
without doubt sans doute
to **witness** assister à
woman la femme
wonder la merveille
wonderful! formidable! terrible!
to **woo each other** se faire la cour
woodwork la boiserie
word le mot
work l'œuvre (*f*), le travail
to **work** fonctionner, marcher, travailler, être de service
worn usé
worry le souci
to **worry** craindre, inquiéter, s'inquiéter
worse pire

worse and worse de mal en pis
the **worst** le pire
the **worst of it is . . .** le pire c'est que . . .
to be **worth** valoir
to **write** écrire
writer l'écrivain (*m*)
wrong mauvais
the **wrong way** en sens interdit

Y

to **yawn** bâiller
year l'an (*m*), l'année (*f*)
yellow jaune
yes oui, si
yes (you will etc.) mais si
yesterday hier
yesterday evening hier soir
you te, toi, tu, vous
(to) **you** te, vous
you (too) toi, vous (aussi)
you're joking! vous voulez rire!
young jeune
young girl la jeune fille
young man le jeune homme
young people les jeunes
your ton, ta, tes, votre, vos
yours, your one à toi, à vous, le tien, le vôtre
yours truly je vous prie d'agréer l'expression de mes sentiments distingués
youth la jeunesse

Appendix

Verbs

Auxiliary verbs: *avoir, être*

Avoir

Simple tenses	Compound tenses	Simple tenses	Compound tenses	
INDICATIVE		SUBJUNCTIVE		IMPERATIVE
Present	Perfect	Present Que (qu'...)	Perfect Que (qu'...)	
J'ai	**J'ai eu**	**j'aie**	**j'aie eu**	
Tu as	**Tu as eu**	**tu aies**	**tu aies eu**	**aie**
Il a	**Il a eu**	**il ait**	**il ait eu**	
Nous avons	**Nous avons eu**	**nous ayons**	**nous ayons eu**	**ayons**
Vous avez	**Vous avez eu**	**vous ayez**	**vous ayez eu**	**ayez**
Ils ont	**Ils ont eu**	**ils aient**	**ils aient eu**	
Imperfect	Pluperfect			PARTICIPLES
J'avais	**J'avais eu**			Present:
Tu avais	**Tu avais eu**			**ayant**
Il avait	**Il avait eu**			Simple past:
Nous avions	**Nous avions eu**			**eu**
Vous aviez	**Vous aviez eu**			Compound past:
Ils avaient	**Ils avaient eu**			**ayant eu**
Past historic				
J'eus				
Tu eus				
Il eut				
Nous eûmes				
Vous eûtes				
Ils eurent				
		CONDITIONAL		INFINITIVES
Future	Future perfect	Present	Past	Present:
J'aurai	**J'aurai eu**	**J'aurais**	**J'aurais eu**	**avoir**
Tu auras	**Tu auras eu**	**Tu aurais**	**Tu aurais eu**	Past:
Il aura	**Il aura eu**	**Il aurait**	**Il aurait eu**	**avoir eu**
Nous aurons	**Nous aurons eu**	**Nous aurions**	**Nous aurions eu**	
Vous aurez	**Vous aurez eu**	**Vous auriez**	**Vous auriez eu**	
Ils auront	**Ils auront eu**	**Ils auraient**	**Ils auraient eu**	

Etre

Simple tenses	Compound tenses	Simple tenses	Compound tenses	
INDICATIVE		**SUBJUNCTIVE**		**IMPERATIVE**
Present	Perfect	Present Que (qu'...)	Perfect Que (qu'...)	
Je *suis*	J'*ai été*	je *sois*	j'*aie été*	
Tu *es*	Tu *as été*	tu *sois*	tu *aies été*	*sois*
Il *est*	Il *a été*	il *soit*	il *ait été*	
Nous *sommes*	Nous *avons été*	nous *soyons*	nous *ayons été*	*soyons*
Vous *êtes*	Vous *avez été*	vous *soyez*	vous *ayez été*	*soyez*
Ils *sont*	Ils *ont été*	ils *soient*	ils *aient été*	
Imperfect	Pluperfect			**PARTICIPLES**
J'*étais*	J'*avais été*			Present:
Tu *étais*	Tu *avais été*			*étant*
Il *était*	Il *avait été*			Simple past:
Nous *étions*	Nous *avions été*			*été*
Vous *étiez*	Vous *aviez été*			Compound past:
Ils *étaient*	Ils *avaient été*			*ayant été*
Past historic				
Je *fus*				
Tu *fus*				
Il *fut*				
Nous *fûmes*				
Vous *fûtes*				
Ils *furent*		**CONDITIONAL**		**INFINITIVES**
Future	Future perfect	Present	Past	Present:
Je *serai*	J'*aurai été*	Je *serais*	J'*aurais été*	être
Tu *seras*	Tu *auras été*	Tu *serais*	Tu *aurais été*	Past:
Il *sera*	Il *aura été*	Il *serait*	Il *aurait été*	avoir été
Nous *serons*	Nous *aurons été*	Nous *serions*	Nous *aurions été*	
Vous *serez*	Vous *aurez été*	Vous *seriez*	Vous *auriez été*	
Ils *seront*	Ils *auront été*	Ils *seraient*	Ils *auraient été*	

Other verbs

I Verbs ending in -*ER*

A **aimer** type (IA): **observer, arriver, regarder, examiner,** etc.

PRINCIPAL PARTS	TENSES	MOODS	INDICATIVE	IMPERA-TIVE	SUBJUNCTIVE	PARTICIPLES	
Present indic. 1st person: **J' aime**	PRESENT		J'aime Tu aim**es** Il aim**e**	aime	Qu(e) J'aime Tu aim**es** Il aim**e** Nous aim**ions**	Present participle: aim**ant** Simple past: aim**é**	SIMPLE TENSES
			Nous aim**ons** Vous aim**ez** Ils aim**ent**	aim**ons** aim**ez**	Vous aim**iez** Ils aim**ent**	Perfect: ayant aim**é**	
Present participle: aim**ant**	IMPERFECT		J'aim**ais** Tu aim**ais** Il aim**ait** Nous aim**ions** Vous aim**iez** Ils aim**aient**				
Past historic: **J'aimai**	PAST HISTORIC		J'aim**ai** Tu aim**as** Il aim**a** Nous aim**âmes** Vous aim**âtes** ils aim**èrent**				
					CONDITIONAL	INFINTIVES	
Present infinitive: aim**er**	FUTURE		J'aim**erai** Tu aim**eras** Il aim**era** Nous aim**erons** Vous aim**erez** Ils aim**eront**		Present conditional: J'aim**erais** Tu aim**erais** Il aim**erait** Nous aim**erions** Vous aim**eriez** Ils aim**eraient**	Present infinitive: aim**er** Past: avoir aim**é**	
Past participle: aim**é**			The compound tenses are formed in the same way as for **AVOIR**				COM-POUND TENSES

N.B. All verbs which belong to this category, which we will call IA, are conjugated in the same way as **aimer**: the endings are the same; only the root has to be changed.

j'aim**e**	tu aim**es**	il aim**e**
j'observ**e**	tu observ**es**	il observ**e**
j'arriv**e**	tu arriv**es**	il arriv**e**

The following note applies to all regular verbs, irrespective of the category to which they belong:

There are five *main parts of a verb*, from which all others are formed. These are:

1　The PRESENT INDICATIVE (1st person), from which are formed
the SINGULAR OF THE PRESENT TENSE and
the SINGULAR OF THE IMPERATIVE:

	tu aim*es*	2nd person singular of the pres. indic.
j'aim*e*	**il aim*e***	3rd person singular of the pres. indic.
	aim*e*	singular form of imperative

2　The PRESENT PARTICIPLE, from which are formed the PLURAL forms of the PRESENT INDICATIVE and IMPERATIVE, the IMPERFECT INDICATIVE and the PRESENT FORM of the SUBJUNCTIVE:

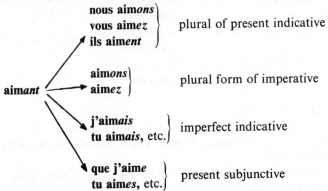

nous aim*ons*
vous aim*ez* ⎫ plural of present indicative
ils aim*ent* ⎭

aim*ant*

aim*ons* ⎫ plural form of imperative
aim*ez* ⎭

j'aim*ais* ⎫ imperfect indicative
tu aim*ais*, etc. ⎭

que j'aim*e* ⎫ present subjunctive
tu aim*es*, etc. ⎭

3　The PRESENT INFINITIVE, from which are formed the SIMPLE FUTURE and the PRESENT CONDITIONAL:

aim*er*

j'aimer*ai* ⎫ simple future
tu amer*as*, etc. ⎭

j'aimer*ais* ⎫ present conditional
tu aimer*ais*, etc. ⎭

4　THE PAST PARTICIPLE, from which are formed all the PAST COMPOUND TENSES and the PASSIVE:

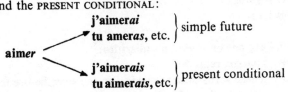

j'ai		perfect
j'avais	**aim*é***	pluperfect
j'aurai		future perfect
j'aurais		past conditional

je suis	**aim*é***	passive
j'étais		

5 THE PAST HISTORIC, from which is formed the imperfect subjunctive, which is a tense used only in written language, and which is not used in this course.

If you know these five primary forms, you will be able to conjugate any regular verb.

A **Important note on the compound tenses of the active form:**
In the active form, all compound tenses of all verbs (transitive, intransitive, reflexive) are formed by the simple tenses of **avoir** or **être** followed by the past participle of the verb.

1 Conjugated with **avoir**:
a all transitive verbs **j'*ai* regardé**
　　　　　　　　　　　　　　j'*avais* fini
b most intransitive verbs **j'*ai* téléphoné**
　　　　　　　　　　　　　　j'*avais* parlé
c the verbs **avoir** and **être** **j'*ai* eu**
　　　　　　　　　　　　　　j'*avais* été

2 Conjugated with **être**:
a some intransitive verbs (mainly verbs of movement):
　　　aller, arriver, descendre, s'enfuir, entrer, mourir, partir, rester, tomber, venir
　　　je *suis* allé   je *suis* descendu à l'Hôtel du Nord   j'*étais* arrivé
b all reflexive verbs:
　　　je me *suis* regardé dans la glace
　　　ils se *sont* regardés
　　　ils se *sont* levés

B **Verbs which have one or several peculiarities:**
　　I.B a **-eler** **appeler, rappeler**
　　　　　　　These verbs take a second **l** in the stem before the silent **e**: **j'appell-e,** but **nous appel-ons**
　　I.B b **-eter** **jeter**
　　　　　　　A second **t** before the silent **e**: **je jett-e,** but **nous jet-ons**
　　I.B c **-ger** **manger, soulager, voyager, déranger**
　　　　　　　An **e** must be added after the **g** before **a** and **o**:
　　　　　　　mange-ant, nous mange-ons, but **vous mang-ez**
　　I.B d **-cer** **agacer, commencer, annoncer, remplacer**
　　　　　　　A cedilla accent must be placed under the **c** before **a** and **o**:
　　　　　　　agaç-ant, nous agaç-ons; but **vous agac-ez**

I.B e *-yer* envo*y*er, appu*y*er, pa*y*er, netto*y*er, emplo*y*er, essa*y*er, s'ennu*y*er

The **y** changes to **i** before a silent **e**:

je pa*i-e*, il netto*i-e*, but vous netto*y-ez*

I.B f *-eter* ach*e*ter

      -ener se prom*e*ner, am*e*ner, emm*e*ner

      -ever enl*e*ver, l*e*ver

In the case of these verbs, **e** becomes **è** before a consonant followed by a silent **e**: j'ach*è*te, je me prom*è*ne, j'am*è*nerai, je me l*è*ve . . . but: vous ach*e*tez, vous vous prom*e*nez, vous vous l*e*vez

I.B g *-éter* inqui*é*ter

      -éder poss*é*der

      -érer préf*é*rer

      -éler rév*é*ler, h*é*ler

In the case of these verbs, **é** becomes **è** before a consonant followed by a silent **e**:

-je m'inqui*è*te, je poss*è*de, je préf*è*re, je rév*è*lerai, il se refl*è*te

C Two irregular verbs:

I.C a aller

Present indicative	Imperative	Present subjunctive
je vais		que j'aille
tu vas	va	que tu ailles
il va		qu'il aille
nous allons	allons	que nous allions
vous allez	allez	que vous alliez
ils vont		qu'ils aillent
Future	Present conditional	Present infinitive
j'irai	j'irais	aller
Future perfect	Past conditional	Past infinitive
je serai allé	je serais allé	être allé
Simple past	Imperfect	Present participle
j'allai	j'allais	allant
Perfect	Pluperfect	Past participles
je suis allé	j'étais allé	allé, étant allé

N.B. All the past compound tenses can be conjugated with the past participle of **être - été**, instead of **allé**. The auxiliary **avoir** is used: **j'ai été j'avais été j'aurai été j'aurais été**, etc.

335

I.C b   Envoyer

Envoyer is conjugated like **payer** (I.B e), except in the FUTURE and the CONDITIONAL tenses, which are irregular:

j'en*verrai*, tu en*verras*, il en*verra*, etc.

j'en*verrais*, tu en*verrais*, il en*verrait*, etc.

II   Verbs ending in -*IR*

A   **finir**, type (II.A): **chois*ir*, gross*ir*, réfléch*ir*, rempl*ir*, gém*ir*, mûr*ir*, vieill*ir*, réuss*ir*, grand*ir*, sais*ir***

PRINCIPAL PARTS	TENSES	MOODS	INDICATIVE	IMPERA-TIVE	SUBJUNCTIVE	PARTICIPLES	
Present indic. 1st person: **Je fin*is***	PRESENT		Je fin*is* Tu fin*is* Il fin*it*	fin*is*	Que (Qu') je fin*isse* tu fin*isses* il fin*isse*	Present participle: fin*issant* Simple past: fin*i*	SIMPLE TENSES
			Nous fin*issons* Vous fin*issez* Ils fin*issent*	fin*issons* fin*issez*	nous fin*issions* vous fin*issiez* ils fin*issent*	Perfect: ayant fin*i*	
Present participle: **fin*issant***	IMPERFECT		Je fin*issais* Tu fin*issais* Il fin*issait* Nous fin*issions* Vous fin*issiez* Ils fin*issaient*				
Past historic: **Je fin*is***	PAST HISTORIC		Je fin*is* Tu fin*is* Il fin*it* Nous fin*îmes* Vous fin*îtes* Ils fin*irent*				
					CONDITIONAL	INFINITIVES	
Present infinitive: **fin*ir***	FUTURE		Je fin*irai* Tu fin*iras* Il fin*ira* Nous fin*irons* Vous fin*irez* Ils fin*iront*		Present conditional: Je fin*irais* Tu fin*irais* Il fin*irait* Nous fin*irions* Vous fin*iriez* Ils fin*iraient*	Present infinitive: fin*ir* Past: avoir fin*i*	
Past participle: **fin*i***			The compound tenses are formed in the same way as for **AVOIR**				COM-POUND TENSES

336

B. **sortir** type (II.B) **par***tir*, **men***tir*, **sen***tir*

PRINCIPAL PARTS	TENSES	MOODS	INDICATIVE	IMPERA-TIVE	SUBJUNCTIVE	PARTICIPLES	
Present indic. 1st person: **Je sors**	PRESENT		**Je sor***s* **Tu sor***s* **Il sor***t*	*sors*	**Que (Qu')** **je sor***te* **tu sor***tes* **il sor***te*	Present participle: **sor***tant* Simple past: **sor***ti*	SIMPLE TENSES
			Nous sor*tons* **Vous sor***tez* **Ils sor***tent*	*sortons* *sortez*	**nous sor***tions* **vous sor***tiez* **ils sor***tent*	Perfect: **étant sor***ti*	
Present participle: **sor***tant*	IMPERFECT		**Je sor***tais* **Tu sor***tais* **Il sor***tait* **Nous sor***tions* **Vous sor***tiez* **Ils sor***taient*				
Past historic: **Je sor***tis*	PAST HISTORIC		**Je sor***tis* **Tu sor***tis* **Il sor***tit* **Nous sor***tîmes* **Vous sor***tîtes* **Ils sor***tirent*				
					CONDITIONAL	**INFINITIVES**	
Present infinitive: **sor***tir*	FUTURE		**Je sor***tirai* **Tu sor***tiras* **Il sor***tira* **Nous sor***tirons* **Vous sor***tirez* **Ils sor***tiront*		Present conditional: **Je sor***tirais* **Tu sor***tirais* **Il sor***tirait* **Nous sor***tirions* **Vous sor***tiriez* **Ils sor***tiraient*	Present infinitive: **sor***tir* Past: **être sor***ti*	
Past participle: **sor***ti*			The compound tenses are formed in the same way as for **AVOIR**				COM-POUND TENSES

N.B. The compound tenses of **sortir** and of **partir** are formed with the auxiliary **être: je** *suis* **sorti**
je *suis* **parti**

337

C ouvrir type: souffr*ir*, offr*ir*, couvr*ir* (II.C)
   ouvr*ir*, j'ouvr*e*, ouvr*ant*, j'ouvr*is*, ouv*ert*

D ven*ir* type: ten*ir*, reten*ir*, deven*ir* (II.D)
   ven*ir*, je v*iens*, ils v*iennent*, ven*ant*, je v*ins*, ven*u*
   N.B. The compound tenses of **venir** are formed with the auxiliary
         être: **je** *suis* **venu**

E Irregular verbs ending in -*IR* (II.E)
   cueill*ir*, je cueill*e*, cueill*ant*, je cueill*is*, cueill*i*
   cour*ir*, je cour*s*, cour*ant*, je cour*us*, cour*u*
   mour*ir*, je meur*s*, ils m*eurent*, mour*ant*, je mour*us*, *mort*
   fu*ir*, je f*uis*, ils f*uient*, fu*yant*, f*uis*, f*ui* (s'enfuir)
   N.B. The compound tenses of **mourir** and of **s'enfuir** are formed
         with the auxiliary **être**: **il** *est* **mort, il** *s'est* **enfui** (cf. L14, N8a).

   serv*ir*, je ser*s*, serv*ant*, je serv*is*, serv*i*
   dorm*ir*, je dor*s*, dorm*ant*, je dorm*is*, dorm*i*

III Verbs ending in -*RE*

A Verbs ending in -**ENDRE** (III.A)
   descendre type (III.A): **attendre, entendre, prétendre, vendre, rendre,
                                défendre**

B Verbs ending in -**RDRE** (III.B): **perdre**, are conjugated like **descendre**
   perd*re*, je perd*s*, perd*ant*, je perd*is*, perd*u*

C Verbs ending in -**AÎTRE** (III.C): **connaître, reconnaître, paraître,
                                        disparaître, apparaître**
   conna*ître*, je conn*ais*, (il conn*aît*), connais*sant*, je conn*us*, conn*u*
   N.B. Be careful: There is a circumflex accent on the **i**, and a **t** at the
         end of the third person singular of the present indicative.
   N.B. **Apparaître** is conjugated with **être** in its past compound tenses:
         il *est* **apparu.**

D Verbs ending in -**UIRE** (III.D): **conduire, introduire, cuire**
   cond*uire*, je cond*uis*, (il cond*uit*), condui*sant*, je conduis*is*, cond*uit*
   N.B. Be careful! There is a **t** at the end of the third person singular
         of the present indicative.

PRINCIPAL PARTS	TENSES	MOODS INDICATIVE	IMPERA-TIVE	SUBJUNCTIVE	PARTICIPLES	
Present indic. 1st person: **Je descends**	PRESENT	Je descend**s** Tu descend**s** Il descend	descend**s**	**Que** je descend**e** tu descend**es** il descend**e**	Present participle: descend**ant** Simple past: descend**u**	SIMPLE TENSES
		Nous descend**ons** Vous descend**ez** Ils descend**ent**	descend**ons** descend**ez**	nous descend**ions** vous descend**iez** ils descend**ent**	Perfect: étant descend**u** ayant descend**u**	
Present participle: descend**ant**	IMPERFECT	Je descend**ais** Tu descend**ais** Il descend**ait** Nous descend**ions** Vous descend**iez** Ils descend**aient**				
Past historic: **Je descendis**	PAST HISTORIC	Je descend**is** Tu descend**is** Il descend**it** Nous descend**îmes** Vous descend**îtes** Ils descend**irent**				
				CONDITIONAL	INFINITIVES	
Present infinitive: descend**re**	FUTURE	Je descend**rai** Tu descend**ras** Il descend**ra** Nous descend**rons** Vous descend**rez** Ils descend**ront**		Present conditional: Je descend**rais** Tu descend**rais** Il descend**rait** Nous descend**rions** Vous descend**riez** Ils descend**raient**	Present infinitive: descend**re** Past: être ⎱ descend**u** avoir ⎰	
Past participle: descend**u**		The compound tenses are formed in the same way as for **AVOIR**				COM-POUND TENSES

N.B. All the compound tenses of verbs ending in **-ENDRE** which are found in this course are conjugated with **avoir**. But **descendre** is conjugated with **être** when it is used as an intransitive verb:

Il *est* **descendu à la gare du Nord.**

But   **J'***ai* **descendu le boulevard Haussmann.**

339

E   Irregular verbs ending in -RE (III.E): -prend*re*, apprend*re*,
comprend*re*

prend*re*, je prend*s*, tu prend*s*, il prend, nous pre*nons*, vous pre*nez*,
ils pre*nnent*
pren*ant*, que je p*renne*, que tu p*rennes*, qu'il p*renne*, que nous
pren*ions*, que vous pren*iez*, qu'ils pre*nnent*
je pr*is*, pr*is*

-vain*cre*, convain*cre*
vain*cre*, je *vaincs*, (il *vainc*), vain*quant*, je vain*quis*, vain*cu*

General comment: All the following irregular verbs ending in -RE,
take a **t** in the third person singular of the present indicative (like
connaître, III.C, and like **conduire** . . . **il conduit** . . . III.D).

-craindre — se plaindre, plaindre, teindre, déteindre, peindre, rejoindre
-craind*re*, je crain*s*, (il crain*t*), craign*ant*, je craign*is*, crain*t*
viv*re*, je v*is*, viv*ant*, je vé*cus*, vé*cu*
lir*e*, je l*is*, lis*ant*, je l*us*, l*u*
batt*re*, je bat*s*, batt*ant*, je batt*is*, batt*u*
conclu*re*, je concl*us*, conclu*ant*, je conclu*s*, conclu
boir*e*, je bo*is*, tu bo*is*, il bo*it*, nous b*uvons*, vous b*uvez*, ils bo*ivent*,
buv*ant*, que je b*oive*, que tu bo*ives*, qu'il bo*ive*, que nous b*uvions*,
que vous b*uviez*, qu'ils bo*ivent*
tair*e*, je ta*is*, tais*ant*, je t*us*, t*u*
plair*e*, je pla*is*, (il pla*ît*), plais*ant*, je pl*us*, pl*u*
rir*e*, je r*is*, ri*ant*, je r*is*, r*i*

Be careful! There are two **i**'s in the first and second person plural of
the imperfect, and of the present subjunctive:

$$\left.\begin{array}{l}\text{nous r}iions\\ \text{vous r}iiez\end{array}\right\} imperfect$$

$$\left.\begin{array}{l}\text{que nous r}iions\\ \text{que vous r}iiez\end{array}\right\} present\ subjunctive$$

suiv*re*, je su*is*, suiv*ant*, je suiv*is*, suiv*i*

N.B. **Je suis**, therefore, may be either the first person of the present
indicative of **être** or of **suivre**.

dir*e*, je d*is*, vous di*tes*, dis*ant*, je d*is*, d*it*
-écrire, prescrire
écri*re*, j'écr*is*, écriv*ant*, j'écriv*is*, écri*t*

-mettre, promettre
mett*re*, je met*s*, mett*ant*, je m*is*, m*is*
naît*re*, je n*ais*, il n*aît*, nai*ssant*, je na*quis*, *né*
N.B. The past compound tenses of **naître** are conjugated with **être**:
  je *suis né*

-faire
Present indicative: **je f*ais*, tu f*ais*, il f*ait*, nous f*aisons*, vous f*aites*,**
                   ils f*ont*
Future: **je f*erai*, tu f*eras*,** etc.
Conditional: **je f*erais*, tu f*erais*,** etc.
Present participle: **fai*sant***
Present subjunctive: **que je f*asse*, que tu f*asses*, qu'il f*asse*,**
                   que nous f*assions*, que vous f*assiez*, qu'ils f*assent*
Past historic: **je f*is*, tu f*is*,** etc.
Past participle: *fait*

croi*re*, je croi*s*, ils cr*oient*, croy*ant*, je cr*us*, cr*u*
distr*aire*, je distr*ais*, distray*ant*, distr*ait*

IV Verbs ending in -*OIR* (IV.A)

A **recevoir** type: **décevoir**
Present indicative: **je re*çois*, tu re*çois*, il re*çoit*, nous rece*vons*,**
                   vous rece*vez*, ils re*çoivent*
Future: **je rece*vrai*, tu rece*vras*,** etc.
Conditional: **je rece*vrais*, tu rece*vrais*,** etc.
Present participle: **rece*vant***
Present subjunctive: **que je re*çoive*, que tu re*çoives*, qu'il re*çoive*,**
                   que nous rece*vions*, que vous rece*viez*,
                   qu'ils re*çoivent*
Past historic: **je re*çus*, tu re*çus*,** etc.
Past participle: **re*çu***

B **Irregular verbs ending in -OIR (IV.B)**
-vouloir
Present indicative: **je v*eux*, tu v*eux*, il v*eut*, nous v*oulons*,**
                   vous v*oulez*, ils v*eulent*
Future: **je v*oudrai*, tu v*oudras*,** etc.
Conditional: **je v*oudrais*, tu v*oudrais*,** etc.
Present participle: **vou*lant***
Present subjunctive: **que je v*euille*, que tu v*euilles*, qu'il v*euille*,**
                   que nous v*oulions*, que vous v*ouliez*,
                   qu'ils v*euillent*
Past historic: **je vou*lus*, tu vou*lus*,** etc.
Past participle: **voul*u***

-pouvoir

Present indicative: **je p*eux*, tu p*eux*, il p*eut*, nous p*ouvons*,
vous p*ouvez*, ils p*euvent***

Future: **je p*ourrai*, tu p*ourras*,** etc.

Conditional: **je p*ourrais*, tu p*ourrais*,** etc.

Present participle: **pouv*ant***

Present subjunctive: **que je p*uisse*, que tu p*uisses*, qu'il p*uisse*,
que nous p*uissions*, que vous p*uissiez*,
qu'ils p*uissent***

Past historic: **je p*us*, tu p*us*,** etc.

Past participle: **p*u***

-savoir

Present indicative: **je s*ais*, tu s*ais*, il s*ait*, nous s*avons*, vous s*avez*,
ils s*avent***

Future: **je s*aurai*, tu s*auras*,** etc.

Conditional: **je s*aurais*, tu s*aurais*,** etc.

Present participle: **s*achant***

Past historic: **je s*us*, tu s*us*,** etc.

Past participle: **s*u***

-voir

Present indicative: **je v*ois*, tu v*ois*, il v*oit*, nous v*oyons*, vous v*oyez*,
ils v*oient***

Future: **je v*errai*, tu v*erras*,** etc.

Conditional: **je v*errais*, tu v*errais*,** etc.

Present participle: **voy*ant***

Present subjunctive: **que je v*oie*, que tu v*oies*, qu'il v*oie*,
que nous v*oyions*, que vous v*oyiez*, qu'ils v*oient***

Past historic: **je v*is*, tu v*is*,** etc.

Past participle: **v*u***

-devoir

Present indicative: **je *dois*, tu *dois*, il *doit*, nous *devons*, vous *devez*,
ils *doivent***

Future: **je dev*rai*, tu dev*ras*,** etc.

Conditional: **je *devrais*, tu *devrais*,** etc.

Present participle: ***devant***

Present subjunctive: **que je *doive*, que tu *doives*, qu'il *doive*,
que nous *devions*, que vous *deviez*, qu'ils *doivent***

Past historic: **je *dus*, tu *dus*,** etc.

Past participle: ***dû***

-valoir

Present indicative: **je *vaux*, tu *vaux*, il *vaut*, nous *valons*, vous *valez*,
ils *valent***

Future: **je vaud*rai*, tu vaud*ras*,** etc.

Conditional: **je vaud*rais*, tu vaud*rais*,** etc.

Present participle: **val*ant***

Present subjunctive: **que je *vaille*, que tu *vailles*, qu'il *vaille*,
que nous *valions*, que vous *valiez*, qu'ils *vaillent***

Past historic: **je val*us*, tu val*us*,** etc.

Past participle: **val*u***

C **Two impersonal verbs ending in -OIR (IV.C)**
-pleuvoir
il pleu*t*, il pleu*vra*, il pleu*vrait*, pleuv*ant*, il pl*ut*, pl*u*

-falloir
il *faut*, il fau*dra*, qu'il *faille*, il fall*ut*, fall*u*

Pronominal verbs

Certain verbs are accompanied by an unstressed personal pronoun
or a reflexive complement (direct or indirect) which represents the
same person as the subject.

Je *me* demande pourquoi. Il *se* plaint. Vous *vous* parlez.

According to the meaning, these verbs may be categorised as:

1 Reflexive: the action comes back to . . . reflects upon . . . a
complement which is the same person or the same thing
as the subject:
Je *me* regarde dans la glace.
(me is the direct complement)
Les arbres *se* reflètent dans l'eau.
(Se is the direct complement)
Je *me* dis . . .
(**me**: indirect complement)
Je ne *me* pardonne pas.
(**me**: indirect complement)

N.B. **a** The reflexive pronoun of the third person is **se**:
je *me* regarde dans la glace.
tu *te* regardes dans la glace.
il *se* regarde dans la glace.
nous *nous* regardons dans la glace.
vous *vous* regardez dans la glace.
ils *se* regardent dans la glace.

b A reflexive pronoun may be reinforced with the help of: **moi-même, toi-même, lui-même, elle-même, nous-mêmes, vous-mêmes, eux-mêmes, elles-mêmes.**

2 Reciprocal: when two or more subjects are involved in action between each other:

Paul et moi, nous *nous* parlons. (2 people)

Les Delon et les Levoisin *se* comprennent. (several people)

N.B. A reciprocal verb may be reinforced with the help of **l'un l'autre** or **les uns les autres:**

Paul et M. Levoisin *se* comprennent *l'un l'autre*.

Ils *se* battent *les uns les autres*.

3 Simply pronominal: when the second pronoun has no real reflexive or reciprocal meaning and adds nothing to the meaning of the verb:

Je *m'*ennuie

Je *m'*assois

Je *me* rappelle

Je *me* promène

These constructions are really Gallicisms.

4 Pronominal verbs which have a passive meaning: **se trouve, se vendent, s'appelle** have a passive meaning in sentences such as:

L'aéroport *se trouve* près de Paris.

Les légumes *se vendent* bien.

Il *s'appelle* Paul.

General comment

The compound tenses of pronominal verbs are formed with the auxiliary **être**:

Je *me suis* dit . . . Paul et Valérie *se sont* parlé. Ils *se sont* ennuyés.

Passive verbs

Transitive verbs — and only transitive verbs — have a passive form:

Ma ferme *est entourée* de champs.

La rivière *est bordée* d'arbres.

N.B. In the passive form the past participle must agree with the subject:

Paul **n'est pas convain*cu*.**

Valérie **n'est pas convain*cue*.**

Ils **ne sont pas convain*cus*.**

Elles **ne sont pas convain*cues*.**